OUR LORD PRAYS FOR HIS OWN

thoughts on John 17

OUR LORD PRAYS FOR HIS OWN

thoughts on John 17

MARCUS RAINSFORD

Foreword by W.H. Griffith Thomas
Introduction by S. Maxwell Coder

KREGEL PUBLICATIONS
Grand Rapids, Michigan 49501

Our Lord Prays for His Own by Marcus Rainsford
Copyright ©1950, 1978 by Moody Bible Institute,
Chicago. Published in 1985 by Kregel Publications, a
division of Kregel, Inc. under special arrangements with
the copyright owner. All rights reserved.

Moody Press edition 1950
Kregel Publications edition 1985, 1986

Library of Congress Cataloging in Publication Data

Rainsford, Marcus, 1820-1897.
    Our Lord Prays for His Own.

    Reprint. Originally published: Chicago: Moody Press,
1950.
    Bibliography: P.
    1. Bible. N.T. John XVII—Criticism, interpretation,
etc. I. Title.
BS2615.2.R34   1985   226'.506   85-8095
ISBN 0-8254-3617-6

Printed in the United States of America

CONTENTS

PREFACE TO THE FOURTH EDITION

THE FOLLOWING EXPOSITION has been for some time out of print, and I have been requested by many valued Christian friends to revise and remodel it. I have attempted the task with much pleasure. Each year's additional experience of self and need tends to convince me of the paramount importance of being more and more fully established in the inestimable truths set forth in this precious portion of God's Word, and with sincere desire that each reader of my book may enjoy the light and teaching of the Holy Ghost in the study of it, I send it now forth to the praise of the glory of Him whose prayer for His people it was, and is.

MARCUS RAINSFORD

Belgrave Chapel

FOREWORD

AT THE REQUEST of my friend, Mrs. Rainsford, who was a member of my congregation at St. Paul's, Portman Square, London, W., I gladly preface a new edition of one of the valuable works of her late husband with a few words of personal testimony. It would be as unbecoming as it is unnecessary for a younger man to write even a word of "introduction" to such a father in Israel, and one so well known as the late Mr. Rainsford. What I would wish to do is to pay a little tribute of gratitude to his memory.

I have personal reasons for great thankfulness to God for Mr. Rainsford's teaching. In the early days of my Christian life I was much helped and strengthened by his clear, solid, and scriptural presentation of Christian truth; and from the time I first read one of his books, I learned to look out for anything that came from his pen. Mr. Rainsford was truly remarkable for his firm grasp of essential evangelical doctrine, and for his peculiarly strong hold on the great foundation realities connected with the believer's standing in Christ.

It is well known that he was greatly valued by Mr. Moody for his clear-cut definitions of doctrine, and for his lucid and convincing statements of spiritual truth.

The present volume deals with the "Holy of Holies" of our Lord's earthly life, and those who prayerfully read it through, Bible in hand, will find ample reward in its exposition of doctrine and its application of truth to mind and heart. I shall regard it as a great privilege if my words serve to call the attention of some, who are just commencing their ministry, to a work which will afford them the very clearest guidance and no little establishment in the faith.

W. H. GRIFFITH THOMAS

INTRODUCTION

IN THE PROVIDENCE OF GOD, Marcus Rainsford was the chosen vessel through whom has come the greatest classic ever written on Christ's high priestly prayer for His people recorded in the seventeenth chapter of John. First published, as far as can be determined, under the title *Lectures on St. John 17*, the book went through a number of editions before going out of print early in the present century.

Our Lord Prays for His Own now takes its place again as a true masterpiece both of devotional and expository literature. It is an example of the kind of ministry which made such men as Rainsford outstanding servants of Christ in their generation, and caused the evangelical movement in Britain to prosper under their leadership.

It is a privilege to bring out of their places of obscurity not only these rich meditations by an expositor of rare ability, but also something of the life of their author, whose name is hardly known today. The gospel dialogues which he carried on with D. L. Moody are another forgotten treasure from another day which many will appreciate.

We are confident that the blessing of God will rest upon these pages, penned by one who, though he died more than fifty years ago, "yet speaketh" because he searched the Scriptures while he lived, then gave to the world the results of his Spirit-guided search. It is to be hoped that such fine examples of what constitutes a true Bible teaching ministry may stimulate some to become more proficient in the Word today, when multitudes are hungering for the old truths which their fathers loved so dearly.

W. H. Griffith Thomas said in his preface to the fifth English edition of this classic, "The present volume deals with the 'Holy of Holies' of our Lord's earthly life, and those who prayerfully read it through, Bible in hand, will find ample reward in its exposition of doctrine and its application of truth to mind and heart." There is indeed a heart-warming experience awaiting everyone who will peruse these pages, whether he studies with care, or uses the book for occasional devotional reading.

S. M. C.

BIOGRAPHICAL INTRODUCTION

IT IS A STRANGE THING that the life of Marcus Rainsford has never been written. In fact, careful research in some of the largest libraries in the United States does not disclose so much as a line of biographical reference to one of the greatest Bible expositors of the nineteenth century. Here was a man of God much sought after by D. L. Moody and other evangelical leaders of his generation, a man who wrote several volumes of expository studies which are collectors' items today, a man who was given such a deep spiritual insight into our Lord's high priestly prayer of John 17 that *Our Lord Prays for His Own* is still considered the greatest masterpiece ever penned on that part of the Word of God, and yet it has been almost impossible to discover what manner of man Rainsford was or what he did beyond writing the books which we treasure so much today.

It seemed for a time that the present work would have to appear without a biographical introduction. Several persons, including capable librarians, had given assistance in an unsuccessful attempt to discover something about this honored servant of Christ.

Then one day, when the last promising lead had ended in failure, the writer was walking near a certain library (already searched in vain for data on the life of our author), when a line of Scripture came to mind, "Ye have not, because ye ask not" (James 4:2). He lifted up his heart in prayer for help, entered the library, and within a few minutes was providentially directed to a shelf where stood one volume, in that vast collection of more than 300,000 books, which not only mentions Marcus Rainsford, but even takes us into the villages in Ireland where he began to preach, and to the hearthside where he taught his children the Word of God. The volume is the autobiography of his son William Stephen Rainsford, *The Story of a Varied Life,* published at New York by Doubleday, Page and Company in 1922.

This son of Marcus Rainsford was rector of St. George's Episcopal Church in New York City between the years of 1883 and 1905. He wrote one other autobiographical book, *A Preacher's Story of His Work,* which appeared in 1904. By piecing together various incidental references to his father in these volumes, with some data gleaned from contemporary periodical literature and from prefaces to Rainsford's expository works, the material in this biographical sketch was assembled. Of particular value were some details, probably recorded nowhere else, supplied through the courtesy of Mr. Charles T. Cook, Editor of *The Christian,* from a brief article which appeared in that London journal on November 12, 1896, just nine months before Rainsford's death.

When Rollo the Norseman conquered Normandy in the tenth century, one of his fighting men was named Guy Rainsford, an individual who managed to secure for himself a large part of the province. Some of his descendants crossed to England in 1066 with William the Conqueror, and to the Lancashire branch of the family the lineage of Marcus Rainsford may be traced. During the Wars of the Roses his direct ancestors migrated to Ireland, where they acquired a considerable landed estate.

At Rainsford Lodge, County Wicklow, Ireland, Marcus Rainsford was born, probably in the year 1820. The exact date of his birth is not known. When an infant he was thought to be dying, but recovery was granted in answer to the prayers of his Christian father and mother, who dedicated him to the service of Christ should his life be spared.

By the time of his birth, what were once large family posses-

sions had dwindled away to an unpretentious house on a heavily
encumbered property, so that his early days were spent in real
poverty. His father, Ryland, incurred some large debts for
which Marcus afterward made himself responsible, although he
was not legally bound to do so. He considered it a moral obligation to pay these off, in spite of the fact that it kept his own
family poor for many years.

When he was about sixteen years of age, to use his own
words, "a dream of the night awoke me from the sleep of
death," and caused him to inquire what he must do to be saved.
In the providence of God an old copy of Romaine's *Life of
Faith* fell into his hands. That treatise was the means of leading
him to Christ, and to a clear grasp of the simple gospel certi-
tudes which he later preached with great clearness and power.

Young Rainsford attended the Irish schools of his day in
Dublin. In due course he entered Trinity College, where he
earned a B.A. degree in 1843. After ordination in 1844, his
first curacy as a clergyman of the Church of Ireland was at Hill-
town, County Down, where he labored with youthful zeal for
a year and a half. Then came a period of ministry at Holy
Trinity Church, Dromore, in the same county, and his appointment as Secretary of the Irish Society for Promoting Christianity
Among the Jews. He thankfully referred to this office, which
he held for nine years, as one which led him early in his active
life into the privilege of association with a class of believers who
were true Bible students.

Dublin was the next scene of Rainsford's Christian service.
The great evangelical movement had been working in that city
ever since the opening of the nineteenth century. Although it
was not countenanced by the bishop and the fashionable clergy,
the tactless rule of Archbishop Whately threw many of the rich
laity into the movement. These men built free chapels, not
under the Archbishop's control, and one chapel, the Molineux
Asylum in Dublin, was soon filled by the able preaching of

Marcus Rainsford. He was also chaplain of a hospital for the blind. As his son informs us, "the chaplain attached to a hospital like that was often the center of quite an important ministry; the hospital was almost subordinate. My father was a preacher from the very beginning; he had drawn about him quite a large congregation in Dublin. He was a man of remarkable power."

While residing at Coolock, a modest Dublin suburb, Rainsford married the daughter of Stephen Dickson, the rector of Dungarven, in the south of Ireland. At Coolock his son William was born in 1850, to whom we are indebted for most of what we know about the great expositor.

It was also in 1850 that the Earl of Roden, patron of the vicarage of Dundalk, recognizing Rainsford's unusual gifts as a preacher, appointed him as vicar there. Dundalk was a straggling, untidy place of some 10,000 inhabitants, the great majority of them being Roman Catholics. It was an ancient town, a farm center standing at the head of a considerable bay into which emptied a short river rising in the nearby mountains. In the old red brick vicarage seven more children were born during the next sixteen years. The eldest in this large family wrote with great nostalgia later of his early memories of that home in Dundalk, the "vicarage with its row of elm trees facing the mountains and the sea, and the old church with its crooked spire.

"Dundalk was a beautiful place. The old vicarage stood facing the bay. There was an ancient quay and considerable shipping—fishing, coaling and landing of steamers; mountains 2,000 feet high running down to the sea; and jutting into the bay a beautiful mountainous promontory. I can see it as clearly as though it were only yesterday, the yellow patches of golden grain, the purple heather, the light on the mountain. They were treeless mountains except along the base.

"At that time there was quite a strong movement in the religious world both in England and in Ireland. The great revival in Ireland in '59 made a deep impression; the revival swept all over the country and produced some remarkable phenomena. The revivalist's hymnbook was one of the results. Before that time, as I remember, there was no such thing as hymnology in the church. The wave was . . . distinctly evangelical. You will find a number of the hymns that came to life then in the Moody and Sankey book; they were ultra evangelical. . . . It was a new presentation of the doctrine which my father was preaching with all his might.

"By this time he was a noted preacher. His pulpit in Dundalk had become quite remarked. He did not know anything but his Bible; he did not know even his Greek Testament; but he was eloquent—one of the finest exponents of the early evangelical movement in Ireland. The best people in the country were swept along in that wave. Laymen went preaching; my father was in correspondence with scores of people all over the country; the north of Ireland was profoundly moved."

Rainsford's income at Dundalk was $1500. Out of this he managed to feed, clothe and educate his eight children. The family raised its own vegetables, had a cow, chickens and pigs; salted down its own bacon; was able even to relieve the distress of poorer neighbors.

Such a rigorous life took its toll. Wrote William, "Looking back on those years now, from 1855 to 1865, I can see that the strain on my mother was more than even her fine constitution and indomitable courage could endure. She gave her very life for the home. Her babies came too closely, one after the other; her sewing took all her evenings, her careful housekeeping and cooking her days. Her garden, while any vigor remained to her was her delight and recreation. When I was about ten years old, she gradually had to give up gardening. Arthritis, that later made her life a martyrdom, came to fasten its grip on her frail little body and she was never afterwards free from cruel pain until she died in 1887."

Eight hundred people crowded the church to the doors each Sunday morning to hear Marcus Rainsford preach. He is described as having "a fine carrying voice, with an Irishman's eloquence, who profoundly believed that he held a commission to declare God's truth to men, whether they would hear or whether they would forbear. So he had power with the crowds who listened to him for so many years in Ireland and later in Belgrave Square, London. His preaching emptied the parish churches and monopolized the religious teaching of the Protestant population."

At Dundalk and the neighboring curacy of Castletown, for both of which Rainsford was responsible, one who knew him informs us that "his previous devotion to close and systematic study of the Holy Scriptures came into specially practical fruition, in connection with Sunday School and Bible class effort, on which God's richest blessing rested. He has told, in his own vivid and pictorial way, of another branch of service at this time, in gospel effort among the Roman Catholic children in his parish.

"One narrative in this connection which the writer heard him relate was as to the conversion and subsequent persecution of a poor Roman Catholic boy; the lively and pathetic recital alternately convulsed his audience with laughter and melted them to tears.

"All were fish that came to Mr. Rainsford's net. He had a long ride on one occasion on a 'jaunting car,' in a remote part of the country, with an Irish farmer. To this man Mr. Rainsford, like Philip in his chariot ride with the Ethiopian eunuch, preached the gospel, and the truths of salvation were drunk in by the solitary auditor with the utmost eagerness. 'I believe,' said Mr. Rainsford, in telling the story, 'I shall meet that man in heaven, though I never saw or heard of him again.'"

The Dundalk church was cruciform in plan; the pews were of different sizes, but graded in accordance with the importance of the families who occupied them. The membership included all sorts and conditions of men, from earls to the children of the local distiller. In this community Marcus Rainsford gathered around him a band of intensely religious men who sought to evangelize the entire area. His influence must have been great, because the men who stood with him were leaders in the community. One of them was a famous engineer of that time who could rise from a discussion of the technical problems of joining England and France with a tunnel, to enter into conversation with the minister's own children on the question of whether or not they were born again. Members of the band went here and there around the country preaching. Some of them would accompany their pastor when he went on preaching trips, to deal with his converts, of whom there were apparently a great many throughout his ministry.

In 1866 Marcus Rainsford was called to St. John's Church, Halkin Street, Belgrave Square, London. Popularly known as Belgrave Chapel, the church stood in the middle of the most fashionable part of the largest city in the world, a few yards from the northeast corner of its finest square.

Rainsford took the west end of London by storm. There was soon gathered together a congregation impressive not only because it jammed the chapel so that there was not even standing room, but also because of the high social position of many of its members.

The Prince of Wales was seen in the audience more than once; he asked that the preacher should be presented to him. Gladstone came sometimes, in spite of his avowed high churchmanship. The Lord Chancellor Cairns was one of the first to rent a pew. Statesmen, soldiers, bankers and many members of Parliament attended regularly, as well as some of the first families of England who had been touched by the evangelical revival.

Although his sermons were praised, his advice sought, his

friendship courted by many of the leading figures in British life of that day, Rainsford still went quietly about his work with the same earnest regularity he had used in the poor Irish parish. In the morning he shut himself up in his study, in the afternoon he went from house to house visiting, for several hours each day. Not only did he succeed in carrying the true gospel into the homes of the aristocracy who resided in large numbers in the neighborhood; he reached the many domestic servants of the area as well, holding classes on weekday evenings especially for them. All of the volumes which have come from his pen were written during his ministry at Belgrave Chapel.

One morning, in the summer of 1869, while his son William was studying in the same room where his father was writing his sermon, Marcus Rainsford suddenly looked up and said, "Well, have you made up your mind what you want to be? The desire of my heart is that you should become a clergyman."

"At that moment," wrote William afterward, "at that moment I seemed to have a vision of my life work. I had always looked forward to going into the army, but then a vision came to me. I bowed my head and said, 'Daddy, if you will send me to Cambridge I will be a clergyman.' That settled it then and there. . . . Nobody impressed me as did my father; his doctrine was sufficient for me, and his earnestness touched me."

William did go to Cambridge; he did become a clergyman. It is not easy to understand how the son of such a father as Marcus Rainsford, with men like Lightfoot, Westcott and Dean Farrar as his teachers at Cambridge should have become known afterward for his emphasis on the social gospel rather than the gospel his father had lived and preached. Nevertheless, he frankly admitted in his autobiography that he was intellectually unable to accept the doctrines his father had proclaimed.

Something Rainsford suggested to William as he afterward left home to take his first charge as a minister of the established Church is of interest as throwing light upon the careful preparation which went into such expository messages as appear in this volume. He said, "You are going to a place where you will probably have a great deal of speaking to do. You are not well prepared to do it. Let me give you one bit of advice. Give your whole week, if necessary every single morning of the week, to preparing as thoroughly as you can one discourse. If you do that thoroughly, you will never run utterly dry, even if you have to speak five or ten other times during the week without preparation." After he had become an eminent preacher in New York many years later, young Rainsford said, "I owe a great deal of my success to following out that one idea. . . . For this advice I can never be thankful enough, and I have re- peated it in hundreds of cases, I hope with profit to all who have heard it."

Another son, Marcus, carried on in the steps of his father as a staunch evangelical in North London. According to a brief notice appearing in *The British Weekly* on June 22, 1905, "The Rev. Marcus Rainsford, the recently appointed Vicar of Pad- dington, is associating himself very heartily with his brethren of the Free Churches. . . . I hear that the attendance at Pad- dington Church has been steadily growing since Mr. Rainsford came." This son died in 1911.

Information about Marcus Rainsford's private life is rather meager. His eldest son informs us that "he was a lover of nature, though of natural history, except what he had picked up for himself, he knew nothing. He loved a horse and was an excellent judge of its points. In boyhood, he hunted with the 'Kildare,' a famous pack then, and he told me, when he gave me my first mount on a donkey, that he went to his first 'meet of hounds' on the same humble steed. He was a first-class horseman, hands and feet of the best, and could, years after, when he had long given up the hunting field as a worldly and sinful amusement, still take a horse over a good sized gate and hold two pennies, one under each knee, without losing them. When vicar of

Dundalk, he would groom his own horse and see to it that I
did the same for my pony. . . .

["He loved gardening, too,]and was always at work among his
flowers and vegetables long before we had breakfast, and we
breakfasted early. Later, when our means were not so straitened
and he could afford a man of all work, he confined himself to
his roses. These were his joy and pride. He grew standard roses,
budding varieties from England and France and wild hedgerow
stock. These I used to dig up and bring to him from the country-
side, and he would give me a shilling a dozen for them. So the
old, neglected vicarage garden became a beautiful thing to see,
for no one in Dundalk raised such roses as he did."

Rainsford honored the Word of God in everything, including
the management of his home. He himself took the place of
headship; he accorded to his wife the place of honor; his children were in the place of obedience. Hours were kept punc-
tually; no one dreamed of being late for a meal or for family
prayer with which each day began and ended.

The children knew that their parents lived in the company
of the Lord whom they loved and trusted. They consistently
presented the beautiful realities of their walk with God. The
younger ones learned a verse of the Bible every morning. When
they could read, they memorized two verses on weekdays and
six on Sundays. Said one of them, "to our parents the Bible was
not a Word of God, one among many words, but *the* Word of
God, from the first letter to the last, His inspired and inerrant
message to men. In it we children were schooled as soon as we
could understand English, and thankful I am for that rule of my
home.

"Our home was unlike and in advance of most other homes,
in that father and mother were the most wise, tender and patient
parents I ever knew. The evening we looked forward to, when
we all sat around the fire in the drawing room. Father and

mother sang to us (mother had a sweet alto voice) and told us stories. Then, as we grew bigger father read to us. And later still we as well as our parents sang. Father read delightfully, explaining as he went. What an introduction he gave us to *Robinson Crusoe, Swiss Family Robinson,* and *Pilgrim's Progress!"*

Certain things were not tolerated in the Rainsford home. Among these, untruthfulness and disobedience were first. Cowardice, idleness, neglect of pets and cruelty of any kind were to the children "a good second." It never occurred to them to dispute the discipline of their parents. Obedience was not a hardship; it was a matter of course, because the Bible required it. From their earliest years, the young folks were taught to have no secrets from their father and mother. They learned to bring all troubles, whether little or big, to their parents in full confidence that help would be forthcoming, so that the custom of going to them about everything became firmly established.

There is one observation by William Rainsford, made in America as he compared family life in his New York parish with what he had known under his own godly father and mother, which stands as a testimony by a liberal to the folly of departing from the teaching of the Word of God in the home.

"I contrast the memories of my home," he wrote, "with what I see on all hands in families today. Children are taught chiefly to express themselves. If, even in earliest infancy, the very babies are taught to assert themselves, to express their own view of things, to have their own way, one of two things must happen. Either the child wins out and the parent gives in, or parental authority is attained only at the cost of perpetual argument and dispute. All nature cries out against such an idea of child training. What is the stored-up experience of the parent for? That precious heritage, handed down through the ages, so painfully acquired and retained? What is it but a trust for the child? . . . What possible value has the judgment of a child, say, of four

years? Yet how commonly I have been forced to look on the
folly, nay, the tragedy, of a poor ignorant theorizing mother
arguing with her four-year-old little one!"

Just as the son gave thanks that his father had respected the
Word of God in the home, so many people in that generation
had occasion to give thanks that Marcus Rainsford honored the
Word of God in the pulpit.

Moody and Sankey conducted great evangelistic missions in
London in 1875 and 1883–4. No minister of that city entered
more heartily into these campaigns than Mr. Rainsford. The
evangelist was quick to perceive his gift of clear and simple
utterance in clearing away such mental difficulties as are commonly encountered in inquiry room work. Therefore he arranged to have Mr. Rainsford stand with him on the platform
and answer various questions about the teachings of the Scriptures, in the presence of large congregations.

These gospel dialogues attracted considerable attention. They
were published in *The Christian* in 1884, and later reprinted
as a tract booklet by the Bible Institute Colportage Association
of Chicago. They are of such interest and value that they have
been incorporated in the present volume. It may be that the
Lord will lead someone in our own generation to use again this
forgotten method of evangelism and teaching, where a leader
in all humility takes the place of a mere questioner, a learner,
in the presence of another man mighty in the Scriptures, to
bring the blessing of the other man's ministry to his own
congregation.

At Wandsworth, in the great wooden hall where Mr. Moody
was conducting such a gospel dialogue, a working man listened
and was saved. Some time later he told Mr. Rainsford his story.

Mr. Moody had asked, "How long would you give a sinner to
come to Christ and be saved?" Mr. Rainsford replied, "Do you
speak of a real bad one?" Moody said, "Yes, a real bad one!"

The poor sinner testified, "I listened sharp to that, for I knew

I had served the devil for forty years!" Mr. Moody went on, "Would you give him twenty-four hours?"

Mr. R.: "Certainly not. He might awake in hell before half the time!"

Mr. M.: "Well, how long would you give him—one hour?"

Mr. R.: "No, certainly not; but just time enough to say, 'Lord, I believe; thanks be to God for His unspeakable gift!' "

"Oh, sir," said the man to Rainsford, "that did it for me! To think I might come to Christ and get salvation then and there, right off. It was wonderful good of Him, and I just took Him at His word, sir, and I am so happy ever since. I thought I must come and tell you."

In 1886, three years after the London campaign, Mr. Moody invited Marcus Rainsford to the Northfield Conference platform. It was reported that "he speedily won all hearts at Northfield, and none of the addresses of that year were more thoroughly enjoyed than those of the pastor of Belgrave Chapel, whose genial utterance, rich unfolding of the treasures of God's Word, and inimitable faculty of lively narration made him a universal favorite."

Dr. Mahaffy, provost of Trinity College, Dublin, wrote an estimate of Rainsford and his contemporaries, which appeared in the (liberal) *Hibbert Journal* in April, 1903:

"These popular preachers, who included Marcus Rainsford, differed from the early Puritans in that these thought an accurate knowledge of the original Bible essential, while their descendants were quite content with the Authorized Version . . . some of them believed in the verbal inspiration of the English Bible, which they made the absolute rule of faith."

After describing how the preacher read through "the service," devotedly using the Book of Common Prayer, then retired to reappear in a lofty pulpit in black preaching gown and bands for the sermon, Dr. Mahaffy continued,

"In his discourse it was his absolute duty to set forth the

whole gospel (as he understood it) so that any stray person, or
any member of the congregation in a contrite condition, might
then and there attain conversion (which was always sudden)
and find peace. These men were all Calvinists, as their fore-
fathers had been; they were distinctly antiritualists. The doctrine of justification by faith was the cardinal point of their
teaching . . . they did not hesitate to preach that all those
who had not embraced the dogma of justification by faith were
doomed to eternal perdition. They believed as strongly as Mas-
silon in 'the small number of the elect.' They were not afraid
to insist on the eternity and very maximum of torture. On the
other hand, they had the firmest belief in the future bliss of
those who were saved, and upon their death beds looked forward with confidence to an immediate reunion with the saints
who had gone before. They had strong hopes of seeing visions
of glory on their death beds.

"They lived saintly lives, though they inveighed against the
value of good works. They controlled their congregations as
spiritual autocrats, though they denied all efficiency in apostolic
succession. They were excellent and able men, proclaiming a
creed that has over and over again produced great and noble
types of men. . . ."

Evangelicals today will be interested to learn that one of the
compelling motives which fired Marcus Rainsford and his contemporaries with a passion to win the lost to Christ was their
conviction that the Lord Jesus might return at any moment and
bring to an end the present opportunity to engage in the ministry of the gospel.

According to his son William, Mr. Rainsford was "more
than a low churchman; he was a very extreme low church type;
and when I speak of him, I speak of his school: they had no
conception at all of the church idea. They were gospel preachers
seeking only to evoke personal experience . . . they were in-
dividualists of the most marked type.

"The majority of these men believed and preached the imminence of the second coming of Jesus and the gathering to Him of His saints in the air, which belief indeed St. Paul in his earliest teachings held, as we see by the first of his epistles, I and II Thessalonians. . . . The evangelicals of the nineteenth century were the spiritual heirs (of Whitefield and Wesley). They too protested against the worldliness, ignorance and supineness of the national church, and when all preferment was denied them, they went outside Episcopal boundaries, preaching on the streets and in the cottages of the poor."

Early in November, 1896, a writer for *The Christian* visited Belgrave Chapel and afterward wrote his impressions of what he witnessed that day.

"This spot has for thirty years past been the scene of a Christian ministry which for its plain and reiterated setting forth of 'the lovely story of the gospel' could not well be surpassed. The preacher who still occupies the pulpit is the Rev. Marcus Rainsford, and the phrase that we have quoted is his own. No words could better describe the attractive aspect of salvation that he has ever delighted to present to his congregation.

"He revels in the fullness and freeness, the graciousness and complete sufficiency of God's dealings with the sinful sons of men, as embodied in the birth, life, words, acts, death, resurrection, ascension, session, intercession and second advent of Him who is the Son of God and the Saviour of the world.

"For a generation he has been telling within the same building the story of Jesus and His love. Last Sunday morning it was the same inexhaustible theme on which he discoursed. The listener could see that the physical man is decaying through the course of nature, but the spirit is yet full of an ardor and intensity that are not merely the index of a Celtic ancestry. . . .

"As the writer noticed the somewhat feeble gait and pale countenance of this man of God, a petition in one of the Psalms for the day came home to him with a peculiar sense of appropriateness as applied to the preacher. It was, 'O spare me that I may recover strength, before I go hence and be no more.'

When the inevitable hour comes for him to pass within the veil, and to know with grander fullness the comforting truths he has so long taught, he will leave behind him many a cherished memory and many a sanctifying impulse, besides countless seals to his wholehearted gospel ministry."

In Scotland on August 15, 1897, Marcus Rainsford died. Among the Christian leaders of that generation who testified to the debt of gratitude he owed to the ministry of the great expositor was Dr. W. H. Griffith Thomas, who wrote, "I have personal reasons for great thankfulness to God for Mr. Rainsford's teaching. In the early days of my Christian life I was much helped and strengthened by his clear, solid and scriptural presentation of Christian truth. From the time I first read one of his books, I learnt to look out for anything that came from his pen. Mr. Rainsford was truly remarkable for his firm grasp of essential evangelical doctrine, and for his peculiarly strong hold on the great foundation realities. . . . He helped me much to realize my judicial acceptance and standing in Christ— that basis of all peace, satisfaction and growth in the Christian life."

Any writer who could so deeply influence a man of the spiritual stature of Griffith Thomas deserves to be brought to the attention of believers today. This brief account of the life and ministry of a faithful servant of Christ, sketched with so much difficulty after the silence which has surrounded him for more than fifty years, may serve to call attention to the wonderful blessedness attaching to Christian service which honors the Word of God. The reprinting of Marcus Rainsford's expository studies in the great high priestly prayer of Christ for His people will not only provide this generation with a devotional classic, but set a standard for those who would emulate Rainsford's example, and engage in a ministry which is truly biblical and expository.

S. MAXWELL CODER

OUR LORD PRAYS FOR HIS OWN

thoughts on John 17

1

"THESE WORDS SPAKE JESUS, AND LIFTED UP HIS EYES TO
HEAVEN, AND SAID, FATHER, THE HOUR IS COME."
—John 17:1

THIS CHAPTER is emphatically the Lord's prayer. That which
we commonly call the Lord's prayer He taught His disciples, but did not use Himself. The petition, "Forgive *us our
trespasses,*" could never have been uttered by the Lord Jesus
Christ. This prayer, on the other hand, is *His own*—His disciples
were not invited to unite in it; it was a prayer they did not and
could not utter. Evidently the Lord spake so as to be heard, and
the disciples listened. The Holy Ghost has provided that not one
petition should be lost to the Church of God. We often find our
Lord *teaching* His disciples to pray, and we read of Him spending even whole nights in prayer; but we never find Him praying
with His disciples. Indeed, there would seem to be something
incongruous in Christ kneeling down *with* His disciples for
prayer; there must always have been something peculiar in His
petitions.

At this time His work on earth was well-nigh ended: nothing
remained for Him but to die: "I have *finished* the work which
thou gavest me to do" (v. 4). The Last Supper was over. The
Lord had dispensed to His disciples the broken bread and
poured-out wine, memorials of His dying love; He had expressed to them His desire, that in remembrance of Him, they
should often gather together and thus show forth His death in
this *illustration* and their union with Himself and with each

other, until His return to them in glory. He had washed their feet; He had comforted them; He had opened His whole heart to them. He now opens it *for* them to Him before whom "all hearts are open, all desires known, and from whom no secrets are hid"; and having poured out His soul into the ear, and into the bosom of God, He went forth into Gethsemane. May God the Spirit be with us and give unction and understanding to our hearts, while we meditate on His most precious prayer.

A preface to His sacrifice, He left it with us as a specimen of the intercession which even now He carries on for us at the right hand of the Majesty in the heavens.

"These words spake Jesus"; the reference evidently is to His foregoing discourse, and not to the prayer He was about to utter. "These words spake Jesus." From the fourteenth chapter we have the record of them, words of life and joy; words of comfort, peace, and hope; utterances of inexpressible love.

"These words spake Jesus." He had told them who He was!

> "Philip saith unto him, Lord, show us the Father, and it sufficeth us. Jesus said unto him, Have I been so long time with you, and yet hast thou not known me, Philip? he that hath seen me hath seen the Father; and how sayest thou then, Show us the Father?" (14:8, 9).

He had told them why He was about to leave them!—

> "In my Father's house are many mansions . . . I go to prepare a place for you" (14:2).

He had told them, He could hear them still, though in His Father's house—

> "Whatsoever ye shall ask in my name, that will I do, that the Father may be glorified in the Son. If ye shall ask anything in my name, I will do it" (14:13, 14).

"These words spake Jesus." He had told them how He loved them:—

"As the Father hath loved me, so have I loved you" (15:9) of the certainty of His return!—

> "If I go and prepare a place for you, I will come again, and receive you unto myself; that where I am, there ye may be also" (14:3).

He had told them, whom He would send to them!—

> ⌈"I will pray the Father, and he shall give you another Comforter that he may abide with you forever"⌉(14:16).

He had told them of their union with Himself, whether absent or present—

> "I am the vine, ye are the branches" (15:5).

And that vine was now about to have its roots in His risen and glorified humanity on the very throne of God. Henceforth the blood-royal of heaven is in your veins; henceforth identification with Myself is your *position,* and the consequence of that identification is your *portion.*

Then, at the close of chapter 16, He had told them of the legacy He was about to leave them—"Peace I leave with you, my peace I give unto you"—peace in a world full of tribulation; peace in Himself; and triumph also, though the world, the flesh, and the devil were all leagued against them. "Be of good cheer, I have overcome the world."

Moreover, there were words of warning; He had told them of trial, of danger, of difficulty:

> "If the world hate you, ye know that it hated me before it hated you. If ye were of the world, the world would love his own: but because ye are not of the world, but I have chosen you out of the world, therefore the world hateth you.
>
> "Remember the word that I said unto you, The servant is not greater than his lord. If they have persecuted me, they will also persecute you; if they have kept my saying, they will keep yours also. But all these things will they do unto you for my name's sake, because they know not him that sent me" (15: 18–21).

"These words spake Jesus." Little did they contain of the circumstances of His own sorrow; He hints at the betrayal, because He would melt the heart of the betrayer; He tells Peter of his denial, because He would have him know that all the weakness and the waywardness of that wayward heart were fully known to Him when first He called him from his fishing nets to be His servant. But there was nothing of Gethsemane, nothing of the judgment-hall, nothing of Golgotha; they could not bear it *yet*. It was not of His own, but of His people's sorrow the Saviour's heart was full.

"These words spake Jesus." With what object?

> "These things have I spoken unto you, that my joy might remain in you, and that *your joy might be full*" (15:11).
> "These things have I spoken unto you, that you should not be *offended*" (16:1).
> "These things I have spoken unto you, that *in me* ye might have peace" (16:33).

And then, having given those whom "He loved from the beginning and loved to the end," all the comfort, all the instruction, all the encouragement, all the warning, and having expressed to them all the love that filled His soul, He "lifted up his eyes to heaven." Earth had been a wilderness to Him, and He was about to be trodden in its winepress; the baptism with which He was to be baptized, and of which His soul was straitened till it should be accomplished, was about to begin. "He lifted up his eyes to heaven"; His rest was *there,* His throne was *there,* His angels were *there.* Oh, that desiring look! that expectant look! that confiding look! He "lifted up his eyes to heaven," the weary, longing, thirsting eyes, "Father, the hour is come."

Now I ask your attention to two things:

I. The prayer—it is Christ's prayer for His disciples throughout all time.

Our glorious Christ had covenanted with God for all the

things He now proceeds to ask of God; what He purchased, or was about to purchase, with His blood, He here asks His Father to bestow as a favor upon His people. Learn! that God gives us promises in order to incite us to prayer. What the Saviour had spoken from God to them He now speaks to God of them, and for them; so faithful is Christ that He will never say anything to us that He will not say for us. Let us, therefore, have strong confidence; let us rest and triumph in Him.

The Lord Jesus Christ in prayer! What a wonderful theme for study and contemplation! Prayer was the messenger He was wont to send on all His errands, and in this He is an example to us. By prayer He held His constant intercourse with heaven; and we have no better way of doing so. Prayer was the arrow of Christ's deliverance, and the shield of His help,—"Lord, teach us how to pray."

II. Next observe the arguments He uses; they are two, and they are very short.

The first is, "Father!" Who can tell the power of that argument? who can tell how that cry thrilled the heart of God— *"Father."* When He taught His disciples, He said, "When ye pray, say, Father"; He at least knew that Father's heart. Speaking of it, He says,

> "What man is there of you, whom if his son ask bread, will he give him a stone? or, if he ask a fish, will he give him a serpent? If ye, then, being evil, know how to give good gifts unto your children . . . how much more shall your Father which is in heaven give the Holy Spirit to them that ask him?" (Matt. 7:9–11; Luke 11:13).

Again,

> "Your heavenly Father knoweth that ye have need of all these things" (Matt. 6:32).

Again,

> "Fear not, little flock; for it is your Father's good pleasure to give you the kingdom" (Luke 12:32).

"He lifted up his eyes to heaven, and said, Father." A child of God need never seek a more prevailing cry!

Observe how frequently our Lord returns to it. No less than six times in the prayer we find the same expression, more or less varied, "O Father" (v. 5); "Holy Father" (v. 11); "Father" (v. 21); again, "Father" (v. 24); and "Righteous Father" (v. 25). They that know that name will put their trust in Him who bids us call Him Father.

The second argument, "The Hour is Come!" Many an hour had passed on the dial of time since time began, but no hour like this. It was the hour on which His own and His Father's heart had been set, and with the issues of which His own and His Father's thoughts had been engaged from all eternity. It was the hour for which He became incarnate, and for which He came into the world; it was the hour when all God's waves and billows were to pass over Him, and when

> "Judgment also will I lay to the line, and righteousness to the plummet" (Isa. 28:17).

It was the hour when His soul was to be made an offering for sin; when, having been given by God to us He was about to offer up Himself to God for us. "The hour is come." Satan's hour,—"Your hour," as He said to His enemies; the hour of judgment, the hour of His weakness, the hour of death to Him. "Father, the hour is come," *that hour,* out of which Thy love, Thy promise, Thy covenant engagements are pledged to deliver Me and Mine. See! He rests His all on the promises of God.

> "Mine arm also shall strengthen him . . . I will beat down his foes before his face" (Ps. 89:21, 23).
> "Thou wilt not leave my soul in hell; neither wilt thou suffer thine Holy One to see corruption" (Ps. 16:10).
> "In the shadow of his hand hath he hid me" (Isa. 49:2).
> "I will . . . give thee for a covenant of the people, for a light of the Gentiles" (Isa. 42:6).

The promises now fill the soul of the Lord Jesus Christ and He pleads them. "Father, the hour is come"—*Thine hour,* Mine hour, Mine enemies' hour, and My people's hour.

Remember, as we study this chapter, how evidently we are caught that prayer is not intended to move the heart of God— no need for that. The Lord will have His people pray, in order that they may assure *their own hearts,* by bringing their need, their difficulties, and their cases before Him whom they have been taught to know as able and willing to help them. Prayer is the promise sent back in faith and confidence for the performance; and the prayer of faith is a testimony to the same. No other inducements are needed, the Saviour's prayer has taught us this. One cry is sufficient, "Father"; one fact, *"The hour is come."*

2

"THESE WORDS SPAKE JESUS, AND LIFTED UP HIS EYES TO
HEAVEN, AND SAID, FATHER, THE HOUR IS COME;
GLORIFY THY SON, THAT THY SON ALSO MAY
GLORIFY THEE."—John 17:1

IT IS ALTOGETHER NECESSARY to keep clearly before our minds the position, state, and character, in which our blessed Lord was at the time He uttered this prayer. *As God He could not pray.* He would have no one to pray to, nor could He possibly have received any addition to His essential glory. The blessed Lord Jesus is here presenting Himself before His Father in His official and mediatorial office and character. He had undertaken before time was, to take upon Himself the form of a servant, to be made in the likeness of men; and being found in fashion as a man, to humble Himself to death, even the death of the cross. For this end He was born, for this end He came into the world, and He who had been in the form of God, and thought it not robbery to be equal with God, is now presenting Himself before God as the Mediator—the man Christ Jesus.

The hour was come. He had fulfilled all righteousness, He had magnified the law in His life, and now He was about to magnify it in His death. As the Surety for the Church, as its Substitute, He now stands beside the altar on which He was about to lay down His whole person an offering to God for a sweet smelling savor; and as Solomon, when he had constructed the temple, dedicated it to God, whose temple it was, and the glory came and filled the house, so here we have a greater than Solomon, consecrating the mystical temple which the Lord built and not man, that the glory of God shall fill every living stone of the spiritual building—"Glorify thy Son, that thy Son also may glorify thee."

Truly, few portions of God's Word contain deeper or more experimental, precious truth, than this prayer of our most blessed Lord. If we are to grow in Christian life we must live upon the food God has provided—the Bread of God. May He teach us to digest it, to appropriate it, to understand and enjoy it, that we may be "strong in the Lord, and in the power of his might."

Now observe this latter portion of the verse—"Father, . . . glorify thy Son"—the Father in covenant with Christ was the *author* of all His mediatorial glory. Our blessed Lord invariably attributes this to Him; His whole life's object on earth was to show forth the glory of His Father; He gives Him all the credit of the salvation He came to accomplish;

> "He that hath seen me hath seen the Father";
> "God so loved the world, that he gave his only begotten Son."

He would have men read in the tender expressions which *He* uttered, and in the gracious acts which *He* performed, the character of the Father who had sent Him; accordingly He prays, "Father, glorify thy Son." This prayer uttered on earth by Jehovah's Servant, at the throne of the heavenly grace, is the model of the intercession, which, as our risen and accepted Representative, the Lord Jesus Christ now carries on above, seated as He is at the right hand of the Majesty in the heavens, on the throne of glory. "Father, the hour is come, glorify thy Son."

How long the Lord Jesus Christ *waited* upon His Father's will! For thirty years He lived in privacy; and now for near three and a half years He had been engaged in public ministry. He had a baptism to be baptized with, and His soul was straitened till it was accomplished. Yet still He waits for His Father's appointed time to present Himself as a sacrifice for the sins of His

people. What a picture of patient waiting upon God! Truly He
is an example to us in this respect. Observe also how Christ
trusted His Father. Upon Him was laid all the iniquity of the
Church of God; yet nevertheless and with that accumulated load
upon His soul He never questioned His Father's promise to accept His death as the atonement for it all. Oh, for more of His
faith! We sometimes question whether God accepts the blood
of Jesus for our sins; the Lord Jesus never doubted Jehovah's
acceptance of His blood for all the sins of His people.

There are many petitions in this prayer for the people of God;
but only one doth Christ present for Himself—"Father, glorify
thy Son." In the fifth verse it is repeated and expanded: "And
now, O Father, glorify thou me with thine own self, with the
glory which I had with thee before the world was." Wonderful!
wonderful! He asks His Father to take the Son of Man into the
position He as the Son of God occupied before His incarnation;
that there, as the Representative of His people, and as Head of
His Church, and Head over all things to His Church, He might
rule everything in heaven, and earth, and hell, for their benefit.
The prayer means nothing less than that; God only knows how
much more it means. "Glorify thy Son." Our blessed Lord was
now in His appeal entering into the very heart of God with all
the travail He had long ago purposed and undertaken to endure
for us men and for our salvation. In John 12:27, 28, we have
His anticipation of that hour:

> "Now is my soul troubled; and what shall I say? Father, save
> me from this hour: but for this cause came I unto this hour.
> Father, glorify thy name. Then came there a voice from heaven,
> saying, I have both glorified it, and will glorify it again."

The hour had come, and the Saviour prays, "Glorify thy Son."
The Lord was about to fulfill all righteousness. He had taken the
whole responsibility of the salvation of the Church of God
upon Himself; He was about to bear in His own person our
condemnation; and put away sin forever out of God's sight, on

behalf of all who ever did, or ever will put their trust in Him, by the substituted sacrifice of Himself; and to be enabled to affect this, was, in His loving estimation, to be glorified. "Father, *glorify* thy Son."

Oh, if we could enter more fully into the thoughts of God as to the real nature, character, and consequences of sin; and His boundless love for sinners, manifested in the gift of His own Son—descended from heaven into our nature in order to effect our salvation, to vindicate the character of the broken law, and to declare the righteousness of God, that He might be just, and at the same time the Justifier of him who believeth on Jesus, then should we understand what a glorious position Christ did really occupy, and what a marvelous grace Jehovah bestowed upon Him in appointing Him to be the manifestation and incarnation of His Everlasting Love, and "the daysman, to lay his hand upon both."

> "Behold my servant, whom I uphold; mine elect, in whom my soul delighteth; I have put my spirit upon him: he shall bring forth judgment to the Gentiles . . . I the Lord have called thee in righteousness, and will hold thine hand, and will keep thee, and give thee for a covenant of the people, for a light of the Gentiles; to open the blind eyes, to bring out the prisoners from the prison, and them that sit in darkness out of the prison house. I am the Lord: that is my name: and *my glory will I not give to another*" (Isa. 42:1, 6–8).

This was the work Christ was about to accomplish; and to finish it was in His estimation *to be glorified*. Satan, also, the enemy of God and man, was to be overthrown; the Goliath who had defied the armies of the living God was to be trampled under foot: and the Son of Man was to do it. Death, the wages of sin, was to be fully paid; and through death Christ was to "destroy him that had the power of death"; "to abolish death"; to extract its sting; "to swallow up death in victory"; and rise again, to die no more; but with authority to impart His own risen life to His people, so that henceforth they might live in Him, thus "delivering them who through fear of death were all their lifetime subject to bondage." This was the work He had in view, and the accomplishing of it was His glory.

"Father, glorify thy Son"—Thy love-gift to Thy people; by now laying upon Him the iniquity of them all; by accepting the sacrifice He is about to offer to Thee on their behalf; by substituting Him for the sins of Thy people; by sustaining and upholding Him in the tremendous ordeal He is about to undergo; by bursting the bonds of death and delivering Him from the power of hell, not suffering Thine Holy One to see corruption; by consecrating Him to be Thine own High Priest, to transact the affairs of man with God, and of God with man.

> "Christ *glorified* not himself to be made an high priest; but he that said unto him, Thou art my Son, today have I begotten thee" (Heb. 5:5).

Glorify Thy Son by enthroning Him at Thy right hand, and crowning Him as Head of the Church, and Head over all things to the Church; glorify Thy Son by sending down the Holy Ghost to those on whose behalf He suffers, that He may comfort them, that He may quicken them, that He may unite them to their risen Head, and be in them "a well of water springing up into everlasting life"; glorify Thy Son by putting all their foes under His footstool; glorify Thy Son by gathering together Thy people to Him, as it is written, "unto him shall the gathering of the people be"; glorify Thy Son by granting Him by-and-by in the midst of His redeemed and glorified Church to sing praises unto Thee and say—

> "Behold I, and the children which God hath given me."

This was the spirit and meaning of His prayer, and it was answered. In Ephesians 1:20–23, we read of the exceeding greatness of God's power.

> "Wrought in Christ, when he raised him from the dead, and set him at his own right hand in the heavenly places, far above all principality, and power, and might, and dominion, and every name that is named, not only in this world, but also in that which is to come: and hath put all things under his feet, and gave him to be the head over all things to the church, which is his body, the fullness of him that filleth all in all."

Again, Philippians 2:9-11;

> "God also hath highly exalted him, and given him a name which is above every name: that at the name of Jesus every knee should bow, of things in heaven, and things in earth, and things under the earth; and that every tongue should confess that Jesus Christ is Lord, to the glory of God the Father."

Again,

> "God . . . raised him up from the dead and gave him glory; that your faith and hope might be in God" (I Peter 1:21).

See the blessed connection between the glorifying of Christ and the faith and hope of believing sinners!

Now observe the arguments with which He pleads; they are seven.

(1) *His relationship,* "Thy Son," "Glorify thy Son!"

(2) *The glory of God the Father,* "That thy Son also may glorify thee"; that He may be the means of expressing and showing forth the glory, manifesting how great, and holy, and loving, and merciful, and true, Thou art; and how great is Thy glory in the salvation of Thy people. What is glory, but the manifestation of what God is! and Christ is the manifestation of God.

> "God, who commanded the light to shine out of darkness, hath shined in our hearts, to give the light of the knowledge of the glory of God in the face of Jesus Christ" (II Cor. 4:6).

"Whatsoever ye shall ask in My name, that will I do, *that the Father may be glorified in the Son"* (John 14:13). Again,

"Receive ye one another, as Christ also received us *to the glory of God*" (Rom. 15:7).

(3) *The commission God had given to Him,* "As thou hast given him power over all flesh, that he should give eternal life to as many as thou hast given him," therefore glorify Him now, and enable Him to fulfill this commission.

(4) *"Those whom thou hast given me!"* They were the objects for whom He came, for whom He lived, for whom He died, for whom He is now enthroned in heaven; those given to Him, given to be washed in His blood; given to be clothed in His righteousness; given to be united to His person, and presented unto God, "without spot, or wrinkle, or any such thing," before the throne, to the praise of the glory of God. Father, *glorify Thy Son* by enabling Him to fulfill the trust committed to His charge, even to give eternal life to as many as Thou hast given Him—and who are they? Can we set to our seal and say, "Lord, thou hast given me"?

"As many as received him, to them gave he power to become the sons of God, even to them that believe on his name."

Glorify Thy Son, by enabling Him to save them, that Thy Son also may glorify Thee in accomplishing their salvation.

(5) *"I have glorified thee on the earth."* He would have an equivalent for His life spent here on earth for the glory of His Father.

(6) *"I am glorified in them"* (v. 10); and again, "The glory which thou gavest me I have *given them*" (v. 22). He did not ask for glory as God. What could increase the glory of God? But Christ was born into our nature, and came down here and lived and died that He might obtain this glory, even a full equivalent for all that He in His glorious person as God-man either did or suffered, that He might give that glory to us. "I have given them the glory which thou gavest me." Observe how

the glory of the Church, the glory of Christ, and the glory of the Father are all *united*.

(7) *"I have finished the work which thou gavest me to do"* (v. 4).

Now it may well assure our hearts before God to know that the glory of the Father, the glory of the Son, and the glory of the Holy Ghost, are mutually secured and displayed in the salvation of those who come with their cares, their needs, their sorrows, and their sins, for life, pardon, and salvation, to the Lord Jesus Christ. Christ *accepted for us,* is the pledge of our glory; Christ *dwelling in us,* the hope of our glory; Christ *walking with us,* the light of glory; Christ *on* us, the garments of glory; Christ's *fullness,* the measure of our glory; and Christ *Himself,* our crown of glory. Christ crucified and raised from the dead for us, is Christ glorified; and Christ glorified, is God the Father glorified, the Holy Spirit glorified, and the believer glorified. "Father, glorify thy Son, that thy Son also may glorify thee."

These are deep things, but may He who searcheth all things, yea, the deep things of God, instruct us in them for Christ's sake!

3

"AS THOU HAST GIVEN HIM POWER OVER ALL FLESH, THAT
HE SHOULD GIVE ETERNAL LIFE TO AS MANY AS
THOU HAST GIVEN HIM."—John 17:2

THIS VERSE contains an argument drawn by our Lord Jesus
Christ from the nature and character of the commission with
which His Father had entrusted Him. He had prayed, "Father,
glorify thy Son, that thy Son also may glorify thee": the Father
was to be glorified by the Son through His accepting, undertaking, and fulfilling the office of Mediator, "that he should give
eternal life to as many as thou hast given him"; and the Son was
to be glorified by the Father commissioning, sustaining, enabling, and qualifying Him to discharge the trust committed to
Him. To bestow eternal life on lost sinners is the glory of the
Father; and to be the means and channel for the bestowal of that
eternal life on lost sinners is the glory of the Son. The blessed
Saviour here acknowledges this, and pleads it as the motive and
object His Father had in view when the Father and the Son entered into mutual covenant engagements for the salvation of
the Church. Oh, for God's own light to enable us to apprehend
God's precious truth!

Our Lord is speaking in an official character. He appears before the Father here as the Mediator; as God He could not pray,
as God He could not receive any power that did not belong to
Him essentially. On the other hand, as the God-man Mediator,
all He possessed was bestowed upon Him—His office appointed
to Him in the everlasting covenant between Father, Son, and
Holy Ghost; His work assigned to Him; His qualifications sup-

plied to Him; His ability bestowed upon Him. Thus the Father was glorified in calling, appointing, and qualifying the Son to be the Saviour of sinners; and the Son was glorified in undertaking, discharging, and accomplishing the blessed trust. How it should cheer our hearts, establish our faith, and kindle our hope and love, to know that Christ's office of Mediator—which is our security for the possession of eternal life—is founded on the glory of the Father and the glory of the Son. "Glorify thy Son, that thy Son also may glorify thee; as thou hast given him power over all flesh, that he should give eternal life to as many as thou hast given him."

Let us dwell upon three subjects presented to our consideration in the text:

I. The extent of the power committed to Christ—"power over all flesh."

II. The avowed object of the Father in committing that power to Him—"that he might give eternal life."

III. The persons on whom this eternal life is to be bestowed —"as many as thou hast given him."

I. The power—"power over all flesh." Righteously did the blessed Mediator obtain this power. The Son of God was born of a woman!

> "Forasmuch . . . as the children are partakers of flesh and blood he also himself likewise took part of the same" (Heb. 2:14).

The Word which was with God, and was God, and without whom nothing was made that was made, *was made flesh.* Christ suffered in the *flesh,* the Just for the unjust, to bring sinners to God. Sin was judged and condemned "in the *flesh*"; that is, in the flesh of the Lord Jesus Christ. Through the rent veil of His *flesh* He opened a new and living way of access to God; and in that *flesh* He abolished the enmity. And having given His *flesh* for the life of the world, He rose from the dead,

and gave His *flesh* to be life *to* the world. Righteously, then, did
He obtain the power which He here asserts He had received.

Sometimes by the expression "all flesh," the Spirit of God
teaches us to understand all mankind:

> "God looked upon the earth, and, behold, it was corrupt; for
> *all flesh* had corrupted his way upon the earth" (Gen. 6:12).

Again:

> "*All flesh* shall see the salvation of God" (Luke 3:6),

either to bless Him for the grace that led them into the enjoyment of it, or to learn what a grievous thing it was to reject
God's gift. Here, then, Christ asserts that He has had committed
to Him "power over all flesh"—all mankind—to rule, to control, to subdue, to restrain, to remove, to convert, to convict, and
finally to judge them.

> "Who art thou, that thou shouldest be afraid of a man that
>   shall die,
>   And of the son of man which shall be made as grass;
>   And forgettest the Lord thy maker,
>   That hath stretched forth the heavens, and laid the founda-
>   tions of the earth;
>   And hast feared continually every day
>   Because of the fury of the oppressor,
>   As if he were ready to destroy?
>   And where is the fury of the oppressor?" (Isa. 51:12, 13).

We need not fear what man can do unto us; for "Thou hast
given him power over all flesh."

But oftentimes by the flesh is meant the corrupt principles
and depraved faculties of our fallen nature.

> "In me (that is, in my flesh,) dwelleth no good thing"
> (Rom. 7:18).
>   "The flesh lusteth against the Spirit, and the Spirit against
> the flesh" (Gal. 5:17).
>   "The life which I now live in the flesh I live by the faith of
> the Son of God" (Gal. 2:20).

Child of God, you have no reason to fear the flesh, that corrupt thing you carry about with you, and under the pressure of which you groan. It may be you cannot overcome it; it may be there are risings and swellings in that corrupt heart you cannot restrain; but our glorious Christ can: "Thou hast given him power over all flesh." Neither the flesh without, though in league with "principalities and powers, and the rulers of the darkness of this world, and spiritual wickedness in high places," against which we wrestle; nor the power of the flesh within, though grievous and present, and often apparently set on fire of hell—neither the power without, nor the hidden depths within, can "separate us from the love of God which is in Christ Jesus." He has power over all flesh. He can subdue it, though we cannot. He can control it, though we cannot. He can bind or loose it, acquit, forgive, judge it; and finally, He can and will

> "Change this vile body, that it may be fashioned like unto his glorious body, according to the working whereby he is able even to subdue all things unto himself" (Phil. 3:21).

He can deliver from the bondage of the flesh, and He will exercise His prerogative; for "Thou hast given him power over all flesh, that he should give eternal life to as many as thou hast given him."

Observe further, He says: "All power is given unto me in heaven and in earth"—a power He possesses and sways by virtue of His sufferings, and the victory He achieved in that *flesh* which He took on Him, that

> "Through death he might destroy him that had the power of death, that is the devil; and deliver them who through fear of death were all their lifetime subject to bondage" (Heb. 2:14, 15).

And this power was

> "Wrought in Christ, when God raised him from the dead, and set him at his own right hand in the heavenly places, far

above all principality, and power, and might, and dominion, and every name that is named, not only in this world, but also in that which is to come" (Eph. 1:20, 21).

Thus our glorious Christ has power over everything that is named, or can be named, in heaven, or earth—in this world, or in that which is to come.

> "To this end Christ both died, and rose, and revived, that he might be Lord both of the dead and living" (Rom. 14:9).

How delightful it is to dwell upon the royal attributes of our blessed Christ! What encouragement faith finds in the contemplation; what ground of hope and blissful expectation! All power in heaven and in earth—His! All power over the enemies of our souls—His! All power over that which is within us and contrary to us—His! All power over that which is without us and opposed to us—His! All at His absolute disposal and control, and bestowed upon Him for this very end and object, that nothing might be able to hinder Him, or even interfere with Him in the discharge of His office, but "that he should give eternal life to as many as God hath given him." The realms of nature, the boundless stores of grace, the fullness of glory, and power over all flesh, are all lodged in the mediatorial hands of God's Christ; no wonder the apostle says:

> "I am persuaded, that neither death, nor life, nor angels, nor principalities, nor powers, nor things present, nor things to come, nor height, nor depth, nor any other creature, shall be able to separate us from the love of God, which is in Christ Jesus" (Rom. 8:38, 39).

And for this simple reason, they are all in His hands, all at the absolute disposal of Christ; to this end—that "He should give eternal life to as many as God hath given him."

II. The avowed object of the Father, as acknowledged by the Son, in giving Him all this power—"that he should give eternal life." We really know but little what eternal life is; but we know what the Scripture says about it, and by attending to this our minds will be enlightened. We find eternal life to be nothing less than Christ Himself: in the opening of I John it is so stated,

> "That which was from the beginning, which we have heard, which we have seen with our eyes, which we have looked upon, and our hands have handled, of the Word of life; (for the life was manifested, and we have seen it, and bear witness, and show unto you that eternal life, which was with the Father and was manifested unto us;) that which we have seen and heard declare we unto you, that ye also may have fellowship with us: and truly our fellowship is with the Father, and with his Son Jesus Christ" (I John 1:1–3).

This, then, is eternal life—fellowship with the Father, union and communion with His Son Jesus Christ!

"That thou shouldest give eternal life"—including the *present* possession and all-sufficiency for the ultimate fruition of it. This involves the removal of every obstacle in the way to the glory to be revealed, the setting aside of every hindrance, even though all the powers in earth and hell were united to oppose us. Children of God, if the possession of all power in heaven and earth is sufficient to carry us safely through the wilderness, and finally to make us more than conquerors through Him that loved us—then truly no weapon formed against us shall prosper; and every tongue that shall rise against us in judgment shall be condemned. "This is the heritage of the servants of the Lord": "for thou hast given him power over all flesh, that he might give eternal life to as many as thou hast given him."

But further: it is not enough that the hindrances be taken out of the way; we must be qualified to enjoy eternal life. I must have a nature given me suitable to that life—eyes and ears, affections and understanding—else would it be thrown away upon me; but He who gives eternal life, as Mediator, supplies the qualification for the enjoyment of it, putting away sin, renewing the soul, healing its diseases, conquering death, obliterating blindness, undoing and slaying the enmity, and finally subduing even the flesh itself, till "death is swallowed up of life."

"This is the promise that he hath promised us, even eternal life" (I John 2:25).

"And this is life eternal, that they might know thee, the only true God, and Jesus Christ whom thou hast sent."

The promise is Himself—His salvation; His crowns—the crowns of life; His kingdom—the kingdom of God; fellowship with Himself—the power of His resurrection; a new creation answerable to the great love of God in giving His Christ; an inheritance answerable to the great grace of Christ in giving Himself to obtain it; a nature answerable to the glory of the Father, the glory of the Son, and the glory of the Holy Ghost, and the infinite desire of the Godhead, that the people given to Christ should be filled with all the fullness of God.

Who can speak of eternal life? A life spent in the favor of God, in the presence of God, in the image of God, and in the power of God eternally; a life that will satisfy the love of the Father, the love of the Son, the love of the Holy Ghost, and the immortality of man. Just as eternal death is the sum of all misery, so eternal life is the sum of all bliss. Now the avowed object of the Father, in giving all power to Christ, was that He might give eternal life to His people.

III. The persons given to Him—even "to as many as thou hast given him." So, then, God has given a people to Christ; and "all things are for your sakes." This is the truth which, next to the revelation of Christ Himself, shines out most fully in Scripture. For your sakes Christ was incarnate; for your sakes the office of Mediator was appointed; for your sakes Christ died, and rose, and revived; for your sakes all power is committed to Him; and for your sakes all power is exercised by Him. Read God's Word and see if these things be not so.

Now remark here:

(1) A fact—a people given to Christ! To take charge of, to

undertake for, to wash in His blood, to clothe in His righteousness, to feed as their Shepherd, to espouse as their Husband, to
lead triumphantly as the Captain of their salvation, to subdue
their corruptions, to put down their foes, to bruise Satan under
their feet, to communicate to them His own life, to endow them
with His own fullness, to acknowledge them as His own brethren, "heirs of God, and joint-heirs with Christ." He knows them,
though they do not know themselves; and though the discoveries they make of themselves day by day ofttimes startle them,
yet their heavenly Saviour knew it all before. He values them—
oh, who can tell at what a price! He gave *Himself* for them; He
gives Himself to them; He rules heaven and earth for their interests; He is their appointed Head, and it will be the triumph
of His grace "to present them without spot, or wrinkle, or any
such thing"; "to be glorified in His saints, and to be admired in
all them that believe."

(2) *His delight in them;* how He dwells on and acknowledges His portion in them again and again—"as many as thou
hast given me." The language in the original is very peculiar:
"thou hast given him power over all flesh, that to all that thou
hast given him he should give eternal life to them." "All that!"
You have the same language exactly in John 6:37, "All that
the Father giveth me"—"all that." The idea is as if He were
looking over His portion, thinking how much it was, how rich
it was, how delightful it was—"all that I have, all this!" There
is nothing more calculated to bring out the delight the Lord
Jesus has in the possession of this gift to Him, than by noticing
how frequently He alludes to it in this prayer. In seven different
places He speaks of His Father's gift of His people to Him; in
verse 2, "as many as thou hast given him"; in verse 6, "I have
manifested thy name unto the men whom thou gavest me"; and
again, "thine they were, and thou gavest them me"; in verse 9,
"I pray . . . for them which thou *hast given* me; for they are
thine." Why were they so precious? Apparently for another

reason than His own delight in them—His Father's delight in them. "They are thine; and *thou* gavest them to me." In verse 11, "Keep through thine own name those whom thou hast given me." In verse 12, "Those that thou gavest me I have kept"— and finally, for the seventh time, in verse 24, "Father, I will that they also, whom thou hast given me, be with me where I am."

(3) The Lord declares that *the salvation of those given to Him* is an object of the Father's glory, and of His own glory; for, in order that He might be enabled to give them the eternal life He was commissioned to bestow, He prays, "Father, glorify thy Son, that in the accomplishing of this thy Son also may glorify thee."

(4) *Those who are given to Christ have assured safety.* They will lack nothing for time, nor for eternity; if the fullness of divine grace can satisfy them, they shall be satisfied; if the fullness of divine glory can crown them, they shall be crowned; if the Mediator on high can save them, they shall be saved; if God is to be glorified, they shall be glorified. Who are they? We have a description of them (6:37), "All that the Father giveth me shall come to me." They believe on Jesus, they come to Jesus. I cannot read the Book of Life to see if my name be there; but I can read my name in this Book of God, which is the copy of the Book of Life, and I can know assuredly for the comfort of my own soul that my name is written in the Book of Life above. I have come to Christ, I have believed on Christ; this is the description of those whom the Father has given to Him.

Again, we learn from verse 6, that they are those to whom Jehovah manifests Himself. Have we seen the beauty of Jesus? Have we admired the love of the Father in giving Him? Have we learned His name?

"The Lord, the Lord God, merciful and gracious, long-suffering, and abundant in goodness and truth, keeping mercy for thousands, forgiving iniquity and transgression and sin,

and that will by no means clear the guilty . . ." making "him
. . . who knew no sin to be sin for us, that we might be made
the righteousness of God in him"?

Another is—"I have manifested thy name unto them."

Again: "I have given unto them the words which thou gavest
me; and they have *received them,* and have known surely
that I came out from thee, and they *have believed* that thou
didst send me." Here is the Lord's own account of the people
given to Him—is it a description of ourselves? Have we received His Word? Have we known surely that He came forth
from God? Have we believed that the Father did send Him?
Have we believed that

> "God so loved the world that he gave his only begotten Son,
> that whosoever believeth in him should not perish, but have
> everlasting life"

and that such an one is of the number given by the Father to
Christ, that Christ might give him eternal life? and for the
accomplishing of which end all power in heaven and earth has
been given to Christ, that nothing might let or hinder Him in
bestowing, or them in obtaining it? How He pleads for them!
He pleads His covenant engagements; He pleads His own relationship; He pleads the favor bestowed upon Him, the gifts
supplied to Him, the avowed object of their salvation—the
mutual glory of the Father and the Son.

O pleading Saviour, to whom the Father hath given power
over all flesh, overcome our flesh; cleanse the thoughts of our
hearts; bring down within us all that is contrary to Thy Father
and to Thee; kindle our faith; brighten our hope; deepen our
love; make us more than conquerors in Thyself; whilst we hear
Thee say that Thou hast received power over all flesh to give
lost sinners who come to Thee, and to the Father by Thee,
eternal life!

4

HAVING EXPRESSED all His desire to His heavenly Father in these words, "Glorify thy Son, that thy Son also may glorify thee"; having pleaded His commission, and the universal and unlimited power given to Him that He might fully discharge His trust—even to give eternal life to as many as the Father had given Him—our Lord now expresses most fully wherein eternal life doth consist, and the means whereby it is to be obtained and enjoyed. And this He does in the hearing of His disciples that they might fully understand what a privilege the Father's love had purposed for them and for Him; for them, that they might know the only true God; and for Him, that He might be the means for their attaining to it: "This is life eternal, that they might know thee the only true God, and Jesus Christ, whom thou hast sent."

Thus He manifests and magnifies the glory of the Father by declaring that eternal life consisted in the knowledge of Him; and thus He magnifies the grace bestowed on Himself, in that power over all flesh was given to Him in order that He might give eternal life to as many as God had given to Him.

Life is the perfection of being; eternal life is the perfection of life; all life has its fountainhead in God; He is, and He alone, the living One: natural life, spiritual life, and eternal life, all flow from Him. Natural life is His creation; spiritual life is His inspiration; eternal life is His gift, possessed and enjoyed in union with Himself, and in the knowledge and fruition of Himself and Jesus Christ whom He has sent. As all life flows from God, so is it supported and maintained by God. This is true of natural life:

> "Thou takest away their breath, they die, and return to their dust" (Ps. 104:29).

It is true of spiritual life—separation from God is the death of the soul; as God said to Adam:

"In the day that thou eatest thereof thou shalt surely *die*" (Gen. 2:17), spiritual death followed upon disobedience, because sin cut him off from communion with God. It is also true of eternal life—this is the life of God in the soul; it flows from union with God, and is maintained in the communion and fellowship of God with us and we with God, in the knowledge of God, and Jesus Christ whom He has sent.

Oh, how great and inestimable an existence is life eternal—the gift of God's love, the end of Christ's coming!

> "I am come that they might have life, and that they might have it more abundantly" (John 10:10);

the fruit of the indwelling power, energy, and operation of the Holy Ghost, in the knowledge of God, and Jesus Christ whom He has sent. Eternal life is not a faculty—however divine that faculty might be—bestowed on us apart from God; but a principle laid up in Christ for us, "hid with Christ in God," and imparted to the soul by the Holy Ghost, in the knowledge of God, and Jesus Christ whom He has sent. The Father Himself is the source and fountainhead of it; Jesus Christ is the channel; and the Holy Ghost the communicating power. Faith is the heaven-born faculty in the soul, by which we see, hear, taste, receive, know, and enjoy God, and Jesus Christ whom God hath sent. We read the record given to faith thus:

> "God hath given to us eternal life, and this life is in his Son" (I John 5:11).

The text is our Saviour's own definition of life eternal: "This is life eternal, that they might know thee the only true God, and Jesus Christ, whom thou hast sent." Let us carefully examine this statement: (1) Here is the most excellent knowledge conceivable, for it is knowledge which imparts the life of God to the soul. (2) Failing this, all other knowledge is ignorance. (3) For unfallen beings the knowledge of God alone is sufficient for the enjoyment of eternal life. Angels that never fell can possibly enjoy Him in the immediate vision of His glory; but for sinners, there is no knowledge of God but as associated with the knowledge of Jesus Christ whom He has sent. (4) Observe how plainly the equality of the Father and the Son is set before us in this matter of eternal life: "This is life eternal, to know thee the only true God, and Jesus Christ, whom thou hast sent."

The more we know of God the more this eternal life shall energize our souls; the more we know of God the more happiness and peace, and joy, and power, and holiness, and love, and rest, shall be possessed by us, till "we know even as also we are known." On the other hand ignorance of God is the death of the soul.

> "Having the understanding darkened, being alienated from
> the life of God through the ignorance that is in them" (Eph.
> 4:18).

It was in order to dispel this ignorance, and impart to us the knowledge of God, Jesus Christ came; and that through Him we might be made partakers of eternal life—so He states in this address to His Father.

Observe what light is thrown by this passage on Genesis 2:16,17, where we are told God commanded the man, saying,

> "Of every tree of the garden thou mayest freely eat: but of
> the tree of the knowledge of good and evil, thou shalt not eat
> of it: for in the day that thou eatest thereof thou shalt surely
> die."

God did not forbid our first parents to eat of the tree of knowledge with a view of depriving them of any *good* they might obtain by partaking of its fruit; but only to debar them from the *evil*. All that was good they had, all that was enjoyable they had; there was no need to eat of the tree of knowledge of good and evil in order to add to their joy. God Himself was their abundant good—all that they attained by their disobedience was the knowledge of *evil,* involving condemnation and eternal death. Hence we learn how the love of God provided a means to cancel the condemnation and bestow life eternal, in the knowledge of the only true God and Jesus Christ whom He has sent. Even the beginning of this knowledge here on earth is eternal life, commenced in grace: for he that believeth *hath* eternal life, and the consummation of it in heaven by-and-by will be the fruition of eternal glory.

Let us give our attention to the nature and character of this most excellent knowledge; and may it be the one aim and end of our lives to attain unto it! For this the Scriptures were written; they are the means of attaining to this knowledge. *For this* the Holy Ghost came down from heaven, to enable us to study the Scriptures with minds enlightened, and understandings quickened, "comparing spiritual things with spiritual."

> "His divine power hath given unto us all things that pertain unto life and godliness, through the knowledge of him who hath called us to glory and virtue; whereby are given unto us exceeding great and precious promises, that by these we might be partakers of the divine nature" (II Peter 1:3, 4).

What a comment is this on the Saviour's words, "this is life eternal, that they might know thee the only true God, and Jesus Christ, whom thou hast sent." Yes, truly, in the knowledge of God we become partakers of His divine nature. And again in Colossians 3:10, we are told that we are "renewed in knowledge, after the image of him that created" us. This knowledge not only imparts the life of God, but stamps the image of God upon us; and the more we know Him, the more we shall be like Him; and when we know as we are known, we shall be altogether like Him. In Daniel 11:32, we read:

> "The people that do know their God shall be strong, and do exploits."

What an excellent knowledge this is! Again, Ephesians 1:17, the apostle prays that

> "The God of our Lord Jesus Christ, the Father of glory, may give unto you the spirit of wisdom and revelation in the knowledge of him."

In II Peter 1:2, we read,

> "Grace and peace be multiplied unto you through the knowledge of God, and of Jesus our Lord";

not only grace and peace be bestowed upon you, but be multiplied unto you in the knowledge of God.

These passages seem to open out to us what that eternal life is which we have in the knowledge of God, and of His Son Jesus Christ. Again, Philippians 1:9,

> "This I pray, that your love may abound yet more and more in knowledge."

In the knowledge of God we get our love to God; and not only so, but as we know Him, our love *abounds more and more*—love to God, and love to man. What an excellent knowledge this is! In Psalm 9:10, we read,

> "They that know thy name will put their trust in thee."

The knowledge of God begets trust in Him. Then in that beautiful passage in II Timothy 1:12,

> "I know whom I have believed, and am persuaded that he is able to keep that which I have committed unto him against that day."

Lastly, in II Peter 1:8, it is stated that it is this knowledge which causeth us to be neither barren nor unfruitful:

> "For if these things be in you, and abound, they make you that ye shall neither be barren nor unfruitful in the knowledge of our Lord Jesus Christ."

Thus we have fruitfulness as well as love, strength, and confidence, abounding grace, and wisdom, through the knowledge of God, and of Jesus Christ whom He has sent.

How great and glorious our God must be, since it is eternal life to know Him; indeed, our text implies not only that the principle of eternal life is in the knowledge of God, and Jesus Christ whom He has sent, but also that the knowledge of God is the aim and object of its existence, and the consummation, and rest, and crown of all its attributes and all its aspirations. How deep, experimental, and appropriating must this knowledge be, which introduces an eternal life of grace and glory into the soul of its possessor; and how divinely secure its possession has been made: "Thou hast given him power over all flesh, that he might give eternal life to as many as thou hast given him."

Oh, for a more abundant knowledge of the living God! To know Him is life eternal, to be acquainted with Him is peace; His favor is better than life itself, fellowship with Him is salvation. The vision of God is glory; His Word is the foundation for our faith, and hope, and joy, and God Himself is our portion for ever and ever. With Him is the well of life:

> "In thy presence is fullness of joy;
> At thy right hand there are pleasures for evermore" (Ps. 16:11).

Oh, to know Him!—to know Him in His Fatherhood; to know Him as the God of love; to know Him as delighting in mercy; to know Him as the truth itself; to know Him as having so loved this sinful world, that "he gave his only begotten Son, that whosoever believeth in him should not perish, but have everlasting life." "This is life eternal, that they might know thee, the only true God, and Jesus Christ whom thou hast sent."

How precious is this sent One—the Lord Jesus Christ; His Person, God-man, the Daysman, to lay His hand upon us both; how precious to know Him in His offices—High Priest in heaven, laying Himself out in all His fullness to transact our affairs with God, sending down the Holy Ghost to be our Comforter, a well of living water, springing up within us into everlasting life (cf. John 4:14). The King of grace, and the King of glory—what a precious, precious Christ He is! It is eternal life to know Him. How precious His engagements!— undertaking for us; coming down into our nature to accomplish our salvation; paying the debt for us; abolishing death for us; and then rising in the power of an endless life to impart that life to us, so that, as Paul exclaims:

> "I am crucified with Christ: nevertheless, I live; yet not I, but Christ liveth in me: and the life which I now live in the flesh I live by the faith of the Son of God, who loved me, and gave himself for me."

How precious His *commission*—to give eternal life in the knowledge of the only true God, and Jesus Christ whom He has sent, and to rule all things in heaven and earth, so that nothing might hinder our possession and enjoyment of it. Oh, for more of this heaven-born knowledge!—it is the one thing we need; it would dispel all our fears; it would scatter all our doubts; it would well-nigh dry up all our tears; and it would give us joy unspeakable and full of glory. Why are we so ignorant? Alas! alas! is it not because our faith is so feeble?

Faith has a high prerogative; it is the principle in the soul which lays hold upon God, and approaches and enjoys the knowledge of Him, and Jesus Christ whom He hath sent. Oh, that the Lord would increase our faith! It was in order that He might establish and increase our faith, the Lord uttered these words in the hearing of His disciples: for faith comes by hearing, and hearing by the Word of God: "And this is life eternal, that they might know thee the only true God, and Jesus Christ whom thou hast sent."

What a lifelong study these words unfold to the believer born of the Spirit and taught of God! Sweet to study Him here—it is life begun; it will be glory to study Him hereafter, when we shall know even as also we are known. The knowledge of which Christ speaks is not an intellectual, speculative, theoretical knowledge of doctrines; but an experimental, heart-affecting, life-influencing acquaintance with the only true God and Jesus Christ whom He has sent.

The Lord utters these words to His Father in the hearing of His disciples, that they might understand that His mission was to remove all the obstacles which could by any means interfere with their enjoyed vision of God. For this "the Word was made flesh, and dwelt among us"; that He might be made sin for us, and by giving Himself for us, might thus put away forever that which formed the real barrier. For this the brightness of the Father's glory was revealed, that His unveiled face might be seen—because a veil of unbelief had covered our hearts—and for this the Holy Ghost was sent, and—

> "God, who commanded the light to shine out of darkness, hath shined in our hearts, to give the light of the knowledge of the glory of God in the face of Jesus Christ" (II Cor. 4:6).

It was a deep sense of these things which made the great Apostle of the Gentiles count all things but loss for the excellency of the knowledge of Christ Jesus his Lord. No attainment here on earth seemed to satisfy him. Still his cry was evermore,

> "That I may know him, and the power of his resurrection."

Now, everything is to give place to, and shall make way for, this great end; every obstacle interposed by the world, the flesh, or the devil, between God and our hearts, Christ will take away; all other considerations are secondary to this great purpose, and shall in nowise hinder it. Christ is commissioned to give eternal life; and this eternal life is the knowledge of God, and Jesus Christ whom He hath sent. If clouds arise from our own souls, Christ will remove them; whatsoever oppositions from self, Christ will remove them; if we set up idols in our hearts, Christ will remove them; self-ease, Christ will conquer; if pleasure, Christ will thwart it. Thank God He will! His purpose is that we are to know God—to enjoy and possess Him; and all things that come between us and God, whether they be enemies from without, or unbelief and ignorance from within, the Lord Jesus Christ is commissioned, and has undertaken, to remove. And we may say confidently with the apostle Paul:

> "I am persuaded, that neither death, nor life, nor angels, nor principalities, nor powers, nor things present, nor things to come, nor height, nor depth, nor any other creature, shall be able to separate us from the love of God, which is in Christ Jesus our Lord" (Rom. 8:38, 39).

What a panorama of glory this subject opens out to us! Here we have God manifesting Himself: the Father loving; the Son undertaking; the Holy Ghost indwelling; knowledge increasing; ignorance dispelling; heaven opening; Satan falling; man rising—till he loses himself in the fruition of life eternal, knowing as he is known, and evermore enjoying all the fullness of God.

5

"I HAVE GLORIFIED THEE ON THE EARTH."—John 17:4

OUR BLESSED LORD is here engaged in prayer. He evidently opens His whole heart to His Father; His petitions are wonderful; first for Himself, and then for "those whom thou hast given me." As Aaron appeared before the Lord in the Holy Place, with the names, and circumstances, and conditions of Israel borne upon his heart on the breastplate of judgment, for a memorial before the Lord continually, so Christ appears before God in this prayer. A greater than Aaron is here; Christ is all in all—the altar, the sacrifice, the incense, the priest, and intercessor, all in Himself; and He here presents Himself before His Father's throne in all the inestimable worth, preciousness, and perfection of His mediatorial work and office. He pleads, "I have glorified thee on the earth." Truly this prayer and this pleading did ascend into the very Holy of Holies, and perfume the heavens forevermore.

Now it is of the utmost importance that we should understand, as it is also the perfection of blessedness that we should realize:

    I. Who and what is the glorious Person here pleading with the Father.

    II. The circumstances under which He pleads.

    III. The ground on which He rests His plea.

I. The person of the Lord Jesus Christ is the greatest of all the revealed mysteries of God: He was, and ever will be, God and man in one person; the eternal Son of the Father, one essential being in the infinite essence of the Godhead; the Word of God, by whom all things were made, and without whom was not anything made that was made, was made flesh and dwelt among us. The Son of the Father became the Son of Man also; and, as such, He was

> "The brightness of the Father's glory, and the express image of his person" (Heb. 1:3); "we beheld his glory, the glory as of the only begotten of the Father, full of grace and truth" (John 1:14); "in him dwelleth all the fullness of the Godhead bodily" (Col. 2:9).

Therefore, the majesty, the holiness, the blessedness, the preciousness, and the glory of the God-man, Christ Jesus, can never be conceived or expressed; the Father's love for Him, and His delight in finishing the work which the Father gave Him to do, are utterly beyond conception; His love to sinners in working for them, in living for them, in dying for them, must be infinite, and the dignity of His person must stamp eternal value, power, and efficacy upon His words and upon His works.

II. Then the circumstances under which He here presents Himself before God. That Christ undertook the office of mediator between God and man, and consented to take our nature and our place, was in consequence of covenant stipulations, engagements, and settlements between His Father and Himself. If He,

> "Who, being in the form of God, thought it not robbery to be equal with God: but made himself of no reputation, and took upon him the form of a servant, and was made in the likeness of men: . . . humbled himself, and became obedient unto death, even the death of the cross" (Eph. 2:6–8).

He was also to see of the travail of His soul, and be satisfied in the salvation of those for whom He was born, for whom He lived, and for whom He died. The Father covenanted to accept the Offering; the Son covenanted to present His whole self upon the altar of divine justice as an atonement for sin; and the Holy Ghost undertook to reveal the great salvation and apply it with power to the hearts of those whom the Father had given to Christ.

Now this covenant runs all through Scripture. In Psalm 89, from verse 19 and onward, all refers to Christ:

> "Then thou spakest in vision to thy Holy One,
> And saidst, I have laid help upon one that is mighty;
> I have exalted one chosen out of the people.
> I have found David my servant;
> With my holy oil have I anointed him."

The King of Israel, David, was but a picture, and type, and shadow of the David meant here.

> "With whom my hand shall be established:
> Mine arm also shall strengthen him.
> The enemy shall not exact upon him;
> Nor the son of wickedness afflict him.
> And I will beat down his foes before his face,
> And plague them that hate him.
> But my faithfulness and my mercy shall be with him:
> And in my name shall his horn be exalted.
> I will set his hand also in the sea,
> And his right hand in the rivers.
> He shall cry unto me, Thou art my Father,
> My God, and the rock of my salvation.
> Also I will make him my firstborn,
> Higher than the kings of the earth.
> My mercy will I keep for him for evermore,
> And *my covenant* shall stand fast with him" (Ps. 89:
> 22–28).

Then observe this precious part of the covenant:

> "If his children forsake my law,
> And will walk not in my judgments;
> If they break my statutes,
> And keep not my commandments;
> Then will I visit their transgression with the rod,
> And their iniquity with stripes.

Nevertheless my loving-kindness will I not utterly take from
  him,
Nor suffer my faithfulness to fail.
My covenant will I not break,
Nor alter the thing that is gone out of my lips.
Once have I sworn by my holiness
That I will not lie unto David" (Ps. 89:30–35).

This was the Father's part of the covenant. Christ's part was to
glorify Him upon the earth. Now David well knew such language was not intended to have its fulfillment and fruition in
himself. In II Samuel 23:1–4 we read:

"These be the last words of David . . .
The Spirit of the Lord spake by me,
And his word was in my tongue.
The God of Israel said,
The Rock of Israel spake to me,
He that ruleth over men must be just,
Ruling in the fear of God.
And he shall be as the light of the morning, when the sun
  riseth,
Even a morning without clouds; as the tender grass springing
  out of the earth by clear shining after rain."

A beautiful picture of the kingdom, glory, and majesty of
the Lord Jesus! "Although," David adds,

"My house is *not* so with God;
Yet he hath made with me an *everlasting covenant*,
Ordered in all things, and sure:
For this is all my salvation, and all my desire,
Although he make it not to grow" (II Sam. 23:5).

In Acts 13 the apostle Paul teaches that the promises to David
were fulfilled when God raised Christ from the dead, because
this was the seal and confirmation of the everlasting covenant.
Again (Isa. 42: 1–8):

"Behold my servant, whom I uphold;
Mine elect, in whom my soul delighteth;

I have put my spirit upon him:
He shall bring forth judgment to the Gentiles.
He shall not cry, nor lift up,
Nor cause his voice to be heard in the street.
A bruised reed shall he not break,
And the smoking flax shall he not quench:
He shall bring forth judgment unto truth.
He shall not fail nor be discouraged,
Till he have set judgment in the earth:
And the isles shall wait for his law.
Thus saith God the Lord,
He that created the heavens, and stretched them out;
He that spread forth the earth, and that which cometh out
    of it:
He that giveth breath unto the people upon it,
And spirit to them that walk therein:
I the Lord have called thee—

(He is speaking to Christ)—

I the Lord have called thee in righteousness,
And will hold thine hand,
And will keep thee, and give thee for a *covenant* of the people,
For a light of the Gentiles;
To open the blind eyes,
To bring out the prisoners from the prison,
And them that sit in darkness out of the prison-house,
I am the Lord: that is my name:
And my glory will I not give to another,
Neither my praise to graven images."

This was God's part of the covenant—His engagement to Christ; Christ's engagement was to glorify Him on the earth.

Then, if we turn to the prophet Malachi 2:4–6, "That my covenant might be with Levi"; here the true Levi is meant, the Lord Jesus Christ.

"My covenant was with him of life and peace;
    And I gave them to him
    For the fear wherewith he feared me,
    And was afraid before my name.

The law of truth was in his mouth,
And iniquity was not found in his lips:
He walked with me in peace and equity,
And did turn many away from iniquity."

In Luke 1, we come to the fulfillment (vv. 68–75) in the song of Zacharias:

"Blessed be the Lord God of Israel;
For he hath visited and redeemed his people,
And hath raised up an horn of salvation for us
In the house of his servant David;
As he spake by the mouth of his holy prophets,
Which have been since the world began:
That we should be saved from our enemies,
And from the hand of all that hate us;
To perform the mercy promised to our fathers,
And to remember his *holy covenant;*
The oath which He sware to our father Abraham,
That he would grant unto us,
That we *being delivered* out of the hand of our enemies
Might serve him without fear,
In holiness and righteousness before him,
All the days of our life."

This was the provision of the covenant; God's part being to give His only begotten Son: the Son's part being to glorify Him upon the earth; and the Spirit's part to reveal and apply this salvation to the hearts of His people, by His Word and by His grace. Lastly, we find God revealing Himself by His Spirit in a new covenant character, as the God of peace:

"The God of peace, that brought again from the dead our Lord Jesus, that Great Shepherd of the sheep, through *the blood of the everlasting covenant,* make you perfect in every good work to do his will" (Heb. 13:20, 21).

Such were the circumstances under which the Lord Jesus Christ prayed to His Father.

III. The ground upon which He rests His plea—"I have

glorified thee on the earth." The Saviour pleads the performance of His part of the contract. He was at this time standing, bound with the cords of everlasting love, beside the altar of burnt offering. The last act was as good as done; He was on His way to Gethsemane; He stands at the bar of God's justice, faithfulness, and holiness; He represents His people, and He gives them the whole benefit and credit of all the infinite merit belonging to His person, work, and office as mediator, in His life and in His death; and, on this ground, He claims an equivalent from His Father's justice for Himself as their Head, and for His people as members of His body; for Himself as the Son, and for them as those whom the Father had given Him—the people of His love, on whose behalf He had descended from heaven to earth to glorify His Father.

"I have glorified thee on the earth." I conceive that these were the greatest words ever spoken here below, even by the Lord Jesus Christ Himself; and I am sure if we could enter into all their fullness we should be convinced that this is true. Who can express them in their height, and depth, and length, and breadth? "I have glorified Thee on the earth, My Father; I have, according to the good pleasure of Thy will, according to the riches of the glory of Thy grace, and according to the covenant engagements between Me and Thee, performed all that was in Thine heart, and all that Thou didst require of Me for the accomplishing of the salvation of Thy people given to Me. I have opened all Thine heart, I have expressed Thine eternal and everlasting love to poor sinners; I have manifested Thy faithfulness to Thy promises; I have displayed the riches of the grace Thou didst bestow on a lost world. I have come down from heaven to make known the holiness of Thy nature and Thine unspeakable gift; I have magnified the perfection of Thy law by descending from heaven to obey it. I have demonstrated Thy justice and Thine abhorrence of sin to the uttermost, for I am about to lay down My life upon the cross to expiate it; I

have revealed and displayed Thine infinite love, for Thou didst
so love the world that Thou didst give Thine only begotten Son,
that Thou mightest be just and the justifier of him that believeth
in Jesus. This I have done; and all that remains to be done I am
prepared to do and to fulfill to the uttermost. Look upon the
Son of Thy right hand; upon the Son of Man whom Thou
hast made strong for Thyself. Thou knowest Me, Father, that
I am Thy fellow, Thou God of Hosts; Thou King of Saints;
Thou knowest the honor I have done to Thy law by being born
under it, and by My obedience unto death to expiate the guilt
of those who transgressed against it; Thou knowest the preciousness of My blood—Thou knowest its eternal efficacy to put
away sin; Thou knowest that I have more than vindicated the
dishonor done to Thy name, Thy character, Thine attributes,
and Thy will. I have glorified Thee on the earth; that earth so
long a land of darkness to Thee—that earth so long in the
hands of the usurper—that earth which has been so long ar-
rayed in arms against Thee; I have glorified Thee here, and I
will glorify Thee again."

Verily! none but the Son of God Himself could have truly
uttered what is here expressed; not all the angels and archangels
in Jehovah's presence, even though they excel in strength,
though they do His commandments, hearkening unto the voice
of His word; not all those ministers of His, that do His pleasure,
could say individually or collectively, "I have glorified Thee"
in heaven or earth: the great Jehovah has glorified them and
glorified Himself in them and by them; but they never glorified
nor could they glorify Him who "dwelleth in the light which no
man can approach unto." His name, His blessedness, His truth,
His majesty are beyond all expression and surpass all thought;
He is the God of glory, and He cannot but be what He is—essentially happy, holy, glorious, and incomprehensible: universal
nature, the course of Providence, the displays of grace, even
Christ Himself could add nothing to God's essential glory. It is

utterly impossible. God is most blessed for evermore, and His glory is incapable of increase or decrease; and, therefore, while we desire so to explain those words as to put immortal crowns upon the head of the Mediator, we must take heed in doing so not to overlook the essential glory of the Godhead which even He could only manifest but not increase.

Man's sin did not and could not diminish it in the most remote degree. The clouds that flit across the noonday sun may hide his beauty, but cannot mar his splendor; the moon, that beautiful satellite, made to reflect his light, may eclipse, but cannot add one beam to his glory: so sin did rise up, as a dark cloud, and shut out the light, and beauty, and glory of God from our creation, casting back its midnight shadow—its darkness that might be felt—its death-pall upon the hopes, happiness, and destinies of man. It was to remove that cloud, and to put away that sin by the sacrifice of Himself, Jesus Christ came; and, through the rent veil of His own crucified body, He opened a new and a living way, even for the chief of sinners, to God, to holiness, and to rest. It was through that veil, rent from the top to the bottom, the glory in the Holiest shone forth, inviting and encouraging sinners to come boldly to the Throne of Grace; and thus it was that the Lord Jesus Christ glorified God on the earth.

We read in Isaiah 59:2, "your iniquities have separated between you and your God." These were the clouds that had risen from beneath and passed across the ineffable glory of Jehovah, obscuring Him from mortal eye; and Jesus came down to scatter them by the sacrifice of Himself.

The crucifixion of the Lord of glory, and the atoning death of the Prince of Life, was not the extinguishing of a lesser glory, as the light of a star put out by the sun; but it was the glory of a sun hiding itself under the dark cloud of our sins, that the holiness of God might shine out and be magnified by His eclipse; as if one king did descend from his throne to do honor to another king, thus in the substituting of Himself, as a curse for us, in emptying Himself of the glory He had with His Father before the world was, and coming down to be spit upon, rejected, and crucified here on earth, the Lord Jesus did remove the cloud that obscured the glory of His Father, and, at the cost of the eclipse of Himself, could say, "I have glorified thee on the earth."

They are wonderful words. It was not only from the time the Lord Jesus was born in Bethlehem, but from the morning of all time He had been the glorifier of His Father. Creation was the handiwork of Christ.

> "Thou, Lord, in the beginning [to the Son he saith it], hast laid the foundation of the earth; and the heavens are the works of thine hands; they shall perish; but thou remainest; and they all shall wax old as doth a garment; as a vesture shalt thou fold them up, and they shall be changed: but thou art the same, and thy years shall not fail" (Heb. 1:10–12).

And He that made all things doth *uphold* them by the word of His power, therefore creation itself is but Christ's manifestation of the glory of God in one way; and providence is Christ's manifestation of that glory in another way. How early He began to glorify His Father by manifesting His wondrous ways and works and His thoughts which were to usward; how soon He began to make it evident that His delights were with the sons of men, and that creation and providence were but the circumstantials by which Jehovah surrounded the creature He delighted to honor; that the visible universe itself was but a home for man—a platform on which He purposed to manifest to Him all His grace and all His glory!

See Him walking in the garden with Adam; feasting in the tent with Abraham; wrestling, and suffering Himself to be overcome by Jacob; speaking face to face, as a man speaks to his friend, with Moses; bearing His people of Israel out of Egypt as upon eagles' wings; as Captain of the host of God leading them through the wilderness. The *manna* that fed them was Christ; the *rock* that followed them was Christ; the *pillar-cloud* that guided them was Christ. And as He was their companion in the wilderness so He was afterwards their companion in the furnace. "The form of the fourth," in Nebuchadnezzar's furnace, walking in the midst of the fire, with Shadrach, Meshach, and Abednego, was "like the Son of God."

Who was it that sent the prophets, rising up early and sending them? It was JESUS! and "the testimony of Jesus is the spirit of prophecy." Who was it that sent messengers from time to time to His tried and troubled people, suiting the word of hope, or comfort, or faith, to their varied necessities? It was Jesus! How often in times of danger, we read, "Fear not!" How often, in times of difficulty, "I will be with thee!" How often in seasons of sorrow, "I, even I, am he that comforteth you!" How often in seasons of desolation, "I will never leave thee, nor forsake thee!" How often in periods of sin and shame, "I, even I am he that blotteth out thy transgressions"—till at last He came Himself, and the angels of God sang the song of His nativity, "Glory to God in the highest!" He did not begin to glorify God then; but it was a new phase of it—"Glory to God *in the highest,* on earth peace, good will toward men."

What was His whole life here but a continued manifestation of the glory of the Father! When Philip said to Him, "Show us the Father," what was His answer?

> "Have I been so long time with you, and yet hast thou not known *me,* Philip? he that hath seen me hath seen the Father" (John 14:9).

Now only the crowning act was to be accomplished—nothing remained for Him but to lay down His life, "the Just for the unjust to bring sinners to God." And thus He provided the highest of all the high crowns of God—the crown of the glory of His grace, the crown of our salvation. All this, and a thousand times more than this—more than any angel or mortal tongue could tell—the Mediator gathers up into this one plea: "Father, I have glorified thee on earth." There is the set-off against man's sin; there is the set-off against the dishonor done to God's character, God's law, and God's truth. Put this in the one scale, and all the creature could do is but as the small dust in the other.

"I have glorified thee on the earth." May faith rest upon that plea, and come with boldness to the throne of grace, seeing that He who glorified Jehovah on earth is now seated on His throne, with open arms, to welcome those who have never glorified Him—that they may come in, and receive, and enjoy the great salvation which the God of all love and grace has provided for them in the Son of His love.

6

THE LORD is still pleading in reference to His Father's covenant engagements with Him as Mediator. Already we have considered the plea: "I have glorified thee on the earth." Now let us consider His further plea: "I have finished the work which thou gavest me to do." How blessed to listen to those words!—truly it is everlasting life to know them; and peace that passeth all understanding to realize them.

See, He claims the Father's recognition of the fact that He had *fulfilled* the salvation-work assigned to Him; and in consideration of which His Father had engaged to accept Him as the Representative and Saviour of His people: to "raise him from the dead, and set him at his own right hand in the heavenly places, far above all principality, and power, and might, and dominion, and every name that is named, not only in this world but also in that which is to come"; there to invest Him with all power in heaven and in earth, to be administered on their behalf; there to put "all things under his feet, and give him to be head over all things to his church, which is his body, the fullness of him that filleth all in all"—in order that His people's "faith and hope might be in God"; and that nothing, visible or invisible, whether they be thrones, or dominions, or principalities, or powers, should be able to let or hinder Him in being "the author of eternal salvation to all them that obey him"; or, in other words, receive Him, for to receive is to obey,—or, believe Him, for to believe is to obey,—and is therefore called "the obedience of faith."

Now He declares, "I have finished the work which thou gavest me to do." It was as good as done; He was about to be

> "Wounded for our transgressions . . . bruised for our iniquities" (Isa. 53:5)

that the chastisement of our peace might be laid upon Him. One man's disobedience had brought sin into the world, and death by sin; He, by one obedience unto death, was about to bring in everlasting righteousness, and the gift of eternal life through Himself, to the praise and glory of God the Father.

"I have finished the work which thou gavest me to do." It was not only during His earthly ministry the blessed Lord Jesus Christ, the Mediator, did work. He could say:

> "My Father worketh hitherto, and I work" (John 5:17).

Every manifestation of God from the beginning was by Jesus Christ; every communication from God to man from the beginning was through Jesus Christ. From the time the promise was given in Eden—the Seed of the woman shall bruise the serpent's head—His work began; and earlier than that, for in Proverbs 8:22–31 where undoubtedly Christ, "the wisdom of God," is speaking, He says,

> "The Lord possessed me in the beginning of his way,
> Before his works of old.
> I was set up from everlasting,
> From the beginning, or ever the earth was.
> When there were no depths, I was brought forth;
> When there were no fountains abounding with water.
> Before the mountains were settled,
> Before the hills was I brought forth:
> While as yet he had not made the earth, nor the fields,
> Nor the highest part of the dust of the world.
> When he prepared the heavens, I was there:
> When he set a compass upon the face of the depth;
> When he established the clouds above:
> When he strengthened the fountains of the deep:
> When he gave to the sea his decree,

That the waters should not pass his commandment:
When he appointed the foundations of the earth:
Then I was by him, as one brought up with him:
And I was daily his delight, rejoicing always before him;
Rejoicing in the habitable part of his earth;
And my delights were with the sons of men."

Our blessed Lord was the agent in creation, all things visible and invisible were made by Him; He was the pattern, the model after whose image and likeness Adam was created; and before Adam and Eve acknowledged their sin, or repented of their transgression, He was "the Lamb slain" for them "from the foundation of the world." What was "the tree of life in the midst of the garden" but an emblem of Christ? What were the "coats of skin" with which God covered the nakedness of our first parents but early pictures of the righteousness of Christ, covering our nakedness at the cost of the life of Him who procured it? Whose voice was it that brought conviction of sin and promise of redemption to our first parents? It was the voice of Jesus.

If we go through the Old Testament history, we find Him in all the communications of God with men. What did that bow encircling the heavens signify—that pledge to Noah and his posterity that the Deluge should no more cover the earth? It was a picture of Christ! What was the ark that saved them? A picture of Christ! Then came that grand ceremonial law, which from the beginning to the end told of Christ. What were all its sacrifices, but pictures of Christ?—its altars, its tabernacle, its temple, all told of Christ, till at length the Babe of Bethlehem was born.

What was His whole earthly life but one continued occupation about His Father's business? Hear His first discourse in the synagogue of Galilee:

"The Spirit of the Lord is upon me,
Because he hath anointed me

> To preach the gospel to the poor;
> He hath sent me to heal the broken-hearted,
> To preach deliverance to the captives,
> And recovering of sight to the blind,
> To set at liberty them that are bruised,
> To preach the acceptable year of the Lord" (Luke 4:18, 19).

Every miracle He wrought was an illustration and pledge of the work He came to do; when He opened the blind eyes, unstopped the deaf ears, cast out devils and raised the dead, it was but a continued illustration of His great salvation-work. He was about to give sight to blind souls, and hearing to deaf souls; He was to cast out demons from possessed souls, to raise dead souls. All His miracles were pledges of His power to save.

> "Whether it is easier to say . . . Thy sins be forgiven thee; or to say, Arise, and take up thy bed, and walk? But that ye may know that the Son of man hath power on earth to forgive sins, (he saith to the sick of the palsy,) I say unto thee, Arise, and take up thy bed, and go thy way into thine house" (Mark 2:9–11).

But now, "I have *finished* the work which thou gavest me to do." Those blessed hands were about to be bound; the feet that went about doing good were soon to be pierced; the brow, "fairer than the children of men," was now to be crowned with thorns, the emblem of earth's curse: "Cursed is the ground for thy sake . . . thorns also and thistles shall it bring forth to thee," so the sentence ran; and men plaited a crown of thorns to crown the Saviour with. Having plaited a crown of thorns, wherewith in solemn mockery to crown the King, the King of kings and Lord of lords, eternal, immortal, invisible, the only true God, not satisfied with the infliction of the most excruciating physical suffering, men hurled reproach at Him in the hour of His agony, until the prophecy of Psalm 69:20, "Reproach hath broken mine heart," was literally fulfilled. Little knew they what they did. The gentle heart, ever wont to pour forth love, was to break on Calvary; nothing remained but this. "I have finished the work which Thou gavest me to do." He speaks of it as done; and it was as good as done. He speaks of Himself as one passed out of the world at this time: "And now I am no more in the world; but these are in the world, and I come to thee." So completely was He laid upon the altar, His whole self was there, His whole heart, and thought, and soul were there.

Let me call your attention to four things—subjects for great and everlasting praise; sources of infinite and inexhaustible comfort.

I. A work given to Christ, and undertaken by Him for man's redemption. It was a *prescribed* work; a *definite* work; a *complete* work; there was no uncertainty about it. "The work which thou gavest me to do." We have a beautiful summary of this work in Daniel 9:24, the great prophecy of the Messiah:

> "Seventy weeks are determined upon thy people and upon thy holy city, to finish the transgression, and to make an end of sins, and to make reconciliation for iniquity, and to bring in everlasting righteousness, and to seal up the vision and prophecy, and to anoint the most Holy."

This was the work given by the Father to the Lord Jesus Christ to do; and this was the work He now declares Himself to have finished. See the evil to be dealt with, in its threefold aspect,— "iniquity," "transgression," and "sin": evil, in the principle, in the character, and in the practice; sin, as a crime, as a debt, and as a disease; and all dealt with by the glorious Christ, and in this way *He* was "to finish the transgression." How did He do that? By fulfilling the law. The law demanded one of two things— obedience; or, failing obedience, satisfaction. Christ met the law in both ways; He obeyed it to the uttermost, and He rendered infinite satisfaction on the behalf of those who had transgressed it. He *finished* the transgression—put it out of the way; so that God can never look at any sinner standing before Him in Christ, as chargeable with a single transgression.

Again, He was "to make an end of sin." What a wonderful

expression! To seal it up. The original gives the same idea as that in Revelation 20:3 where Satan is shut up in prison, and a seal put upon him that he might do no further harm. Thus the Mediator was to deal with sin—to make an end of sin; to shut it up; to put it away; to abolish it; to take it out of God's sight forevermore. How little we enter into the fullness of Christ's great salvation!

Again, He was "to make reconciliation (to expiate, to make atonement) for iniquity"; to satisfy the justice of God; to meet and suffer the righteous sentence pronounced against iniquity. We know how He did this—by giving up Himself, "the Just for the unjust." "I have finished the work which thou gavest me to do." What a wondrous incarnation of love and power Christ appears to the mind and heart of the believer, while we listen to Him uttering such words as these!

But He had to do more. He was "to bring in an everlasting righteouness." Himself, the righteousness of God, He was to bring in—to our emptiness, to our poverty, to our ruin, to our death; nay, more: He was to bring in this everlasting righteousness, into the very heaven of heavens, for our benefit and in our behalf to bring it in meritoriously, actually, effectually, absolutely, and acceptably, a righteousness, from everlasting and to everlasting:

> "Now the righteousness of God without the law is manifested, being witnessed by the law and the prophets; even the righteousness of God [there is the everlasting righteousness] which is by faith of Jesus Christ unto all and upon all them that believe: for there is no difference: for that all have sinned" (Rom. 3:21-23).

See also II Corinthians 5:21:

> "[God] hath made him to be sin for us, [that is, in our place] who knew no sin; that we might be made the righteousness of God in him."
> He was "to bring in everlasting righteousness" for us.

Again, He was to "seal up the vision and prophecy"; that is, to consummate them, to ratify them, to fufill them, to secure all their precious promises, and to preserve them for His people —as a seal protects and preserves. All that rich treasury of promise to be obtained, fulfilled, secured, and laid up for His people; all that rich salvation He was pledged to accomplish and to apply; all those visions that patriarchs and righteous men desired to see, the Lord Jesus was to embody, to fulfill, to accomplish, to consummate. "The testimony of Jesus is the spirit of prophecy"; and when He came, He fulfilled to the utmost all the conditions of all the promises; He became the substance of all the shadows, and He was the glory of all the visions.

Finally, and most glorious, "to anoint the most Holy." I need not tell you there is an allusion here to the Holy of Holies in the Tabernacle and in the Temple; that Most Holy Place, the sanctuary of God, where His throne was between the wings of the cherubim, the mercy seat, Jehovah's habitation; where He held intercourse with Israel; yes, where the high priest ministered, and the glory was revealed. What a costly structure it was! what care was bestowed upon it! what a variety of materials it was composed of! The plan was God's own; the materials were all appointed by him; the workmen inspired by Him; the pattern given by Him, how carefully it was covered with many coverings; how wondrously furnished and anointed! What was it a picture of? for it was but a picture, "a pattern" of something in the heavens. Compare two passages of God's Word, and you will see what it meant.

> "Let them make me a sanctuary; that I may dwell among them" (Exod. 25:8).
> "I will set my tabernacle among you: and my soul shall not abhor you. And I will walk among you, and will be your God, and ye shall be my people" (Lev. 26:11, 12).

The Holy of Holies in the Tabernacle was that sanctuary. It accompanied the Israelites in their wanderings till it was super-

seded by the grander Temple, when they became dwellers in
the land of promise. But still, whether in the Tabernacle or the
Temple the Most Holy place was Jehovah's immediate dwelling place. His throne was there. Compare II Corinthians 6:16:

> "Ye are the temple of the living God; as God hath said, I
> will dwell in them, and walk in them; I will be their God, and
> they shall be my people."

The Most Holy Place in the Tabernacle and in the Temple was
the picture of a great idea that lay very, very near to the heart
of God. His purpose was also to build a home for Himself—an
habitation for God—built not with such materials as suns, and
stars, and skies, and worlds; but with living stones, even redeemed, rejoicing, loving hearts. He laid the foundation in the
incarnation, life, death, resurrection, and ascension of His only
begotten Son.

> "Built upon the foundation of the apostles and prophets,
> Jesus Christ himself being the chief cornerstone; in whom all
> the building fitly framed together groweth unto an holy temple
> in the Lord: in whom ye also are builded together for an habi-
> tation of God through the Spirit" (Eph. 2:20–22).

Yes; sinners believing on the Lord Jesus Christ are "living
stones," gathered out of the quarry of nature. They are cemented
by the blood of Christ into this building, which, when it is complete, Jehovah Himself shall fill: inhabiting the praises of His
people for evermore; revealing to heaven and earth, to angels
and men, the sanctuary of God, where He will dwell forever,
and rest in His love; communing there with His outward creation; and making known by the church [to] "the principalities
and powers in heavenly places . . . the manifold wisdom of
God" (Eph. 3:10). If the Most Holy Place of old was glorious,
what think you will be the glory of this sanctuary which the
Lord Jesus Christ has anointed?—His home of grace and glory;
the habitation of the Most High God; furnished with all His

fullness; provided with all His graces, defended by His omnipotency; adorned by all His attributes; a praise through all the universe; admired by all creation; a monument of what His love could do; of what His power could do; of what His Christ could do—to the praise and the glory of Father, Son, and Holy Ghost, for ever and ever. Well might the prophet say,

"A glorious high throne from the beginning is the place of our sanctuary" (Jer. 17:12).

II. "I have finished the work." So He pleaded; and whether looking backward upon the earth, where His work was over; or forward to the glory, where He was to "see of the travail of his soul and be satisfied," He pleads with His Father, "I have finished the work which thou gavest me to do." "The work given" by the Father to the Lord Jesus Christ is *altogether finished;* "the transgression" *finished;* the making an "end of sin" *finished;* the "making reconciliation for iniquity" *finished;* the bringing in the righteousness of God, the "everlasting righteousness," *finished;* the "sealing up the vision and prophecy" *finished;* the Scripture is fulfilled, the foundation of the Most Holy is laid, and the topstone shall be Christ—and you and I, sinners, who believe, are the living stones of the building—redemption *finished;* the types and the shadows *finished;* forgiveness sealed and *finished;* the separation which sin had made between us and God, and between the members of Christ, *finished;* the distance annihilated; and those "who were afar off are made nigh by the blood of Christ." "I have finished the work which thou gavest me to do."

III. This was no light work—all the angels in heaven could not have accomplished it. Jehovah is represented in the prophecy of Isaiah as wondering that there was no man to accomplish it.

"He saw that there was no man,
And wondered that there was no intercessor:

Therefore his arm brought salvation unto him;
And his righteousness, it sustained him" (Isa. 59:16).

It was no *insufficient* work; the Lord Jesus left nothing for us to do, nothing for angels to do, in order to the completion of that which He had undertaken to accomplish. "I have finished the work which thou gavest me to do." It was no *disappointing* work: it did not disappoint the Father; it did not disappoint the Son, or He would not have pleaded, "I have finished it"; it did not disappoint the Holy Ghost; and it will not disappoint you.

"For the Scripture saith, Whosoever believeth on him shall not be ashamed" (Rom. 10:11).

It was no *uncertain* work; some people seem to think and speak of it as if its completion depended upon whether they consented or not. Christ's work was no *uncertain* work nor is it an *unsatisfying* work; try it; God tried it.

"Behold I lay in Zion for a foundation a stone,
A *tried* stone, a precious corner stone, a sure foundation:
He that believeth shall not make haste" (Isa. 28:16).

Devils tried it in vain; judgment tried it; death itself tried it, but the grave could not hold Him; and many a guilty sinner has tried it. He that falls upon this Stone shall be broken, even though his may be a hard heart; "but upon whomsoever it shall fall it will grind him to powder." Lastly, it was no *unnecessary* work; without this work of Christ being undertaken and finished, no sinner could be saved; you cannot reach heaven by any other way; you cannot approach God in any other name. Talk not of your works, your prayers, your intentions, your charity. It is written,

"I am the way, the truth and the life: no man cometh unto the Father, but by me." (John 14:6).

And now, the Father is satisfied; the Son is satisfied; and the Holy Ghost is satisfied. I ask you, in the presence of God, individually, are you *satisfied* with Christ as your "all in all" for acceptance with God? I tell you the issues of eternity hang upon your answer.

IV. The whole mediatorial work and office of Christ was appointed and provided for by the Father; thus He glorified Himself, and thus He glorified Christ: and through this work will He glorify whosoever believes and claims this finished work of Christ as the Father's gift and pledge for the salvation of lost sinners. Observe how, by the person and work of Christ, Jehovah vindicated His wisdom in creating man.

(1) The life of Christ on earth has proved that sin is no necessity of our nature; here was a true Man without sin.

(2) The life of Christ proved that sin is no consequence of the circumstances in which we are placed; Christ was "tempted in all points like as we are, yet without sin"; such is the record concerning Him.

(3) By the Lord Jesus Christ's life and work our God has vindicated His goodness in eternally punishing those who sin against Him; for He has provided and proclaimed such a salvation as "eye hath not seen nor ear heard, neither hath it entered into the heart of man to conceive." Consider what an aggravation of sin is the rejection of the gift, the neglect of that Christ, the refusal of that salvation! And yet how many of the sons and daughters of men live in the practical neglect and rejection of Christ. Was there ever such a message as He brings? Was there ever such a salvation accomplished as that He has finished! Were there ever terms so easy as, Believe and live! Were there ever such cogent motives—"God so loved the world that he gave his only begotten Son, that whosoever believeth in him should not perish, but have everlasting life"?

(4) Through the work of Christ, God has proved that He can be just while He is "the justifier of him which believeth in Jesus."

(5) And thus, too, God has vindicated His righteousness

in raising poor sinners from the dunghill, and putting them at
His own right hand in the heavenly places. What doth not
union with the Son of God entitle me to, and qualify me for!
—and if I myself, my happiness and my glory, are to be the reward of "the travail of his soul," what crowns too bright, what
kingdoms too glorious, what majesty too divine to be bestowed
upon me as the reward of what Christ did and suffered for me!
Look at God's commended love to you in Christ Jesus; come to
the marriage feast He has prepared for you in Christ Jesus;
listen to His appeal to you, for while Christ pleads with His
Father—"I have glorified thee on the earth; I have finished
the work which thou gavest me to do"—the Father Himself
by those very words appeals to you; for

> "Herein is love, not that we loved God, but that he loved us,
> and sent his Son to be the propitiation for our sins" (I John
> 4:10).

O wondrous love of God in Christ, following us evermore
through evil report and good report, and resting forever where
it delights to dwell!

> Like some bright river that from fall to fall
> Through many a maze descending—bright through all,
> Finds some low valley where, each labyrinth passed,
> In one broad lake of light it rests at last.

7

ALREADY THE LORD had prayed, "glorify thy Son." He meant, as you will remember, that His Father would be pleased to support, sustain, and accept Him in the tremendous ordeal He was to undergo: He was about to offer His soul a sacrifice for sin; to be wounded for our transgressions, bruised for our iniquities, and to have the chastisement of our peace laid upon Himself, that by His stripes we might be healed; He was about to sustain in His own blessed person the curse due to the sins of His people; to be made answerable for all the iniquities, transgressions, and sins of all who ever did or ever will trust in Him. This was the baptism with which He was to be baptized; and His soul was "straitened till it was accomplished." To be permitted to render this great atonement by the sacrifice of Himself was, in His loving estimation, to be glorified; and the Father's acceptance of His offering and of His undertaking to give His redeemed the benefit of the travail of His soul was, in His estimation, to be crowned with glory. We have a precious proof that it was so in Hebrews 2:9, where we read:

> "Jesus . . . was made a little lower than the angels for the suffering of death [and] crowned with glory and honor; that he by the grace of God should taste death for every man."

The petition He now presents is altogether different and additional; He here pleads to be glorified, not only on earth as it is in the former case, but in heaven; not in suffering, but on the ground of suffering, and as having finished the work which as Mediator He had undertaken.

Our blessed Lord appears before His Father, here, as His commissioned Mediator, to whom power over all flesh had been promised; and as having completely, effectually, and absolutely finished the work assigned to Him. His language is, "Now, O Father, glorify thou me . . . with the glory which I had with thee before the world was." He seems to say, "Father, Thou knowest the understanding existing between Us, in consideration of which I endure the cross, despising the shame; Thou knowest, Father, Thine own covenant engagement, that on condition of My making an offering for the sins of Our people acceptable to Thy justice, Thy holiness, and Thy truth, Thou wouldst raise Me up into the glory which I had with Thee before the world was, in order that I might rule heaven and earth on their behalf, and dispense as their Head eternal life to as many as Thou hast given Me. Father, the hour is come, and the work *is finished,* I am about to lay down My life a sin offering, and Myself a whole burnt offering, and peace offering, on the altar of My Godhead; and I claim as the recompense of My life-labor and the reward of My entire obedience unto death, even to be now glorified; and that My whole self, My whole Person, My whole manhood shall be taken up into the glory which I possessed with Thee before the world was." Oh, what a prayer!

There are four great and essential principles of gospel truth brought out in this petition, so distinctly and so simply expressed that he that runs may read.

I. *That before all worlds our glorious Saviour was associated with the Eternal God in His essential glory!* In the opening of the Gospel of John, and in the opening of the Epistle to the Hebrews, this great truth is stated very simply. It is well, in such days as those we live in, to have our minds fully established as to who He was who bowed the heavens and came down to save us. The higher and more worthy our views of Him, the greater will be our appreciation of His salvation; and the more we understand Him who loved us, the greater will be our confidence and the repose of our souls in Him. In John, we read,

> "In the beginning was the Word, and the Word was with God, and the Word was God."

And in Hebrews 1:2, 3 we read of:

> "His Son, whom he hath appointed heir of all things, by whom also he made the worlds; who being the brightness of his glory, and the express image of his person, and upholding all things by the word of his power, when he had by himself purged our sins, sat down on the right hand of the Majesty on high."

II. *That this glorious Saviour, who was with the Father, in the glory before the world was, did suffer that glory to be eclipsed.*

> "The Word was made flesh, and dwelt among us."

"The brightness of the Father's glory, the express image of his person," that He might purge our sins with His own blood, came down into our nature, was made flesh, and dwelt among us.

> "We beheld his glory, the glory as of the only begotten of the Father";

but it was beheld in flashes only, for the glory was veiled in flesh. The apostle evidently alludes to the occasion when, upon the Mount of Transfiguration, with Peter and James, he beheld the glory of the Mediator.

III. *The Lord Jesus here pleads with His Father to be reinstated in glory;* even the glory that He had with Him before the world was. Now He did not pray thus as God. As the only begotten Son, Jehovah's Fellow, He could not receive either power or glory not already essentially His own; the Godhead is incapable of any increase of glory or addition of happiness; but as

God-man Mediator all was received, all was bestowed. Our Lord is here speaking as God-*man,* our blessed Saviour, bone of our bone, not more truly God than He was man; and He prays as man to be taken up personally in that human nature He descended from heaven to assume, and to be reinstated in the essential glory that, as the Son of God, He had with the Father before the world was.

Oh, what a mystery is the Person of Christ! God-man one glorious Person; but man—true man—enshrined evermore in the essential glory of the Godhead. It is an amazing grace; and the Spirit in revealing it, has taught us what

> "Eye hath not seen, nor ear heard, nor hath ever entered into the heart of man to conceive" (II Cor. 2:9, lit.).

IV. As we contemplate these truths we seem to ascend to a climax of glory, and I think this is the summit.

> "As he is, so are we in this present world."

Christ represents His Church. He is the head of His mystical Body, and cannot be separated from it. See I Corinthians 12: 12–26:

> "As the body is one, and hath many members, and all the members of that one body, being many, are one body: so also is Christ" (I Cor. 12:12).

Christ the head thereof can never be separated from His members, nor His members separated from Him.

> "Whether one member suffer, all the members suffer with it; or one member be honored, all the members rejoice with it. Now ye are the body of Christ, and members in particular" (I Cor. 12:26, 27).

When the Lord Jesus Christ made His soul an offering for sin, He did so as representing His whole Body; and His covenant with the Father secured that His offering should be accepted for His whole Body. And now He claims to be exalted with all His members into the glory which He had with His Father before the world was; and the light that falls down from that glory tells us that

> "If one member be honored, all the members rejoice with it."

If this be so, what a divine and unutterable petition was this prayer of our Mediator: "Glorify thou me, O Father, with the glory which I had with thee before the world was."

It was a prayer of *faith*—a faith that embraced all the purposes and promises of the everlasting covenant. It was a prayer of *hope;* it looked out beyond the wilderness, beyond the conflict with death and hell, beyond the wrestling against flesh and blood, and the rulers of the darkness of this world, in which both He was engaged and His people, into the bright sunlight of the glory that was beyond. It was a joyous prayer in which "the joy set before him" was never more full than when He uttered it. And it was the prayer of *love;* He speaks as Mediator: the salvation, the triumph, and the glory of His people were inseparable from His own. When He said, "Glorify thou me," He prayed as Head of His Church; the God-man mystical was included, and in His person all the members of His mystical Body.

Now, the prayer of our Lord has been answered. He is in the glory! You remember how the Holy Spirit brought the tidings down:

> "The God of Abraham, and of Isaac, and of Jacob, the God of our fathers, hath glorified his Son Jesus" (Acts 3:13).

Nay, the apostle who had been in the third heaven tells us that "It pleased the Father that in him should all the fullness dwell." There is the full answer to His prayer; "glorify thou me with thine own self, with the glory which I had with thee before the world was." And what saith the Spirit? What an object for hope, for triumph, for praise, and for glory is our Emmanuel! "It pleased the Father that in him should all fullness dwell";

and all fullness *doth dwell in Him*. And the soul that receives Him is complete in Him who is the head of all principality and power; and "of his fullness have all we received, and grace for grace."

Moreover, not only is it a fact that His prayer is answered; but the steps by which He ascended into that glory are revealed— the stages of its consummation are all recorded. They are deeply interesting to us, for they are divinely associated with our own resurrection and ascension to glory. The glorifying of the Son of Man and His assumption into the glory He had with His Father before the world, began with His resurrection! Till then it was veiled; we saw "no form nor comeliness" in Him; He was "a man of sorrows, and acquainted with grief" until He died upon the cross; but at His resurrection all was changed. In Romans 1:4, we read that He was

> "Declared to be the Son of God with power, according to the spirit of holiness, by the resurrection from the dead."

And Acts 13:32, 33, which we compare with this, records that

> "The promise which was made unto the fathers, God hath fulfilled the same unto us their children, in that he hath raised up Jesus again; as it is also written in the second psalm, Thou art my Son, this day have I begotten thee."

Taken up out of death, the curse, the grave, exalted out of humiliation into the essential glory of the only begotten Son— how deeply associated are His people's salvation, happiness, and security with that resurrection! On that occasion it was that our great High Priest entered on His heavenly office, as it is written:

> "Christ glorified not himself to be made an high priest; but he that said unto him, Thou art my Son, today have I begotten thee" (Heb. 5:5).

Manifested Sonship is associated with His resurrection; so also is His Priesthood; and so also is our salvation—and all three rest upon the same blessed foundation: the manifested relationship of the only begotten Son to the Father.

Acts 2:33 records a further benefit to us in connection with the exaltation of our risen Head. His first act when as consecrated High Priest He ascended up on high, was to send to us the Holy Ghost:

> "Therefore being by the right hand of God exalted, and having received of the Father the promise of the Holy Ghost, he hath shed forth this, which ye now see and hear" (Acts 2:33).

The descent of the Holy Ghost the Comforter on the day of Pentecost was the priestly blessing of our glorified Mediator.

But He is enthroned King as well as Priest; and His portion and His inheritance is in His people. In Ephesians 1:18–23, the apostle prays:

> "That the eyes of your understanding being enlightened; that ye may know what is the hope of his calling, and what the riches of the glory of his inheritance in the saints, and what is the exceeding greatness of his power to us-ward who believe, according to the working of his mighty power, which he wrought in Christ, when he raised him from the dead, and set him at his own right hand in the heavenly places, far above all principality, and power, and might and dominion, and every name that is named, not only in this world, but also in that which is to come: and hath put all things under his feet, and gave him to be the head over all things to the church, which is his body, the fullness of him that filleth all in all."

Hence we can understand what lay in the heart of Christ when He said:

> "O Father, glorify thou me with thine own self, with the glory which I had with thee before the world was."

And, again:

> "When he ascended up on high, he led captivity captive, and gave gifts unto men. (Now that he ascended, what is it but that he also descended first into the lower parts of the earth? He

that descended is the same also that ascended up far above all
heavens, that he might fill all things)" (Eph. 4:8–10),

fill heaven with His glory; fill earth with His praise; fill the
hearts of His people with the Holy Spirit; and fill the universe
with His name: and yet again:

> "[God] raised him up from the dead, and gave him glory;
> that your faith and hope might be in God" (I Peter 1:21).

These are some of the ends for which He ascended into glory;
and a portion of the gifts bestowed on us as He ascended, for all
these things, and more than these, were in our great Redeemer's
heart when He said—"Now, O Father, glorify thou me with
thine own self, with the glory which I had with thee before the
world was."

Finally, you remember that in I Corinthians 15 Christ's resurrection into glory is said to be as

> "The firstfruits of them that slept,"

the pledge, the sample, the earnest, and the consecration of the
harvest to follow. And in Colossians 3:3, 4, His whole salvation is thus expressed,

> "Ye are dead, and your life is hid with Christ in God. When
> Christ, who is our life, shall appear, then shall ye also appear
> with him in glory."

And in I Timothy 3:16, we have an epitome of all this:

> "Without controversy great is the mystery of godliness: God
> was manifest in the flesh, justified in the Spirit, seen of angels,
> preached unto the Gentiles, believed on in the world, received
> up into glory."

I do not think this passage is usually interpreted according to the
mind of the Spirit. Observe the order of events here: "God was
manifest in the flesh"—we know that means the incarnation of
the Lord Jesus Christ; "justified in the Spirit"—there His death
and resurrection are intended:

"He . . . was declared to be the Son of God with power, according to the Spirit of holiness, by the resurrection from the dead . . . raised again because of our justification" (Rom. 1:3, 4; 4:25).

Next in order follows His ascension into heaven—"seen of angels"; next, "preached unto the Gentiles"; next, believed on in the world." But not until all His redeemed are gathered, raised from the dead, baptized into one Body, and received up with Him into glory, will the mystery of godliness be fulfilled. To interpret this last clause, as fulfilled in the ascension of Christ personally, is evidently to overlook and even invert the divine order. In that case, the verse should read thus: "God was manifest in the flesh, justified in the Spirit, *received up into glory,* seen of angels, preached unto the Gentiles, believed on in the world!"

Thus we have tried to follow some of the wonderful purposes of love and blessing toward us treasured in the heart of Christ, when He said: "Father, glorify thou me with thine own self with the glory which I had with thee before the world was." And as He ascended to the throne, taking possession of all power in heaven and earth, and sending down His Spirit to indwell, seal us and unite us to Himself. So by-and-by He "will come again and receive us into glory, that where he is, there we may be also." But, high above all His communicable majesty, our blessed Head has ascended into the glory which He had with His Father before the world was, He Himself implies that the utmost He can ask for His people is that they may behold it: "I will that they also, whom thou hast given me, be with me where I am; that they may behold my glory." Nay, it would seem as if all the glory that He can communicate to us is but the qualification for our beholding that glory; for He says, "The glory which thou gavest me I have given them; that they may behold my glory." So it is, believing in the Lord Jesus Christ, we are to inherit the fruits of His mediatorial glory, and to behold His personal glory without a veil between. If the anointing oil, descending upon the head of Aaron, went down to the skirts of his raiment, what shall our anointing be when, by-and-by, the descending glory from our God-man Head, enshrined in essential deity, shall come down upon His members to fill them for evermore! If, even now, "we with unveiled face, reflecting as in a mirror the glory of the Lord, are being changed into the same image from glory to glory, even as by the Spirit of the Lord," what shall it be when we are with Him where He is, and see Him face to face? All this and more—Oh, much more!—was in the heart of our loving Saviour, when He said: "Now, O Father, glorify thou me with thine own self, with the glory which I had with thee before the world was."

8

THIS IS the second part of our Lord's prayer. Hitherto He had prayed for Himself in the character and with the views and objects we have already considered, and on this ground: "I have glorified thee on the earth; I have finished the work which thou gavest me to do." Now He prays for His disciples. But not only for His disciples—doubtless they had a special place in His mind, for they were His firstfruits—our Lord prays for all His people to the end of time, as "the men given unto him out of the world." It was not the eleven disciples only who were given to the Lord Jesus Christ; surely it was not of the eleven only He spake when He said,

> "Let not your heart be troubled" (John 14:1);

not to them only He promised,

> "I will come again, and receive you unto myself; that where I am, there ye may be also" (John 14:3);

not merely to encourage them that He said,

> "In the world ye shall have tribulation: but be of good cheer; I have overcome the world" (John 16:33).

In Hebrews 13:5, 6, we have a key as to the divine mind in reference to the universal application of particular promises to individual believers:

> "Be content with such things as ye have: for he hath said, I will never leave thee, nor forsake thee. So that *we* may boldly say, The Lord is *my* helper."

Here the apostle quotes a promise made to wandering Jacob, and applies the comfort of it to the believers in his own day; laying down a general rule for a similar appropriation of all the promises of God in Christ by all His people, at all times.

Again: when the Lord spake to His Father, saying, "I have manifested thy name unto the men which thou gavest me out of the world," how much still remained to be manifested of that name! He had declared, "God so loved the world, that he gave his only begotten Son"; and

> "As Moses lifted up the serpent in the wilderness, even so must the Son of man be lifted up" (John 3:14)—

but this was not yet done. Just as He had said before,

> "I have finished the work which thou gavest me to do,"

so He says here,

> "I have manifested thy name unto the men which thou gavest me out of the world."

The truth is, all power was vested in Him for this purpose; and the Holy Ghost was awaiting His ascension into heaven, in order to descend and be the Revealer, through Christ, of that Father. He therefore refers to it as, in every sense of the word, an accomplished fact; whether He speaks of His own work, "I have finished the work"; whether He speaks of the revelation of the Father's name, "I have manifested thy name unto the men thou gavest me"; or whether He speaks of their reception of that name, "they have kept thy word." The whole is a beautiful illustration of our blessed Lord's intercession at the right hand of God. Not a word *against* His people; no reference to their failings, or their shortcomings; no allusion to what they had done; none to what they were about to do as a body—

> "They all forsook him and fled" (Mark 14:50);

no, He speaks of them only as they were in the Father's purpose, as in association with Himself, and as the recipients of the fullness He came down from heaven to bestow upon them: "I have manifested thy name unto the men which thou gavest me out of the world." Very blessed it is to dwell upon Christ's prayer in this point of view, as giving us an illustration of the mode and character of His intercession for us now at the right hand of God.

Let us, now, endeavor to strengthen faith by directing our attention to the arguments by which He presses His petitions, and also to the petitions themselves. There are seven considerations urged, and seven petitions presented.

1. The first is: "I have manifested unto them thy name." This fact is repeated in the last verse—"I have declared unto them thy name." Thus He enshrines them, as it were, in the name of His Father, baptizing them into all that name involves.

2. He pleads the Father's own interest in them. He seems to exalt this consideration even above His own work for them— "Thine they were." Let us learn to prize this fact, that we belong to God, beyond all others whatsoever; for it is because we belong to God, that we have been given to Christ.

3. He pleads the gift of them to Himself: "Thou gavest them to me." The Father's interest in them first; and then, as the result, His gift of them to Christ.

4. He pleads their reception of Himself and His message— "they have kept thy word." The Word of God proclaiming to them the gospel of His grace; that Word, says Christ, "they have kept." We know how feebly they kept it; and even while He uttered those words, how misty their notions were; how weak their faith; how little after all they practically understood. Even when He had risen again, we are told,

> "As yet they knew not the scripture, that he must rise again from the dead" (John 20:9).

His crucifixion seemed to have extinguished their last hope;

> "We trusted that it had been he which should have redeemed Israel" (Luke 24:21).

But in the strong majesty of His own grace to them, in the fullness and security of His own purposes towards them, He pleads:
"they have kept thy word." Oh, well it is for us that we have
such an Advocate!

5. Then, in verse 10; there is another wonderful plea, in the
power of which He presents them to the Father for the blessing
He is about to ask—"I am glorified in them." He had prayed,
"Father, glorify thy Son"; and now He plainly says, Father, if
Thou wilt glorify Me, remember "I am glorified in them." Oh,
for faith to hear Him say this even for our own very selves!
Truly if faith's ears were sharp, we would hear this wonderful
petition even now ascending on our own behalf to our Father
in heaven.

6. In verse 14 there is another plea, and it falls like balm
upon the soul to read it—Father, "the world hath hated them";
thus He would engage not only the Father's love for His people,
but His sympathy also. "The world hath hated them"; "they are
cast upon Thee, they are far from home in an ungenial wilderness. Father, they are in the world, where temptations, difficulties, trials, distresses, and anguish will follow them; where they
are hated for My name's sake: let this fact fix Thine heart upon
them, secure Thy care for them, and cause Thee to put Thine
everlasting arms round about them, and give Thine angels
charge over them."

7. Again, verse 14—"they are not of the world, even as I am
not of the world." "Redeemed, delivered, I have for evermore
associated them with Myself; and now, Father, hear Me while
I ask Thee what I desire Thou shouldst do for them."

Seven special petitions follow:

1. "Keep them" (v. 11). "Holy Father, keep through Thine
own name those whom Thou hast given Me; let Thy name,
which I have manifested unto them, be their hiding place, their
tower, their refuge, and their rest. Thou seest their need, Father;
Thou knowest Thine own interest in them, and they are Thy

gift to Me. Father, keep them!" Thus He deposits His people into His Father's heart, and commits them to His care.

2. "Sanctify them" (v. 17). How He longed to see His people separated from evil, and united, bound one to another by the cords of His own divine love!

3. "Unite them" (v. 21). "That they all may be one, as thou, Father, art in me and I in thee, that they also may be one in us."

4. Let them be, *"with me* where I am" (v. 24).

5. *Glorify them,* by granting them to "behold my glory which thou hast given me."

6. Let "the love wherewith thou hast loved me . . . *be in them"* (v. 26). (Who can measure this prayer?)

7. Lastly. And *"I myself in them."*

Now, what more could God give? What more could Christ ask? What more could His blood purchase? What more could His Spirit reveal, or enable His people to enjoy, than is here pleaded before God, at the moment when Christ's hour was come, and He was pouring His last words into that Father's heart, whose work He had finished, whose name He had glorified, and whose glorified name He had manifested to His redeemed ones?

By the name of God is signified God Himself—His perfections, attributes, character—God's revealed self. In the Word of God, we have Jehovah manifesting Himself to His people by various names—a precious study it would be to collect them! Let me remind you of a few:

> "The high and lofty One that inhabiteth eternity, whose name is Holy" (Isa. 57:15).
> "The Creator of the ends of the earth" (Isa. 40:28).
> "The God of glory" (Acts 7:2).
> "The Holy One of Israel" (Isa. 43:14).
> "Thy God that pleadeth the cause of his people" (Isa. 51:22).
> "The Lord thy God which teacheth thee to profit, which leadeth thee by the way that thou shouldest go" (Isa. 48:17).

"The God of hope" (Rom. 15:13).
"The God of peace" (Heb. 13:20).
"God is love" (I John 4:8).

Now the manifestation of *the name* of God is that which constitutes the glory of God; because by this name He Himself is made known. Just as light constitutes the glory of the sun, because it shows us what it is; so the name of God reveals God, and in His revealed name we learn what He is. Thus the manifestation of His name is His glory. Now God has manifested Himself in creation:

> "The heavens declare the glory of God;
> And the firmament showeth his handiwork" (Ps. 19:1).

God has manifested Himself in providence, upholding, providing, protecting the universe. The Psalmist says:

> "The eyes of all wait upon thee; thou givest them their meat
> in due season" (Ps. 145:15).

And God has revealed Himself in grace: telling us His purposes; spreading out before us pictures of those purposes in types and shadows; making to us promises; giving us direct communications of the wondrous thoughts that He has to us-ward in association with His own great name. Let us refer to a few passages in the Word. In Exodus 3:13–15, when He sends Moses to deliver His people Israel out of the bondage of Pharaoh:

> "Moses said unto God, Behold, when I come unto the children of Israel, and shall say unto them, The God of your fathers hath sent me unto you; and they shall say to me, What is his name? what shall I say unto them? And God said unto Moses, I AM THAT I AM: and He said, Thus shalt thou say unto the children of Israel, I AM hath sent me unto you. And God said moreover unto Moses, Thus shalt thou say unto the children of Israel, The Lord God of your fathers, the God of Abraham, the God of Isaac, and the God of Jacob, hath sent me unto you: this is my name for ever, and this is my memorial unto all generations."

A God self-existing, all-sufficient, and your God—here is a wonderful name; and who can tell the glory of it!

In Exodus 6:3, He proceeds to reveal the meaning, and open out to them the fullness of His name, "Jehovah." Establishing His covenant (v. 5); hearing the groanings; bringing them out from under their burdens; ridding them from their bondage; and redeeming them (v. 6); taking them to Himself for a people, and pledging Himself to be their God (v. 7); bringing them into the land He had promised to their fathers, and giving it to them for a possession (v. 8). Here is a name!—a glorious name, and a wonderful manifestation of it even in this record! In chapter 33 we have additional light thrown upon the name of God. After considerable intercourse with God, Moses' heart burns with desire for a fuller manifestation of Him, and he says, "I beseech thee, show me thy glory." And God said, "I will make all my goodness pass before thee; and I will proclaim the name of the Lord before thee."

His *goodness,* His *name,* and His *glory* are all the same. This is the name of which He is speaking in the text. In Exodus 34: 5–7, we have the Lord proclaiming His name. The Old Testament proclaims it, Christ manifests it; that is the difference.

> "And the Lord descended in the cloud, and stood with him there, and proclaimed the name of the Lord. And the Lord passed by before him and proclaimed, The Lord, the Lord God, merciful and gracious, long-suffering, and abundant in goodness and truth, keeping mercy for thousands, forgiving iniquity and transgression and sin, and that will by no means clear the guilty."

"Just, and the justifier"—here is the Old Testament manifestation; Christ is the New Testament manifestation: "I have manifested thy name."

Once again, see Numbers 6:24–27, where additional light is thrown upon the name:

> "The Lord bless thee, and keep thee: the Lord make His face shine upon thee, and be gracious unto thee: the Lord lift up his

countenance upon thee, and give thee peace. And they shall put
my name upon the children of Israel."

Observe, here, the threefold name of God, and its destination,
its resting-place, pointed out; "they shall put my name upon the
children of Israel."

There is nothing Jehovah is so jealous of as His own holy
name; how that name has been ignored! how it has been "polluted"! how it has been misrepresented! Alas! alas! How it has
been "blasphemed"! It was a glorious mission for Christ to come
and manifest that name—He counted it His highest glory; as
He teaches us here, that the greatest glory He can bestow upon
His people is to manifest that name to them.

Ignorance of God is our ruin; knowledge of God is our salvation. "O righteous Father, the world hath not known thee; but
I have known thee" (v. 25). He is "the brightness of the
Father's glory, and the express image of his person"—who so
suited to manifest Him? He is "the only begotten Son in the
bosom of the Father"—who so well qualified to make Him
known to the sons of men?

But Christ is not only the manifestor of the Father's name,
He is the *manifestation* of it; Christ, the manifestation of God's
mighty power, put forth for salvation; Christ,

>"the power of God and the wisdom of God" (I Cor. 1:24);

Christ,

>"the hidden wisdom" (I Cor. 2:7);

Christ,

>"The Word of God" (Rev. 19:13),

and

>"who of God is made unto us, wisdom, and righteousness,
>and sanctification, and redemption."

He has manifested the *holiness* of God—a holiness so pure
that He cannot look upon iniquity; He has manifested the *faith-*

fulness of God—a faithfulness so great that even the promise which cost Him His only begotten Son's life was nevertheless fulfilled; Christ was the manifestation of the *fullness* of God—a fullness so vast that it can supply even our need; and Christ was the manifestation of the *love* of God, for

> "God so loved the world, that he gave his only begotten Son, that whosoever believeth in him should not perish, but have everlasting life."

But He was not only the outward manifestation of the name of God to arrest our reason, to convince our understanding, but also the inner power, whereby God manifests Himself to the heart; for it is written,

> "God, who commanded the light to shine out of darkness, hath shined in our hearts, to give the light of the knowledge of the glory of God in the face of [in the person of] Jesus Christ" (II Cor. 4:6).

Lastly; we learn here that the greatest possible blessing which even Christ Himself can bestow upon His people is to manifest the Father's name to them. He puts it first: "I have manifested thy name." Evidently, in His estimation, this included everything else; because all the rest flows from it. If God only manifests Himself to you in Christ Jesus, every blessing that eternity can supply is sure to follow.

This is the first mention He makes of His people in His prayer to His Father: "I have manifested thy name unto the men which thou gavest me out of the world." This was their life; "this is life eternal, to know thee." This was the foundation of their confidence: "they that know thy name will put their trust in thee." Herein consisted their triumph and their victory:

> "Thou hast given a banner to them that fear thee" (Ps. 60:4);
> "In the *name* of our God we will set up our banners" (Ps. 20:5).

This was their protection:

> "The name of the Lord is a strong tower: the righteous run-
> neth into it, and is safe" (Prov. 18:10).

This was the ground of their fellowship with God:

> "In all places where I record my name I will come unto thee,
> and I will bless thee" (Exod. 20:24).

This was the security of their salvation; for as the depositories of the name of the Father, He pleads that the Father should keep them, sanctify them, and glorify them. And by-and-by,

> "They shall see his face: and his name shall be in their fore-
> heads" (Rev. 22:4);

this is the description given of the glory to be revealed! No won-der, then, He should dwell upon this; no wonder He should put it in the forefront of His pleadings with His Father for His people—"I have manifested thy name unto the men which thou gavest me out of the world."

You remember, in Old Testament times, the servants of God were wont to inscribe the names of Jehovah upon the monu-mental pillars where the displays of His grace, His salvation, or of His kindly care had been manifested. When Abraham was taught the lesson of substitution on Mount Moriah,

> "Jehovah-Jireh"—the Lord will provide—(Gen. 22:14)

was the name inscribed there; when a great victory was achieved over Amalek,

> "Jehovah-Nissi"—the Lord my banner—(Exod. 17:15)

was inscribed there; when the "city that hath foundations, whose builder and maker is God," is revealed,

> "Jehovah-Shammah"—the Lord is there—(Ezek. 48:35)

ʋas the title given to it; when the diseases of His people were healed,

> "Jehovah-Ropheka"—the Lord that healeth thee—(Exod. 15:25)

was the memorial written; when the justification of His people is celebrated,

> "Jehovah-Tsidkenu"—the Lord our righteousness—(Jer. 33:16)

is the inscription to celebrate it; and when He spake peace,

> "Jehovah-Shalom"—the Lord send peace—(Judg. 6:24)

was the record of His grace.

But saved sinners are His true monuments, "the men which thou gavest me out of the world." And every name of God shall be inscribed upon them. And Jesus Himself shall be the inscriber; for He has promised,

> "Him that overcometh will I make a pillar in the temple of my God, . . . and I will write upon him the name of my God" (Rev. 3:12);

JEHOVAH-JIREH—

> "And the name of the city of my God" (Rev. 3:12);

JEHOVAH-SHAMMAH,—

> "New Jerusalem, which cometh down out of heaven from my God: and I will write upon him my new name" (Rev. 3:12).

And that new name is the fullest and highest manifestation God can give of Himself; and if even now, "we all beholding, as in a glass, the glory of the Lord, are changed into the same image from glory to glory," how shall we shine by-and-by, when

> "he shall come to be glorified in his saints, and to be admired in all them that believe" (II Thess. 1:10);

and when, with unveiled face, we behold His glory, and see Him as He is? Then we shall understand something of the depth of the meaning of our blessed Mediator, when He presents us in prayer to His Father, saying, "I have manifested thy name unto the men which thou gavest me out of the world."

9

"I HAVE MANIFESTED THY NAME UNTO THE MEN WHICH
THOU GAVEST ME OUT OF THE WORLD: THINE THEY
WERE, AND THOU GAVEST THEM ME; AND THEY
HAVE KEPT THY WORD."—John 17:6

IN OUR EXPOSITION of the first part of this passage, we had a general view of the petitions which our Lord urges in this wondrous prayer for His people, and the grounds on which He presents them to His Father. And as we read the text again, with its context, we feel compelled to acknowledge it is impossible to conceive what more could have been said in their behalf; "I have manifested thy name unto the men which thou gavest me out of the world: thine they were, and thou gavest them me; and they have kept thy word." Wonderful Intercessor! Had they been the most faultless, perfect, constant, faithful, and loving, of all the ministers of God that do His pleasure—instead of being, as they were, a company of needy, weak, failing, unworthy sinners—our blessed Lord could not have said more in their favor.

Hence we learn a most soul-sustaining truth. The Word of God does not tell us one whit more of the privileges belonging to us as believers standing in Christ, than Christ takes credit for as He represents us before the throne of the Majesty in the heavens. If the Spirit of God tells us in His Word,

> "Ye are complete in him" (Col. 2:10),

our Intercessor speaks of us above as complete in Him. If the Spirit of God in His Word proclaims to us that

> "By him all that believe are justified from all things" (Acts
> 13:39),

our glorious Intercessor speaks of us before His Father as "justified from all things." And if the Spirit of God tells us in His
Word,

> "There is no condemnation to them that are in Christ Jesus"
> (Rom. 8:1),

so doth the heavenly Intercessor speak of us before His Father's
throne, as those whom no man can accuse and whom no man
can condemn.

How it must have amazed His disciples to hear such words!
What a world of grace must have been opened out to their understanding! The Lord here reveals to them, and to us, the very
secrets of His Father's heart. He opens to us all the hidden
purposes of the everlasting covenant, and points out the subjects
and objects which it embraces. "Men"—not angels, nor archangels—but men, and sinners—"The men which thou gavest
me"; the men—Thy specially chosen and beloved ones amongst
the sons and daughters of men. From *whence* were they taken?
"Out of the world." It was not that they were better than others:
they were "of the world"; they were "in the world"; they "had
followed the course of this world"; they had been like the world,
carried captive at his will by "the prince of this world"; blinded
as to their understanding by the world and its glittering nothingness; guilty, "children of wrath even as others," condemned,
enemies of God, no love for Him, no desire towards Him, no
knowledge of Him; yet loved with an intensity that only God
can be conscious of and given to the Lord Jesus Christ to be
saved in Him with an everlasting salvation. "Thine they were,
and thou gavest them me." Seven times in this prayer Christ
reminds His Father that He had given His people to Him.

Evidently He regarded this gift as the greatest proof of His
Father's love to *Him;* even as the Holy Ghost teaches the be-

liever to regard the gift of Christ as the greatest proof of our heavenly Father's love to *us*.

> "Herein is love, not that we loved God, but that he loved us, and sent his Son to be the propitiation for our sins" (I John 4:10).

Nay, if we compare the passages in the New Testament, where Christ speaks of His people as the Father's gift to Him, and of His delight in them as His portion, His joy, and crown; if we compare, I say, these passages with those which speak of the gift of Christ as the pledge of the Father's love *to us,* and as being our portion and joy, our glory, and our crown, we know not on which side the grace seems to preponderate, and whether the Holy Ghost would teach us most to admire the grace which gave us to Christ or gave Christ to us.

"Thine they were, and thou gavest them me." Christ here traces all the Father's acts and purposes towards His people, whether in creating them, protecting them, bestowing His grace upon them now, or by-and-by crowning them with glory, to the high source and divine foundation of all grace—"Thine they were." This is the origin of all grace—the Father's own interest and property in His people; the Father's own unspeakable and everlasting love. Oh, what a blessed resting place for faith is here! Yes, God *has*—He ever *had* and ever *will have*—an inheritance of glory in His people; "he formed them for himself." The world, the flesh, and the devil, have sought to rob God of His glory, mar His inheritance in His people, and eclipse the majesty of His name:

> "And he saw that there was no man, and wondered that there was no intercessor; therefore his arm brought salvation unto him; and his righteousness it sustained him" (Isa. 59:16);
> God "laid help on one that was mighty" (Ps. 89:19);

and He gave His people over into the hands of Christ—the most fitted, the most able, the most precious one to Him—and wherefore? That He might redeem them from all iniquity; that He might regenerate them with the divine nature; that He might restore them to the position they had lost; and much more than this: that He might raise them to a position which they never had—even unto union and communion with the only begotten Son of God. "Thine they were, and thou gavest them me." Christ's people, being His Father's property, are not entrusted themselves with the happiness and fullness intended for them; but are given over to Christ to be preserved and qualified for all the Father's love has provided for them.

In reading these words, I confess that it seems hard to discover whether Christ most prizes His people, as His Father's property: His love-gift to Himself; or as His own beloved ones; evidently all these considerations fill His heart while He pleads for them. "Thine they were, and thou gavest them me." Truly, it is divine and irresistible pleading; written for our sakes, that our faith may be feasted, and our hope established, that we may love the Lord our God, and go on our way rejoicing.

Here, then, let us trace our divine lineage, as the people of God—"Thine they were." God's own property; and because God's own *given* to Christ: and because given to Christ, *saved.* Observe; it was no part of the work of Christ to make us God's people, and it was no part of the work of Christ to secure God's love for us. Hear His own testimony: "Thine they were, and thou gavest them me." How clearly and beautifully the Spirit opens out this subject in Ephesians 1. The apostle is addressing the saints, the separated ones, God's people: observe the position in which He addresses them (v. 1) *"in* Christ Jesus"; there they are the given ones, they are in Christ Jesus, and (v. 3)

> "*Blessed* with all spiritual blessings in heavenly places in Christ";

(v. 4)

> "According as he hath *chosen* us in him";

(v. 6)

"He hath made us *accepted* in the beloved";
(v. 7)

"In whom we have *redemption* through his blood, the *forgiveness* of sins";
(v. 11)

"In whom also we have obtained an *inheritance*";
(vv. 13, 14),

"In whom ye also . . . after that ye believed, ye were *sealed* with that Holy Spirit of promise, which is the earnest of our inheritance until the redemption of the purchased possession";

and then (vv. 17, 18) the apostle presents this prayer—it is all he desires, it is certainly all our souls need:

"That the God of our Lord Jesus Christ, the Father of Glory, may give unto you the spirit of wisdom and revelation in the knowledge of him: the eyes of your understanding being enlightened; that ye may know what is the hope of his calling, and what the riches of the glory of his inheritance in the saints."

In I Corinthians 3:21, 22, we have the very same teaching. Why is it that we have an inheritance? Why are all things ours?

"All things are yours; whether Paul, or Apollos, or Cephas, or the world, or life, or death, or things present, or things to come; all are yours; and ye are Christ's, and Christ is God's."

We might think perhaps it is because Christ is ours. *Not so,* but because we are Christ's, a very much higher reason. Christ's interest in His people is their security, even more than their interest in Christ; His love for me is my security, His property in me much more than my property in Him, which is but the consequence; and there is a still higher reason, Christ is God's. Here we are taken up to the thought in our Lord's mind—the origin of all grace, which is not our interest in God, but God's interest in us. "Thine they were, and thou gavest them me." All things are ours, for we are Christ's, and Christ is God's—such is the pleading of our blessed Lord, while He prayed for "the men whom the Father had given him out of the world."

But why, being taken out of the world, were they given to Christ? Because Christ is Lord of all, the Head of creation, the Head of grace, and the Head of glory. If there could have been one higher than Christ, God would have given them to Him; but Christ is "head over *all things* to His church": and as we are to inherit creation, we are given to the Head thereof; and, as God's purpose is to crown us with all grace, we are given to the Head of all grace; and, as God's purpose is to glorify His people, He has given them to Christ, who is the Head of glory!

Now, all things were created for Christ; the greatest thing created for Him is His Church. The worlds were created for Him; there would have been no creation, but that Jehovah purposed Christ should have a kingdom. The heavens were created for Him; there would be no heaven, or heaven of heavens, but that Jehovah purposed that His Son should have a kingdom; but "the church" is more than the kingdom, more to Him than earth and heaven. Angels were created for Christ; no angel would ever have winged his way through infinite space, but that it was Jehovah's purpose that His Son should have attendants: but the Bride is more than the attendants. Whatever be the thrones our blessed Christ is to occupy; whatever be the dominions He is to possess; whatever be the principalities over which He is to rule—He will give to us "to sit with him on his throne, even as he also overcame, and is set down with his Father on his throne."

Christ was set up as Lord of the universe; but His people are "the members of his body"—His own flesh and blood, and

"No man ever yet hated his own flesh; but nourisheth and cherisheth it, even as the Lord the church" (Eph. 5:29).

All other creations are from without; the Church, in some mysterious ineffable way, is from *within*.

This was pictured to us in the Garden of Eden, when Adam, the great type of Christ, was created, and dominion was given him over all creatures, and he gave them names; but there was no "companion meet for Adam amongst them all." And the Lord God caused a deep sleep to fall upon Adam, and while he slept, God took part of him and formed it into a woman, and presented her to the man. "This," said Adam, "is now bone of my bones, and flesh of my flesh." And the apostle (Eph. 5:31, 32) tells us:

> "For this cause shall a man leave his father and mother and shall be joined unto his wife, and they two shall be one flesh. This is a great mystery: but I speak concerning Christ and the church."

Christ is the image and glory of God; His people are to be the image and the glory of Christ. Christ is the Man of God's right hand; the people of Christ are His royal diadem.

Human language sinks burdened under the expressions of His love—the love of Christ to His people. He calls them His jewels, His peculiar treasure, His flock, His temple, His Bride, His all! The world may look coldly upon the people of God; the world may speak hardly of them; and may think lightly of them —but hear what Jesus says of them. Oh, it is sweet to retire from a cold world and listen! "Thine they were, and thou gavest them me." He is not speaking of the *heavens* given to Him; of the *earth* given to Him; of the *thrones,* and dominions, and principalities, and powers, and crowns given to Him; but "Thine *they* were, and thou gavest *them* me." Given to Him to be His *charge,* doubt not He will take care of them; given in *trust* to Him, He will keep them, He will teach them, He will qualify them, He will clothe them, He will wash them, He will present them without spot or wrinkle, or any such thing, to the everlasting praise of the glory of His love.

They are His "flock"—a scattered flock, but He will gather them. Remember the beautiful passage in Ezekiel 34 where we have the Lord's own definition of the office of a shepherd, and how He Himself will fulfill it (vv. 11–16):

"Thus saith the Lord God;
Behold, I, even I, will both search my sheep, and seek them
   out.
As a shepherd seeketh out his flock
In the day that he is among his sheep that are scattered;
So will I seek out my sheep,
And will deliver them out of all places where they have been
   scattered
In the cloudy and dark day.
And I will bring them out from the people,
And gather them from the countries,
And will bring them to their own land,
And feed them upon the mountains of Israel
By the rivers, and in all the inhabited places of the country.
I will feed them in a good pasture,
And upon the high mountains of Israel shall their fold be:
There shall they lie in a good fold,
And in a fat pasture shall they feed upon the mountains of
   Israel.
I will feed my flock, and I will cause them to lie down,
Saith the Lord God.
I will seek that which was lost,
And bring again that which was driven away,
And will bind up that which was broken,
And will strengthen that which was sick."

Jesus Christ is the good Shepherd; He will take care of the flock
committed to His charge. They are His Bride—

   "As the bridegroom rejoiceth over the bride, so shall thy God
rejoice over thee" (Isa. 62:5).

They are His "children"—

   "Like as a father pitieth his children, so the Lord pitieth
them that fear him" (Ps. 103:13).
   "The mountains shall depart, and the hills be removed; but
my kindness shall not depart from thee, neither shall the covenant of my peace be removed, saith the Lord" (Isa. 54:10).

They are His "poor and needy." What have they but Himself?
Not in all the wide world has the soul of the child of God a

single resting place but in the love of his Lord and Saviour; not a hiding place but His heart; not a portion but Himself. He knows it. They are His "weary" ones. The journey has been long, and the path rough; and weary eyes are looking to Him; weary hands are stretched out to Him; weary hearts are longing for Him: and He knows it. They are His "stricken and wounded ones." Their warfare has been very constant, and often gone hardly with them; but He has pledged Himself to make them more than conquerors, and He will. They are His "temple," and He will inhabit them; they are His "inheritance," and He will protect and possess them; and He hath made them His "priests and kings" to show forth "the praises of him who hath called them out of darkness into his marvelous light"; for Thine they were, Thine they are, and Thine they ever shall be, and Thou gavest them Me.

There is rest for the weary in truth like this. May our hearts enter into it by faith, for His name's sake who uttered this prayer for our comfort and encouragement!

10

"THEY HAVE KEPT THY WORD."—John 17:6

OUR LORD'S PURPOSE is evidently to commend His people to His Father in the highest possible way, and He does it thus: "Thine they were, and thou hast given them me; and they have kept thy word." When shall we value that Word as we ought? We have, in this statement, some wonderful characteristics of our precious Saviour's intercession. He evidently considers Himself responsible not only for the full discharge of the mission upon which His Father sent Him, but also to give an account of His success: "I have manifested thy name unto the men which thou gavest me out of the world"; but more—I have succeeded: "they have kept thy word." Surely He here gives them credit not only for what He had Himself done in teaching them; but also for what the Holy Ghost was about to do in confirming the instructions He had given them. He not only pledges Himself to the completion of His own work for them, but also to the completion of the work the Holy Ghost was about to accomplish in them, when He says "they have kept thy word." Nor will He allow them to appear before God in anywise but as altogether acceptable and altogether accepted: for "I have manifested thy name unto the men which thou gavest me out of the world; and they have kept thy word."

Truly, faith in God's Word is a divine and a mighty principle. It is the most acceptable obedience the heart of man can render. Faith is that principle which lays hold upon God, through His Word; it is the work of the Spirit of God in the soul; it is omnipotent power, because it lays hold upon the strength of God Himself; and it overcomes the world; faith honors God, and therefore God honors faith. And here we are taught something more, namely; that it is the first practical evidence of our relationship to God: "they have kept thy word." We cannot look into the Book of Life and see whether our names are amongst those of whom the Lord says, "thine they were, and thou gavest them me"; but we can look into the Word of God, and if we can honestly say we have received that Word of God, and do rest our souls upon the promises contained therein, and upon the faithfulness of Him whose Word it is, then we have the first and all-sufficient evidence of our relationship to God.

It is by the Word so kept, that, as by an instrument, our conversion is effected and our souls renewed. It is by the Word of God so kept that we "grow up into him, in all things, which is the head"; and old things pass away, and all things become new. It is by the Word so kept that Christ manifests to us His Father; and bestows upon our souls the precious name which He so manifests to us. See John 14:22:

> "Judas saith unto him, not Iscariot, Lord, how is it that thou wilt manifest thyself unto us, and not unto the world?"

You observe the fact—the Lord Jesus is manifested to His people, and is not manifested to the world; His people have their joy, their peace, their hope in Him: not so the world. How is this?

> "Jesus answered and said unto him, if a man love me, he will *keep my words:* and my Father will love him, and we will come unto him, and make our abode with him" (John 14:23).

It is in our keeping the Word of God that the Holy Ghost manifests to us the God of the Word. The world doth not keep the Word of God, therefore God is not manifested to them. In the same degree as His people keep the Word, is the God of the Word manifested in their souls.

Notice how the Lord commends those who keep His Word. Writing to the church at Philadelphia, a church without a fault before God, it is said,

> "Thou hast a little strength, and hast kept my word, and hast not denied my name . . . Because thou hast kept the word of my patience" (Rev. 3:8, 10).

A striking expression! The Lord oftentimes allows a long interval to elapse between the promise and the performance of it; the meantime is for the exercise of patience, "the word of my patience." How long the Church had to wait for Christ!—how long she is waiting for Christ's coming again! But He who has given the Word will fulfill the promise.

> "Because thou hast kept the word of my patience, I also will keep thee from the hour of temptation, which shall come upon all the world, to try them that dwell upon the earth" (Rev. 3:10).

It is only as we keep the Word that we are prepared for temptation. The time is coming when we shall need, yea, the time is come when we do need, to keep the Word of God. What strange doctrines we hear of, what new notions, what new-fangled theories are everywhere being circulated!—we have no security against being entangled and carried away by them, if we are not established in the Word of God. Alas! there are but few amongst us sufficiently acquainted with the Word of God to be able to bring to the test of its standard the manifold heresies that are abroad.

> "Behold, I come quickly: hold that fast which thou hast, that no man take thy crown" (Rev. 3:11).

The Word of God is his crown.

> "Thou hast magnified thy word above all thy name" (Ps. 138:2).

Crown you with it, brethren! Hide it in your hearts; and let it be as frontlets between your eyes, that you may not sin against

God. Once again, see how the Lord commends the keeping of His Word. We read in Luke 11:27, 28,

> "A certain woman of the company lifted up her voice, and said unto him, Blessed is the womb that bare thee, and the paps which thou hast sucked. But he said, Yea, rather, blessed are they that hear the word of God, *and keep it.*"

And now He says, speaking to His Father of His people: "They have kept *thy* word."

Observe the emphasis. The words spoken by Christ were the Father's words. He does not say, They have kept *My* words; but "They have kept *Thy* word." He spake nothing of Himself.

> "My doctrine is not mine, but his that sent me" (John 7:16).

So of His works—

> "The Father that dwelleth in me, he doeth the works" (John 14:10).

So of His mission: as we read—

> "Neither came I of myself, but he sent me" (John 8:42).

And, seeing the words of Christ were the Father's words and the works and the mission of Christ were the Father's works and mission, He tells us,

> "Verily, verily, I say unto you, He that heareth my word, and believeth on him that sent me, hath everlasting life, and shall not come into condemnation; but is passed from death unto life" (John 5:24).

"They have kept thy word." Note the blessed teaching here! It is very deep and very precious. He makes no distinction between disciple and disciple; some were much more instructed than others; some were much more faithful than others; some walked much more closely with Him than others. Doubtless it was so; but He makes no distinction, He speaks of them as one body—yes, and He speaks of the whole Church as one body: "they have kept thy word."

We may notice here with profit and instruction the great difference between our standing in Christ, and our personal and actual experience. In the one case, God sees us only as He sees Christ; no spot, no stain, no possible accusation can be brought against us, no possible condemnation can be pronounced against us, we are *"complete* in him." This is as much the case with one child of God as another; the least in the family, the feeblest believer in Christ Jesus is complete in Him, and as accepted as was Paul, or as John, who lay upon His bosom. "They have kept thy word," is Christ's account of them, speaking of them as standing in Himself, and as represented by Him before God.

As to our own experience, and as to the disciples' experience, it is far otherwise: believe me, they were very much like what we are ourselves. There is a habit nowadays of deifying the disciples; it is a very great mistake. They were a company of poor, needy sinners, such as we are, full of failures; and very faithfully the Scriptures of truth record their failures. Their knowledge was very dim; their faith was oftentimes very feeble; their hopes were very much mingled with what was earthly and sensual. And so it is with ourselves. Oh, how limited our knowledge! *We* keep His Word! Why, most of us, even the best taught of us, know very little about it. What a scanty knowledge ours is of the Word of God! How small our attainments in the knowledge, the enjoyment, and the fullness of that Word! We learn, by daily experience, to confess it is so, and like the apostle it behooves us to say:

> "Forgetting those things which are behind, and reaching forth unto those things which are before, I press toward the mark for the prize of the high calling of God in Christ Jesus" (Phil. 3:13, 14).

And like him, too, to pray as for others, so for ourselves,

> That "the eyes of your understanding being enlightened; that ye may know what is the hope of his calling, and what the

riches of the glory of his inheritance in the saints" (Eph. 1:18).

Thus we should learn, by the sense of our own need, to watch, to pray, to strive, to fight. But when Christ pleads for His disciples, He says, "They have kept thy word." There is no mention of their forsaking Him; yet He had just told them, "Behold, the hour cometh, yea, is now come, that ye shall be scattered, every man to his own, *and shall leave me alone.*" His plea is "Father, they have kept thy word." Precious, glorious, adorable Intercessor!

Having thus guarded the higher truth in this passage, we must not overlook the fact that the little company around the Lord, for whom He prayed, had sincerely and truly received His testimony; they did trust in Him; with all their failures and shortcomings, they could appeal to Him, and He did not deny their appeal; "Thou knowest all things; Thou knowest that we love Thee." They had left their little all—it was not much, but is *was* their all—to follow Him; and His word was their law, Himself their all; still they could not say of themselves what He said of them—"they have kept thy word."

There is a very blessed emphasis upon *"thy word."* If the disciples did not apprehend it, the Father Himself did, and Christ did. It seems to me as if the Lord Jesus was calling His Father's attention to His own Word. Oh, what a treasury it was —of divine promise, grace, hope, blessing, and faithfulness! What a deposit it was of everything the love of God could give or pledge Himself to, or the faith of His people embrace, or their need require: now He says, "Father, they have kept *thy word.*" "They little realize all which that Word means: They have but dimly apprehended all which that Word pledges Thee to. But I know, and Thou knowest; and 'I have manifested thy name unto them, and they have kept *thy word.*' "

"Remember the word unto thy servant, upon which thou hast caused *me* to hope" (Ps. 119:49).

We further gather how greatly Christ desires that all His people should keep His Father's Word; for, while He utters this high commendation of them, "they have kept thy word," surely He looks at us, and teaches us how closely it lies upon His very heart, that we should keep that Word; and why? because He loves us, and He delights in the evidences of our love. "If a man love me, he will keep my words" (John 14:23). Now, the loving heart of the Lord Jesus looks for responsive love, and it is thus His children express and manifest their love; they keep His words. But there is something more; He desires communion with us, and it is in our keeping His Word He enjoys our society, for we read:

> "If a man love me, he will keep *my words:* and my Father
> will love him, and we will come unto him, and make our abode
> with him" (John 14:23).

And yet more; the Lord longs for His people's joy as well as for their society.

> "These things have I *spoken* unto you, that my joy might remain in you, and that your joy might be full" (John 15:11).

Therefore, would He have us keep His Word. Again, He longs that we may possess His *peace* in our souls.

> "These things I have *spoken* unto you, that in me ye might
> have peace" (John 16:33).

He longs, too, that we should be comforted: He sends the Holy Ghost the Comforter to teach us all these things, to bring all these things to our remembrance. He longs for His people's security; and what is our security? *His Father's Word*—the foundation of our faith, and our hope, the motive for our love, the lamp for our path, the light for our feet, our refuge in danger, our food in the wilderness, and our sword for the battle. He longs for His people to enjoy realized union with Himself; and this is in keeping of His Word:

"If ye abide in me, and *my words* abide in you" (John 15:7).

Here lies the power: we abide in Him only as He abides in us; and we realize our union with Him, and abide in Him only as His *words* abide in us. Finally, He longs to see His people's desires granted, and that there should be no unanswered prayers, no unsuitable petitions:

"If ye abide in me, and my words abide in you, ye shall ask what ye will, and it shall be done unto you" (John 15:7).

"O, let Thy Word be impressed on our souls, expressed in our lives, confessed by our faith, and professed by our conversation. We bless Thee, Father, that Thou hast given us Thy great name, that Thy Son might manifest it. We bless Thee, Son of God, that Thou didst come down from heaven to manifest to us our Father's name; we bless Thee, O Holy Ghost, that Thou hast taken away the veil, and shown us that name. Our God, Thou hast said:

"'My word . . . shall not return unto me void; but it shall accomplish that which I please, and it shall prosper in the thing whereto I sent it' (Isa. 55:11).

Oh, grant us grace to keep Thy word!" It is all we need while here below. When we keep Thy Word, we find that Word can keep us, comfort us, enlighten us, strengthen us, establish us. But when conscience tells us we have but kept it feebly; and we have to accuse ourselves of forgetfulness, ignorance, and unbelief—may our faith ascend to Him who has gone *within the veil,* and with His own blood sprinkled the mercy seat, pleading that our unbelief may be pardoned; and let faith listen while our Advocate says for us and of us—"They have kept thy word." Even now, Lord Jesus, in Thine own name, say it *in us,* by Thine own Holy Spirit—"They have kept thy word"!

11

"NOW THEY HAVE KNOWN THAT ALL THINGS WHATSOEVER
THOU HAST GIVEN ME ARE OF THEE."—John 17:7

IN THIS PART of His prayer, our blessed Lord is wholly engaged in commending His people to His Father. No allusion of the slightest kind is made to any of their many deficiencies, no reference to any of their frequent failures; we search in
vain throughout the whole prayer for anything like an accusation against them, directly or indirectly. This is a beautiful
comment on what the apostle afterwards urges,

> "Who shall lay anything to the charge of God's elect? . . .
> Who is he that condemneth? It is Christ that died!" (Rom.
> 8:33, 34).

In the fullness of His mediatorial office, in the virtue of His
atoning blood—for the hour was come—in the greatness of
His salvation, in the height, and depth, and length, and breadth
of the love that passeth knowledge, in which He had received
them at His Father's hands, and had manifested to them that
Father's name; enshrined in that name He now presents them to
His Father, accredited with all His own work of salvation for
them, and with all the covenant work the Holy Ghost was about
to perform in them. All judgment, the Scripture says, is given
unto the Son; the Father judgeth no man: and thus He, to
whom all judgment is committed, speaks of them: "they have
kept thy word; and, now they have known that all things whatsoever thou hast given me are of thee." How little they actually
knew at this time! How imperfectly they had kept that Word!

How deficient had been their faith! This fact is evident from our Lord's own frequent rebuking of them; only a short time before, we find Him saying to them, "Do ye now believe?" And how often do we find such rebukes as these—"O ye of little faith"! And again, "Where is your faith? . . . How is it that ye do not believe?" Let us evermore remember this most precious fact, that however in His wondrous grace our blessed Teacher may discover to ourselves our deficiencies; however He may correct and rebuke us, discovering to us in our daily experience how needy, how feeble we are, and of how little faith —yet our standing before God is in the fullness of our Head and Representative; and He will never allow us to appear before His Father otherwise than as endued with all the completeness of His own righteousness. When we know, even as we are known, though our experience shall be more blessed, yet shall not our standing or acceptance be more complete than it is now while He pleads for us and of us—"Now they have known that all things whatsoever thou hast given me are of thee."

What a remarkable illustration we have in these words of the fact that the whole of His life on earth, all His acts, and all His doctrines, bore witness that He sought not His own glory but the glory of Him that sent Him. It is of the utmost importance, and it most deeply concerns our worship of God, and our estimation of our heavenly Father's love, that we should have right views of that which the Lord here takes such pains to teach. It is possible to think and speak of the person and work of the Lord Jesus Christ, so as to disparage the Father's grace. It appears to me one of the simplest proofs in Scripture, of the Godhead of our Lord Jesus Christ, that if He is not very God, then God would have set up a rival to Himself in our world and in our hearts, by sending the Lord Jesus Christ to be our Saviour.

I will illustrate what I mean by a story told in ancient history.

Cyrus had conquered and taken captive a prince with his wife and children; and when they were brought before the

King, Cyrus, who could sometimes manifest a very generous disposition, demanded of the prince, "What will you give me if I set you at liberty?" "I will give my kingdom," was the reply. "And what ransom can you then give for your wife and children?" Quickly the answer came, "I will give *my life* for them." "Well," said Cyrus, "I will restore your kingdom, your wife, and your children—you may have all"; he was pleased with the devoted love expressed by the father and the husband. Of course the prince was very grateful, and fell at the feet of Cyrus; and expressed his thanks, and his admiration of the generosity of the giver and the royalty of the gift. But one was silent—the wife said nothing—and her husband anxiously up-braided her, and said, "Why do you not thank the king?" She answered, "I am thinking only of the man who said he would give his life for my liberty." All thought of Cyrus' generosity was obliterated in her heart; she was thinking only of a love that would substitute his own life for hers.

Now this is something like the case before us. If the Lord Jesus Christ's person, mission, and salvation work be not all ascribed to our Father's love, as the Lord Himself did so faithfully and diligently teach His disciples, what would the effect be? That God would become the object of awe and fear; while Christ would have all our love, all our sympathy, and all our gratitude. The teaching of our blessed Master was evermore—"all things, Father, are of Thee." And He would lead us to see in Himself, and in His work, but the manifestation of the Father's love, and the Father's grace; and thus the Holy Spirit teaches us in Scripture:

> "Scarcely for a righteous man will one die . . . but God commendeth his love toward us, in that, while we were yet sinners, Christ died for us" (Rom. 5:7, 8).

Examine a few passages on this subject:

> "For I came down from heaven, not to do mine own will, but the will of him that sent me. And this is the Father's will which

hath sent me, that of all which he hath given me I should lose nothing, but should raise it up again at the last day" (John 6: 38, 39).

"All things that I have heard of my Father I have made known unto you" (John 15:15).

He evidently would have us ascribe to the Father all the comfort, peace, and happiness His words produce, or were calculated to produce. See also that remarkable passage in chapter 10:17, 18:

"Therefore doth my Father love me, because I lay down my life, that I might take it again. No man taketh it from me, but I lay it down of myself. I have power to lay it down, and I have power to take it again. This commandment have I received of my Father."

You see He attributes to the Father all His own atoning work, and tells us it was an act of obedience on His part to His Father's will. As the Lord taught, so did His disciples. Dwell on this because it is so very important.

"All things *are of God,* who has reconciled us to himself by Jesus Christ" (II Cor. 5:18).

"It became him, for whom are all things, and by whom are all things, in bringing many sons unto glory, to make the Captain of their salvation perfect through sufferings" (Heb. 2:10).

All this is fully comprehended in our text: and thus He taught His disciples; "Now they have known that all things whatsoever thou hast given me are of thee."

Let us endeavor, God helping us, to grasp this great subject.

I. The Speaker. He had been in the form of God. He was not so now; He was in the form of a servant—He was Jehovah's servant, His obedient, submissive, dependent Servant, emptied of all the glory that was His own, and which He had with His Father, before the world was. He was here "In the likeness of sinful flesh," "doing his Father's will," occupied with "his Father's business." The man of God's right hand, provided,

qualified, appointed by the Father, to be His salvation to the
ends of the earth; a new and divine source of life, joy, peace,
righteousness, grace, and glory to the Church of God. All was
pure grace to Him, and pure grace to us; faithfully and
diligently our blessed Lord and Master taught us so. "A body
hast thou prepared me," "a people prepared," the "salvation
prepared," "mercy and truth prepared"; and when He admits
them by-and-by into the kingdom, it shall be "the kingdom
prepared for you from the foundation of the world"; and when
into the glory, it shall be the glory that was prepared. Christ,
and Christ's salvation, were but the manifestations of the Father's name, the commended love of God; "he that hath seen
me hath seen the Father."

II. What are the things given to Him? "They have known
that *all things* whatsoever thou has given me are of thee." He
had spoken (v. 2) of *the persons* given to Him: "As thou hast
given him power over all flesh, that he should give eternal life
to as many as thou hast given him." Now he speaks of all things
given to Him. The persons were given that He might give
eternal life to them; now all things are given to Him, that He
might carry out this purpose, aim, and object, even to give
eternal life. I know not how many "alls" we read of in the
Scripture as given to Christ: "all grace," "all mercy," "all
might," "all dominion," "all long-suffering," "all power in
heaven and earth" given into His hands; all enemies of His
people, whether they be thrones or dominions, or principalities,
or powers put under His feet; "Head over all things to his
church." "It pleased the Father that in him should all fullness
dwell." And again, "In Him dwelleth all the fullness of the
Godhead bodily." "Do not I fill heaven and earth?" said the
Lord; and if so, heaven and earth would be empty without
Him. Yet from Ephesians 1:23, we learn that He would be
empty without His people; for there we read, "The church,
which is his body, the fullness of Him that filleth all in all."

III. Let us now endeavor to gather from Scripture how He will dispense His fullness. In John 1:16, we read, "Of his fullness have all we received, and grace for grace." So that the Lord Jesus will impart to His people all the fullness which it hath pleased the Father should dwell in Him for their supply. There are two or three passages connected with this subject well worth remembering:

> "Jesus knowing that the Father had given *all things into his hands,* and that he was come from God, and went to God; he riseth from supper, and laid aside his garments; and took a towel, and girded himself . . . and *began to wash his disciples' feet"* (John 13:3, 4).

Here He illustrates the use He intends to make of the power and fullness vested in Him, even condescending to the most menial office, if necessary, for the supplying of all the needs of all His blood-bought ones. In Matthew 28:18, 19, we have a similar connection. Jesus said to His disciples,

> "All power is given unto me in heaven and in earth. Go ye therefore, and teach all nations."

Observe the connection between His possessing all fullness and all power, and the proclamation of free grace and everlasting salvation to poor sinners.

Again, in I Corinthians 3:21, a very wonderful statement is made.

> *"All things* are yours; whether Paul, or Apollos, or Cephas, or the world, or life, or death, or things present, or things to come; all are yours; and ye are Christ's; and Christ is God's."

Nothing more can be said of *Him* than that all things are His; and nothing *less* is said of us in Him than that "all things are yours." And why? for "ye are Christ's, and Christ is God's"—the root and source of all. Again, in that wonderful vision the Evangelist had of our Priest and King in heaven (Rev. 1:17, 18):

"And when I saw him, I fell at his feet as dead. And he laid
his right hand upon me, [all things are given into those hands]
saying unto me, Fear not; I am the first and the last: I am he
that liveth, and was dead; and, behold, I am alive for evermore,
Amen; and have the keys of hell and of death."

See then how He will exert the power given to Him; see how
He will dispense the fullness entrusted to Him, even in protecting, in blessing, sustaining, comforting, and keeping His
people.

Once again (Ps. 68:18, cf. Eph. 4:8):

"Thou hast ascended on high, thou hast led captivity captive; thou hast received gifts for men; yea, for the rebellious
also, that the Lord God might dwell among them."

Now, in quoting this passage in Ephesians 4:8, the apostle says:
"Wherefore he saith, When he ascended up on high, he led
captivity captive, and gave gifts unto men." The psalmist said:
"He received gifts." The Holy Ghost has since then come down
from heaven to tell us what He intended to do with the gifts
He had received—even to *give* them. And thus the apostle com-
ments on the passage:

"He that descended is the same also that ascended up far
above all heavens, that he might fill all things."

This is our glorious Saviour's present work; thus it is He is engaged and employed in reference to the fullness it pleased the
Father should dwell in Him; thus He exercises the power—*all
power*—in heaven and in earth, power which it pleased the
Father should be vested in Him. Filling all things: filling
heaven with the glory of His eternal name; filling earth with
the praise of His great salvation; filling the hearts of His people
with Himself: and, by-and-by, He will fill their bodies, too,
with glory; He will be admired in His saints; they shall reflect
the beauty and glory of Him who bought them with His
blood, who represented them on the cross, and now represents

them in heaven, sending down the Holy Ghost to inhabit them, "that they might be filled with all the fullness of God" (Eph. 3:19). And "all things, Father, whatsoever thou hast given me, are of thee." The glorious person of the Mediator, His office, and salvation; His fullness, glory, and majesty—all of Thee! and "his glory is great in thy salvation." Thus the Mediator prays.

> "His name shall endure for ever. His name shall be con-tinued as long as the sun: and men shall be blessed in him: all nations shall call him blessed" (Ps. 72:17).

Now and evermore He is the Christ—"the same yesterday, and today, and forever"; full of grace, full of power, full of pardon-ing love. And His mediatorial throne shall continue till God be all in all. He who sits thereon is ready to receive all who come to Him. He is unchangeable in His love, unceasing in His com-passion, and endless in His grace and truth; rich in mercy to all that call on Him.

> "Let us therefore come boldly unto the throne of grace, that we may obtain mercy, and find grace to help in time of need" (Heb. 4:16).

Christ is King of grace, and, therefore, can dispense it; He is head of creation, and therefore can control it; He is first-born from the dead, that in all things He might have the pre-eminence. "On his head are many crowns"; but highest, and richest, and fairest of all—the crown of His people's salvation. "Go forth, O ye daughters of Zion, and behold King Solomon, with the crown wherewith his mother crowned him in the day of his espousals, and in the day of the gladness of his heart."

"Now they have known that all things whatsoever thou hast given me are of thee." "Herein is love, not that we loved God, but that he loved us, and sent his Son to be the propitiation for our sins." There is a very beautiful comment on this, showing how the Holy Ghost did subsequently establish the disciples in this great truth:

"We have known and believed the love that God hath to us. God is love, and he that dwelleth in love dwelleth in God, and God in him. Herein is our love made perfect, that we may have boldness in the day of judgment: because as he is, so are we in this world" (I John 4:16, 17).

Thus we stand, henceforth, before God in Christ. However He may rebuke us, or teach us our failings and infirmities, our standing is evermore in Himself; we are accepted in the Beloved, and this is God's appointment.

Lastly, as we remarked before, that Christ while pleading with His Father, "They have kept thy word," seems at the same time to speak to our hearts and tell us how much it is for His glory and our own happiness, that we also should keep His Word; so, while we listen by faith as He addresses the Father, saying, "Now they have known that all things whatsoever thou hast given me are of thee," let us assure our hearts that the work of Christ, the person of Christ, the salvation of Christ, the triumphs of Christ, the merit of His precious blood, and all that shall ever flow from it now and throughout eternity, joy and peace, and happiness to our souls are *all from God*. All was from the Father's love; all was through the Father's wisdom; all was in the Father's covenant. "Now they have known that all things whatsoever thou hast given me are of thee." Thus also the disciple that Jesus loved draws a distinction between believing children, young men, and fathers (I John 2:14), and puts the crown upon the head of the fathers, for saith he:

"Ye have known him that is from the beginning."

12

"FOR I HAVE GIVEN UNTO THEM THE WORDS WHICH THOU
GAVEST ME; AND THEY HAVE RECEIVED THEM,
AND HAVE KNOWN SURELY THAT I CAME OUT
FROM THEE, AND THEY HAVE BELIEVED
THAT THOU DIDST SEND ME."
—John 17:8

THERE ARE seven things given to Christ, as Mediator, of
which He makes great account in this prayer.

First. A people given to Him (v. 2).

Second. Eternal life to bestow upon that people (v. 2).

Third. Power over all flesh (v. 2).

Fourth. A work given Him to do (v. 4). That work was,
to die,

> "That through death he might destroy him that had the
> power of death, that is the devil; and deliver them who through
> fear of death were all their lifetime subject to bondage" (Heb.
> 2:14, 15).

He was to finish the transgression, and bring in an everlasting
righteousness; He was to save the Church.

Fifth. The Father's name was given Him that He might
manifest that name to His people (v. 6), that they might be
kept in that name (v. 12), united (v. 21), and filled with the
love of God (v. 26).

Sixth. "I have given unto them *the words which thou gavest
me*" (v. 8).

Seventh. "The glory which thou gavest me I have given
them" (v. 22).

Here, then, are *seven* gifts to Christ; praise be to God they are given to *Christ,* given to One who can take care of them, One who can dispose of them, One who can make no mistake about the use of them: the people; the eternal life for the people; the power over all flesh; the work of salvation; Jehovah's name, that they may be kept in that name, united in that name, and filled with love divine in that name; the words,—the means by which He manifests that name—and the glory to be yet revealed.

Now, observe, all these gifts are *for His people,* and given to them by Christ. This He confesses to His Father, acknowledging He had received them for that end, and this in the hearing of His disciples, that they might have everlasting consolation, yea, that *we* too may have everlasting consolation; for these things are written that—

> "My joy might remain in you, and that your joy might be full."

When our Lord speaks of "the words which thou gavest me," He evidently alludes to the testimony concerning Himself now written for us in the Scriptures. How precious those words are, seeing the fourfold channel through which they have come down to us.

First, we have Jehovah, the Father, conceiving the plan of salvation, purposing, promising, and giving His plan, so conceived, purposed, and promised, to Christ to be executed.

Next, we have Christ, the Son, coming down from heaven to fulfill His Father's words, and to convey them to His people, and so He pleads, "I have given them the words which thou gavest me."

Finally, we have a third channel; "He through the Holy Ghost gave commandments unto the apostles" (Acts 1:2). When the Lord had fulfilled the words which the Father had given to Him, He committed to the Holy Ghost the prerogative

of communicating them to the apostles; it was not till the Holy
Ghost descended, on the day of Pentecost, they really ap-
prehended "the words," yet the Lord takes credit, here, for hav-
ing given them, and gives them credit for having received them;
He might well do so; He had given them the words, and the
Holy Ghost would come in due time to be the Remembrancer.

> "When the Comforter is come, whom I will send unto you
> from the Father . . . he shall teach you all things, and bring
> all things to your remembrance, whatsoever I have said unto
> you" (John 15:26; 14:26).

See all the three Persons of the Godhead engaged about these
"words." The Father giving them; the Son executing them; and
the Holy Ghost revealing, applying, and communicating them.
And the apostles "received them"; they preached them during their lifetime, and then they wrote them; and the same
Spirit that revealed the words to them must reveal them to us,
and write them on our hearts, else we read them in vain.

Here, then, are four communications of the Word—from
the Father to Christ, from Christ *through the Holy Ghost* to
the apostles, and from the apostles, as inspired by the Holy
Ghost, to ourselves. How this language of Christ ought to make
us value the Holy Scriptures! How much He makes of them.
"Thy word . . . The words which thou gavest me . . . The
words which I have given unto them." The words which they
have received, kept, understood, believed. Next to God Himself,
there is nothing greater, nothing more precious than the word
which reveals God; the greater the Intelligence, whose wisdom,
love, and truth His words represent, the more precious the words
are. A fool's words go for nothing, a wise man's words are precious, but Christ is here speaking of the words of the All-Wise
One, the All-True One, the All-Faithful One; the words of God,
and "God is light," and "God is love." "I have given unto them
the words which *thou* gavest me." They are words of promise,
full of power; they are words of salvation, everlasting and free;

they are spirit, and they are life; they comfort and they quicken
all who receive them. By those words souls are begotten into
the family of God;

> "Of his own will begat he us with the word of truth" (Jas.
> 1:18);

by those words souls are filled with joy, and peace, and hope, and
power, and holiness, and love; all these things come into the
soul in the hearing and in the believing of "the words which
thou gavest to me."

Observe the word *"for"* with which the text commences connects with what precedes and with what follows. *"For* I have
given unto them the words," connects with "I have manifested
unto them thy name." It was by means of the *words,* He had
been enabled to manifest the Father's name. Then follows,
"They have *received* them, and have *known surely* that I came
out from thee, and they have *believed* that thou didst send me."
It was through these *words* our Lord was enabled to teach
them to know these things. It was through these words, the
Lord was enabled to assure them whence He came, and for what
purpose. It was through these words, also faith was begotten
in their souls—that faith which united them to Himself; for
He says, "They have believed that thou didst send me." Having
thus taken a general view of the passage, let us endeavor to
gather the more direct instruction.

I. We learn here and from many similar passages both in
the Old and New Testaments that the gospel of our salvation
was originally a covenant of promise *made with Christ,* and
given to Him to carry out.

> "Listen, O isles, unto me; and hearken ye people from far;
> The Lord hath called me from the womb;
> From the bowels of my mother hath he made mention of my
>   name.
> And he hath made my mouth like a sharp sword;
> In the shadow of his hand hath he hid me,

> And made me a polished shaft;
> In his quiver hath he hid me; and said unto me,
> Thou art my servant, O Israel, in whom I will be glorified"
> (Isa. 49:1).

Then follows a complaint—"for who hath believed our report, and to whom is the arm of the Lord revealed?" "He was in the world, and the world was made by him; and the world knew him not; He came unto his own and his own received him not."

> "Then I said, I have laboured in vain, I have spent my strength for nought, and in vain: yet surely my judgment is with the Lord, and my work with my God" (Isa. 49:4).

"And now, saith the Lord that formed me from the womb to be his servant, to bring Jacob again to him, Though Israel be not gathered, yet shall I be glorious in the eyes of the Lord, and my God shall be my strength. And he said, It is a light thing that thou shouldest be my servant to raise up the tribes of Jacob, and to restore the preserved of Israel: *I will also give thee for a light to the Gentiles,* that thou mayest be my salvation unto *the ends of the earth.* Thus said the Lord, the Redeemer of Israel, and his Holy One, to him whom man despiseth, to him whom the nation abhorreth, to a servant of rulers, Kings shall see and arise, princes also shall worship, because of the Lord that is faithful, and the Holy One of Israel, and he shall choose thee. Thus saith the Lord, In an acceptable time have I heard thee, and in a day of salvation have *I helped thee;* and I will preserve thee, and give thee for a *covenant of the people, to establish the earth,* to cause to inherit the desolate heritages; *that* thou mayest say to the prisoners, Go forth; to them that are in darkness, Shew yourselves. They shall feed in the ways, and their pastures shall be in all high places. They shall not hunger nor thirst; neither shall the heat nor sun smite them: for he that hath mercy on them shall lead them, even by the springs of water shall he guide them" (Isa. 49:5–10).

And again:

> "The Lord God *hath given* me *the tongue* of the learned, that
> I should know how to speak *a word in season* to him that is
> weary: he wakeneth morning by morning, he wakeneth mine
> ear to hear as the learned. The Lord God hath opened mine ear,
> and I was not rebellious, neither turned away back. I gave my
> back to the smiters, and my cheeks to them that plucked off the
> hair: I hid not my face from shame and spitting. For the Lord
> God will help me; therefore shall I not be confounded: there-
> fore have I set my face like a flint, and I know that I shall not
> be ashamed" (Isa. 50:4–7).

Thus all was arranged between Christ and His Father:

> "As for me, this is *my covenant with them,* saith the Lord;
> My spirit that is upon thee [Christ] and my words which I
> have put in thy mouth, shall not depart out of thy mouth, nor
> out of the mouth of thy seed, nor out of the mouth of thy seed's
> seed; saith the Lord, from henceforth and forever" (Isa. 59:
> 21).

Under the titles of David and Levi in the Old Testament, the
covenant was established in Christ (see Ps. 89:19–22):

> "Then thou spakest in vision to thy Holy One, and saidst,
> I have laid help upon one that is mighty;
> I have exalted one chosen out of the people,
> I have found *David my servant;* with my holy oil have I
>   anointed him:
> With whom my hand shall be established:
> Mine arm also shall strengthen him.
> The enemy shall not exact upon him;
> Nor the son of wickedness afflict him."

And on to verse 37 is a continuous promise to Christ of triumph
and dominion. In the strength of these and similar promises
He came; they contained the joy set before Him. "And I have
given unto them *the words* which thou gavest me."

In II Samuel 23:3–5, compared with Psalm 110, we have
further light. The marginal reading is,

> "The God of Israel said, the Rock of Israel spake to me, He
> that ruleth over men must be just, ruling in the fear of God.
> And as the light of the morning, when the sun riseth, even a
> morning without clouds; as the tender grass springing out of
> the earth, by clear shining after rain. Although my house be not
> so with God: yet he hath made with me an everlasting cove-
> nant, ordered in all things, and sure: for this is all my salvation,
> and all my desire, although he make it not to grow."

David looked beyond himself and his house to the Messiah as
the fulfillment thereof. In Psalm 110:1–4, where we have almost the same language, David alluding no doubt to the same
communication:

> "The Lord said unto my Lord, Sit thou at my right hand,
> until I make thine enemies thy footstool. The Lord shall send
> the rod of thy strength out of Zion: *rule thou* in the midst of
> thine enemies. Thy people shall be willing in the day of thy
> power, in the beauties of holiness *from the womb of the morn-
> ing:* thou hast the dew of thy youth. The Lord hath sworn, and
> will not repent, Thou art a priest for ever after the order of
> Melchizedek."

Here, undoubtedly, the promise is to Christ, the true Melchize-
dek, and the covenant was with Him. These were the words
given to Christ, and Christ came to effectuate and to establish
them, that all their conditions might be fulfilled.

Again, under the character of Levi, in Malachi 2:4–6:

> "And ye shall know that I have sent this commandment unto
> you, that my covenant might be with Levi, saith the Lord of
> hosts. My covenant was with him of life and peace; and I gave
> them to him for the fear wherewith he feared me, and was
> afraid before my name. The law of truth was in his mouth, and
> iniquity was not found in his lips; he walked with me in peace
> and equity, and did turn many away from iniquity."

Now let us come to the New Testament. In Galatians 3:16,
we have the apostle commenting upon an expression frequently
met with in the Old Testament—*"thy seed."*

"Now to Abraham and *his seed* were the promises made. He
saith not, And to seeds, as of many: but as of one, And to thy
seed, *which is Christ.*"

The promise is made to Christ.

There is a remarkable passage in the opening of the Book
of Revelation—"The revelation of Jesus Christ *which God
gave unto him.*" Not—"The revelation of Jesus Christ which
God gave *unto us.*" No, all that is here opened out to us in
prophecy, was first mapped out to Christ, God gave it *unto
Him;* He showed Him the white-robed multitude, and the city
with the pearly gates; He showed Him the foundations thereof,
and caused Him to listen to the song of the redeemed; and
gladly He came down here to die that He might bring the things
to pass. "Lo, I come to do thy will, O God," and for the joy set
before Him He endured the cross, despising the shame; the
love of Christ for us constrained Him then, and, as we realize
it, it will constrain us now.

II. Christ takes credit for having acted as God's commissioned Ambassador. See Deuteronomy 18:18, 19.

"I will raise them up a Prophet from among their brethren,
like unto thee, and will put *my words in his mouth: and he
shall speak unto them all that I shall command him.* And it
shall come to pass, that whosoever will not hearken unto my
words which he shall speak *in my name,* I will require it of
him."

"I have given unto them the words which thou gavest me."

Let us compare two passages, John 3:33, 34, "He that hath
received his testimony [that is Christ's] hath set to his seal that
God is true." And why? "For he whom God hath sent, speaketh
the words of God . . . *the words which thou gavest me.*"
Chapter 7:16, "Jesus answered them, and said, My doctrine is
not mine, but his that sent me." For this reason, principally,
Christ is called *the Word of God;* His words are God's words,
He was the mouthpiece of God, the voice of God. He is *"The*

faithful and true witness." "This is my beloved Son," said the voice from heaven, "hear him." Now let us hear His testimony preached in the synagogue, and quoting from Isaiah 61:1–3,

> "The Spirit of the Lord God is upon me; because the Lord hath *anointed me to preach good tidings* unto the meek; he hath sent me to bind up the broken-hearted, to proclaim liberty to the captives, and the opening of the prison to them that are bound; *to proclaim* the acceptable year of the Lord, and the day of vengeance of our God; to comfort all that mourn; to appoint unto them that mourn in Zion, to give unto them beauty for ashes, the oil of joy for mourning, the garment of praise for the spirit of heaviness; that they might be called trees of righteousness, the planting of the Lord, that he might be glorified."

"I have given unto them *the words* which thou gavest me."

III. "They *have* received them." Observe, He takes credit for the success of His embassy, and that as Mediator, He is entrusted with *"the words,"* and the fulfillment of *"the words,"* and the preservation of *"the words,"* and also with the communication of *"the words,"* and the application of *"the words"* to His people. He always speaks in His prayer, as responsible for them, and as being the condition of the fulfillment of the covenant between the Father and Himself. This is the account He renders: "I have given unto them the words which thou gavest me; and they have received them"—not as *notions,* not as *opinions,* but as Thy very words. And "they have known"—in the reception of them—"that I came forth from thee, and they have believed that thou didst send me." All His teaching and example were intended and calculated to bring our hearts up to the Father, that we might see in that Father's love the *reason* for all things, even the reason why He was here to intercede for us, and to claim the reward of the merit of the travail of His soul on our behalf.

Now, let us draw a few practical conclusions from this statement.

The knowledge of God, as our Father, and of His Son Jesus

Christ, as that Father's gift to sinners, is *the end of all revelation*. If we have not attained to this knowledge, so far as we are concerned, in vain the Scriptures have been written.

Here we learn what is the surest, truest, and most unchangeable ground and resting place for our faith, *the words Christ spake,* for He says: "I have given unto them the words which thou gavest me." Not His *miracles;* He does not allude to them; they are evidence—no doubt glorious evidence, precious evidence; "the works bear witness of me," He says; but there is higher evidence. Much less was it their *frames* and *feelings* which He spoke of as the ground of their assurance and confidence. No, no, *"the words* which thou gavest me" I have given them. Oh! to examine them more carefully, and to live upon them more abidingly! Here, too, we have the ground of peace, and joy, and comfort, and hope, and blessing. May we hide *the words* in our hearts for His name's sake who gave them to us.

The words which the Lord Jesus Christ gave unto us are only received truly by us when they lead us to believe in Him. We may listen to them, we may talk about them, we may profess them to any amount, but until the words which the Father gave to Christ, and which Christ has given to us, are so received by us that we believe on Him whom God hath sent, we have never profited, we have never truly received them. Then, added to this (read John 5:24):

> "Verily, verily, I say unto you, He that heareth my word, and believeth on him that sent me, *hath* everlasting life and shall not come into condemnation; but is passed from death unto life."

So that if we do not know we have passed from death unto life, if we do not know that we shall not be condemned, if we do not know that we are forgiven, we have really never taken *in the full truth of the testimony,* even the words which the Father gave unto Christ to give unto us; and this is a very practical consideration.

Remember what Christ considered the highest commendation of *His people*. "They have received the words which thou gavest me, they have known surely that I came out from thee, and they have believed that thou didst send me."

And observe what the Lord Jesus evidently considers one of the highest commendations *He can give of Himself*, when He now presents Himself as Mediator before His Father. "I have given them the words which thou gavest me." *Precious words they are!* When shall we value them as we ought? When shall we take them to our hearts, and receive them with meekness, with gladness, and with faith, and having received them, witness of them to others?

13

"I PRAY FOR THEM: I PRAY NOT FOR THE WORLD, BUT FOR
THEM WHICH THOU HAST GIVEN ME; FOR THEY
ARE THINE."—John 17:9

PROPERLY SPEAKING, this is the actual commencement of
our Lord's prayer. His previous utterances were but intro-
ductory. Was ever prayer so introduced before? He who pleads
is the Son of God—the Mediator. He could say to His Father,
"I know that thou hearest me always." What mighty pleadings
are here! He pleads, *the occasion*—"The hour is come" (next
day He was to die). He pleads His relationship, *"Father, the
hour is come."* He pleads *His commission*, "Thou hast given
him power over all flesh, that he should give eternal life to as
many as thou hast given him." He pleads *His consecrated life,*
"I have glorified thee on the earth," "I have manifested thy
name." He pleads *His finished work,* "I have finished the work
which thou gavest me to do . . . I have kept them in thy
name"; I am now about to wash their sins away; glorify Thy
Son by receiving My sacrifice; let the fire of accepting love come
down upon the altar and the offering, and then, Father, "glorify
thou me with thine own self, and with the glory which I had
with thee before the world was . . . that thy Son also may
glorify thee."

His prayer *has been answered,* our blessed Lord Jesus Christ
is in the highest heavens now—that glorious Man (and it is like
a foretaste of heaven to realize it), who is bone of our bone,
flesh of our flesh, our own Brother,—for albeit He is our King
and God, He is our Brother,—our Husband, our Friend, our

Shepherd, Priest, and King, He is at the right hand of God now, and all the powers of heaven and earth are committed into His hands,—those same hands which were once pierced for us upon the cross. Moreover, "God . . . raised him up from the dead, and gave him glory; that our faith and hope might be in God" (I Peter 1:21).

> "He hath set him at his own right hand in the heavenly places, far above all principality, and power, and might, and dominion, and every name that is named, not only in this world, but also in that which is to come: and hath put all things under his feet, and gave him to be the head over all things to the church, which is his body, the fullness of him that filleth all in all" (Eph. 1:20–23).

Oh, for faith to grasp this great fact! We often tremble here below in the contemplation of the weakness of self, the malice of our enemies, and the difficulties we have to grapple with; yet our risen Head and King is above them all; they have all been put *under His feet*,—is it possible He could have them under His feet, and yet allow them really to hurt us? *It is impossible.* The fact that the crown of the universe is upon His head secures us; the fact the principalities and powers are beneath His feet, and subject to His sway, secures the soul that looks to Him by faith, and enables us to say as the apostle did,

> "Neither death, nor life, nor angels, nor principalities, nor powers, nor things present, nor things to come, nor height, nor depth, nor any other creature shall be able to separate us from the love of God which is in Christ Jesus."

This intercession of our Lord for His disciples, and "for all who shall believe on him through their word," is but an illustration of the intercession He is now carrying on for His people at the right hand of God. As our great High Priest He has ascended into the highest heavens "by his own blood." What Aaron did upon the great day of atonement on earth, the Greater than Aaron has done in the temple of heaven; He has gone in, not to the mercy seat made with hands, which is the image of the true, but to the very throne of God; not with the blood of bulls and of goats, which could not take away sin, and which were but pictures and emblems of the true, but with His own precious blood, and there He appears "in the presence of God *for us.*" He came "for us," He lived "for us," He died "for us," He rose "for us," ascended "for us," entered into the highest heavens "for us," presents His blood "for us," intercedes "for us," prepares a place "for us," claims the mansions "for us," has caused the Holy Scriptures to be written "for us," has sent down the Holy Ghost "for us," and will come again "for us." Oh, what a precious Christ! With mortal ears we cannot listen to Him *there*, but faith, gathering its inspiration from His prayer *here* on earth, can enter somewhat into the spirit of that inter-cession. "Behold Me, My Father, Thy co-equal Son! Thou knowest the glory which I had with Thee before the world was; Thou knowest how I emptied Myself, and became so poor that I had not where to lay My head; Thou knowest how Thy judg-ment due to sin did fall on Me; Thou knowest how Thou didst make My soul an offering for sin; Thou knowest the reward of My travail is that those who believe on Me might never suffer." "I am about to be wounded for their transgressions, bruised for their iniquities, the chastisement of their peace is upon Me, that by My stripes they might be healed: Father, it is *I who call,* it is *My* voice Thou hearest, I have glorified Thee on the earth, and I pray for them."

When men urge a petition they use such arguments as they believe likely to influence most the parties with whom they plead, and so does Christ in His prayer. He, who was eternally in the Father's bosom, well knew the delight that Father had in His beloved people; He knew the intense complacency with which He regarded them, the interest He had in them, and that He had given them to Him to be gathered from their wander-ings, washed from their sins, have their ignorance instructed, be clothed in the best robe that heaven's wardrobe could provide for them, made members of His own body, and presented by Him without spot or wrinkle, accepted in Himself, to share' His kingdom, to live in His life, to share His joy, to know His peace, and to sit upon His throne forever. He received them as the pledge of His Father's love: "Thine they were, and thou gavest them me." I am glorified in being their High Priest (Heb. 5:5). I know how their salvation redounds to Thine honor, and fills Thee with joy, and shall yet fill heaven and earth with Thy praise. "I pray for them!" They have destroyed themselves, but in Me is their help. "I pray for them!" They have polluted their souls, but I am their salvation. "I pray for them!" They have been lost, but I am come to seek and to save that which was lost; they have been blind, and naked, and poor, and captives, and in prison, but Thy Spirit is upon Me, because Thou hast anointed Me to open the eyes of the blind, to unstop the ears of the deaf, to open the prison doors to them that are bound, to proclaim liberty to the captives, and the acceptable year of the Lord. "I pray for them," for I have received them *at Thy hand,* I undertake for them, I lay out My fullness for them, and I will lay down My life for them. I ask nothing for Myself, apart from them, I ask no return for the travail of My soul, I seek no honor, I desire no exaltation, no glory apart from them. *"They are thine";* they are Thine Hephzi-bahs, Thy delight is in them; they are Thy Beulahs, Thou art married to them; they are Thine own "peculiar treasure," they were created for Thy glory; they shall show forth Thy praise; Father, "I pray for them"; they oftentimes tremble in the consciousness of their weakness and their unworthiness, but "I pray for them." Satan desires to have them, that he may sift them as wheat, but "I pray for them"; true, they are poor, tempest-tossed, oftentimes sore let and hindered in running the race set before them, but "I pray for them." They are needy—so needy that no one but Myself and Thyself can understand the depth of their need, but "I pray for them." They often forget to pray for themselves, but "I pray for them."

> "*Keep them* through thine own name;
> *Sanctify them* through thy truth;"
> *Unite them* in thine own self:
> "And *I will that* they . . . be with me where I am;
> That they may behold my glory, which thou hast given me;
> For thou lovedst me before the foundation of the world."

This is the Lord's prayer, and as faith rises into the contemplation of it, we are enabled to exclaim with the apostle—

> "Who shall lay anything to the charge of God's elect? It is God that justifieth. Who is he that condemneth? It is Christ that died, yea rather, that is risen again, who is even at the right hand of God, who also maketh intercession for us. Who shall separate us from the love of Christ? shall tribulation, or distress, or persecution, or famine, or nakedness, or peril, or sword? As it is written, For thy sake we are killed all the day long; we are accounted as sheep for the slaughter. Nay, in all these things we are *more than conquerors* through him that loved us" (Rom. 8:32–37).

There is a very solemn exception in this prayer, which we must not overlook. Men of the world! as some love to call themselves; women of the world! as some are not ashamed to style themselves, what do you make of this? *"I pray not for the world."* Oh, this weary, wretched, disappointing, condemned world! how is it that people cling to it as they do? Its god is not our God. "The god of this world"—you know who he is? Its prince is not our Prince;

> "The prince of this world cometh, and hath nothing in me."
> "I pray not for the world, *but* for them which thou hast given me; for they are thine." There are two classes: one He calls the world; He does not pray for it;—the other He describes as those "thou hast given me out of the world . . . who have received my word [who] have believed that thou didst send me," and those who "have known surely that I came out from thee."

Let us consider this solemn matter.

1. The world contrasted with the Lord's people.
2. The character of the world.
3. The judgment of the world.
4. The message of God to the world.
5. The command of God to His people in the world.

We know very well that this is not fashionable teaching, but it is God's truth for all that.

1. See verse 14, "I have given them thy word"; and the world hath *hated* them, "because they are *not of the world, even as I am not of the world.*" Let us keep that contrast before our minds; for just in proportion as we keep His Word, and live closely with God, the world will hate us, and call us very disagreeable, peculiar, unpleasant sort of people; and is it not in order to escape this so many who call themselves Christians lower their standard? They have not enough of love to Christ to endure the brunt of the world's sneer and contempt, that is the reason there are so many unsatisfactory Christians. It is a very easy Christianity which admits of our being all day long in the world, and half an hour with God in the morning and evening; the world will never despise us for that, nay, it will applaud us as the right sort of Christians! In Luke 16:8, the Lord distinguishes between the children of the world and the children of light. As two distinct families: "the children of this world are in their generation wiser than the children of light." Again, John 8:23: "Ye are from beneath; I am from above: ye are of this world; I am not of this world." Now, if this means anything, it means this—that they who are truly of this world are from beneath; all that appertains to the world, its prince, its principles, and its practice, are from beneath, and tending to beneath. This is so, else what does the Lord mean? Do not gloss over those contrasts; we ought to think and pray over them. See also I John 5:19:

"We know that we are of God, and the whole world lieth in wickedness";

all unconscious even of their danger, asleep, careless, and lost! To this contrast add the fearful words of our text, *"I pray not for the world."*

2. The character of the world? This has been described in the passages quoted, but let us add some others. Galatians 1:4: "Jesus Christ . . . gave himself for our sins, that he might deliver us from *this present evil world,* according to the will of God and our Father." See John 15:18: "If the world hate you, ye know that it hated me before it hated you." When our Lord was here on earth, it was not the ignorant—the uneducated and the depraved—that hated Him, it was the rulers, the priests —*aye, the priests, and the high priest at the head of them.* They hated Him, they were "the world," although ordained priests, and the Pharisees, the religionists of the day, they hated Him also and persecuted Him to the death. And again, I John 2:16: "All that is in the world, the lust of the flesh, and the lust of the eyes, and the pride of life, is not of the Father, but is of the world." Also James 4:4: "The friendship of the world is enmity with God; whosoever, therefore, will be a friend of the world, is the enemy of God." *"I pray not for the world."*

3. The judgment of the world? It is condemned; it is under sentence. Not more truly was Sodom condemned to destruction than is the world. "The earth also and the works that are therein shall be burned up." And the apostle Peter charges men with being willingly ignorant of the fact that as the first world was destroyed by water, so "the world that now is, is reserved unto fire against the day of judgment and perdition of ungodly men." In John 16:8–11 we read that the Comforter, when He should come, would "reprove the world of sin . . . because they believe not on me; of righteousness, because I go to my Father, and ye see me no more; *of judgment,* because the prince of this world is judged." It is only the longsuffering of God which brings it to pass that this world is yet spared; God is longsuffering to us, and He waits till His message is heard and His people

gathered; He waits if peradventure those led captive by Satan at his will may recover themselves from the snare of the devil, and claim that repentance, forgiveness, conversion, and faith, which He delights to bestow.

"The world passeth away. . . . If our gospel be hid, it is hid to them that are lost: in whom the god of this world hath blinded the minds of them which believe not, lest the light of the glorious gospel of Christ, who is the image of God, should shine unto them" (I John 2:17; II Cor. 4:3).

4. God's message to the world:

"Behold! the Lamb of God which taketh away the sin of the world" (John 1:29).

"God so loved the world that he gave his only begotten Son, that whosoever believeth in him should not perish."

"And as Moses lifted up the serpent in the wilderness, even so must the Son of man be lifted up: that whosoever believeth in him should not perish, but have eternal life" (John 3:14, 15).

5. The command of God to His own people in the world:

"Come out from among them, and be ye separate . . . and touch not the unclean thing; and I will receive you, and will be a Father unto you, and ye shall be my sons and daughters, saith the Lord Almighty" (II Cor. 6:17, 18).

"Be not conformed to this world: but be ye transformed by the renewing of your mind" (Rom. 12:2).

"Love not the world, neither the things that are in the world. If any man love the world, the love of the Father is not in him" (I John 2:15).

"Pure religion and undefiled before God and the Father is this, to visit the fatherless and widows in their affliction, and to keep himself unspotted from the world" (Jas. 1:27).

Sinner! you are no more safe in the world than Lot would have been in Sodom; "Escape for your life." You are no more safe in the world than Noah would have been upon a mountain top; *"Come into the ark."* "I pray not for the world." There is no atonement for an *unbelieving* world. Therefore no intercession of Christ; His intercession is at all times founded upon His atonement. There is no hope for the world; it is a lost world, a condemned world; it is the enemy of God; it is the kingdom of him the world worships. There is no safety but in flying from it to the Rock cleft to shelter you. Come to Me, says Christ, I will save you, I will shelter you, I will keep you, I will pray for you. But, Father, "*I pray not for the world,* but *for them which thou hast given me . . . out of the world . . .* for they are thine.*" The curse of our day is that people are trying to serve two masters—the world on the one hand and God on the other; *it cannot be done:* we must either come out of the world and be with Christ, or we must sink with the world into the condemnation of those who reject Christ.

May God grant a blessing with these words, for the sake of Him who is at the right hand of God, and who ever liveth to make intercession for all those who come unto God by Him; "*I pray not for the world.*"

14

"AND ALL MINE ARE THINE, AND THINE ARE MINE;
AND I AM GLORIFIED IN THEM."—John 17:10

PERHAPS it would have been better not to have separated this verse from that which precedes it; reading them together we are enabled more distinctly and fully to appreciate the amazing argument of our blessed Lord—"I pray for them: I pray not for the world, but for them which thou hast given me; for they are thine. And all mine are thine, and thine are mine; and I am glorified in them."

Here is a distinct and emphatic assertion by our blessed Lord of His equality with God; the most convincing proofs of this fact are not found in direct assertions, but in those statements which imply and take for granted His Deity. In the original, the word "all" is neuter, *"all things* that are mine, are thine." All things belonging to Me personally, essentially, and relatively, are Thine, Father; and "thine are mine," all that belongs to Thee—Thy nature, Thy name, Thine eternity, Thy perfections, Thine attributes, Thy fullness, Thy dominion, all that Thou hast an interest in, Thy kingdom, Thy heavens, Thy throne, Thy people, Thy glory—"all thine are mine"; "We are *mutually, equally,* and *alike* interested in them; for all things that are mine are thine, and all that are thine are mine." Imagine an archangel using language such as this; imagine the absurdity of the highest created being making such a statement —it would be blasphemy; and, therefore, we are led to this most blessed conclusion, Jesus Christ is very God, of very God.

See a parallel passage (16:14, 15). The Lord is promising

the Comforter; He says, "He shall glorify me: for he shall receive of mine, and shall show it unto you." Then He explains,

> "All things that the Father hath are mine: therefore said I, that he shall take of mine, and shall show it unto you" (John 16:15).

The Holy Spirit doth not take directly from the Father and show the things of the Father to the people of God, because Jesus is *the Mediator,* Jesus is the medium. It pleased Jehovah that in Him should all His fullness dwell, and it is of the fullness that is in Jesus, the Holy Ghost receives, in order to show and bestow it upon us. (See another passage, I Cor. 2:9–11.)

> "Eye hath not seen, nor ear heard, neither have entered into the heart of man, the things which God hath prepared for them that love him; but God hath revealed them unto us by his Spirit: for the Spirit searcheth all things, yea, *the deep things* of God. For what man knoweth the things of a man, save the spirit of man which is in him? even so the things of God knoweth no man, but the Spirit of God. . . . For who hath known the mind of the Lord, that he may instruct him? But we have the mind of Christ" (I Cor. 2:9, 10, 16).

Thus it is the Spirit through the Son who reveals and communicates to the people of God *"the all things"* of the Father.

In Hebrews 2:8, we have the Holy Spirit's own commentary upon the extent of the expression—"all things."

> "Thou hast put all things in subjection under his feet. For in that he put all in subjection under him, *he left nothing* that is not put under him."

Apply this rule to the passage before us; all things that belong to Thee are Mine—without *exception,* and without *limitation.*

Taking these passages together, the great truth brought out is—that there is a mutual interest *in each other,* and in the things that pertain to *and belong to each other,* between the Persons of the glorious and adorable Trinity; the Eternal Three

are united together in the divine essence, they have equal communion and fellowship in the divine attributes, and an equal
and mutual interest in their redeemed people. This is precious
truth, but it stands upon *a rock*. The Father has as much interest
in the salvation of the redeemed as Christ has, and Christ and
the Holy Ghost have as much interest in them as the Father
has. The Father's love gave Christ to them, Christ's love gave
Himself for them, and the Holy Ghost's love reveals and applies to them the salvation of God.

"They are thine," "They are mine," and "I am glorified in
them." *All* of them are Mine, all of them are *Thine*—the weak,
the needy, the most ignorant of them, the veriest babe in the
family, as much so as the most fully grown towards the measure
of the stature of the fullness of Christ. All of them and *all
things pertaining to them* "are Mine," "are Thine"; they are
Ours mutually, equally, alike, and everlastingly.

What a secret our blessed Lord revealed to His listening
disciples! How they must have wondered as He thus spake concerning them, and not only concerning them, but, thank God,
concerning us, if we believe on Him; for verse 20 includes us,
"Neither pray I for these alone, but for them also which shall
believe on me through their word; that they all may be one;
as thou, Father, art in me, and I in thee, that they also may be
one in us." "All mine are thine, and thine are mine." It was Thy
love gave them to *Me,* and gives Me *to them,* and Our mutual
love to them secures that the Holy Ghost shall *dwell within
them;* Our interest in them brought Me down to be their Saviour to take upon Mine own self their debt, and die in their
place; Our interest in them leads Me to give my life to be their
life, and Myself to be their portion, and the glory Thou gavest
Me to be their crown. *"Thine* they were" eternally and by election, purpose, and grace; *"mine* they are irrevocably, by creation, for I made them; *Mine* they are by gift, for "thou gavest
them to me"; *Mine* by purchase, for I lay down my life for

them; *Mine* by the conquest of My grace, for "I have manifested to them thy name"; *Mine* by the voluntary surrender of them-selves, for they believed Thy Word and have come to Me as their Refuge, their Saviour, their Hiding-place, and their Friend; *"mine* they are"—My portion; the members of My body, of My flesh, and of My bones; *Mine* they are—My Bride whom I shall present unto Thee without spot or wrinkle, or any such thing, adorned with heavenly jewelry, clothed in the garments of My salvation; *Mine* they are—My Body and My fullness! What would My kingdom be without them? or *My* throne? they are My glory, "I am glorified in them."

Wonderful language! But He meant it all; *and He means it all.* His words were the result and the expression of *God's com-mended love!* "All mine are thine, and thine are mine; and I am glorified in them." They are God's children, they are Christ's Church, they are the Holy Ghost's habitation,—they are His beloved ones, they are His Bride, they are the Holy Ghost's charge, and He shall educate them for the positions that the Son's love and Father's love have appointed for them. They are Jehovah's portion, therefore they are Christ's purchase, and the Holy Ghost dwells in them "the earnest of their inheritance until the redemption of the purchased possession." They are the people of God "formed for himself": "created for his glory": and they are "the glory of Christ." He will come by-and-by "to be glorified in them," and meanwhile, even in their tribulations "the Spirit of glory doth rest upon them," till "God be all in all."

Really, thought becomes giddy, and our poor feeble minds weary, in contemplating truths like these, but they are resting places for faith; and it was in order that our faith might be strengthened, our hope established, and our love deepened, that the Lord uttered these words to His Father—not in private, but in the hearing of His disciples, "All mine are thine, and thine are mine." We are mutually engaged in choosing, redeeming, sanctifying, saving, keeping, and glorifying them; and We are mutually interested in their persons, wants, troubles, difficulties, temptations, and warfare; in the formation of their characters, and the consummation of their happiness.

God Himself then and the fullness of God is our "portion," God is our "rock," God is our "refuge," God is our "high tower," God is our "redeemer," God is our "sanctifier," God is our "preserver," God is our "Father," God is our "husband," God is our "salvation," and "our God for ever and ever." How secure must they be who have believed on His name!

We are taught in Scripture that our security flows from three great facts. The Father has *loved us* with an everlasting love—a love that never changes; Christ, who died for our sins, is now at God's right hand in resurrection glory and ever lives to make *intercession for us,* pleading His work finished and accepted; and God the Holy Ghost *dwelleth in us.*

"A threefold cord is hard to be broken!" (Eccles. 4:12).

Will God lose those He has loved with an everlasting love? Will Christ forget those for whom He ever lives to intercede? Will God cast off those to whom He has sent the Holy Ghost, to dwell in them, for ever be in them—

"And be in them a well of living water springing up unto everlasting life" (John 4:14),

and that they might be builded together for His own habitation through the Spirit? See our Redeemer prays not only for the final salvation of those for whom He intercedes, but for their *preservation* in this present evil world (see v. 11), "Holy Father, keep through thine own name those whom thou hast given me." He prays, in verse 17, for their *sanctification,* "Sanctify them through thy truth; thy word is truth." In verses 23, 26, He prays for *their comfort,* that they may know they have been loved by the Father, even as the Father loves Him; and, in verse 22, that they may be *glorified* with Him, beholding

the glory that He had with the Father before the world was.
Now, if these things be so, we *are safe,* completely safe, and we
ought to be happy. Only unbelief and distrust can interfere with
our abiding happiness. Our peace ought to be as a river, and
our righteousness like the waves of the sea. If these things be
so, we may well be assured that *all things are working together
for our good.* Can it be true that Father, Son, and Holy Ghost
are mutually, equally, and alike interested in us, and that anything can go wrong, really wrong with us? We may be tried,
we may be tempted, we may be troubled on every side; we may
be in deep waters; but we shall come out of the tribulation, and

> "The trial of your faith being much more precious than
> gold that perisheth, though it be tried with fire, might be found
> unto praise, and honour, and glory, at the appearing of Jesus
> Christ" (I Peter 1:7).

If "all mine are thine, and thine are mine," then *our interests*
temporal and spiritual, for time and for eternity, are *the care of
God,* we are fully *"accepted* in the beloved," the *ear of God* is
open to our prayers; our *inheritance* is chosen for us, *"all things
are yours,"* and "ye are Christ's and Christ is God's."

Three practical results grow out of this statement of privileges. The first is II Corinthians 7:1:

> "Having therefore these promises, dearly beloved, let us
> cleanse ourselves from all filthiness of the flesh and spirit, per-
> fecting holiness in the fear of God."

Another is II Timothy 1:12:

> "I know whom I have believed, and am persuaded that he is
> able to keep that which I have committed unto him against
> that day."

And a third is John 14:1 and 16:33:

> "Let not your heart be troubled: ye believe in God, believe
> also in me. . . . In the world ye shall have tribulation: but be
> of good cheer: I have overcome the world."

15

WHEN WE REMEMBER who it is that speaks, to whom, of whom, and the circumstances under which He speaks, these words are very wonderful. Like the apostle of the Gentiles, we must be content to contemplate them, and exclaim "O the depths!"

Already the prayer has ascended—"Father, glorify thy Son, that thy Son also may glorify thee"; glorify Him by supporting Him through death, by accepting His sacrifice, by raising Him from the dead, and giving Him glory, that Thy people's faith and hope may be in Thee (I Peter 1:21). Such is evidently the meaning of the first part of the prayer. Then, again, He had prayed, "Father, glorify thou me with thine own self with the glory which I had with thee before the world was." A wonderful petition. It cannot mean less than this; exalt Me in My manhood into the majesty which, as Son of God, I enjoyed with Thee before all worlds; and then He adds, "all mine are thine, and thine are mine; and I am glorified *in them*"—by which words He not only pleads that they should be glorified, but that their glory should be associated with His own,—glorify them with Me, and glorify Me in them. We have a somewhat similar prayer in II Thessalonians 1:10–12, where the apostle speaks of the time when "Christ shall come to be glorified in his saints," and then adds, "Wherefore also we pray always for you, that our God would count you worthy of this calling, and fulfill all the good pleasure of his goodness, and the work of faith with power: that the name of our Lord Jesus Christ may be glorified

in you, and ye in him, according to the grace of our God and
the Lord Jesus Christ."

"I am glorified in them." Let us endeavor to enter by degrees
(for it is only in this way that we can possibly do so) into this
great statement. He who speaks is "the Lord of glory"; He had
for a time laid aside that glory, and taken upon Him the form of
a servant; the great salvation work He came to do was all but
done, and He was about to ascend into the glory He had with
the Father before the world was. He *has gone* into that glory,
He is reigning there *now,* and He will continue to reign there
until, according to His own sure word of promise, He shall
come again "in the Father's glory, and his own glory, and of the
holy angels." In heaven He is "the brightness of the Father's
glory, and the express image of his person"; He fills the heaven
of heavens with His glory, and by-and-by he will fill earth as
well as heaven with His glory; yet, hear Him, *"I am glorified
in them."* The conclusion is much more easily drawn by the
spiritual mind than can be expressed by mortal tongue.

What is glory? Glory is the display of the fullness of God,
the glory of Christ is the manifestation of what *Christ* is. So we
read (John 16:14), speaking of the Spirit,

> "He shall glorify me: for he shall receive of mine, and shall
> show it unto you."

The manifestation and communication of Christ is the glory
of Christ, as the light of the sun is the glory of the sun; as the
manifested beauty and fragrance of the flowers of the field are
their glory.

> "The heavens declare the glory of God; and the firmament
> sheweth his handywork";

but here is something far more wonderful, "I am glorified in
them." As it was in the temple of old, the glory of the Lord was
manifested there more than in all the earth beside, so it is with
Christ's people, they are the temple where He doth display,

and will display, His glory more than in all the earth, aye, more than in all heaven beside; therefore He says, "I am glorified in them."

Again, the glory of the Lord is manifested in the kingdom of His providence; He upholds all things that He hath made with the word of His power,

> "By the greatness of his might, for that he is strong in power not one faileth" (Isa. 40:26).

But much more in upholding, sustaining, keeping, blessing, and supplying the need of His people, is He glorified. It is in His dealings with the sons of men that the Lord Jesus Christ most manifests, and, therefore, most glorifies Himself, as it is in giving the Lord Jesus Christ to the sons of men, Jehovah has most glorified Himself. We are the empty vessels, into which the Lord Jesus Christ pours the fullness of His grace, and into which, by-and-by, He will pour forth the fullness of His glory. It is in redeeming sinners Jesus is most glorified; it cost Him but a word to create the worlds, but to redeem a sinner's soul cost Him all that He had, including His tremendous stoop from heaven's glory to earth's wilderness, the cross, and the curse. It is in regenerating sinners that the Lord Jesus manifests His glory. Who but Himself could take a dead soul, and re-generate it with His own eternal life? This is truly a wonderful display of the glory of His grace; matter does not resist His power, the sinner does; sun, moon, stars, earth, and skies gave Him no opposition when He created them—but the world, the flesh, and the devil do their utmost to resist Him in His new creation; and if His glory is manifested in the natural creation, which never did or could resist His power, how much more in His new creation. It is in the conversion of sinners Christ is glorified, turning them

> "from darkness to light, and from the power of Satan unto God" (Acts 26:18).

Filling their eyes with new objects, their hearts with new affections, their hopes with new themes; going forth for their
salvation, delivering them from the lowest state of ruin, bursting the bonds with which the devil had enthralled them, securing to them liberty, even liberty of access to God, washing
their sins away in His own blood, clothing them with the spotless robe of His own righteousness,—but this is not all,—opening the fullness of God to them, and sending the Holy Ghost
to qualify them to enjoy it. Oh *here* it is that Christ is most
glorified. *"I am glorified in them."* By-and-by when He sets the
crowns upon their heads, and listens to their song, ascribing to
Him the kingdom, and the glory, and the praise for having redeemed them to God by His blood, out of every kindred and
tongue, and made them kings and priests unto God and unto
His Father (see Rev. 5:9, 10), then shall be consummated that
saying,

> "He shall see of the travail of his soul and be satisfied" (Isa.
> 53:11);

He shall be glorified in their glory, for they shall be glorified in
Him.

"I am glorified in them." We feel as if we could dwell on this
sentence, and never weary of the wonderful Theme it presents
to us. It is a precious prism, every aspect of it sheds forth divine
radiancy. Angelic might cannot display Christ's strength so
much as our weakness does; the riches of heaven cannot display
Christ's fullness so much as our poverty does; the holiness of
archangels cannot speak His praise so much as the covering of
our unrighteousness does; the anthems of the seraphim cannot
utter His glory as shall the praises of His redeemed; and not all
the worship of heaven's hosts can render to Him so grateful an
offering, or crown Him with so rich a crown, as the love of His
pardoned people. "I am glorified in them."

Yes, and every attribute of God shall be glorified in them: when

"Unto the principalities and powers in heavenly places shall be made known by the church the manifold wisdom of God" (Eph. 3:10).

His power shall be glorified in them; and His faithfulness shall be glorified in them. For notwithstanding all their failings and wanderings, and notwithstanding all their unworthiness, He never will forget His promises to them. And His goodness shall be glorified in them, goodness that bears with them, long-suffering, and abundant in its truth, never lowering the standard of His justice, or abating one jot of His law, or disparaging the holiness of His character, and yet providing a salvation which makes them "heirs of God, and joint-heirs with Christ." Moreover His mercy shall be magnified in them, and His divine and inexhaustible love! Every office of Christ is glorified in them: He would have nothing to do as a teacher but for them; He would have nothing to do as a High Priest but for them; He would have no redeemed subjects to reign over but for them. We read (II Cor. 4:6), that "the light of the knowledge of the glory of God is manifested in the face of Jesus Christ"; and, here, Jesus Christ tells His Father, "I am glorified in them." Wonderful! Wonderful!

Doubtless, the apostles were uppermost in His mind when He uttered the words of our text. He *had been* glorified in them, for "they had first trusted in Christ"; they had left their little "all" to follow Him, and Jesus is thus glorified; He acknowledges this to His Father, saying, "I am glorified in them." But we must not overlook how very little they knew, how very little they had attained unto, when the Lord uttered these words; but Christ doth ever regard His own grace, planted by His own Spirit in the heart of His child; it may be hidden there; it may be well-nigh *overwhelmed with corruption,* but the Lord recognizes it; He knows that His own Word, the incorruptible seed, is the germ of eternal glory, and He takes credit for it. "I am glorified in them." And He was *about to be* glorified by them. When the Lord Jesus had ascended into heaven, the Holy Ghost would come down upon these men and lead them into all truth, and make them the inspired communicators of the Word of God to the sons of men; their testimony to His name was to overspread the earth,

> "And they loved not their lives unto the death" (Rev. 12:11);

they knew whom they had believed, and were persuaded he was able to keep that which they had committed unto him against that day (II Tim. 1:12); and they counted not their lives dear unto them so that they might finish their course with joy, and the ministry which they had received of the Lord Jesus, to testify the gospel of the grace of God (Acts 20:24); He was about to send them to open blind eyes, to turn sinners "from darkness to light, and from the power of Satan unto God"; He knew that He would be glorified in them, therefore He says, Father! "I am glorified in them." Their subsequent life's history was just a story of the goodness, the love, the care, the patience, the gentleness, the tenderness, of the Lord Jesus Christ toward them. He walked with them through the waters, according to the Word in which He caused them to hope; when all men forsook them, the Lord stood by them and strengthened them, delivering them from every foe and from every fear; He drew them out of many waters, and set their feet upon a rock and established their goings (II Sam. 22:17; Ps. 40:2), putting a new song into their mouths, cheering their hearts, enlightening their paths, and scattering their foes on every side. *"I am glorified in them."*

And we may not confine the Lord's words to the eleven apostles. "Neither pray I for these alone, but for them also which shall believe on me through their word." And, if *we* have believed upon the Lord Jesus Christ, He is glorified *in us;* only think of it—the Lord glorified in us! Verily, He is not glorified by what He *gets from us,* but by what He *bestows upon us;* we are the empty vessels into which He pours grace, and in doing so He is glorified in us; by-and-by, having filled us with grace, He will fill us with glory too; and in doing so He will be glorified in us. The only possible way in which we can glorify Him here is by receiving Him:

> "What shall I render unto the Lord for all his benefits toward me? I will *take* the cup of salvation, and call upon the name of the Lord" (Ps. 116:12, 13).

The utmost we can do to glorify Him here is to live upon Him, to abide in Him; never to go beyond Himself for comfort or guidance, or look to other than Him for faith and hope; never to be beyond His own bosom for a resting place; never beyond the fountain He has opened for sin and for uncleanness to get rid of our sin; and ever to make mention of His righteousness, and of His righteousness only! The life we live, if we are living souls, is *His life;* the light we walk in, if we have any light, is *His light;* every victory we gain is *His triumph;* every stone in the spiritual building is *grace,* every bright beam of our spiritual day is *grace.* All our fruitfulness, all our gladness, all our comfort, the foundation upon which we stand, and by-and-by the top-stone with which we shall be crowned *is all of Christ,* that He may be glorified. Therefore He says, "I am glorified in them."

Now, consider the evident object which the Lord here had in view in thus pleading for His people. It was as if He had said: "Father, My glory is Thy special delight; I know it; Thou knowest it; Thou hast created the universe for My glory; there is not an angel that wings his way through heaven's space that has not been created for My glory; providence, in all its departments, is for My glory, and eternity is for My glory; that glory is dear to Thee, Father, *'I am glorified in them.'* I cannot be glorified if they are not blessed." This is God's own truth, and we ought not to take a lower standing; why should we when God gives us such a high and glorious one? Our glory (if we have come to Christ by faith and taken Him for our Saviour) is as sure as His own: "whom he called, them he also justified: and whom he justified, them he also glorified" (Rom. 8:30).

Truly, the glory of the sinner who believes on Jesus, and for whom Jesus intercedes, is bound up with God's own glory. In Jeremiah 14:20, 21, we find a marvelous argument in prayer, apparently founded on this fact:

> "We acknowledge, O Lord, our wickedness, and the iniquity of our fathers: for we have sinned against thee. Do not abhor us, for thy name's sake, *do not disgrace the throne of thy glory:* remember, break not thy covenant with us."

Again, "I am glorified in them," in *all of them!* The Lord has laid on His Father's heart the cases of all His children, all His believing ones, to the end of time; every one who ever did or ever would believe and trust Him. To confine this statement merely to the eleven would be to ascribe to Christ but a very limited glory indeed. Nay, He prays *for all* who shall believe upon Him "through their word"—all of them, the weakest as well as the strongest, the neediest (perhaps most of all for the neediest), for the greater the need He supplies, the greater the glory He manifests, and the more He manifests glory, the greater the glory He receives. For the debtor that owed Him five hundred pence will love Him most.

"I am glorified in them." I believe it means at least as much as this: "Father, let them have all the blessing they can contain; let them have all the communicable fullness of God; let them have all the happiness the Holy Ghost can enable them to enjoy; give them as much of Thy strength, as much of Thy love, as much of Thy righteousness, as much of Thyself, *as it is possible for creatures in union with the Son of Thy love to possess,* for 'I am glorified in them.' " Let their interests be Thy care; let all that pertains to them belong to Thee, except their sin, which I am about to put away by the sacrifice of Myself. Watch over them in their weakness, comfort them in their sorrow, direct them in their difficulties, carry them in Thine everlasting arms, bear them to Thy banqueting house, and let Thy banner over them be love. Keep them, sanctify them through Thy truth, unite them, that they may be one, ever as We are, and finally let them behold My glory which I had with Thee before the world was, that I may see of the travail of My soul and be satisfied, for "I am glorified in them."

What a destiny awaits the people of God! The Lord is glorified in creation and in providence. He is glorified in redemption, more than in either. He is glorified in regenerating His people, and He will be glorified by-and-by in raising them from the dead, for Christ is the first-fruits of the glory of the resurrection. Thus, when "he shall see of the travail of his soul, and be satisfied," there will not be a department of the manifested glory of God which shall not find its center and its resting place in His people; they are His *new creation;* they are the watched and cared-for objects of His providence; they are the purchase of His blood; they are the regenerated of His Spirit; they shall be the risen ones of His power, and the glorified of His glory. "He shall change our vile body that it may be fashioned like unto his glorious body, according to the working whereby he is able even to subdue all things unto himself." Whatever *creating* power can accomplish, whatever *providential* power can accomplish, whatever *regenerating* power can accomplish, whatever *resurrection* power can accomplish, whatever the power of the *glory of God* can accomplish, shall be manifested in us. It is enough, henceforth may

"Our conversation be in heaven, from whence also we look
for the Saviour, the Lord Jesus Christ" (Phil. 3:20),

who pleaded for us on earth in prayer, and now pleads for us in
heaven in the glory, "I am glorified in them." Soon, soon, may
He come again to be "glorified in his saints, and admired in all
them that believe"!

16

"AND NOW I AM NO MORE IN THE WORLD, BUT THESE ARE
IN THE WORLD, AND I COME TO THEE."—John 17:11

IN A GENERAL WAY, and with such arguments as we have
tried from time to time to explain, our Lord had commended
His disciples, and all His believing people, to His Father's care.
He now offers *particular* petitions for them, such as He knew
by His own experience, learned in our nature, they needed, such
as was suited to their circumstances, their state, and their various
exigencies. He knew the path that lay before them, and the ungenial place in which He was so soon to leave them, for He had
trodden that way before.

Observe, they all relate to spiritual things; all have reference
to heavenly blessings; the Lord does not ask riches for them, or
honors, or worldly influence, or great preferments, but He does
most earnestly pray that they may be kept from evil, separated
from the world, qualified for duty, and brought home safely to
heaven. Soul prosperity is the best prosperity; and, in truth, all
temporal prosperity, as it is so called, is only real when it is in
proportion to the prosperity of the soul. Remember how the
beloved disciple brings out this thought in his third epistle.

> "Beloved, I wish above all things that thou mayest prosper
> and be in health, even as thy soul prospereth" (III John 2).

Soul prosperity is the index of true prosperity.

Before the petition which follows, "Holy Father, keep them,"
our Lord's prayer is prefaced with the words we have just read.
They seem to open out His whole heart to us. What depths of

thoughtful love, tenderest sympathy, devoted consideration, and interest for us these words express, "And now I am no more in the world, but *these are in the world,* and I come to thee." Observe the pronouns, "I, these, they," all through the chapter, all through the prayer "I, thou, they." How He entwines them together! "Now I am no more in the world, but *these* are in the world, and *I* come to *thee."* He had been with them hitherto, and while with them He was their Light, their Comforter, their Companion, their Counselor, their very present Help. Were they accused, He was present to defend them; were they cast down, He was always ready to raise them up; were they mistaken, He was always near to teach them; were they troubled, He was their constant and unfailing Comforter. Now, circumstances were about to be altered. His bodily presence was to be no longer with them. "I am no more in the world."

There are many in our day who profess to worship the *bodily presence* of Christ; they are idolaters in doing so. "I am no more in the world." The body of Christ is at the right hand of God, not here on earth, and all sensuous worship of Him as present in body, whether in religious ordinances, or in the more gross form of matter supposed to contain or represent the person of the Lord Jesus Christ, is idolatry. *"I am no more in the world."* Would to God that this sentence were written over many a ritualist "altar" as it is called, and carried out in the worship of many a professing Christian congregation!

"I am no more in the world." Hitherto He had been.

> "He was in the world, and the world was made by him, and the world knew him not. He came unto his own, and his own received him not" (John 1:10, 11).

He had been hated in the world, and now the world, having hated Him, was about to reject Him, and finally to crucify Him. His had been a weary and a suffering pilgrimage. "He looked for judgment, but behold oppression; for righteousness, but behold a cry." He asked for bread, and they gave Him a stone;

He sought a rest amongst us, the world gave Him a grave; misrepresented, neglected, calumniated, refused, and soon to be killed; the "heir of all things" was about to return home from the vineyard to which God had sent Him. "I am no more in the world." For thirty-three years He dwelt amongst us, "a man of sorrows and acquainted with grief, and we hid as it were our faces from him; he was despised, and we esteemed him not"; the foxes had holes, and the birds of the air had nests, but the Son of Man had not where to lay His head. The baptism with which He was to be baptized, and of which He said His soul was straitened till it was accomplished, was now about to descend upon him; His travail of soul was nearly over, the Captain of our salvation was about to lay aside the shield and the sword, and the entire panoply; His last tear was soon to be shed, His last sorrow experienced, His last sigh uttered, His last conflict over; "I am no more in the world, *but these are in the world.*" The train of thought evidently in the Lord's mind as He uttered these words is truly wonderful, beautiful, subduing, touching, "I am no more in the world, but *these* are in the world, and I come to thee." I come, My Father, to be with Thyself, "I come to thee,"—My rest, My portion, My home,—but *"these* are in the world." I come to Thy presence where there is fullness of joy, and to "thy right hand where there are pleasures for evermore." "I come"—to where the river of the water of life flows from the Throne of God; but *these, these* are in the wilderness. "I come"—where no enemy can follow Me, where no temptation can assail Me, where no weariness can distress Me; but *these, "these* are in the world." "I come"—to reap the trophies of My great victory. "I come"—to grasp the scepter, to wear the crown, and to ascend the Throne. I have been weary here, but I shall soon be weary no longer; the way has been rough and thorny, but it is all over, My haven is almost reached; yet *these, "these* are in the world!" "I come to thee!" I come to see Thy face, I come to listen to the angels' praises and the redeemed ones' song, but "these are in the world"; I come where the harps are tuning, and hearts are waiting, and diadems are sparkling,— "I come to thee"—but these, *these are in the world.*" How beautiful! how full of sympathy! Whatever reasons made it expedient for us that He should go away, it is very evident He was leaving His heart behind Him; and that, however exalted He may be at the right hand of the Majesty in the heavens, He does not and cannot forget His poor struggling followers here in the wilderness. As it was when He spent *that night* in prayer with God, He looked down upon the tempest-tossed Lake of Galilee and saw the little boat struggling, and the disciples toiling in rowing; although for a purpose He left them there till the *fourth* watch of the night, yet in the end He came down to them walking upon the sea. As it was then, so it is now, and so it will be by-and-by; from the height of the glory He remembers His tempted, buffeted, and tempest-tossed followers in the wilderness. "I am no more in the world, but these are in the world."

See how, even in the anticipation of Gethsemane, and of the cross, He was thinking *of them;* although the glory was before Him, and the gates were trembling to fall back upon their everlasting hinges that the King of Glory might come in, He was thinking of His people rather than of Himself; neither the agony of the cross, nor the glory of the throne, could make Him overlook the fact *"these are in the world."* Nay, He founds a double argument in petitioning His Father concerning them—a double reason why His Father should specially take care of them; first, because He is no more with them in their troubled lot here; and, secondly, because He was coming to the glory and they were not coming with Him. "Now I am no more in the world, but these are in the world, and I come to thee." Thus it is, whatever be the circumstances in which our glorious Mediator may be placed, whether with them, or in heaven, He will draw forth arguments and reasons therefrom that His people may have the benefit.

"These! are in the world." We might almost imagine Him looking at them, in the intensity of His love, and stretching forth His hands toward them, as He speaks—"these!" Thine own gift to Me, My Father, Thine own portion, My Father; *these!* the children, the helpless ones, the flock, My redeemed; "these are *in the world,*" they are My life, My Bride, My joy, My glory, My portion, My all; "these are in the world"; they are not of the world, Our love hath taken them out of it, they are raised above it, yet they are in the world.

Now consider the position that infinite love and wisdom has assigned to the people of God—*"in the world"*—the ungodly, unkind, ungenial world, which, however it may "love its own," hates Christ and the things of Christ, and will always persecute those who are *for* Christ and *like* Christ. "These are in the world"—the place of *trial,* where every principle shall be tested; the place of *danger,* where they are surrounded on every side with foes; the place of *temptation,* where every means will be taken by the enemy of their souls, to draw them aside; the deceiving world—so fair, so fascinating, and oh! so disappointing; the world—which offers and promises much, but gives little; the world—where hope withers, and joy is a mockery, and where there is nothing abiding, where corruptions are strong, and foes numerous, and the flesh weak; the world—that "lieth in wickedness," where the devil, as a roaring lion, walketh about, seeking whom he may devour;

"A dry and thirsty land, where no water is" (Ps. 63:1).

"These are in the world"—an unfruitful place, an unsatisfying place, an unsafe place, where each one must in his or her own way learn more or less quickly, and more or less deeply,

"This is not your rest; because it is polluted" (Mic. 2:10).

Such is the position the God of all grace and love has placed His people in; not the garden of the Lord, but the wilderness, where every particle of food for their souls must drop upon them from heaven, where all the waters that can really refresh their spirits must flow to them from the "rock," where the only guide that can be depended upon is "the *pillar*" of their God. Not in peace are they placed—far from it—but in conflict; not in the midst of friends—far from it—in the midst of foes, ready to take advantage of them at every turn; not in plenty, but oft-times in the conscious want of all things; not clothed in glory, but in "the earthly house of this tabernacle"; not in the banqueting house—not yet; "these are in the world."

Our heavenly Father has good reasons for this; not without His own wise purposes has He chosen the position for His people. Perhaps we may gather from the Word of God *three* reasons why the Lord's people are left in the world. He *might* immediately take them to glory. The moment the blood drops upon them, the moment the Spirit of God enters into them to show them themselves, and to show them Christ, the Lord might translate them, and send a chariot of fire for them, as He did for Elijah; but He does not, and why?

First, the Lord leaves His people in the world in pity to the world. "Ye are the light of the world." They are left here to illuminate this dark world; oh, that they did it more faithfully! There is not a ray of light to bless the world's darkness but that which emanates from the people of God. Would that we were more faithful as light-bearers in this dark world! Would to God that our homes, our families, our circle of acquaintance, and the world around us were the better for our light!

"Ye are the salt of the earth." The only hope for it, that which saves it from falling into absolute corruption are the churches of God scattered over it. Alas! Alas! that the salt so often loses its savor. There is nothing under the heavens so worthless as a savorless Christianity; and nothing so useless, few things more filthy than a smouldering lamp! We are left here for the world's sake, to witness for our Lord, to tell the sweet story of His love, to gather the wanderers, to comfort the sorrowing ones, and, by God's grace, to point heavenward, and lead the way. "These are in the world."

Another reason why the Father leaves us in the world is—for the formation of our Christian character. We are here to learn what it is to live by trust; we are here to be exercised in faith and hope and love. And that we may learn to live upon God. In the storms of life we cast our anchor upon God, look for the day:

"Here is the patience of the saints . . . and the faith of Jesus" (Rev. 14:12).

Were there no trial of faith, and hope, and love, how could faith, or hope, or love be exercised and strengthened? But when Christ left us in the world, He gave us this comfort:

"As the Father hath loved me, so have I loved you; continue ye in my love" (John 15:9).

For circumstances will arise to lead you to question My love; you will often times feel alone, deserted, utterly weak, apparently forgotten; oh! remember that Mine eyes are always on you, My heart always with you, My arms always around you:

When you "walk in darkness, and have no light" (Isa. 50:10),

trust still in Me; hope still in Me; I change not, "I will never leave you, or forsake you."

A third reason why we are in the world is—for the honor of His own dear name—that He may be glorified. Salvation, under any circumstances, is difficult. Suppose us to be surrounded with all possible appliances, advantages, and supplies, even under such circumstances, even as strong and not weak, as full and not empty, as holy and not unholy, our salvation would be a very difficult thing. The storms are tremendous, the foes are numerous,

"For we wrestle not against flesh and blood, but against
principalities, against powers, against the rulers of the darkness
of this world, against spiritual wickedness in high places"
(Eph. 6:12).

But here is a bark so frail that it needs not a wave but a ripple
to upset it; and see, it rides over the wildest storms and steers
its way through the most fatal breakers. How is this?—Jesus is
there! See a reed—a reed bruised, that can be scarcely kept together, and yet all the powers of hell cannot crush it. See the
smoking flax, that a puff of wind would extinguish, and yet all
the powers of hell cannot extinguish it. How is this?—Jesus is
there! Just like the bush in the wilderness burning but not con-
sumed; so are His people here: we are

"Kept by the power of God through faith unto salvation"
(I Peter 1:5),

outriding every storm, resisting every temptation, carried triumphantly over death and hell in spite of the world, the flesh,
and the devil; and all that His blessed name may be glorified,
and that we may each learn to acknowledge that

"It is no more I that live, but Christ that liveth in me: and
that life which I now live in the flesh I live in faith, the faith
which is in the Son of God, who loved me, and gave himself
for me" (Gal. 2:20, R.V.).

Not with our strength but in our *weakness,* not with our fullness but in our *emptiness,* not with our wealth but in our *poverty,* He conquers and overcomes the world, that He may be
glorified; these are among the reasons why we are in the world.

But the *comforts* He leaves us while in the world are not
small. "These are in the world." How assuring it is to hear Him
say this. *He knows the fact;* we are not here unknown to Him,
He pleads the fact with His Father as a reason why His Father
should keep us: He has provided for every emergency, He has
measured the world's storms, He holds the winds in the hollow

of His hand, He has weighed its billows, He has counted its difficulties,

> "In the world ye shall have tribulation: but be of good cheer: I have overcome the world" (John 16:33).

His words imply that it is only while we are in the world sorrow can assail us; the trials, the difficulties, the conflicts, and the dangers *are only here,* none of these things are in that world to which we are going; its joys are without clouds, its smiles without tears, its songs without sorrows, its eternity without sin; only in the world does any difficulty exist.

"But these are in the world"!!! See, He accounts Himself so identified with us, that He seems jealous that He should be in glory while we are in the world, or that we should be in the world, and He not with us here, and because the Father's glory, our salvation, required that we should be parted for a time. He turns it into an argument in our behalf, "Now I am no more in the world" with them, therefore, "Holy Father, keep them!" for I come to Thee, and My heart is *there with them.*

17

TRULY, we have here the expression of "love that passeth knowledge." When in the anticipation of His sufferings, and in the immediate prospect of entering into the glory He had with the Father before the world was, He seems to tell His Father, in the hearing of His people, that glory would be no glory to Him if they were not safely kept, as in the hollow of His hand, in that wilderness world in which He was about to leave them. Holy Father, keep them!

If any question arises in our mind suggesting "Why leave them in the world?" why say, "I am no more in the world"? Why not say, "And now *we* are no more in the world"? Any such question is silenced and answered by the Saviour's prayer. Surely there is a needs-be. Not only is it expedient that He should go away, but truly it is equally expedient that His people should be left behind. What though it be a world of temptation, of disappointment, and of conflict, in which He leaves them, where trial that well-nigh breaks the heart, and sorrow that goes far to overwhelm the soul, surrounds them on every side: He into whose hands they are committed

> "Is able to keep . . . from falling, and to present . . . faultless before the presence of his glory with exceeding joy" (Jude 24).

That Holy Father has power enough, and wisdom enough, and love enough, to remove His people out of the world if it was for

His own glory, or if it was for their *real* good that He should do so. And since they are left in the world, be sure it is neither for the glory of their Father, nor for the real welfare of their souls, that they should be removed out of it. Observe the Lord does not pray for it or even desire it; for He says (v. 15)—"I pray not that thou shouldest take them out of the world, but that thou shouldest keep them from the evil."

The truth is, it must cost our Lord Jesus Christ far more to leave His people in the world than it costs *them* to be in the world. If it be true,

> "He that toucheth you, toucheth the apple of his eye" (Zech. 2:8);

If it be true that

> "In all our affliction he was afflicted" (Isa. 63:9);

If it be true that

> "We have not an high priest who cannot be touched with the feeling of our infirmities" (Heb. 4:15),

then what the apostle Paul says of himself in Colossians 1:24, is equally true of every member of Christ's Body here in the world so long as we are exposed to trials and difficulties, we are

> Filling up "that which is behind of the afflictions of Christ in his flesh, for his body's sake, which is the church."

It is through the great grace and *long-suffering* of God, His people are left here in the wilderness: many are the lessons to be learned here. They are absolutely necessary, and not to be learned elsewhere, for practical experience with which, the people of God are left in the world.

1. We are left here to learn—*What we are.* A humbling lesson to be spelled out day by day, and hour by hour; the unworthiness, the weakness, and worse than weakness, of self; the

poverty, the worse than poverty—the *corruption* of self. Where so likely or suitable a place to learn this, as in the world?

2. We are left to learn by practical experience *the emptiness of the creature.* We have our hopes, our affections, our desires, and we try to satisfy them, and find a resting place for them in the creature; we make the effort only to be disappointed. It is well to learn that there is not a resting place in all creation for our poor hopes and hearts; we know of no position so calculated to teach us the lesson as "in the world," and depend upon it, God knows this, else He would not leave us here, but would take us to the place where we could learn most effectually these two great lessons—the unworthiness of self, and the emptiness of the creature.

3. We are left here to learn *the glory of Christ,* the abundance of His grace, the constancy of His love, the inexhaustible fullness, laid up in Him for our help. When the creature disappoints us, we are taught to look to Christ for rest, and there we shall never be disappointed. The grace that is in Him is manifested and enhanced all the more fully in contrast with the unworthiness of self. Here we are taught the value of the blood that cleanseth from all sin. Here we are taught by practical experience that His strength is made perfect in our *weakness.* Oh! well for us if in our earthly training, the flesh goes down, and self is prostrated in the dust, while Christ alone is exalted. Well for us, if when hope fails to find its rest in the creature, we learn to cast our anchor upon Him, where Christ's love, and tenderness, and sympathy are experienced most clearly and distinctly amidst the weariness and disappointments of time.

4. We are left "to be *made partakers* of Christ," and to have fellowship with Him in His sufferings. The *only* thing in which He can have fellowship with us here is in *suffering.* He can have none with our unbelief, distrust, corruptions, or sin—only with our sufferings, and most of all, our sufferings for His name's sake. The world which hated Him hates us, and the principles

of the world which are opposed to Him, oppose themselves to us. He was a stranger here; and just in proportion as His people are like Him, they will learn that they too are strangers here. Now, is it not well to be in a position where He can have fellowship with us in some things? In this wilderness He comes down to us in our sorrows, and has fellowship with us in our sufferings; it was in this wilderness He sorrowed and suffered, and deeply and tenderly He sympathizes with His tempted members; nay,

> "If ye be reproached for the name of Christ, happy are ye; for the Spirit of glory and of God resteth on you" (I Peter 4:14).

5. We are left here to learn *the power of God*. If it were not for the mighty power of God, the world, the flesh, and the devil would be too much for us, they are all leagued against our souls; it is the power of God alone that keeps us; it is not by might of our own, or power or wisdom of our own, but by the strong arm of our God round about us that we are kept; and we are left in the world, to learn the lesson.

6. We are left here to learn *the faithfulness of God*. There is no more important lesson we can learn in the wilderness than this—the faithfulness of our God; that He is true to His promise, always has been, and always will be; that He does not and will not change, though we do; that He does not vary in His love to us, as we do in our love to Him; that He is "the same yesterday, and today, and forever," our faithful Friend, our faithful God.

7. And we are left here to learn *to believe His Word*. In all the varieties of our frames—and where can there be a position imagined in which a greater variety of frames and feelings is brought out as in this weary world—where so much disappointment, conflict, and temptation? where so many deep, deep afflictions—in all the variety of our frames, and in all the phases of our need, we are here to learn to believe His Word notwith-

standing, to hope in His name, to watch, to pray, to wrestle, to fight, and, by His grace, to conquer through Him that loved us.

O God our Father, teach us our wilderness lessons, grant that we may learn them well, grant that we may learn them deeply; let us not lose one stage of our pilgrimage; let us not lose one practical lesson that any of the conflicts, difficulties, and trials of our way were intended to impart; only keep us in the hollow of Thy hand, keep us from evil! Soon the wilderness will be past forever, and *then* the white robe, and *then* the palm branches of victory, and *then* the crown of life, and *then* the throne of glory. Let us try and feed our faith, if we have any; and if we have not, may God Almighty *beget* faith in us while we ponder over our Lord's Prayer, "Holy Father, keep them."

He was looking at the world in which He was leaving them, thinking of its difficulties, its dangers, and sorrows. He knew, He knew them all. "Holy Father, keep through thine own name those whom thou hast given me, that they may be one, as we are." I am leaving them, leaving them in the world; I have no more to ask for Myself, Father, I come to Thee; now all My interest is with them, all My sympathy is with them, all My thoughts, and My prayer is for them. "Holy Father, keep them." Observe the position in which He would have them kept, in *union, and identified with Himself.* Holy Father, keep them "that they may be one, as we are."

We might have expected Him to say, *Merciful* Father, keep them, or *Gracious* Father, keep them, or *Loving* Father, keep them. No; Christ fixes upon His *holiness,* and again, in verse 25, on His *righteousness,* pleading also His relationship to God. *"Holy Father,* keep them." Now why does He fix upon the holiness of God? It is the crown of all God's attributes; it is the beauty and the perfection which sets off the whole. When God would swear,

> "Because he could swear by no greater, he sware by himself" (Heb. 6:13).

Yet He selected this attribute to swear by, as representing His own name—Himself. See Psalm 89:35 to which, no doubt, Christ alludes,

> "Once have I sworn by *my holiness* that I will not lie unto David."

Now, therefore, the true David pleads, *"Holy Father."* In pledging His holiness, Jehovah pledged that which is the crown of all His attributes—that which represents all. The crown of the Godhead is *holiness,* and that is pledged to Christ, and Christ claims the pledge.

Again, Christ had *finished* the work which the Father gave Him to do; and, therefore, He pleads the pledged holiness of God to keep His people. He is not asking that which He had no right to claim; accordingly He also pleads the *righteousness* of God, for it is as righteous a thing with God to keep His people, as it is to "recompense tribulation to them that trouble them." It was in order that they might be kept, Jesus left His throne, and took their nature upon Him; in order that they might be kept, He was about to die for them; and all this in covenant arrangement with His Father. He now pleads the pledged oath, the holiness of His Father, and the fulfillment of His promise that

> "He shall see of the travail of his soul, and be satisfied" (Isa. 53:11).

There is another reason why He pleads the holiness of God; remember the place He was leaving them in; remember the nature they possessed: He was leaving them in an unholy world, He was leaving them in an unholy nature in that world. Oh! there is a close connection between the holiness of God unto which He commits them, and the purpose in His heart for them that they might be kept in the unholy world, and in spite of the unholy nature in which they were to tread that world's wilderness. "Keep them," keep their *lives,* keep their *faith* from dying out, keep their *hope,* let it never be extinguished, keep their *comforts,* keep their *souls,* keep them in their going out, and in their coming in. "Holy Father, keep them through thine own name." It does refresh the spirit to think of these things.

Remember how often in Old Testament times the Spirit of God was pleased to illustrate the "Keeper" of His people. See in Ezekiel 34 Jehovah, the Shepherd, keeping His helpless, diseased, threatened and trembling flock.

> "Thus saith the Lord God; Behold, I, even I, will both search my sheep, and seek them out. As a shepherd seeketh out his flock in the day that he is among his sheep that are scattered; so will I seek out my sheep, and will deliver them out of all places where they have been scattered in the cloudy and dark day. And I will bring them out from the people, and gather them from the countries, and will bring them to their own land, and feed them upon the mountains of Israel by the rivers, and in all the inhabited places of the country. I will feed them in a good pasture, and upon the high mountains of Israel shall their fold be: there shall they lie in a good fold, and in a fat pasture shall they feed upon the mountains of Israel. I will feed my flock, and I will cause them to lie down, saith the Lord God. I will seek that which was lost, and bring again that which was driven away, and will bind up that which was broken, and will strengthen that which was sick" (34:11–16).

Again, see Isaiah 27:2, 3 Jehovah as a *husbandman* keeping His vineyard:

> "In that day sing ye unto her, A vineyard of red wine. I the Lord do keep it; I will water it *every moment:* lest any hurt it, I will keep it *night and day.*"

Our blessed Mediator knew whom He was addressing when He said, "Holy Father, keep them"; He would have them kept in safety every moment, watered every moment, kept day and night. Again in Psalm 121:3–5, Jehovah a watchman, keeping His people,—

"He that keepeth thee will not slumber. Behold, he that keepeth Israel shall neither slumber nor sleep. The Lord is thy keeper."

Oh, to realize that we have such a Keeper; what need of being kept when no other could keep us, what dangers from within, what dangers from without; not all the hosts of angels from heaven could keep us,

"Jehovah himself is thy keeper."

In Psalm 18:2, we have other figures; where the Lord Jehovah is represented as a rock and a fortress: yea, the munitions of rocks, a deliverer, a buckler, a horn of salvation, and a high tower. But all these illustrations of God's power to keep His people are included and *surpassed* in this prayer of our blessed Lord. He actually enshrines us into the Deity itself. "Holy Father, keep through thine own name those whom thou hast given me, that they may be one, as we are."

Observe, He pleads for five things:

1. That they should be kept in the holiness of God.

2. That they should be kept in the Fatherhood of God.

3. That they should be kept through the name, the holy, holy, holy name, the ineffable name. Keep them in Thy name, in the knowledge of it, in the love of it, in the enjoyment of it, in the experience of it, in the power of it, and keep them *by* Thy name. Doubtless, the full meaning of the Lord's Prayer embraces the gift of the Holy Ghost, who was to come personally to them after He left the world. Again, Keep them *for* Thy name; keep them for the praise of the glory of Thy name; keep them so as to manifest that Thou *canst* keep them in the most unfavorable circumstances, and against all conceivable foes. Put Thy name upon them, My Father, and let it be as a bulwark for them, against the world, the flesh, and the devil.

4. "Keep . . . those whom thou hast given me." They are *Thine own;* Thy name is upon them; Thine interests are with

them; Thy glory surrounds them; and they are left here in the world to prove Thy power to deliver them: for Thine own sake, Father, keep them, for they are Thine.

5. Then, lastly, He pleads, keep "those thou hast given me," for they are *Mine own portion;* if they are lost My portion is gone; if they are lost the travail of My soul is for nothing; if they are lost devils will mock; if they are lost the world may triumph; it will be a proved matter that the world, the flesh, and the devil are stronger than Thou art; Thou gavest them to Me to be saved, I died for them, "Holy Father, keep through *thine own name* those whom thou hast given me, that they may be one, as we are."

Observe, He asks that *all* those for whom *He* pleads may be *"one,* as we are," because He knew, and the Father knew, and He would have us know that the safety of the Church consists in union with Himself. Adam was not in union and he fell; angels which kept not their first estate were not in union and they fell; there can be no fall for those who are in union with the living God. This is the ground upon which the loving heart of the Mediator pleads for His people that they may be one. We have, here, an illustration that no mind of man can fully enter into, we find our Lord frequently teaching us about union, comparing the union between Himself and His people to the union between the branches and the vine, and between the members of the body and its head; but here all illustrations are thrown aside, and the union on which hangs the universe, and in which the Deity itself rests is pleaded, "that they may be one, as we are." And He explains afterwards why and how this may be, "I in them, and thou in me, that they may be made perfect in one."

This prayer has been *heard.* How safe, then, must be those who have come to the Lord Jesus Christ, and have taken Him for their portion and their Saviour. The answer to the prayer of Christ is written in I Peter 1:5, where the Spirit of God by the apostle describes the people of God as in the wilderness, and though now for a season, if need be, in heaviness through manifold temptation, yet

> "Kept by the power of God through faith unto salvation, ready to be revealed in the last time" (I Peter 1:5).

For Christ prayed, "Holy Father, keep through thine own name those whom thou hast given me."

Here, then, we have our Lord committing those who believed upon Him, and those who shall believe upon Him through the teaching of His apostles to the *fatherhood* of God, to the *holiness* of God, to the *name* of God, as God's own *property,* and as Christ's own *portion,* as given to Him by His Father to be kept. Now what we need, is faith to *draw* upon these things. We listen to them. Oh! for faith to *live* upon them, to *act* on them, to imbibe the love, the power, and the life they contain, and to go on our way singing, as Israel of old was taught to sing,

> "Happy art thou, O Israel: who is like unto thee, O people saved by the Lord, the shield of thy help, and who is the sword of thy excellency! and thine enemies shall be found liars unto thee; and thou shalt tread upon their high places" (Deut. 33:29).

18

OUR LORD, as we have before said, is in this prayer committing His people to His Father's care. He pleads. As the High Priest appeared before God on the day of atonement with the names of the tribes on his shoulders and on his heart, so Christ presents Himself before His Father. It is the voice of "the only begotten Son of God" that speaks. It is the voice of the Lamb of God even now on His way to the altar of sacrifice, and He thus prays, "Holy Father, keep through thine own name those whom thou hast given me, that they may be one, as we are. While I was with them in the world, I kept them in thy name"; or perhaps more literally, "Holy Father, keep them in Thine own name which Thou hast given Me, that they may be one, as We are. While I was with them in the world I kept them in Thy name, which Thou hast given Me." They are wonderful words; they breathe nothing but love, and grace, and truth, and tenderness. He brings no charge against them, He finds no fault with them, He hints at no deficiency: and yet we know they had many faults, many deficiencies; the disciples were not angels, but men. Hitherto they had not been great saints, but on the contrary very feeble ones, not persons of high attainments, but "slow of heart to believe," and ready to halt; not very eminent for any grace, and at times full of failure and of corruption; but the Lord takes no notice of this in all His prayer. Our Lord Jesus Christ is a great Saviour, and a divine Mediator; He is full of grace and truth and love; He is exactly suited to the need of His people, whether as regards their sins, their corruptions, their miseries, or their temptations; and the whole of His dealings with them have been, are, and ever will be one grand display of abundant mercy; this prayer, expressing His thoughts, revealing His purposes, uttering His will and His anxieties concerning them, are sufficient evidence of this.

"While I was with them in the world, I kept them in thy name." He was with them in the world; "the Word was made flesh, and dwelt among us."

> "Forasmuch as the children are partakers of flesh and blood, he also himself likewise took part of the same" (Heb. 2:14).

He would not only save us with an high hand, but He would *know* our sorrows, He would *experience* our trials, would be *tempted* as we are, and, like His brethren, would learn

> "Obedience by the things which he suffered";

He was with them in the world, not only in their company, but in their *nature*. Every stage of our wilderness-journey has been trodden by the Lord Jesus Christ Himself; in childhood, in boyhood, in manhood, He was with us,

> "In weariness and painfulness, in watchings often, in hunger and thirst, in fastings often, in cold and nakedness" (II Cor. 11:27);

and as He had His nativity with us, so He was about to make His grave with us. "I was with them in the world." Were they in trouble—so was He. Were they offended—so was He. Were they in danger—so was He. Were they neglected—so was He. Were they hated by the world—"if the world hate you, ye know that it hated me before it hated you." "I was with them in the world." However true it may be that His great aim and object in descending from heaven into our nature and dwelling upon the earth was to die, that

"Through death he might destroy him that had the power
of death, that is the devil" (Heb. 2:14),

it is also true that for thirty-three years He was with us in the
world, and He knows, as only He can know, our difficulties, our
dangers, our infirmities, and our foes. He was compassed with
them all His life, and He

"Can have compassion on the ignorant, and on them that
are out of the way" (Heb. 5:2).

He is now far removed from trial, from conflict, and from pain,
but

"We have not an High Priest which cannot be touched
with the feeling of our infirmities" (Heb. 4:15).

He was with us in the world.

We observe He speaks in the past tense. "I *was* with them."
He was about to leave them now, but He suggests this is an
argument and reason why the Father's special care and keeping
should be with them, "I was with them in the world," and while
I was with them, "I kept them in thy name." Probably the true
reading is, "I kept them in thy name, which thou hast given
me." If we take the sentence as it is in our Bibles, "I kept them
in thy name," then He means that He did so by His Father's
appointment and authority. He was God's chosen Shepherd, and
He kept those given to Him in His Father's name. But taking
it in the other reading, "I kept them in thy name, which thou
hast given me," then He means that by His counsel, His teaching, His example, and His constant care, He kept them in the
fullness of the blessedness, the privileges, and the salvation
which that name implies and involves.

Our Lord here fully declares and acknowledges before His
Father, in the hearing of His disciples, and for our instruction
and comfort, *seven* all-important facts.

1. That He was commissioned by His Father to be their
Keeper; He was not here on His own account, He was sent from

heaven to keep in the name of God the people given to Him; therefore in keeping them He only fulfilled His commission, in keeping them to the end He only discharged the obligation and responsibility, which the office He had undertaken involved, the duty which, as Mediator, He bound Himself to render to the Father that sent Him. What a great truth is here! Depend on it He fulfilled His office well, and here He gives an account like to that He will render at the last day. "While I was with them, I kept them in thy name."

2. We learn that in Himself was contained the salvation, strength, and supply in which He was commissioned to keep them, "I have kept them in thy name which thou hast given me."

> "It pleased the Father that in him should all the fullness dwell" (Col. 1:19),

and His commission here was to keep the people of God in the enjoyment, possession, and fruition of the fullness laid up in Himself for their supply: not even the commissioned Mediator can do more than keep His people in the fullness laid up in Himself for their supply.

3. Learn how unspeakably precious to God His people must be. Was the Son of God sent from heaven to keep them, and are they not precious? Was the name of Jehovah committed to Christ, and all the fullness of God laid up in Him *for their supply,* and are they not precious? Oh! inestimably precious. Well the Lord Jesus Christ knows it, and well He pleads the fact, "Keep through thine own name those whom thou hast given me."

4. Our Lord is here pleading His Father's covenant engagement. "Holy Father, keep them." The Father had pledged His holiness that He would do so, and now the pledge is claimed. "I have kept them in Thy name as Thy commissioned servant; My work is done, and now I pledge Thee by Thy holiness." Father,

keep them in Thy name, while I am away from them. Very beautiful and very wonderful this is!

5. There is no safety for us, even though God Himself be our Keeper, but in that *name,*

> "There is none other name under heaven given among men, whereby we must be saved" (Acts 4:12).

There is no *rest* for us but in that name, no *security* for us but in that name, no *salvation* for us but there. Oh, may His name be precious to us, may we prize it, may we hide in it, and live upon it till we are with Him where He is!

6. The Lord had no hope that we could keep ourselves in that name. He knows our helplessness, and He pleads it in His prayer. "While I was with them in the world, I kept them in thy name," and now that it is expedient for Me to go away, "Holy Father, keep them."

7. The character of our blessed Lord's constant intercession. As He was in the days of His flesh, so is He now at the right hand of God; our Mediator! And here is the keynote of His intercession: "Holy Father, keep through thine own name those whom thou hast given me." The *name* of Jehovah was early revealed. In Exodus 3:13–15, we read,

> "Moses said unto God, Behold, when I come unto the children of Israel, and shall say unto them, The God of your fathers hath sent me unto you; and they shall say to me, What is his name? what shall I say unto them? And God said unto Moses, I AM THAT I AM: and he said, Thus shalt thou say unto the children of Israel, I AM hath sent me unto you. And God said moreover unto Moses, Thus shalt thou say unto the children of Israel, the Lord God of your Fathers, the God of Abraham, the God of Isaac, and the God of Jacob, hath sent me unto you: this is *my name* forever, and this is my memorial unto all generations."

We have a further revelation of this *name* in Exodus 34:5–7.

> "The Lord descended in the cloud, and stood with him there, and proclaimed the name of the Lord. . . . The Lord, the

> Lord God, merciful and gracious, long-suffering, and abundant
> in goodness and truth, keeping mercy for thousands, forgiving
> iniquity and transgression and sin, and that will by no means
> clear the guilty."

The Lord Jesus had kept His people in that name, He had revealed to them that name, taught them that name, and now He would have His Father keep them in that name. Oh, this is a precious resting place for the faith, and peace, and happiness of His people. He came Himself to suffer, "the just for the unjust," because He would not, and could not otherwise "clear the guilty."

> "[The Lord Jesus Christ was made] to be sin for us, who
> knew no sin; that we might be made the righteousness of God
> in him" (II Cor. 5:21).

In Numbers 6:23–27, we find the *name* committed to the High Priest, and disposed of by him as the representative in his official character of the Lord Jesus Christ Himself:

> "Speak unto Aaron and unto his sons, saying, On this wise
> ye shall bless the children of Israel, saying unto them, The
> Lord bless thee, and keep thee: the Lord make his face shine
> upon thee, and be gracious unto thee: the Lord lift up his
> countenance upon thee, and give thee peace. And they shall
> *put my name* upon the children of Israel."

Not My names, but My name, Father, Son and Holy Spirit. The New Testament version of that name is familiar to us all,

> "The grace of the Lord Jesus Christ, and the love of God,
> and the communion of the Holy Ghost, be with you all"
> (II Cor. 13:14).

Christ in our nature was the *depositary* and the *manifestation* of Jehovah's name. And now He tells the Father, "While I was with them in the world, I kept them in thy name."

To declare how He did so would be to give an outline of His entire private life and public ministry. Suffice it to say we invariably find the Lord Jesus Christ attributing to the Father all the power He exercised, all the doctrine He taught, the fact that He was sent, and the success of His mission. When men wondered at the gracious words He spake,

> "The word . . . is not mine, but the Father's which sent me" (John 14:24).

And so of His works (cf. John 5:36). So of His people,

> "Thine they were, thou gavest them me,"

therefore they are *Mine*. A Father—loving, gracious, long-suffering; a Shepherd protecting and about to die for His flock, was the name of God manifested to His people by Christ. And He also promised them another Comforter who was to dwell with them, and be in them, abiding forever, leading them into all truth, and being in them a well of water springing up into everlasting life; yes, a Father for them, a Saviour with them, a Holy Spirit in them, was *the name* in which Christ kept His disciples while He was with them in the world, and into which He commanded them to be baptized, and He now pleads with His Father to keep them in it when He is parted from them.

Observe the evident *equality* existing between the Father and Himself, implied by our Lord's words. "While I was with them in the world, *I kept them* in thy name." "Now I am no more in the world . . . Holy Father, *keep them* in thy name." He compares His power and success in keeping them to the Father's own power and ability to keep them. This would be utter folly if there was not equality between the Father and the Son.

> "Beware, lest any man spoil you through philosophy and vain deceit, after the tradition of men, after the rudiments of the world, and not after Christ. For in him dwelleth all the fullness of the Godhead bodily, and ye are complete in him" (Col. 2:8–10).

Oh! dwell in Him, abide in His love, hold fast by Him, lay hold upon the promise that God is able to keep you in Him, and the fact that the Holy Ghost has come down from heaven for this end. See I John 2:27,

> "The anointing which ye have received of him abideth in you, and ye need not that any man teach you: but as the same anointing teacheth you of all things, and is truth, and is no lie, and even as it hath taught you, *ye shall abide in him.*"

Remember also the appointed means whereby He kept them in the name. "I have given *unto them the words* which thou gavest me, and they have received them." It is by the Word of God we are *taught* the fullness of the name; it is by the Word of God we are *invited* to hide in the name; it is by the Word of God we are *introduced* to our Lord Jesus Christ, God's name of salvation among us; and it is by the Holy Ghost that we are taught of and kept in Him.

> "The natural man receiveth not the things of the Spirit of God" (I Cor. 2:14).
>
> "God hath revealed them unto us by his Spirit: for the Spirit searcheth all things, yea, the deep things of God."

Let the Word of God dwell richly in you, and never attempt to study it without asking for the Holy Ghost to teach you; remembering

> "The natural man receiveth not the things of the Spirit of God."

Let us also carefully observe the instruction we here gather as to the nature of this keeping, because we often make great mistakes about it, and go heavily on our pilgrim way, because of our ignorance as to the manner of His keeping. We complain when we feel corruption warring in our members, when our spirits are dark and our hearts are troubled; we complain when we find ourselves compassed with difficulties, oppressed with cares, involved in conflicts temporal and spiritual, when the tears are forced from our eyes, and oftentimes wrung from our very hearts, and we say, can it be that we are kept? Are we in

the care and keeping of that Father to whom Christ committed
His people? If indeed He is our Keeper, could it be possible
we should be tried and troubled, and tossed and worried, and in
agony of heart and of spirit so frequently and so painfully as we
are? Well, I suppose it will be admitted that when our Lord
Jesus Christ said, "I kept them in thy name," He did it *well,* and
yet mark the history of the disciples. They were not kept from
infirmities—they were full of infirmities; they were even not
kept from *sin,* they were certainly not kept from doubts and
from unbelief, for the Lord often charged them with *both.* They
were not kept from failures—oh! how sadly they failed; think
of Peter! They were not kept from

> "The same afflictions [which] are accomplished in the
> brethren" (I Pet. 5:9).

He who was not one whit less than the chief of the apostles,
wrote,

> "We that are in this tabernacle do groan, being burdened"
> (II Cor. 5:4);

they were not so kept as not to confess and complain that they
were often

> "In the heaviness through manifold temptations" (I Pet.
> 1:6).

When our blessed Christ kept His disciples in His Father's
name, He kept them in such a way as to humble them in themselves, while He greatly exalted His own grace toward them.
There is an infinite variety and fullness of grace laid up in the
Lord Jesus for the supply of His people's almost infinite necessities, and it is for the glory of God that His children should enter
into all the departments of that supply. God's glory requires
that there should not be any fullness in Christ, which they shall
not taste and know and enjoy. The grace is all in Him, "my
grace." And the need is all in us that it may be manifested. Are
our necessities almost infinite? He can keep us amid all possible

phases of our life's troubled history, making His strength perfect in our weakness, and demonstrating that His grace is sufficient for us. He kept Jacob in all his wanderings, and fed him
all his life long, even when he said

> "All these things are against me" (Gen. 42:36);

He kept the king of Babylon, but it was by driving him from
the haunts of men, sending him to have his dwelling with the
beasts, that he might learn "that the heavens did rule"; He put
Daniel into the lions' den, and kept him *there;* He put Shadrach, Meshach, and Abednego into the burning fiery furnace,
and kept them *there;* when the great apostle of the Gentiles
had been carried up to the third heaven, and heard things which
it was not lawful for him to utter, and there was a danger of his
being "exalted above measure,"

> "[God sent] the messenger of Satan to buffet [him—and
> kept him there]" (II Cor. 12:7),

confessing most

> "Gladly . . . will I rather glory in my infirmities, that the
> power of Christ may rest upon me" (II Cor. 12:9).

Peter was an ardent, zealous, self-confident character; and the
Lord permitted his fall, and kept him notwithstanding, for

> "I have prayed for thee, that thy faith fail not: and when
> thou art converted, strengthen thy brethren" (Luke 22:32).

One principal way in which our precious Saviour kept His
people *"in His name,"* and the Holy Ghost now keeps His people *"in His name,"* and in which the Holy Father keeps His
people *"in His own name,"* is by allowing them to learn in their
daily experience all varieties of *their needs,* and manifesting at
the same time that they have not a need, or a phase of a need,
for which there is not abundant supply in the fullness and faithfulness of their God. Thus they are kept in such a way as to be
humbled in themselves, while He is glorified; and all the praise

is given to Christ, and no merit is attributed to themselves. It is very trying to the self-righteousness of flesh and blood, but it is the way the Son of God kept His disciples, and it is the way our heavenly Father *keeps us now.*

We are often very much distressed by supposing—and doubtless correctly—that there is something peculiar in ourselves, something which we think contrary to and inconsistent with the possibility of our being Christians; we imagine, if our trials were anything but what they are, if our temptations were of any other sort than the peculiar kind we suffer from, we might possibly be Christians, but the consciousness of having an infirmity which we are not aware that anyone else ever suffered from, and knowing that we are assailed, and sometimes fall before temptations which we never heard or read of in the experience of any other Christian, we stagger in unbelief, we write bitter things against ourselves, we go heavily, and perhaps let go *"the name"* —at least we are sorely tempted to do so. Now, there is not a single sample of fallen humanity, there is not a phase of human infirmity, there is not a conceivable illustration of human character or of human ruin, that there is not a remedy for in the Lord Jesus Christ; and *this is to be proved* and manifested to the glory of Christ, and to the glory of the Father. Suppose I *am* a unit in the Church of God, suppose I *have* a constitution like none other, suppose the history of my experience *is* unlike that of any other Christian, suppose my temptation to be peculiar, my trial unparalleled in the history of the Church of God, *there must be a case just like mine* in order to make it manifest to the glory of God, that there is a provision in Christ's fullness for such a case as mine, and I might as well be that individual as another; would it be better that I should change with you, or that you should change with me? What I want to learn is that there is in the name of my Christ that which meets *my* need, that there is in "the fountain open for sin and uncleanness," that which has washed away *my* guilt, and my song will not be less loud when the chorus of redeemed songsters sing His praises, because my need was the greatest.

Alas! there is comparatively very little joy or liberty or love among us Christians; I do not speak of professors, I speak of *real* Christians; how little as compared with what might be, and with what *ought* to be. What is the reason? We do not "keep his *word,*" we do not make ourselves acquainted with "his *name,*" we do not "abide in him"; if we did so we should have much more happiness, much more triumph, much more joy, much more *fruitfulness.*

The words of our blessed Christ did not imply that He would cease to care for and to watch over us, now that He was returning to His Father. No, ere He left us He said,

"Lo, I am with you always, even unto the end of the world" (Matt. 28:20);

and He promised the Holy Ghost, not merely as a substitute for Himself, but as *another Comforter,* something additional to that which we had before. He is still the Shepherd of the sheep,

"Where two or three are gathered together in my name, there *am* I in the midst of them" (Matt. 18:20).

The fact is, our Lord's mission on earth was to be in Himself the link uniting the whole Godhead to us for our safety and security. His person in human nature taken into the Godhead is the bond uniting Father, Son, and Holy Ghost in Himself to His people. It is "a threefold cord, hard to be broken." Our *Father* keeping us, our *Christ* keeping us, and our indwelling *Holy Spirit* keeping us; our Lord Jesus Christ had done *His* work; and now He pledges the Father to fulfill His promise; even to send the Holy Ghost as on the day of Pentecost to dwell in us—a well of living water, springing up into everlasting life, not only as an influence from without—but as an unfailing power from within till He Himself returns to take us to Himself that where He is we may be also!!

19

LET US READ this according to what is probably the more correct version—"While I was with them in the world I kept them in Thy name which Thou hast given Me, and guarded them, and not one of them perished, but the son of perdition; that the Scripture might be fulfilled." Our blessed Lord is committing His people to His Father's care. He is giving an account of His own faithful discharge of the trust committed to Him by His Father, "While I was with them in the world, *I kept them*"; and such an account He will give in the last great day when as the King, and the Shepherd of His people, He shall give a true and faithful account of all those committed to His trust. Remember a passage or two on the subject. In Ezekiel 20:37, Jehovah promises,

> "I will cause you to pass under the rod, and I will bring you into the bond of the covenant,"

"*a delivering covenant*," as we read in the margin; there the rod is the shepherd's rod, that rod of which David said that it "comforted him." Again, Leviticus 27:32,

> "They pass under the rod for *marking*" (lit.).

And in Jeremiah 33:13, we read,

> "There shall the flocks pass again under the hands of him that telleth them, saith the Lord."

They pass under the rod for numbering, the whole tale is to be faithfully brought forth and presented to the Lord, "without spot or wrinkle, or any such thing"; by Him who, as their Shepherd King, was entrusted with the charge of them, and who will render not only a general, but a *particular* account of those entrusted to Him, "not one of them is lost."

There are three things taught here concerning Christ's people.

I. Their character and condition.

II. Their inestimable value in the sight of God.

III. Their security in the care of our Shepherd for evermore.

1. "I kept them." They had need of being kept. Oh, what need, what need! The apostles were men of like passions with ourselves, they had the same dangers we have. The weakest thing on earth is a child of God. Look at him in whatever light you will, no language can express the need which exists for his being kept. Scripture speaks of us as lambs in the midst of wolves; accounted as sheep for the slaughter; as exposed to storms and tempests, and frosts—as "bruised reeds," and a "shadow that declineth"; as exhibiting the helplessness of infancy, the silliness of doves; these and I know not how many more such expressions are used by the Spirit of God to teach us our need of being kept. Moreover, we are *in the world,* the most ungenial place for God's children, where we are exposed to corruption from within and from without, to snares besetting us on every side, to devils surrounding us, and watching us like roaring lions seeking how and where and when they may devour us.

> "We wrestle not against flesh and blood, but against principalities, against powers, against the rulers of the darkness of this world, against spiritual wickedness in high places" (Eph. 6:12).

What need of being kept! Our path is a dreary and a difficult one; the Scripture speaks of it as sometimes being "through the waters," at other times "through the floods," again in the "fires," deep valleys to descend, rugged heights to scale, where there is danger every moment. What need of being kept!

"I kept them," all their own wisdom collectively and individually could not keep them for one moment; all their own watchfulness, all their gathered experience during the many months and years of their fellowship with Christ, could not keep them in one single difficulty; all their resolutions could not keep them for one hour; all their gifts—and many of them had great gifts—could not keep them in one solitary temptation; all their privileges, all their zeal, all their love, and the frequent warnings with which they had been warned, and the example daily before them utterly failed, and must fail, to keep them in one single difficulty or for one single moment. How soon Peter fell when the temptation came; when danger presented itself, *all* forsook Him and fled, but "I kept them in *thy* name." Carefully He kept them, faithfully, prayerfully, constantly, He kept them, and He claims credit from His Father for this. I know not a more important practical study in the revealed Word of God than this keeping wherewith He kept them; it was of a nature to humble them to the very dust, while it magnified the grace of Him that kept them. They were not kept from learning their own emptiness, they were not kept from proving their own weakness, they were not kept from grievous failures. He kept them, though in a way deeply humbling to them, yet glorifying to Him, and so He keeps His people still. The Lord seems to boast of His ability to keep His people, He teaches us to say,

"The Lord is thy keeper" (Ps. 121:5).

"[He] is able to keep you from falling, and to present you faultless before the presence of His glory with exceeding joy" (Jude 24).

"I know whom I have believed, and am persuaded that he is able to keep that which I have committed unto him against that day" (II Tim. 1:12).

2. Their inestimable value in the sight of God. "I kept them." Whatever we may be in our own sight we *are worth keeping* in God's sight, and worth keeping at such a price as that which it cost God when He sent Christ to be our Keeper and our Saviour. Remember how the Spirit of God multiplies expressions to teach us how valuable we are to Him: His "chosen," "precious" ones, dear to Him as "the apple of His eye," His "purchased people," graven upon the palms of His hands that He cannot forget them (cf. Isa. 49:15, 16). "His peculiar treasure." It is easy to enumerate such expressions, but, oh, to have the Spirit of God showing us the meaning of them! God's "peculiar treasure!" not angels or archangels, but His people! redeemed sinners who put their trust in Him, who come to Him in Christ and believe His Word,

"The Lord's portion is his people" (Deut. 32:9),

a crown of glory, a royal diadem in the hand of their God,

"Members of his [Christ's] body, of his flesh, and of his bones. . . .
"No man ever yet hated his own flesh; but nourisheth and cherisheth it even as the Lord the church" (Eph. 5:30, 29).

How strikingly this was pictured in Aaron's breastplate. The high priest stood before the Lord with the breastplate dotted over with jewels, all differing in their shades and their circumstances, but equally borne before the Lord continually. And not only a memorial before the Lord, but a token of how precious in the sight of Him before whom Jesus stands as our High Priest *is each child of God;* our circumstances may be various, our characters and constitutions may differ, but He loves each soul that trusts Him, one as much as another; He has the case of each one on His heart, one as much as another; His eye watches the path of each one that trusts Him, and one as much as another; all are collected into the heart of Christ, all are individualized *there*. "I kept them"; ofttimes by reason of the peculiarity of our circumstances and the nature of our temptations, or, perhaps, of our very constitution, we are led to think we stand alone, and that no other in all the family is like unto us. Nevertheless, each one has his own place in the Lord's heart, and the Lord *thinks* for me, *cares* for me, *provides* for me, *intercedes* for me, *sprinkles* me, *represents* me as truly as if I *were the only one* in all the world He intercedes for! atones for! cares for! What we need is this precious knowledge of the Lord Jesus Christ; I want to realize that my Saviour is to me in the firmament of God's grace, what the natural sun is to me in the firmament of His power; I may enjoy the *whole* of Him as if there were no other on earth to enjoy Him, and yet rob no brother by my possessing and enjoying *all my Christ*.

"I kept them." His love passeth knowledge; He rested not in creation until He had made man in His own image; and when man fell, He rested not in His redeeming love till He came down from heaven into man's nature to restore him again to the image he had lost. And then since He went up to the throne, He rests not until in the marvelous abundance of His grace we are all filled with the Holy Ghost; nor will He rest in the glory until He can say, Come and sit with Me in My throne.

> "Even as I also overcame, and am set down with my Father in his throne" (Rev. 3:21).

3. "I kept them in thy name which thou hast given me," I kept them by Thine appointment, I kept them at Thy charge, I possessed them, I surrounded them with all the fullness contained in Thy holy, holy, holy name. Nothing less than this is our gospel. The Shepherd of the sheep keeps His people in the eternal *power* of God! in the eternal *wisdom* of God! compassed in the eternal *faithfulness* of God! enshrined in the eternal *love*

of God! quickened with the eternal *life* of God! possessed with the eternal *grace* of God! and to be crowned with the eternal *glory* of God!

> "Kept by the power of God through faith unto salvation" (I Pet. 1:5).

Ascribing praise to Him who is

> "Able to keep you from falling, and to present you faultless before the presence of his glory with exceeding joy" (Jude 24).

Observe, He not only renders a general, but a *particular* account; "none of them perished, none of them is lost." A blessed emphasis, *not one of them.* We read in John 6:39,

> "This is the Father's *will* which hath sent me, that of all which he hath given me I should lose nothing"—

nothing—not even their dust, much less their souls, nothing,

> "But should raise it up again at the last day."

Perhaps it may be said the apostles were a better order of men than we are! Not so, the Lord Jesus Christ sought, and found them, for they were lost; He quickened them, for they were dead; and He kept them. Everything but God was against them; the world against them, the flesh against them, the devil against them, everything against them but God, and everything is against us but God. When shall we learn to view God in this light? If we did—if we learned to know God thus, nothing would keep us from Him. We have too much the habit of regarding God as if He were against us: we go here and there for some motive or reason to induce God to be for us. Everything is against us *but* God, and God is not against us, *but for us.* And Christ in our nature is a pledge of it, the Holy Ghost in the Church is a pledge of it, the Book of God is a pledge of it. Think of the variety of the characters, constitutions, temptations, and difficulties of God's children, and yet not one of them lost. Oh!

the sufficiency of Christ, the fullness of the fountain open for sin, the glorious righteousness to cover, the strength of the Lord to keep—"I kept them."

Then follows a very solemn and awful word, "the son of perdition is lost, that the Scripture might be fulfilled." There is something unutterably mysterious about the person and character of Judas Iscariot. The Lord says he was—"the son of perdition." The only other place in the New Testament, indeed in the Bible, where this expression occurs is in II Thessalonians 2:3, 4:

> "Let no man deceive you by any means: for that day shalt not come, except there come a falling away first, and that man of sin be revealed, *the son of perdition;* who opposeth and exalteth himself above all that is called God, or that is worshiped; so that he, as God sitteth in the temple of God, showing himself that he is God."

The Lord also declares (John 6:70) that he was "a devil." As God was in Christ, so Satan was in Judas. But, of course, we only express an opinion. It is a remarkable fact that the Lord should call him by the same name that Antichrist is styled by, and that He should also say of him that he was "a devil."

Some reading this verse have been puzzled, as if it implied that Judas had been given to Christ to be saved, and that Christ had lost him. Those who are acquainted with the original, and who look closely to it, will see that the very opposite is implied. You find the same mode of expression in Luke 4:25–27, "I tell you of a truth, many widows were in Israel in the days of Elias, when the heaven was shut up three years and six months, when great famine was throughout all the land; but unto none of them was Elias sent, *save* unto Sarepta, a city of Sidon, unto a woman that was a widow. And many lepers were in Israel in the time of Eliseus the prophet; and none of them was cleansed, *saving* Naaman the Syrian." Do you observe— "many widows were in Israel . . . and to none of them was

Elias sent, save to" *one who was not in Israel;* "and many lepers were in Israel . . . and none of them was cleansed saving Naaman," *who was not in Israel.* The word *"but"* in the passage we are considering is not exceptive, it is in opposition— "those thou hast given me I have kept, and none of them is lost but the son of perdition," *is lost,* that the Scripture might be fulfilled.

Judas Iscariot never fell from grace, for he never had it, he was "the son of perdition," he was "a thief," he was "a devil," and the Scripture was fulfilled in his fall, for long ago it had been foretold. And the Lord Himself alludes to the fact,

> "I speak not of you all: I know whom I have chosen: but that the Scripture may be fulfilled, He that eateth bread with me hath lifted up his heel against me" (John 13:18).

He *did* fall from an exalted office, and a successor was appointed to take "part in this ministry and apostleship, from which Judas by transgression fell." Judas had a high and an exalted office in the Church of God. Oh! let us remember that it is one thing to have an office in the church, and quite another thing to be saved. Judas had unspeakable privileges; for years he had been the constant companion of Christ, he had seen Him, handled Him, he had been taught from His own lips, yet he was not saved. I have heard people rash enough to say that if the Church of God did its duty, the whole world would be brought to the knowledge of Christ. This is not so; did not Christ do His duty? Will anyone say Christ was not a faithful minister? And yet one of His twelve apostles was lost. Judas had great gifts, for it is very evident the Lord made no exception with reference to him when He sent them forth "to heal the sick, to cast out devils, and to preach the kingdom," and if there had been any difference with regard to Judas Iscariot, when the Lord said at supper, "One of you shall betray me," suspicion would at once have fallen upon him, but each disciple said: "Lord, is it I?" No one thought of suspecting Judas, which would not have been the case if the Lord had made any difference in His dealings personally or relatively between him and the other disciples, as to his office, privileges, or gifts; here, then, is a most solemn fact; we might have the highest office possible in the Church of God, and be lost; we may sit under the most privileged ministry, and be lost; we may see what patriarchs and prophets desired to see and never saw; we may hear what patriarchs and righteous men desired to hear and never heard, and be utterly lost.

I have also heard it said that if only a minister be properly ordained his flock are bound to hear him. There is no difficulty in tracing "the apostolic succession" *here,* and yet "one of you is a devil." Oh! we may have all the externals of religion, we might receive the bread and wine from Christ's own hands, we might have our arms round His neck and our lips on His cheek, as Judas had, and yet be lost. When shall we learn not to rest in external things, in forms, or in outward privileges, when shall we learn not to rest in offices! We have no resting place but Christ; there is no hiding place but Himself, and no fountain to wash our sins and pollutions away but in His precious blood.

But a question suggests itself, and a most interesting one it is —Why was there a Judas among the Twelve?

It may be this: our dear Lord, when He came to this world, came to be tried; He came to taste the sorrows and the difficulties of His people, so that He might know them all; there is not a greater trial or greater sorrow for a tender heart than unkindness and ingratitude. Here was one bound up with Him in the family circle, the constant companion of Christ, admitted to the closest fellowship, and yet a traitor to Him in heart, watching Him with malice, and betraying Him for thirty pieces of silver. I believe it was one of the bitterest of the sorrows which He tasted here! Or, it may be this. Here was a traitor in the camp, a spy upon Christ, and if he had discovered a fault in thought, or word, or deed, he would have been ready to tell it, ready to expose and exaggerate it, but it is something glorious to hear this enemy forced to confess:

> "I have sinned in that I have betrayed the innocent blood" (Matt. 27:4).

And why does the Lord here dwell upon the fact? "The son of perdition is lost, that the Scripture might be fulfilled." It is a word of comfort for poor hearts who come to Christ. There was a Judas mixed up with the twelve apostles, his lot was cast in with them, and he *seemed* to be altogether one of those who were committed to Christ, yet he was lost. How it would crush any poor sinner's heart if for one moment he could entertain the thought—"I may be lost though I have come to Christ and cast myself upon Him, and though I plead Christ, with God, though I have no hope but in Him, no rest but in Him, perchance I may yet be lost." Now, to silence any such doubt, our Lord declares that Judas was lost that the Scriptures might be fulfilled. He had office with them, but had not their grace, nor did he ever seek it.

There is not a little difficulty connected with this passage, but there is one lesson for all to carry away. Do not rest in a name to live; do not rest satisfied with being employed in the service of God; do not rest in the fact that your knowledge is great, that your attainments are many, that your privileges are peculiar. Judas had all these, and more than any of us have, and yet he was lost. There is one refuge for the sinner, one hiding place for the soul, one name, and they that know that name will put their trust in it, "I kept them in thy name," and in pleading thus with His Father He tells us of the only safe place for you or for me:

> "The name of the Lord is a strong tower: the righteous runneth into it, and is safe" (Prov. 18:10).

20

"AND NONE OF THEM IS LOST, BUT THE SON OF PERDITION;
THAT THE SCRIPTURE MIGHT BE FULFILLED."—John 17:12

OUR STUDY of the mysterious account of the loss of Judas
suggested three lessons.

1. In some sense all men have been given to Christ, some
given to Him to be His members, His portion, His bride, His
kingdom; others given to be His servants.

> "The servant abideth not in the house forever: but the son
> abideth ever" (John 8:35).

Judas was a servant, not a son; angels, devils, and men are
God's servants; earth and heaven, and hell equally at His disposal. A name is given to our blessed Lord,

> "A name above every name: that at the name of Jesus every
> knee should bow, of things in heaven, and things in earth, and
> things under the earth; and that every tongue should confess
> that Jesus Christ is Lord, to the glory of God the Father"
> (Phil. 2:9–11).

Master! Ruler! King! Sovereign! Lord! Whether the name be
in this world or in the world to come, *His* name is above every
name. But "the servant abideth not in the house forever: the
Son abideth ever." Some are given to the Lord Jesus Christ to
be adopted into God's family, kept in God's name, and of them
He can and will say—"not one of them is lost."

2. No gifts, however great they may be, prove that we are
saved souls; no office in the Church of God, however high that
office may be, even though the office be that of *an apostle,* neces-

sarily involves the salvation of the soul; no attainments, however desirable, can save the soul; as the apostle says,

> "I [may] have all faith . . . [to] remove mountains; . . . and I [may] have all knowledge, and understand all mysteries, and [yet be] nothing" (I Cor. 13:2);

nothing external can secure our salvation, or warrant our being justified in saying, I have mine inheritance where Christ is all and in all; nothing, nothing but participation in that covenant of grace by which the Father hath given to the Lord Jesus Christ a people for His name, united to Him by faith, "quickened," "taught," "kept," "saved" by Him, and

> "[Presented] without spot, or wrinkle, or any such thing . . . before the presence of his glory with exceeding joy" (Eph. 5:27; Jude 24)

secures the salvation of any man.

3. When we believe upon the name of the Lord Jesus Christ, and receive God's great gift, then we *have* the divine testimony and evidence that we have been given to Christ to be saved by Him and kept by Him; and that He will, in the faithful discharge of His duty, as the Shepherd of the sheep, feed us, and keep us, and bless us; for He Himself says,

> "Neither pray I for these alone, but for them also which shall believe on me through their word; that they all may be one; as thou, Father, art in me, and I in thee, that they also may be one in us: that the world may believe that thou hast sent me" (vv. 20, 21).

The particular Scripture to which our Lord alludes, and which was fulfilled in this case, was probably Psalm 109. It is quoted by the apostle Peter, in reference to the fall of Judas, in Acts 1:20,

> "It is written in the book of Psalms, Let his habitation be desolate, and let no man dwell therein: and his bishoprick let another take."

The apostle also states (v. 25) that he fell "by transgression," that he might go unto his own place. *His own place!* an awful statement; undoubtedly it means hell-fire, and in his fall the Scripture was fulfilled.

We are living in days when many, and great, and daring attempts are made to tamper with God's Word; evil days when men would set aside Scripture and substitute

> "Profane and vain babblings, and oppositions of science falsely so called: which some professing have erred concerning the faith" (I Tim. 6:20, 21);

proposing to us to accept the fooleries of their own reasonings as the rule for Christian doctrine, walk, and character. Doubts are cast upon the inspiration of Scripture; and men profess to decide, by some power they claim to possess, an internal faculty which it is impossible for them to define or others to understand, what is and what is not the Word of God, in the book we call the Bible; they tell us the Bible is not the Word of God, but that it *contains* the Word of God, and that it belongs to this discerning power of theirs to determine what is of man and what is of God. How very much in contrast with such theories and reasoning do we find the practice of the Lord Jesus Christ Himself; there is nothing of this spirit in the way in which He dealt with Scripture and taught the Scriptures; whether in His private life or in His public ministry we search in vain for the least indication of any sympathy on His part with this rationalism; on the contrary, if there is one thing more remarkable than another in the recorded life of the Lord Jesus Christ, it is His constant endorsement of Scripture, and His evident faith in, and constant use of Scripture. If any being was qualified to speak without the assistance of the written Word of God, on matters pertaining to God and man, that individual was the Lord Jesus Christ: but *where do we ever find Him doing so from the beginning to the end of His earthly history?* His appeal to the Scriptures in all matters, when reference is made to Him as regards any question concerning God or man, His own habit of submission to them, His faith in the promises of the Word of God, and His constant assertion of their paramount authority, as His Father's word, His Father's will, His Father's doctrine, must be familiar to every ordinary reader of the New Testament.

Now let us inquire; first, what does the Lord Jesus Christ mean by "the scriptures"? We have His own definition in Luke 24:44, 45:

> "These are the words which I spake unto you, while I was yet with you, that all things must be fulfilled which were written in the *law of Moses* and in *the prophets,* and in *the psalms,* concerning me. Then open he their understanding, that they might understand *the scriptures.*"

You observe the threefold division, Moses, the Prophets, and the Psalms, and then we are told distinctly that they were the Scriptures. In II Timothy 3:15–17, Paul, speaking of his beloved Timothy, says:

> "From a child thou hast known the holy scriptures, which are able to make thee wise unto salvation through faith which is in Christ Jesus. All scripture is given by inspiration of God, and is profitable for doctrine, for reproof, for correction, for instruction in righteousness; that the man of God may be perfect, throughly furnished unto all good works."

The apostle Peter states:

> "The word of the Lord endureth for ever. And this is the word which by the gospel is preached unto you" (I Peter 1:25).

In his second epistle we have a very remarkable statement. He writes (1:16–21),

> "We have not followed cunningly devised fables, when we made known unto you the power and coming of our Lord

Jesus Christ, but were eyewitnesses of his majesty. For he received from God the Father honor and glory, when there came such a voice to him from the excellent glory, This is my beloved Son, in whom I am well pleased. And this voice which came from heaven we heard, when we were with him in the holy mount."

He is referring to the transfiguration,—

"We have also *a more sure word of prophecy*"—

more sure, more to be rested upon than even that vision; we *saw* that, but the Word of the prophecy *is more sure*,—

"Whereunto ye do well that ye take heed, as unto a light that shineth in a dark place, until the day dawn, and the day star arise in your hearts: knowing this first, that no prophecy of *the scripture* is of any private interpretation"—

of any private mission,—it is not sent forth at man's suggestion, but by God's command,—

"For the prophecy came not in old time by the will of man: but holy men of God spake *as they were moved by the Holy Ghost.*"

The prophets of the Old Testament all assert this. If we take up the writings of Moses we hear him say, "The Lord saith . . . Thus saith the Lord." We hear the prophets say, "The word of the Lord by Isaiah . . . The word of the Lord came to Jeremiah . . . Thus saith the Lord." Not, Thus *I* say, but "Thus saith *the Lord*" by me. This is their own account of the message which they were privileged to deliver. Hear David:

"*The Spirit of the Lord spake by me, and his word was in my tongue*" (II Sam. 23:2).

And here, in this passage, and in countless others, we have Christ quoting the Scriptures, submitting to the Scriptures, and endorsing the Scriptures of the Old Testament.

The testimony of the Lord Jesus Christ was the spirit of the

Old Testament; what the Scriptures foretold, the Lord Jesus Christ in His person, life, and work made to be *history*. It is very interesting to trace this in the New Testament. His birth for instance (Matt. 1:21–23). Why is He called Jesus? Why was He born among us? *We* might say, Because God is Love, and because Jesus the Prince of love would come among us to save us. That is all true, but it is not the reason the Word of God gives.

> "All this was done, that it might be *fulfilled* which was spoken of the Lord by the prophet, saying, Behold, a virgin shall be with child, and shall bring forth a son, and they shall call his name Emmanuel, which being interpreted is, God with us."

And so of the divers incidents in His earthly life. Trace them. See Matthew 2:14–17. Yes. But that is not the reason Scripture gives:

> "[Joseph and Mary] took the young child . . . by night and departed into Egypt."

Why—because there was danger? because Herod would slay the child? That also is true. But the reason Scripture gives:

> "[He] was there until the death of Herod: that it might be *fulfilled* which was spoken of the Lord by the prophet, saying, Out of Egypt have I called my Son."

The Scripture must be *fulfilled;* this is our point. Again, see verses 17, 18.

> "[Herod] sent forth, and slew all the children which were in Bethlehem."

Why did he do that? Because he was cruel? Yes. Because he wanted to slay the Lord Jesus Christ? Yes. But that is not the reason Scripture gives:

> "Then, was *fulfilled* that which was spoken by Jeremy the prophet, saying, In Rama was there a voice heard, lamentation,

and weeping, and great mourning, Rachel weeping for her children, and would not be comforted, because they are not."

Again, verse 23:

"He came and dwelt in the city called Nazareth."

Why did He dwell there? No doubt Joseph had his reasons for dwelling there, no doubt Mary had her reasons for dwelling there, and circumstances made it necessary that He should dwell there, but that is not the reason Scripture gives: but

"That it might be *fulfilled* which was spoken by the prophets, He shall be called a Nazarene."

Now see Matthew 8:16, 17, where we have an account of the *divers miracles* wrought by the Lord Jesus Christ.

"They brought unto him many that were possessed with devils: and he cast out the spirits with his word, and healed all that were sick."

Why did He do so? Was it because He was gracious? Yes. Because He came to seek and save the lost? Yes. But that is not the reason Scripture gives:

"That it might be *fulfilled* which was spoken by Esaias the prophet, saying, Himself took our infirmities and bare our sicknesses."

Observe His *use of the Scriptures.* In Matthew 4:1, after His baptism, He was

"Led up of the spirit into the wilderness to be tempted of the devil."

He does not attempt to deal with Satan on any other ground than as a man of faith dealing with God's truth; thus with

"The sword of the Spirit which is the word of God" (Eph. 6:17).

He defended Himself against the assaults of Satan, and overcame him. When the Sadducees came to Him with their questions, endeavoring to disparage the truth of the resurrection, how did the Lord answer them? He refers them to *the Scriptures* (Exodus), where God speaks to Moses at the bush. The Lord quotes the Book of Exodus as *"spoken by God,"* although people living in our day would tell you it is old wives' fables. Observe, He does not give His own opinion, He quotes the Scriptures in refuting the error of the Sadducees. When divers charges were brought against Him for inconsistency, because He had healed the sick and allowed His disciples to do what the elders conceived to be breaking the law of the Sabbath on the Sabbath day, how did He answer them? Not by reasonings of His own, but by referring to *the Scriptures.* When He prepares for the trial—the awful trial hanging over Him He goes to the Scriptures. See Luke 18:31,

> "Then he took unto him the twelve, and said unto them, Behold, we go up to Jerusalem, and all things that are written by the prophets concerning the Son of man shall be accomplished."

And in His deep sorrow where does He go for comfort? See Mark 14:26, 27:

> "And when they had sung an hymn, they went out into the Mount of Olives. And Jesus saith unto them, All ye shall be offended because of me this night: for *it is written,* I will smite the shepherd, and the sheep shall be scattered."

And when He was undergoing the sentence due to our sin (John 19:28), just before He bowed His head and gave up the ghost, we read—

> "After this, Jesus, knowing that all things were now accomplished, *that the scripture might be fulfilled,* said, I thirst."

Even on the cross He was thinking of what the Scripture had declared concerning Him, and while the bitterness of death was upon His soul, and the prospect of coming glory was before His gaze, His thoughts were upon the fulfillment of Scripture; and

remembering there was a prediction concerning Him so far un-
fulfilled,

> "In my thirst they gave me vinegar to drink . . . *that the*
> *scripture might be fulfilled,* he said, I thirst" (Ps. 69:21;
> John 19:28).

And when He rose from the dead, did that alter His view of the
importance of the Scriptures, or His estimation of them? See
Luke 24:25, 27. He is speaking to the disciples with whom He
had been going on the way to Emmaus:

> "O fools, and slow of heart to believe all that the prophets
> have spoken: Ought not Christ to have suffered these things,
> and to enter into his glory? And beginning at Moses, and all
> the prophets, He expounded unto them in all *the Scriptures*
> the things concerning himself."

How one would like to have a copy of that discourse, a record
of that exposition of the Scriptures! The Spirit has not been
pleased to give it to us, because doubtless all that it contained is
to be found elsewhere scattered through the teaching which
the Holy Ghost came down from heaven to impart. Again
(vv. 44, 45),

> "These are the words which I spake unto you, while I was
> yet with you, that *all things must be fulfilled,* which were writ-
> ten in the law of Moses, and in the prophets, and in the psalms,
> concerning me. Then opened he their understanding, that they
> might understand *the Scriptures.*"

Even after His resurrection, and since He has ascended up into
glory, His testimony for the Scriptures is the same. See Revelation 22:18–20, "I testify."—Who is speaking? See verse 16,
"*I, Jesus,*" it is the same speaker all through to the end, "I Jesus,"
the exalted One, the girded Priest, walking in the mist of the
seven golden candlesticks,

> "I, Jesus, have sent mine angel to testify . . . I testify unto
> every man that heareth the words of this book, If any man

shall add unto these things, God shall add unto him the plagues that are written in this book: and if any man shall take away from the words of the book of this prophecy, God shall take away his part out of the book of life, and out of the holy city, and from the things which are written in this book. He which testifieth these things saith, Surely I come quickly."

See then He is coming again in glory, and before Him shall be gathered all nations, for God hath

"Appointed a day, in the which he will judge the world in righteousness by that man whom he hath ordained; whereof he hath given assurance unto all men, in that he hath raised him from the dead" (Acts 17:31).

How shall the Word of God, *the Scriptures,* stand in that day? See John 12:48,

"The word that I have spoken, *the same shall judge you in the last day."*

This most important and very interesting line of thought should establish the importance and value of the Scriptures in our estimation, considering how He valued them who came to *fulfill them,* and who best knew their worth.

Moreover, He promised to send us another Comforter. What was to be the great business of that Comforter? To lead His people into all truth and to bring all things to their remembrance whatsoever He had *said* unto them (cf. John 16:13; 14:26); to open their understandings that they might understand *the Scriptures* which He, the Holy Ghost Himself, had indited, for

"The natural man receiveth not the things of the Spirit of God: for they are foolishness unto him: neither can he know them, because they are spiritually discerned" (I Cor. 2:14).

"What man knoweth the things of a man, save the spirit of man which is in him? even so *the things of God* knoweth no man but the Spirit of God. Now we have received, not the spirit of the world, but the Spirit which is of God; that we

might know the things that are freely given to us of God"
(I Cor. 2:11, 12).

The apostles, under the teaching of that Holy Spirit, wrote the
New Testament; that is why we believe the New Testament to
be inspired as the Old. St. Peter claims inspiration for his record,
I Peter 1:25, and he endorses the writing of St. Paul as *the
Scriptures:*

> "Account that the long-suffering of our Lord is salvation;
> even as our beloved brother Paul also according to the wisdom
> given unto him hath written unto you; as also in all his epistles,
> speaking in them of these things; in which are some things
> hard to be understood, which they that are unlearned and un-
> stable wrest, as they do also *the other Scriptures,* unto their
> own destruction" (II Pet. 3:15, 16).

The Scripture must be fulfilled; every prediction infallibly accomplished, every promise carried out to the letter; every warning and every threatening fulfilled, according to the faithfulness
and the sincerity of Him whose warning, whose threatening,
and whose Word it is. What can hinder? Is God not *powerful*
enough to keep His Word? Is He not *faithful* enough to keep
His Word? Where shall we go for a single example or instance
where He failed to keep His Word? Go back to the beginning.
In Eden, we have man in the image of God, with God, and
like God, and God said, "Very good"; a few hours, it may be,
certainly not many days afterwards, see what a wreck he was in
that garden of Eden; all misery where there was all gladness; all
darkness and death where once there was only light, and glory
and God! What brought about the great change? You say, sin;
well, so it was. Man became a rebel; so it was. But the real reason was that God had said, "Of the tree of the knowledge of
good and evil, thou shalt not eat of it; for in the day that thou
eatest thereof thou shalt surely die." *The Scripture was fulfilled.*
When man fell, God gave a gracious promise; He spoke of the
second Adam, and long ages afterwards that glorious One came.

He was born at Bethlehem, *"according to the Scriptures";* He took upon Him our nature, *"according to the Scriptures";* He lived among us a man of sorrows, *"according to the Scriptures";* He gave Himself for our sins, *"according to the Scriptures";* He rose from the dead, *"according to the Scriptures";* He conquered death and hell. Why did He do it all? You say, the love of God; yes. You say, the grace of the Lord Jesus Christ; yes. But God had said, "The seed of the woman shall bruise the serpent's head," that is the true reason, and *the Scripture was fulfilled.*

Where shall we go to find that God does not keep His Word? Shall we go to the Deluge? God sent a preacher of righteousness to the antediluvians, who said that within a hundred and twenty years God would bring a deluge upon the earth, if men did not turn from their evil ways. Did God keep His word? The Deluge is the answer. Shall we go to the cities of the plain? God sent a preacher there, too; would that he had been more faithful! But this was the cry heard in Sodom and Gomorrah, "Up, get you out of this place; for the Lord will destroy this city." Did God keep His word? Answer, the descending fires of the Almighty upon the cities of the plain, the moment Lot entered into Zoar.

Where shall we find evidence that God does not keep His word? Shall we ask of Babylon, that princess of kingdoms, the golden city, who said, "I shall be a lady forever"? God said, she shall be a wilderness,

> "The owls shall dwell there, and satyrs shall dance there" (Isa. 13:21),

and so it is, *the Scripture is fulfilled.* Where shall we find evidence that God does not keep His Word? Look at His dealings with the people of Israel, that people, "found in the waste and howling wilderness," and brought in and planted in their own land, even "the land that he had espied for them, flowing with milk and honey, which is the glory of all lands." Where are they now? Scattered, a byword and an hissing. Why? Because God had said, if they forsook Him, He would scatter them; they did forsake the God of their fathers, and they are scattered, a universal testimony throughout the whole earth that *the Scriptures must be fulfilled.*

Where shall we go for evidence that God does not keep His Word? Shall we ask that white-robed multitude standing before the throne, who have washed their robes and made them white in the blood of the Lamb? (cf. Rev. 7:13, 14). Why are they there? They will answer you with an outburst of Hallelujahs. It is because *the Scriptures must be fulfilled.* "We came to Him in our misery, we sought Him in our ruin, we bathed in the fountain open for sin and for uncleanness, and we are whiter than snow." Shall we ask where "the worm dieth not, and the fire is not quenched,"—what evidence is *there* that God doth not keep His Word? The answer would be from amidst wailing and gnashing of teeth, for it is written,

> "The wicked shall be turned into hell, and all the nations that forget God" (Ps. 9:17),

and *the Scriptures are fulfilled.* God will assuredly carry out every jot and tittle of His Word; the Lord Jesus Christ said,

> "Till heaven and earth pass, one jot or one tittle shall in no wise pass from the law, *till all be fulfilled*" (Matt. 5:18).

He does not mean the Ten Commandments only, He means the whole Word of God, the law of the Lord, which was in His heart, the will of His Father, which He came down from heaven to accomplish, because He delighted to do it. In John 10:35, He tells us

> *"The scripture cannot be broken."*

Men venture a fearful cast who argue either that God's promises are *too great to be true,* or that God's threatenings are *too dreadful to be inflicted.* The answer to both is to be found in *the cross of Calvary;* no promise that even God could give could surpass the promise there *fulfilled,* and no exhibition of judgment can ever exceed that which was there exhibited, when He who was in the form of God, and who *was* God, cried out,

> "My God, my God, why hast thou forsaken me?" (Matt. 27:46).

Let infidels scoff, let skeptics object, let worldlings neglect the Word of God if they will, but God has magnified His Word above all His name! (cf. Ps. 138:2).

> "Forever, O Lord, thy word is settled in heaven" (Ps. 119:89).

Every promise is a warrant for faith, a future for hope, a rest for love, and a challenge to the world, the flesh, and the devil; and every threatening is a warning from Him who would not deceive, and who cannot be deceived, to thoughtless sinners, of the sons and daughters of men, to "flee from the wrath to come," and to hide in the Rock that was cleft to shelter them. For *the Scriptures must be fulfilled.*

21

"AND NOW COME I TO THEE."—John 17:13

THUS A SECOND TIME He pleads with His Father as in verse 11. "I am no more in the world . . . I come to thee." Hitherto *I* have taken care of them, hitherto *I* have entered into their difficulties, been their companion in their sorrows, their fellow-pilgrim through the wilderness; "and now come I to thee." The Lord thus expresses Himself, evidently as an argument with His Father, that the special keeping, the constant and holy love of that Father, might surround and enshrine them, during the period which it was expedient for them that He should be parted from them. Such pleadings might well have demonstrated to His disciples (who were listening to Him) and to us, how much of His heart He was leaving behind, even while He could say, "I come to thee,"—not even in glory could He rest, but as He had the assurance and conviction, that the Father's tenderest care would be with His people, that

> The secret place of the Most High should be their refuge, and their dwelling place in the shadow of the Almighty (cf. Ps. 91:1).

Our blessed Lord was about to ascend to "where he was before." For nearly three-and-thirty years He had been on earth engaged about His Father's business. God had promised long before to send Him; and the promise had been fulfilled;

> "The Son of God was manifested, that he might destroy the works of the devil . . . and deliver them who through fear of death were all their lifetime subject to bondage" (I John 3:8; Heb. 2:15).

He had come forth empowered, commissioned, and enabled to

> "[Spoil] principalities and powers, [making] a shew of them openly, triumphing over them in it."

He had come into life's wilderness

> "To gather together the children of God that were scattered abroad"—

to be their "life," their "righteousness," their "sanctification," their "redemption," their "resurrection," their "all in all." He had come

> "To finish the transgression, and to make an end of sins, and to make reconciliation for iniquity, to bring in everlasting righteousness,"

and to be anointed the mystical temple of the living God. He could say, "I have glorified thee, on the earth: I have finished the work which thou gavest me to do." He could say in the hearing, and for the comfort of His disciples, and for our comfort, too, "Thou hast given me power over all flesh, that I should give eternal life to as many as thou hast given me" (v. 2).

Now He was returning, His glorious work divinely accomplished: "I come to thee"—the Conqueror of death and hell, the crowned Saviour and Captain of the people, and of the hosts of God: as their Forerunner, He was now to enter heaven in their names, and take possession of their mansions,

> "The firstfruits of them that slept" (I Cor. 15:20);
> "The first-begotten from the dead" (Rev. 1:5);
> "The first-born among many brethren" (Rom. 8:29);

God's own appointed Mediator, commissioned by the Father to transact His affairs with men, and men's affairs with God. He was returning,—the Head of grace, and the Head of glory; like Joshua returning to Makkedah after the slaughter of the kings, *"and all Israel with him,"* our Lord Jesus Christ was returning home to His Father, as the Leader and Head of His mystical

Body; every spiritual member of that Body virtually going with Him, mounting the vault of heaven with Him, triumphing over death and judgment with Him, sitting down at God's right hand in the heavenly places with Him, and remaining enthroned in the person of their Head till He shall return to take them to Himself, "that where He is there they may be also." Meantime, every foe that could, by any means, hinder their ultimate rest, and joy, and triumph, and salvation, was utterly put down.

"I have overcome the world" (John 16:33).

The law which man had broken, He had magnified; the justice of God which man as a sinner had challenged, He had vindicated; infinite atonement had been made by Him for sin; the remainder of His work was to be fulfilled in heaven—"Now come I to thee." The veil that had hitherto separated the sinner from Jehovah was, through His death and resurrection, to be rent from the top to the bottom, and Himself, as our Forerunner, was the first to enter.

"Christ is not entered into the holy places made with hands, which are the figures of the true; but into heaven itself, now to appear in the presence of God for us: . . . neither by the blood of goats and calves, but by his own blood, he entered in once into the holy place, having obtained eternal redemption for us" (Heb. 9:24, 12).

An high priest, not of the tribe of Levi, or family of Aaron, but "after the order of Melchisedek," was henceforth to officiate for us, not in an earthly tabernacle, or before an earthly sanctuary, but in the heaven of heavens, in the immediate presence of God. This work could not be done on earth,—there was no temple here worthy of our Priest; the temple in the heavens is that in which the Lord Jesus Christ—His people's High Priest —officiates. "Now come I to thee." The blood He was bringing in, and wherewith He sprinkled not an earthly mercy seat, but the very throne of God, was His own blood, in order that the

Holy Ghost might come forth—descending along the path by which He had ascended—commissioned to be our Comforter, in virtue of that atoning blood wherewith our High Priest had "sprinkled heaven itself." "Oh! it was expedient for Him to go, —the Comforter could not come else." "Now come I to thee." The words do press upon one's spirit, they contain so much, there is nothing earthly in them, they are altogether heavenly. Perhaps the best way of examining them is to consider them.

    I. As they refer to Himself.

    II. As they refer to His Father.

    III. As they refer to His people.

I. "I come to thee." Marvelous achievement of grace, of triumph, of faith, and of love! Who comes? The Man, the God-man! There was a time when man in the image of God could come to God, a welcomed and accepted worshiper. But sin had come between, and man could not pass it. But our Christ in wondrous and unutterable grace, had to come down into our nature, and humble Himself, even to the form of a servant, nay, lower than any servant, till He became obedient unto death, even the death of the cross; and now, with the travail of His soul as the payment made to God's justice, He is gone back to God, *not as a private individual,* but as the representative Head of His redeemed family. "I come to thee—I"—My people's Representative; "I"—*the pledge* of Thy love to them, *the seal* of Thy salvation to them; *the earnest* of Thy glory in them—I "come to thee."

I come, not invited as a matter of mercy, but in the right of My atoning finished work, and on the ground of justice and truth. "I come to thee," to Thy very throne, to Thy very heart, to Thy very glory, My Father, and their Father, My God, and their God. What *words of grace,* what *triumph!* What *love!*

And this was His *joy,* for He adds,

> "These things I speak in the world that they might have my joy fulfilled in themselves."

It was that He might thus draw near to God, and claim God, and take possession of God for His Church, and as representing it, that He "endured the cross, despising the shame." This was "the joy set before Him," thus to save His people, bringing them in Himself, as bone of His bone, and flesh of His flesh, nigh to God: and now He is triumphing in its accomplishment, —"I come to thee." How little He seems to think of all that terrible valley which lay between, and of the principalities and powers of hell which were all confederate to oppose His passage. He is thinking only *of the glorious issue,* "I come to thee."

Some of God's children shrink from death! See how the Lord contemplated His death, and yet never was such a death as His. No child of God can ever die as Christ died; His death has taken away the sting of death from all His people. Yet, how brightly He speaks of death—*"I come to thee."* The glory that was beyond! The rest beyond! The songs beyond! The Father beyond! filled His gaze, and filled His heart, and the light from God's glory falling down upon His soul, scattered all the darkness that lay between. Oh, if it did so in *His* case, how much more may it do so in our case! We have not to bear the curse He bore, nor writhe under the sting of death, which He endured in our stead.

The words are words of *faith*—"I come to thee." No *shadow of doubt* passes over His mind as to His welcome. "I come to thee." All the iniquities, all the transgressions, all the sins of omission and commission of all the individuals of the Church of God were laid upon Him; and the only satisfaction which could be made for them was His own outpoured blood—*His substituted life. He* knew the virtue of that blood, *He* knew the Father's estimation of that blood, and it is written by the Spirit of the living God for our joy of faith, that, although conscious He was about to bear the whole sin of the Church laid upon His individual soul, yet such was the virtue of the blood He was about to offer upon the cross, and, as our great High Priest, to plead in resurrection within the veil, that He knew it would cancel every debt with which He was charged, and be His title to enter as our Representative notwithstanding! How is it that we can ever doubt the merit of the Lord Jesus Christ, or the efficacy of His precious blood, to deal with our own individual and lesser portion of sin and iniquity? I would not be understood to disparage or make light of the sin and iniquity of any child of God; but what is the amount of any one man's sin as compared to the burden laid upon the Lord Jesus Christ? When He bore our sins in His own body upon the tree, *He* knew the blood would meet it, *He* knew the faithfulness of the Father who had promised to accept His offering, under the imputation of it all, and in the full consciousness of His liability to atone for all, He said, Father, "I come to thee."

They are words of *love*. Deep indeed is the love which dictated them. "And now come I to thee." What is He thinking of? Not of Himself, but of His people; His heart is full of the salvation He is about to provide for them; He is thinking of the crowns that await them, He is thinking of the songs they shall sing, He is thinking of the joy unspeakable and full of glory into which He would introduce them. In the view of these considerations, He thinks not of the cross, He thinks not of Gethsemane, He thinks not of the dark and terrible valley that lay between Him and the height to which He is going, He only thinks of the consequences of His being there with His people and for His people.

II. Now consider His words as they refer to His Father. "I come to thee." Oh, that we had similar views and thoughts of God! Our dear Lord was weary, He was longing for rest, and thus He expresses Himself in reference to all His realizations and anticipations of rest, *"I come to thee."* Jehovah had promised that He should "see the travail of his soul" and "be satisfied," and now He sums up all His expressions, desires, and expectations of satisfaction thus! "Now come I *to thee*." Crowns were awaiting Him, songs of angels were silent for Him, the heavenly hosts were ready for their shout of welcome,—

> "Lift up your heads, O ye gates; and be ye lift up, ye ever-lasting doors; and the King of glory shall come in" (Ps. 24:7)—

but *not* the starry heights, *not* the songs of angels, *not* the throne of glory fills His heart. Father, "I come *to thee*"—the crown of all My joys, the rest of all My love, the fullness of all My bliss. Would to God we had such views of our Father!

III. Lastly, consider His words as they refer to His people. He has gone to God, the heavens have received Him, and He is now sitting at the right hand of the Majesty on high, in the place of power, and in the place of prospect. God has glorified Him by consecrating Him High Priest in heaven, His whole office being in order to transact sinners' affairs with God—He

> "Can have compassion on the ignorant, and on them that are out of the way" (Heb. 5:2).

He has learned in His own human experience every phase of human sorrow, every class of human temptation, every variety of human difficulty. With all His experience gathered here among us during the days of His flesh, when He went in and out among us, He is now enthroned where no temptations can reach Him, and no unkindness assail Him, where no tears are shed, where no sighs are heard, and no death can enter. The Holy Ghost, the Comforter, sent forth by Him has taken up His eternal dwelling place in our hearts, and tells us His message,

> "Because I live you shall live also" (John 14:19).
> "I go to prepare a place for you. And if I go and prepare a place for you, I will come again, and receive you unto myself, that where I am there ye may be also" (John 14:2, 3).

Oh! let us cast all our care upon Him for He careth for us. Let us tell Him our temptations, He is

"Touched with the feeling of our infirmities" (Heb. 4:15);

"For in that he himself hath suffered being tempted, he is able to succour them that are tempted" (Heb. 2:18).

Let us bring our anxieties to Him, let us roll our burdens upon Him—He is "bone of our bone," though He be the Lord of glory—He is "flesh of our flesh," though sitting upon the throne of God, He is our Head of grace, and Head of glory. It cost Him His life to come down and save us, but it costs Him *nothing* to bless us now—it costs Him *nothing* to open His hand and give us liberally of the "all fullness" that it pleased the Father should dwell in Him, that out

"Of his fullness" we might receive "grace for grace" (John 1:16).

While we wait for His return, let us imitate His confidence. Hath He not prepared the way, hath He not paid the debt, hath He not opened the kingdom of heaven to all believers? What if death and judgment, the world, the flesh, and the devil are all united to oppose us, they were all united to oppose *Him,* and He scattered them, and ascended more than conqueror over them all. May not *we,* seeing we follow Him who "spoiled them," that they should not spoil us, also say, We come to Thee? Let us rejoice in His triumphs. Our enemies are His enemies, His victories are our victories, and His people overcome

"Through the blood of the Lamb, and the *word of their testimony"* (Rev. 12:11).

He has said,

"In the world ye shall have tribulation, but be of good cheer, I have overcome the world" (John 16:33).

Justice is satisfied; judgment is on our side; God is our Father. Oh! plead His blood! make mention of His righteousness only; there is no other righteousness,—God accepts *no other.* He hath given the Lord Jesus to us to be our title; plead His merit; make mention of His name. It is an all-prevailing name with the Father; He delights to hear it. And as you plead, imitate His confidence, and rejoice with joy. Come boldly to the throne of grace; draw near to God, and say, my Father, my Father, "I come to thee."

Oh! it was a glorious sunset. How majestically, how confidently, with what peace and joy and love doth "The day-spring from on high," gather around Him all the trophies which He hath purchased by the travail of His soul, and present them in Himself, and with Himself, to the Father whose love gave Him for us. Father, "I come to thee."

22

"AND THESE THINGS I SPEAK IN THE WORLD, THAT THEY
MIGHT HAVE MY JOY FULFILLED IN THEMSELVES."
—John 17:13

A^{S WE LISTEN}, we get an insight into our dear Saviour's heart, and we discover that He would not only have us safe here, and "more than conquerors through him that loved us," but also a happy people, that He would have us go on our way through the pilgrimage of life not only secure, but singing; fully realizing that He *is* all, that He has *done* all, and that He has *said* all that is necessary for our comfort, as well as our safety, for our joy, as well as for our salvation.

"These things," He alludes to what He had already spoken to His Father in their hearing. He had been unfolding secrets which had been hidden in Himself from the foundation of the world; He had been revealing the purposes and thoughts of God towards His people in Christ, that they might know them. He had been uttering them *in prayer* to His Father that they might be assured of them, and of their interest in them. Wonderful were the facts He had just enumerated in their hearing! *His* Father was their Father. *He* had manifested to them His name! His Father's portion and interest in them,—"*they are thine* . . . I am glorified in them." They were His Father's prized and precious gift to Himself: "Thou gavest them" to Me; and, in order that their joy might be full and their salvation secure, and their enemies surely conquered, "Thou hast given him power over all flesh." He reminds His Father in their hearing, "I have given them the words thou gavest me, and they have kept them, they have believed surely that thou hast sent me." The Lord had spoken much of His people in His prayer; but all was in praise of them, everything for them, and in their favor, and *nothing against them.* We can hardly believe our eyes as we read and hear Him tell the Father, "They have kept thy word." They know that "all things that thou hast given me are of thee." "I pray for them, for they are thine." Surely, He presents them in the perfection of His own fullness, in the glory of His own person, in the plenitude of His own grace!

"These things" (containing and being the expression of God's rich purposes of grace and truth and salvation towards them, and His eternal love for them) are uttered, for their instruction, for their comfort, for their security, for their confidence, and for their joy.

"These things . . . I *speak* in the world." This was no silent communion, no whisper in the Father's ear which His people could not hear. It was an open, audible communication that they all might hear it, and, as they heard, be filled with "joy unspeakable and full of glory."

And "these things" were spoken in prayer that they might understand how near to the heart of Christ, and how secured to them, in the Father's love, those petitions were.

"These things I speak in *the world*"—the world that lieth in "wickedness"—the world henceforth to be the scene of their temptations, their conflicts, and their sorrows—the world in which He had dwelt with them—the world where He was now about to leave them—the world which He had overcome for them. Thus, in the house of the strong man, the Lord Jesus proclaims His triumphs, spoils him of all his armor wherein he trusted, lighting up the kingdom of darkness with the rays of His heavenly love, teaching His pilgrim people how to sing as they pass through it to their heavenly rest. "These things I speak in the world, that they might have my joy fulfilled in themselves."

I know not how to open out these words: it is quite overwhelming to think of them. That they might have—*"joy,"* joyless as they were; poor, weak, needy, helpless ones; that sin had marred, that sorrow had dimmed, and the fear of death had long held subject to bondage. "That they might have joy," —what joy?—*"my joy"*—heavenly joy, this! Nothing of earth in it; joy like His who came down from heaven—"my joy *fulfilled,"* —not merely presented and proposed to them; joy fulfilled, apprehended, realized, and entered into; joy complete, satisfying, sustaining; joy fulfilled, and *"in themselves"*—not in another but in themselves; joy with which no stranger could intermeddle. The joy of the Lord is the strength of His people (Neh. 8:10), and He would have them take their stand in His own joy! Speaking to His Father, but still to them, *words* evermore sufficient to fill us

> "With all joy and peace in believing, that ye may abound in hope, through the power of the Holy Ghost" (Rom. 15:13).

"My joy." We may regard His words in *three* points of view.

I. "My joy." The *joy* which is Mine to bestow; joy of which He is the Author and Giver.

II. "My joy," of which He is *the object, subject,* and *element.*

III. "My joy." *His own personal joy.* Truly, the words comprehend and compromise those *three* aspects of His joy.

First. He came down from heaven to give us joy,

> "The oil of joy for mourning, and the garments of praise for the spirit of heaviness" (Isa. 61:3).

Thus sang the angel of the Lord at His nativity,

> "Behold, I bring you tidings of *great joy* which shall be to all people. For unto you is born this day, in the city of David, a Saviour, which is Christ the Lord" (Luke 2:11).

"My joy"—joy realized in the soul through the knowledge of that Father, whose love He came to reveal; the salvation He came to bestow, the relationships He came to sustain toward us, and the Comforter He sent to dwell in us; joy resulting from the assurance of our acceptance, the consciousness of our justification from all things, the realization of our adoption into God's family, and the fact that

> "[Even] now, we are the sons of God . . . If children, then heirs, heirs of God, and joint-heirs with Christ" (I John 3:2; Rom. 8:17).

Abiding joy and peace, and rest—rest from all our fears, rest from all our foes, rest from all our anticipations of ill, rest found in Him—He calls this "my joy," because He purchased it for us, and because it is His to bestow.

Secondly. "My joy" as the joy of which He is the object and subject, as distinguished from all other grounds and sources of joy whatsoever. We are too apt to look for grounds and sources of joy in ourselves. We examine into our attainments and experiences; or (which is a more *unsuspected* form of self-righteousness) into the graces which God, for Christ's sake, may have bestowed upon us, in order to discover in *them* grounds and occasions for spiritual joy. But there is not—there cannot be—real abiding, soul-satisfying joy, save in the knowledge and enjoyment of the Lord Jesus Christ Himself. He must be the foundation and the element of all our heavenly joy. In the fifteenth chapter of this Gospel and the eleventh verse, we find a similar statement,

> "These things have I spoken unto you, that my joy might remain in you, and that your joy might be full."

He had referred to two matters which might be considered as difficulties, if not exceptions. First, in the twenty-eighth verse of the fourteenth chapter He spake of leaving them. If He was about to leave them, how then could He love them so? And if anything could cast a doubt upon His love, it would darken joy. "Nay," He says,

> "If ye loved me, ye would rejoice, because I said, I go unto
> the Father. . . . If I go not away the Comforter will not come
> unto you; but if I depart, I will send him unto you" (John
> 14:28; 16:7).

His absence was thus declared to be one of the greatest proofs
of His love, and reasons for their joy.

The other matter alluded to, and which might suggest a
doubt as to the constancy of His love, we find in the opening of
the fifteenth chapter, where He enjoins fruitfulness upon His
people, and the necessity of abiding in Him, to this end warning
them of the consequences of not abiding: injury to themselves
and dishonor to Him. Now when we begin to realize our constant failure in all these matters, our feebleness and carelessness
in duty, our shameful neglect and forgetfulness as to abiding in
Him, and how little after all is the amount of our fruitfulness,
we are tempted to question our love to Him, and then, as a
consequence His love to us; but if for any cause whatsoever we
doubt His love, then would our joy be darkened, therefore He
says,

> "As the Father hath loved me, so I have loved you: continue
> ye in my love" (John 15:9).

Whatever be your circumstances, wherever you go, however
you may be situated; with the same unchanging, full, abiding,
and abounding love with which the Father loveth Me, so have
I loved you. Let nothing tempt you to doubt that love. "Continue ye in my love."

> "These things have I spoken unto you, that my joy might
> remain in you, and that your joy might be full."

Remember the *character* of His joy, it is full, complete, abiding, unchanging joy, for He is the object and the subject and the
element of it, and the elements and the reasons of it are all in
Himself. There are two motives for joy in Christ; what He has

done for us, and what He is in Himself. St. Peter writing on this subject says (I Peter 1:8),

> "In whom, though now ye see him not, yet believing, ye rejoice with joy unspeakable and full of glory."

By joy "unspeakable" He does not mean joy that we cannot tell of, joy we cannot express so far as we may realize it, but that if our tongues were set on fire, and we were to begin day and night, and year by year, to tell of His worth and the inexhaustible fullness of the joy He bestowed upon us in Himself and by Himself, still we could never tell it all, for it is "full of glory." We must be in glory before we can fully apprehend the reasons and the motives and matters for exceeding joy which the Lord has given us. Beginning to rejoice in Him, even on earth, is glory begun, it is joy unspeakable, because it is full of glory.

Thirdly. "My joy" as being *His own joy*. When He speaks of the peace He bestows upon His people, it is *"my peace* I give unto you"; when He speaks of the rest into which He introduces them, it is *"my rest"*; when He speaks of the strength He imparts to them, it is *"my strength"*; when He speaks of the life He bestows upon them, it is His own, *"I am . . . the Life"*; when He speaks of the way opened out for them, *"I am the way"*; when He speaks of the fullness He supplies to them, it is *"His fullness"*; and of the grace which supplies it, it is *"my grace."* So here when He speaks of the joy He would have His people possessed of, it is *"my joy."* What was His joy? *God Himself was His joy.* If David could say in Psalm 43,

> "I will go . . . to God, my exceeding joy"

(the gladness of my joy), how much more the Lord Jesus Christ! His God was His joy; God, as His *own God,* was His joy. He only knew Him fully that He might rejoice in Him. The only begotten Son, which was in the bosom of the Father, alone knew the Father, so as fully to apprehend how much ground of joy was in Him. The doing of that Father's will was His joy; the fulfilling of all that Father's pleasure for the salvation of His people was His joy; the being in Himself all in all—the Mediator between God and man—was His joy. The fullness and freeness of His salvation—the fact that all power in heaven and earth was committed to Him for men was His joy! the constancy and complacency of His Father's love to Him, and to His people, which He knew so well and so deeply was His joy; the gift of His people to Him was His joy; their union to Himself for their full enjoyment of grace here, and their full possession of glory hereafter was His joy; and these things I speak in the world, that they might have *"My* joy fulfilled in themselves."

There are *three* occasions of joy which the Lord Jesus Christ shares with His people—all of them are emphatically His own joy. The joy of the Bridegroom over the Bride;

> "As the bridegroom rejoiceth over the bride, so shall thy God rejoice over thee" (Isa. 62:5).

The joy of harvest,

> "They joy before thee according to the joy in harvest" (Isa. 9:3).

As men rejoice when they gather in the harvest, so will the joy of Jesus be shared with His people when He reaps the field of earth, and gathers into the garner of His Father, and His God, *all His sheaves.* The joy of those who divide the spoil,

> "As men rejoice when they divide the spoil" (Isa. 9:3).

Oh! haste the day when our glorious Lord Jesus will gather together His people to partake with Him in His joy as the Conqueror of death and hell; as the Rifler of the tomb; as the Overcomer of the world; and of him who is the god of this world—even the devil; the joy of opening paradise to His blood-bought ones; the joy of presenting them to Himself without spot or wrinkle, or any such thing; the joy of keeping them in the meantime without falling, and presenting them

> "Faultless before the presence of his glory with exceeding joy" (Jude 24).

This was His joy,—and He says, "these things I speak in the world, that they might have my joy fulfilled in themselves." See John 15:11; John 17:13—and Matthew 25:21, "Enter thou into the joy of thy Lord."

If we desire to realize this joy, and to fulfill the Lord's will concerning us, "rejoice always," "rejoicing in hope of the glory of God." If we would be "filled with all joy and peace in believing," never seek for the motive or measure of our joy in the amount of our love. Joy in the Lord can never be according to our love, nor indeed according to anything in us. It must ever be according to our faith. Many persons make a great mistake; they try to find in their love to Jesus a ground for their joy. Try it the other way; seek the ground for your joy in His love to you, and say with the apostle in faith,

> "We have known and believed the love God hath to us" (I John 4:16).

Thus your joy will be according to your faith in that which He has spoken, for

> "These things I speak in the world, that they might have my joy fulfilled in themselves."

Our Lord has told us enough to give us "joy and peace in believing," and what the Lord has spoken in order that we might have joy, God the Holy Ghost has *written* with the same object. See I John 1:4,

> "These things write we unto you, that your joy may be full."

And what things?

> "Truly our fellowship is with the Father, and with his Son Jesus Christ" (I John 1:3).

It was the joy of the Lord that He should be the link between His Father and His people, that they might have fellowship with the Father in Himself. *That* was His joy—the ground of it is Himself, and the proclamation of it the gospel.

Enough has been written to prove how much more a rejoicing people we might be than we are. Enough, to impel us to humble our souls before Him who came down from heaven to *be* our joy, who went back to heaven because He *is* our joy, and who sent the Holy Ghost down that we might have meantime *"the joy of the Holy Ghost"* till we are with Him, entering into His joy.

Oh! may we henceforth in His strength resolve to deal more with God's Word, to wrap our souls in God's promises, to lie down in the green pastures and by the still waters, and then joy, and peace, and rest, which the world cannot give, and which the world cannot take away, will flow deeply into our souls, as we trust in Him,

> "Who, for the joy that was set before him, endured the cross, despising the shame, and is set down at the right hand of the throne of God" (Heb. 12:2).

23

"I HAVE GIVEN THEM THY WORD; AND THE WORLD HATH
HATED THEM, BECAUSE THEY ARE NOT OF THE WORLD,
EVEN AS I AM NOT OF THE WORLD."—John 17:14

OUR MOST GRACIOUS LORD, being about to leave this world, and to enter into His glory, had prayed, "Glorify thou me with thine own self with the glory that I had with thee before the world was." But in presenting this petition, He does it in such a way as to leave no doubt with *those* in whose hearing He was pleading, that the glory He was about to enter into, would be no glory to Him, if His absence was to be any loss to them. Accordingly, we find from the fifth verse to the end of this prayer, all His thoughts, all His words, and all His desires, even in the anticipation of glory, have reference to His people.

These are the three principal desires for His people in the heart of our Lord Jesus Christ expressed to His Father.

Verse 11—That they might be kept in His name;

Verse 13—"That they might have [his] joy fulfilled in themselves";

Verse 17—That they might be sanctified through the truth. Three times He pleads.

> "I have given them thy word."
> "The words thou gavest me."
> "And they have kept thy word."

He did not give them the work to do: "I have *finished the work*," but "I have given them *thy word*." Note well the importance He attaches to His Father's Word.

That Word was the means whereby the accomplishment of all the desires He had expressed to His Father for His people was to be effected. Were they to be kept from evil? The Word is the means whereby the Father keeps His people from evil. It is by the Word He manifests Himself to us; it is by the Word He guides us; it is by the Word He warns us; it is by the Word He comforts us: and just as that Word enters into our hearts, and takes possession of our thoughts, we are kept safely in passing through the wilderness,

> "By the words of thy lips I have kept me from the paths of the destroyer" (Ps. 17:4).

The Word is the means for fulfilling the joy of the Lord in His people. The Word is the testimony of the love of the Father, and of the Son, and of the Holy Ghost to us; the testimony of the triumphs of the Son of God for us. It is as His Word enters into our hearts, joy enters into our hearts, and His joy in accomplishing the Word for us is fulfilled by the reception of the Word in us. And the Word is also the means for the sanctification of His people:

> "Sanctify them through thy truth: thy word is truth."

Oh! it is the discovery of what God is to us, as revealed in His Word, the knowledge of what God is for us, and the assurance of what He has laid up in Christ our portion, as revealed in His Word, which is the means in the hand of the Spirit of God for separating us from the world, and sanctifying us.

"I have given them thy word"—Thy faithful Word, the Word of life, of peace, and of promises all Yea and Amen in the Lord Jesus Christ, now and forevermore, to every one that believeth. As the broken law had been laid up in the ark—the emblem of the Lord Jesus Christ—so the Word of the gospel is laid up by the Lord Jesus Christ in His people, to be fulfilled in them. "I have given them thy word."

Let us endeavor to apprehend our Lord's words, in such

measure as we may. All Christ's gifts are great gifts. When He gave Himself, it was a great gift; when He gave His Spirit, it was a great gift; when He gave His Word, His Father's Word to us, it was a great gift—three great gifts. He gave His people all that He had received for them. Jehovah had given Him *life* for them, *righteousness,* and a *title* to heaven, and He gave them all. The Word, too, which was the divine record of all God's love and purposes towards them, so full of grace, so full of peace, and mercy, truth, and love, He gave to them. "I have given them thy word."

Now, if we take this passage in its highest and fullest meaning, there can be no doubt it applies, in the first instance, to His apostles, individually, affording precious proof from the Lord's own word in prayer to His Father, that what we have from the apostles subsequently, *is the word of God*—"I have given them thy word." He promised also that He would, on His departure, send the Holy Ghost to them, to bring all things to their remembrance, whatsoever He had said unto them. We have, moreover, the apostles claiming for their teaching that it was not the word of man, but the Word of God (I Thess. 2:13),

> "For this cause also thank we God, without ceasing, because, when ye received the word of God which ye heard of us, ye received it not as the word of men but, as it is in truth, the word of God, which effectually worketh also in you that believe."

When our Lord, therefore, declares, "I have given them thy word," He, in the first instance, alludes to that great gift to His apostles of the testimony of God, given to them as a trust, to be faithfully communicated to us; given to them as a testimony to sinners, and against the unbelief of the world—given to them as a light from God to irradiate this world's darkness, and that His people might be gathered out of it to walk in the light, even as He Himself was in the light—and they have faithfully discharged that trust.

But this saying also applies to believers in every day, and in every age. "I have given them thy word." The Word is the *element,* where faith, and hope, and love have their existence and their exercise. It is the field over which faith, and hope, and love are invited to range. *There* we may find everything to comfort; *there* we may find everything to supply our need; *there* we may find everything to direct us in our difficulties, to cheer us in our pilgrimage, to light up for us the valley of the shadow of death; and *there* we may learn the song of Moses and of the Lamb, and begin to sing it even ere we reach our home, beguiling the weariness of the way.

When heaven and earth shall have passed away, we shall find that Word, which has been our guide, our source of help, and comfort, and consolation, in our difficulties by the way, like a rock beneath our feet, which has sheltered and supported us in many a storm, and it will sustain us until we reach the calm sunshine, where storms can never come, and temptations can never weary us.

"I have given them thy word." As truly as the law was given upon Mount Sinai by God,—and it was His Word, His law,— so truly the gospel sent us by Jesus Christ is God's Word, God's law. Peter never forgot this part of the prayer. You remember, in Acts 10:36, 37, when speaking to Cornelius and his family, he says,

> "The word which *God* sent unto the children of Israel, preaching peace by Jesus Christ . . . that word, I say, ye know."

Oh! it is a blessed thing to realize that the gospel, so full of joy, and peace, and liberty, and triumph for us, is God's fulfilled law, is God's Word of salvation to us, that we may triumph in it, and trust in it. You observe Our Lord as Mediator *claims* that He has faithfully discharged His office! "I have given unto them the words which thou gavest me." As we read a sentence like this, how should our hearts be stirred up to study that Word. If it has come down to us from such a source, if it has been given to us by such a Saviour, and in such a way, and at such a cost, how should we value that Word. Well argues the apostle in Hebrews 2:

> "Therefore we ought to give the more earnest heed to the things we have heard, lest at any time we should let them slip. For if the word spoken by angels was stedfast, and every transgression and disobedience received a just recompense of reward, how shall we escape, if we neglect so great salvation, which at the first began to be spoken by the Lord, and was confirmed unto us by them that heard him?"

But He goes on to say, "the world hath hated them." He is speaking to His Father. How sweet it is to know, to realize that the Father is acquainted with all His poor people's trials and difficulties, whether arising from the world, the flesh, or the devil. The fact that they have difficulties, conflicts, and trials, secures for them sympathy and help from their Father. I would not have my Father ignorant of a solitary corruption of my heart, or a difficulty in my way, or an anxiety in my soul; I would have Him know all, that I might be rid of the burden from my own self, and that I might be sure I had the Father's tender sympathy with me in my difficulties.

"The world hath hated them." The dear Lord would have His people count the cost before they enlist under His banner. If we suppose that as servants of Christ, and as recipients of the Word of God, we shall have a smooth passage through life, we are very greatly mistaken. The Lord here reminds His Father and tells His people they shall have no downy pillow on which to rest; He presents to them no false colors; He allures them with no path strewn with flowers, but tells His Father, "the world hath hated them." But how comes the world to hate them? It is the consequence of His having given them God's Word, and this He tells the Father in their hearing. The very fact which makes the world hate the servants of God, namely, that they are the depositaries of God's Word, makes God love them all the more. Observe, how the Lord evidently regards this as an irresistible argument with the Father, securing to His tried people His special presence and His constant care; for at the same time that He is pleading, Father, keep Thy people, fulfill Mine own joy in them, sanctify them through Thy truth, He puts this also before Him—"The world hath hated them."

Observe another very important lesson. God's Word entering into a sinner's heart gives light, revealing to him what eye hath not seen, what ear hath not heard, and what it hath never entered into the heart of man to conceive (cf. I Cor. 2:9), revealing new worlds to him, a new society, new hopes, new joys, and making him a stranger and a pilgrim here. To every true believer in the Lord Jesus Christ, who fully believes the Word of God, and the promises contained in that Word, this world becomes a waste and howling wilderness, a foreign land, an enemy's country. His country—who has God's Word, and the hopes that Word communicates in his heart—"his country is in the heavens," and the consequence is, the man is separate from the world, finds his occupations and tastes other than the world can supply him with, and the world hates him, for the world hates every one who really lives out the Word of God in this world.

There must be a change somewhere! Do not think this a hard saying. What has changed? Has God's truth changed? Has the devil changed? Has the world's enmity to God and to His truth changed? Nay, but professing Christians have changed. Christians are not so like Christ as they ought to be or as they once were. Professing Christians are a vast deal more like the world than they *used* to be, or *ought* to be, and the consequence is, they let the world alone, the world lets them alone. They make a sort of compromise with the world. They are worldly enough to suit the world, and not Christlike enough to *offend* the world, *that is the honest truth.* But if those to whom God in Christ hath committed His Word were more under its influence, that is, if they lived it out more, it would be just as true now as it was in the days when the Lord spake, "I have given them thy word, and the world hath hated them."

But

> "If the world hate you, ye know that it hated me before it hated you" (John 15:18).

These words also apply, in the first instance, to the disciples, then to believers of every age. To the disciples first; they in a special degree practically experienced the truth of our Lord's words. If we refer to I Corinthians 4:9, you read,

> "We are made a spectacle unto the world, and to angels, and to men";

and in verses 11–13,

> "Even unto this present hour we both hunger, and thirst, and are naked, and are buffeted, and have no certain dwelling-place; and labor, working with our own hands, being reviled . . . being persecuted . . . being defamed . . . we are made as the filth of the world, and are the offscouring of all things unto this day."

And why? Christ tells the Father why! "I have given them thy word." But this is true of real Christians now as then. Do not suppose that Word of God is obsolete, which says,

> "All that will live godly in Christ Jesus shall suffer persecution" (Phil. 1:29).

But the world has different ways and means of manifesting its hatred to those who are really living out the Word of God. Satan has tried many a plan; the alteration of his plans does not prove that his purpose has ceased to exist. In the early days he tried persecution, but the Church grew under persecution; then

Satan changed his plan; believers in the Lord Jesus Christ are not persecuted in our day; the age of persecution is at least in abeyance. But Satan had other resources; he has tried to corrupt the truth, and he is working hard to do so still, corrupting the gospel, lowering the standard of God's Word, suggesting "oppositions of science falsely so called," and casting doubts upon the reality and the truth of revelation; he has succeeded far more to injure the cause of God in this way than he ever did by persecution. It seems in our own day especially, Satan has another and a more subtle plan for paralyzing God's Word, namely, the *worldliness of those who profess it.* Alas! it is but too apparent that in order to escape the cross, and to avoid the hatred of the world, and the charge of being peculiar, the Word of God is to a great extent neglected among us, and remains ineffectual and inoperative in the hearts, and in the lives, and even in the profession, of many of those who call themselves Christians.

Then again observe, the world hates all true believers—you will say, perhaps, this is a very uncharitable assertion; but the statement is Christ's own, and we must abide by what the Word of God declares. The world is too religious (?) professedly to display its hatred to Christlikeness, Godlikeness, and holiness, in God's people; therefore, to be consistent with itself, it gives disparaging names to those who are living for Christ, it hates them and sneers at them, not because they are Christians,—oh, no!—but "because they are so disagreeable, so unsociable, because they are such kill-joys, they do judge people so"; and thus they invest the Christian character with what is odious in their own estimation, and present the caricature to others. But this only proves what the Lord asserts, "I have given them thy word, and the world hath hated them."

"If ye were of the world, the world would love his own: but because ye are *not of the world*, but I have chosen you out of the world, therefore the world hateth you" (John 15:19).

Yes, *hates*,—hates the persons, *hates* the principles, *hates* the profession, and *hates* the presence of all true Christians; because their nature is different from the world's nature, their spirit is different from the world's spirit, their worship is different from the world's worship, their conduct is different from the world's conduct, their character is different from the world's character, and their portion, God knows, is different from the world's portion, and the world cannot bear their living testimony against itself, and therefore the world hates them.

But "I have given them thy word,"—that will compensate them for all the world may deprive them of, nay, more. That Word, received by them, with all its promises and privileges, had been manifestly effectual in renewing their souls, and transforming them into the likeness of Christ, else the world would have taken no notice of them. The world hated them in consequence of their having ceased to be conformed to the world.

And "they are not of the world." He who was thus addressing His Father knew all that these words implied, "They are not of the world,"—nay, they are the children of the Lord God Almighty. Their world is where the sun is not needed, where the Lord Jesus Christ is the "light," where the shadows never come, and where death cannot enter. Their joys are the joys at God's right hand for evermore; they are not of this world, they have been "delivered from this present evil world," Christ has died for them, they are the children of light, journeying along the bright path that shineth brighter and brighter unto the perfect day. They have overcome the world by the blood of the Lamb, they are not of the world, and thus they may well bear its neglect, and suffer its hate.

But the Lord further adds what is marvelously calculated to comfort the believer under the cold neglect he may meet with in the world through which he is passing: "They are not of the world, *even as I am not of the world.*" Identified with Him, members of His body, of His flesh, and of His bones, they live in the power of His risen and eternal life, which hath quickened them—they are already more than conquerors, through Him that loved them—"they are not of the world, even as I am not of the world." Absolute union and entire conformity to the Lord Jesus Christ Himself, is surely *enough* to console them under that opposition from the world, which is, after all, only the evidence and the manifestation of the fact that the world has recognized that union. Our Lord's words imply not only "they are not of the world," but the converse also, they *are* of God, heirs of God and joint-heirs with Christ; God is their portion, God's love is their home, God's promise is their joy, God's everlasting arms their security—"they are not of the world." And in the meantime, and till He calls them out of the world, they are the subjects of Christ's constant intercession. And yet more, the objects of the Father's unceasing care, for thus Christ grounds His appeal in their behalf,—Holy Father, keep them, and sanctify them, for "they are not of the world, even as I am not of the world." Well might the great apostle say,

"I reckon that the sufferings of this present time are not worthy to be compared with the glory that shall be revealed in us" (Rom. 8:18).

24

"I HAVE GIVEN THEM THY WORD; AND THE WORLD HATH
HATED THEM, BECAUSE THEY ARE NOT OF THE WORLD,
EVEN AS I AM NOT OF THE WORLD."—John 17:14

W E HAVE ENDEAVORED to gather some of the fruits which
hang so abundantly upon this bough of the tree of life.
Much more remains.

In the midst of many arguments with which our Lord Jesus
Christ pleads for His people with His Father, He says, "I have
given them thy word." I have made them the chosen depositaries of that Word which Thou hast magnified above all Thy
name; that Word which is the seal and the consummation of
all Thy loving purposes and dealings toward them; that Word
which is the ministration of Thy Spirit, the revelation of Thy
Son, the communication of Thy righteousness, and the proclamation to the ends of the earth of Thy great salvation. "I have
given them thy word," the divine means and instrument
whereby faith shall be begotten in their souls, hope be kindled,
and the love of God be shed abroad in their hearts by the Holy
Ghost which is given unto them. Observe the irresistible pleadings which our Lord Jesus Christ presents on His people's behalf
to God.

1. He pleads *the Father's own interest* in them—"I have
given them *thy word*"—that Word in which Thy glory is revealed; that Word in which Thy grace is displayed, and Thy
love made known; that Word in which Thy glorious name is
proclaimed, Thy character revealed, and Thy truth sealed; that

Word which contains, reveals, and communicates the unsearchable riches of Thy Christ; that Word which is Thy promise and Thine oath to the sons of men, never to be repented of or recalled. I have committed it to them, I have engrafted it into their hearts, I have sealed them with Thy Word, I have identified it with them; Father, "keep them."

2. He pleads their own weakness, helplessness, and need, and their absolute dependence upon the love, and care, and keeping of the Father. The Lord seems to say, they are but dust and ashes, and "I have given *them* thy word." Father, where Thy treasure is there let Thine heart be also; and "keep them," for they are utterly incapable of keeping themselves.

3. He pleads *their position*—they are not in heaven, Father; they are not where temptations cannot assail them, or where Our enemies, and their enemies, cannot hurt them, "they are in the world"; *they* are there to learn what they are, and they are there to learn what *Thou* art. Father, "keep them."

4. He pleads (v. 18) *that they were not in the world by their own selection.* It is the position *I have chosen for them;* "I have *sent* them into the world" to be the light of the world, to be the salt of the earth, and I have given them Thy Word to be their blessing, and that they may be made blessings to the world into which I send them. Father, "keep them."

5. He pleads (v. 14) their *calling*—"they are not *of* the world," Father. They are in it, but not of it, they are redeemed by My precious blood, they are delivered and emancipated from this evil world in which they dwell; "they are not of the world."

6. He pleads *their dignity* as being identified with Himself —"even *as I* am not of the world, they are not of the world."

7. And lastly, *their danger*—"the world *hates* them." Because I have given them Thy Word, I have opened heaven to their gaze, I have revealed to them Thy love, I have discovered to them their Heavenly destiny, Thy Word has made them strangers and pilgrims here; they are, therefore, separate from

the world, they care not for it, they are living witnesses against it, and "the world hates them."

The testimony of the Lord Jesus Christ which He had taught them, and which they had received, was of such a nature as to excite the utmost opposition of the world. The cross of Christ is an offense to the world, although it be the glory of the saint; the apostle says,

> "God forbid that I should glory, save in the cross of our Lord Jesus Christ, by whom the world is crucified unto me, and I unto the world" (Gal. 6:14).

The Word which the Lord Jesus Christ taught His people to bear witness to, brought down upon them the world's hatred, because it condemned the world. As the angels said to Lot, so the Word of God says to us, "Get ye out of this place, for the Lord will destroy it, because the cry of it is waxen great before the face of the Lord" (cf. Gen. 19:13).

The world cannot bear testimony of this sort; such teaching cuts at the root of the world's pride, and is entirely opposed to the world's ways, principles, tastes, and pursuits. We have but to be faithful to God's Word, and live out the truths which that Word inculcates, and we shall learn, in our experience, what the apostles of the Lord Jesus Christ bitterly learned in theirs—"the world hath hated them."

This hatred of the world only manifests its enmity to God *Himself.*

> "Whosoever therefore will be a friend of the world is the enemy of God" (James 4:4).

How can we expect the world to submit to testimony of this kind, or to approve of the principles, or creed of the men who believe and act on such testimony? And yet that Word is forever settled in heaven, it was conceived in the everlasting love of God, it is being fulfilled in God's eternal grace, it shall be consummated in God's everlasting glory, and the Lord Jesus

Christ. The Fulfiller of that Word has meantime given it to the sons and daughters of men, that they might have all joy and peace in believing it, that they might abound in hope through the power of the Holy Ghost (cf. Rom. 15:13), and that they might witness to the perishing world into which He sent them, that

> "God so loved the world, that he gave his only begotten Son, that whosoever believeth in him should not perish, but have everlasting life" (John 3:16);
> "But he that believeth not is condemned already" (John 3:18).

The world cannot suffer a religion truly founded upon the Word of God; the principles it inculcates are as opposed to the principles of this world *as light is opposed to darkness;* and hence comes the temptation to be ashamed of Christ and of His Words; hence the apostle was led to warn his beloved Timothy,

> "Be not thou therefore ashamed of the testimony of our Lord, nor of me his prisoner" (II Tim. 1:8).

The men who have been most faithful to God's Word have always been designated "men who have turned the world upside down." So it was said of the apostles, so would men now say—if they were to speak out their hearts and minds—of all who are really faithfully and consistently fighting under the outspread banner which the Lord God Almighty hath given us "to be displayed because of the truth." It is an easy thing to fold the banner up, it is an easy thing to hide our colors as we go through the world; but it was not for this that Christ gave His Father's Word to His disciples, it was not for this that Christ sent His disciples into the world. Has the world then no religion? Yes. It has, it always had, but it is a religion which changes and varies just as it suits the convenience, the prejudices, and superstitions of men. But the truths and doctrines of the everlasting gospel *are contrary to all nature's highest attainments,* and declare to us that

"For that which is highly esteemed among men is abomination in the sight of God" (Luke 16:15).

Just attend to a few specimens of the teaching of the apostles, in the discharge of their trust as the receivers of God's Word. One cardinal truth they proclaimed, and which runs through all their teaching, is the *absolute ruin* of fallen humanity—that there is not a redeeming point in human nature, not one; not a single principle, not a single tendency or attainment, but what is utterly vile, corrupt, and abominable in the sight of God. Can we imagine the world submitting to such teachers or such teaching? Such opinions it calls "narrow-minded bigotry"; yet, after all, it is God's truth. We have in Romans 3:10, the portrait of every natural man. We have also a statement corresponding to this, in the Lord's conversation with Nicodemus, John 3:6, and repeated by St. Paul in Romans 8:8,

"That which is born of the flesh is flesh,"

and

"They that are in the flesh cannot please God."

By the flesh is meant unrenewed human nature, the natural man as he is; don't suppose it means the gross and sensual merely, there is such a thing as refinement and taste in the world; but whether it be the refined or the degraded, "that which is born of the flesh is flesh," and "they that are in the flesh"—whether elegant or moral, or inelegant and immoral—"cannot please God." We can understand how intensely the world hates and must hate truths like these. It therefore tries to disparage them, to ignore them, and to make light of those who believe and endeavor to act upon them.

Then follows the glorious gospel which the apostles were taught to proclaim, and did proclaim—that the Son of God, the Lord Jesus Christ, became man and "died for the *ungodly*" —not for the good but for the bad, not for people who are sorry for sin, but for people who are not even anxious to be sorry for sin. The world overlooks this truth, because it likes to get credit for penitence and good resolutions. The Word of God, on the other hand, declares that when man was utterly bankrupt! an enemy of God! alien! afar off! and the servant of the devil! God the Son took human nature, and died for him in his *ungodliness;* that He came from heaven, not to call the righteous, simply because there were no righteous to call; but He came to call guilty lost sinners. All this is blessed news when a man knows he *is* a guilty lost sinner, but it is exceedingly insulting to the self-righteous spirit of the world, therefore the world will not receive it.

Then the apostles taught that the finished work of the Lord Jesus Christ has completely settled the question of sin *forever,* and that no matter who the sinner is, how bad he may have been, or how far wandered from God, the moment he receives, by faith, the Lord Jesus Christ's and God's testimony concerning His atonement upon the cross, that moment he is *justified from all things;* the blood of Christ has met all that sin hath done, and this, without reference to the tears, the prayers, the sorrow, the repentance, the religion, or the religiousness of the sinner; *He did it Himself,* His own glorious self:

> "[With] his right hand, and his holy arm, hath [He] gotten him the victory" (Ps. 98:1).

Will the world endure teaching like that? Not so! For it makes nothing of all the world's religiousness, nothing of all its good intentions, its piety, its churchgoing, or its prayers!

The apostles proclaim Christ is risen from the dead, and become the new and living resurrected Head of the people of God, and that our life on earth *is the life Christ Himself lives at the right hand of God.* That there is no life in which the sinner can stand before his Judge, no life in which the child can enjoy its Father, no life in which the saint can be accepted and glorified, but the risen life of Christ!

"Because I live, ye shall live also" (John 14:19)—

as I live, as long as I live, and where I live! Oh! this is the joy
of the man who believes, and it is God's testimony, the precious
"word" He commissioned our Lord to give to His people.

The apostles also taught

> "If any man be in Christ he is a new creature; old things are
> passed away; behold all things are become new" (II Cor.
> 5:17);

henceforth his face will be set against the things he before followed, he turns his back upon the world he before loved. In
fact, the Word of God creates *a revolution* in the soul when
once it enters into it. How very contrary to all this is the world's
religion. Alas! the truth of God had not been long proclaimed
before the world, the flesh, and the devil invented a counterfeit,
a caricature of it. There is a vast deal of religiousness on every
side exactly suited to the pride and the self-righteousness of
men, a religion of sentiment, a religion of pious talk, and of
good resolutions never carried out; a religion that will converse
about ministers and doctrines, but hates to speak of Jesus, or of
the precious blood He shed for us; "that is too sacred a subject
to be introduced into common conversation," says the world, "it
is too solemn to be enjoyed, except in the church and on Sundays!" and thus under the guise of exceeding reverence for it,
the Word of God is neglected; a religion of externals, attending
on forms, ordinances, and ceremonies, a material religion is substituted, a yearning for something that the senses may deal with;
where faith in God's Word is laid aside, and faith in sacraments
takes its place. Alas! this is not faith, but *credulity!* Men will
believe anything but that which is revealed—that which is true.
Jesus forewarned the world that it would be so when He said,

> "I am come [to you] in my Father's name, and ye receive
> me not: if another shall come in his own name, *him ye will
> receive*" (John 5:43).

A religion in which man is exalted, in which the priesthood of the Lord Jesus Christ is interfered with and intruded on, in which puppets of the earth call themselves sacrificing priests; a religion in which idolatry is perpetrated as truly as ever it was when Aaron and Israel made the golden calf and proclaimed a feast to Jehovah, is being imposed on us. Remember, it is written they proclaimed a feast *to Jehovah* and worshiped a calf! It might be said they understood and intended by the calf only something which *represented* Jehovah. Exactly so, but therein consisted *their idolatry* before God. Have we forgotten the second commandment?

> "Thou shalt *not* make unto thee any graven image, or *any likeness* of anything that is in heaven above, or that is in the earth beneath, or that is in the water under the earth: thou shalt *not bow down* thyself to them, nor serve them" (Exod. 20:4, 5).

And who will tell us that in the day in which we live there is not a practical worship of sacramental emblems; the worship of bread and wine. We may hide it from ourselves as we like, but who has not observed at the Lord's table, the superstitious, unscriptural way in which some receive that bread and wine? A material, sensuous religion is the world's delight. Christ gave to His people *the Word of God;* faithless churches substitute for it their priesthood and their sacraments. Until lately, the sort of religion I am rash enough to describe, was confined to the Church of Rome; there you have a sensuous religion in perfection, visible, material objects, for worship—an earthly and pompous priesthood claiming a divine right to be the exclusive channels of almighty grace, professing to have power and authority to impart spiritual life *"in baptism,"* a life to be subsequently nourished and maintained by what they call the action of the divine *"sacrifice on the altar,"* but which blessed sacrament is in truth our Lord's own loving memorial left with us that we may show forth His death until He come. Nor is this all. Confession of sin is demanded and absolution given, and all spiritual transactions between God and the soul are professedly undertaken and accomplished by *sinful men,* calling themselves priests of God. Can we wonder at the almost absolute power and control exercised by them over the consciences and feelings of those who believe in them? Until lately, I say, this religion was *Roman!* now, alas! it is becoming *Anglican.* And when we think of this being in a Bible-flooded, privileged land, we are reminded of the apostle's indignant and yet sorrowful expostulation—

> "Ye suffer fools gladly, seeing ye yourselves are wise. For ye suffer, if a man bring you into bondage, if a man devour you, if a man take of you, if a man exalt himself, if a man smite you on the face" (II Cor. 11:19, 20).

May God Almighty keep us close to His Word. You will *not* find *these things* in the Word of God, however you may find *plausible arguments* for such things in the naturally *imperfect* forms and ceremonies men have invented or compiled.

Well, the world's religion is a common one, and the world's religionist is *an everyday character.* Let me try and describe him for you,—he is regular at ordinances, careful to observe seasons *ordained by the church;* he gives his money liberally to the church, and to relieve the poor; he tries to do his duty, and is pretty confident that he is not altogether unsuccessful in performing it to God and to man; he leaves it to bigots and to clergymen to argue about creeds, and he thanks God that he is much more open-hearted and liberal than many he sees about him! Here is just a companion for the Pharisee who stood in the temple and thanked God that he was not as other men are, "or even like this publican." You will say, And is not such a man in a fair way to heaven? Amiable, kind, generous, doing his best, surely such an one *is* on his way to heaven! But the Word of God declares, *if that be all,* he shall never enter into the kingdom of God. The glorious home into which the Lord Jesus Christ entered to prepare a place for those who receive His Word has only *one door,* and that door is *Himself;* if we do not enter by that Door we cannot enter at all. There is but *one title* to that inheritance, and that is the *precious blood* of Jesus; away with all our titles, if we have not this title we shall be utterly refused, and all the more disappointed when we present ourselves, to find all our own arrangements, all the church arrangements, and all the priest's arrangements ignored, for there is only *"one name* under heaven given among men whereby we must be saved," the name of the Lord Jesus Christ. And if we have not that name in our heart, and in our creed, if His love, His life, His salvation are not *made ours* by faith, we will never enter the kingdom of God. This is the word the Lord Jesus left with His disciples.

There is also *one meetness* for heaven, and that is the Holy Ghost dwelling in us; there is *one means* whereby the Holy Ghost, and life, and joy, and peace may be obtained—*the precious Word of God;* for which men substitute services, ordinances, sacraments, confessions, and I know not what. The Lord did not say, I have given them *these,* but *"I have given them thy word";* "and the world hath hated them, because *they are not of the world,* even as I am not of the world."

There are three requisites laid down in the Word of God as essential to true Christianity. One is *regeneration*—a new and divine life in the soul; another is *separation* from the world; and another is *consecration* to God. There is no divine religion, no true Christianity without these. Regeneration is not by baptism, it is by the Word of God, which liveth and abideth forever. I suppose St. Peter knew how this life was bestowed; read I Peter 1:23, and you find

> "Being born again, not of corruptible seed, but of incorruptible by the word of God, which liveth and abideth forever."

Separation from the world is the result of the reception of Christ into the heart; it does not consist in sisterhoods, and monasteries, or ascetic communities, it consists in the heart having learned Him; and the heart that has received Him, can be with Him even in a crowd. The third principle is consecration to God, and that not upon saints' days and holy days, or at Lenten times only. It is strange how much larger our congregations are in Lent than when Lent is over. Is it only for Lent, people come? Is it only for Sabbath days, men consecrate themselves to God? This is the world's religion. People will attend to all ordinances and then spend the rest of the day as *the world invites them,* and go to the world's pleasures, to the world's follies, and to the world's sins. Such religion the world will never disapprove of, nor can it, because it ministers to the world; *but it is not the way to God.*

Probably there is nothing in the Word of God which more excites the enmity of the world against the saints of God, as receivers of His Word, than the sovereignty of the grace it teaches them to profess, and the assurance of salvation it enables them to enjoy.

The world calls the first bigotry, and the latter presumption! But every man who has been called out of darkness into light will acknowledge that he owes to the sovereign grace of God that he has ever been brought to know the Lord Jesus Christ; that grace, whose breadth, and length, and depth, and height no man can fathom or describe, has made him to differ. However men may theorize about the doctrine, yet, in the individual case, no man has ever come to Christ who has not been made conscious that omnipotent grace laid hold upon him, and omnipotent love constrained him, and would not let him go, and that it was the sovereign grace of God alone which brought him out of darkness into His own marvelous light, and from the power of sin and Satan unto God. The world's self-esteem is offended, as it reads:

> "I thank thee, O Father, Lord of heaven and earth, because thou hast hid these things from the wise and prudent, and hast revealed them unto babes. Even so, Father, for so it seemed good in thy sight" (Matt. 11:25, 26).

How it wounds proud human nature to be told that all the world's boasted learning goes for nothing, that all the world's great wisdom goes for nothing, that

> "The natural man receiveth not the things of the Spirit of God" (I Cor. 2:14),

and that

> "After that in the wisdom of God the world by wisdom knew not God, it pleased God, by *the foolishness* of preaching, to save them that believe" (I Cor. 1:21);

that Christ crucified is unto

> "The Jews a stumbling-block, and unto the Greeks foolishness; but unto them that believe, both Jews and Greeks, Christ the power of God, and the wisdom of God" (I Cor. 1:23, 24).

The world hates such teaching; then our assurance of salvation which the Lord gives His people, enabling us to rejoice with joy unspeakable and full of glory,—knowing that He has given us eternal life, and that He gave it to us in Christ Jesus, *before the world was!* The world asks, How do we know? Because He says it!

> "We know that when he shall appear we shall be like him, for we shall see him as he is" (I John 3:2).

How do we know? His Word reveals it.

> "I know that my redeemer liveth, and that he shall stand at the latter day upon the earth: and though, after my skin, worms destroy this body, yet in my flesh shall I see God: whom I shall see for myself, and mine eyes shall behold, and not another" (Job 19:25–27).

The devil and unbelieving men try to impose other substitutes for the Word of God; the professing church, her sacraments, priestism, forms, rites, ceremonies and traditions—alas the churches of Christendom have neglected God's Word! And while men slept the devil has sown tares (cf. Matt. 13:25). People now almost worship the church; God *will judge the church.* There was a time when the church was in danger of being corrupted by the world; take heed if we be not in danger of seeing the world corrupted by the church. Let us judge all things and all men by the Word of God, and not the Word of God by human systems—many of them human follies,—for by the Word of God we stand or fall.

"And the world hath hated them." This is the world that men love, and pet and pursue and fondle and imitate—*the world for which men educate their children;* this is the world whose society men love to mix with, and whose smiles they court—whose ways and principles and habits and worship they imitate, and where they find their choicest companions. Christians escape the cross by doing so, but do not please Him who said, "I have given them thy word; and the world hath hated them, because they are not of the world even as I am not of the world."

25

AS EACH PETITION is expressed for His dear people, our Lord seems to open out His whole heart afresh, and this shows how dearly He loved them, how fully He knew them, and how deeply intent He was upon providing for all their need, for all their cases of difficulty, and for all their circumstances of sorrow. Our Lord Jesus Christ could not express more; nor could His disciples, under any circumstances that ever might arise in their earthly history, need more than our blessed Lord asks for them. His petitions were not for His disciples alone, but for them also which should believe on Him through their word; and they embrace every blessing of the Father's everlasting love. Yet methinks the words we have just now read must have sounded very strangely in their ears, "I pray not that thou shouldest take them out of the world." They had heard Him say, "All mine are thine, and thine are mine; and I am glorified in them." They had heard Him plead, "These are in the world, and I come to thee"; and yet He says, "I pray not that thou shouldest take them out of the world." Our Lord was soon to leave His dear people, and He speaks as He here does in their hearing, that when He should be in glory they might remember what He had said while He was with them on earth, and not only so, but that the remembrance of what He had said might comfort them in all their tribulations, and that, notwithstanding the many trials in the wilderness, "they might have his joy fulfilled in themselves."

Perhaps it may have occurred to us as exceedingly strange, perplexing, and mysterious, that we should find ourselves in a world such as this, in which we are subject to evil thoughts and evil desires; prone in ourselves to what is evil, and impotent for anything that is good, surrounded on every side by difficulties and temptations,—fightings without and fears within: where we are constantly solicited by an evil heart of unbelief to do what we ought not to do, and to be what we ought not to be— a world which is filled with the peculiar attractions suited to our fallen corrupt nature; where we have to

> "Wrestle not only against flesh and blood, but against principalities, against powers, against the rulers of the darkness of this world, against spiritual wickedness in high places" (Eph. 6:12);

forces which, humanly speaking, it is impossible for us either to avoid or to overcome. And to hear our Lord say under such circumstances, "I pray not that thou shouldest take them out of the world," is surely something very wonderful, if not very mysterious.

Let us enquire how is it, and why is it He thus speaks? Is it that He was not able to remove His people out of the trials and temptations, the difficulties, disappointments, and snares of this world?

> "All power is given unto me in heaven and in earth" (Matt. 28:19).

Is it that He was not willing to take them out of the world, if the removal were really for their good? Oh, no! He

> "Gave himself for our sins, *that he might deliver* us from this present evil world" (Gal. 1:4).

Is it that His victory over the world was not complete? We have His own word for it,

> "I have overcome the world" (John 16:33).

Is it that He was not aware of the character and enmity of this world in which He was leaving His people?

> "In the world ye shall have tribulation. . . . If the world hate you, ye know that it hated me before it hated you" (John 16:33; 15:18).

Father, "the world hath hated them."

> "And all that is in the world, the lust of the flesh, and the lust of the eyes and the pride of life, is not of the Father, but is of the world" (I John 2:16).

He knew all! Is it that He did not love them, or that He was indifferent to the trials, disappointments, difficulties, and persecutions which awaited them? By no means. He loved them, and gave Himself for them, and

> "Having loved his own which were in the world, he loved them unto the end" (John 13:1).

The sufferings of His people in this present time are the

> "Filling up that which is behind of the afflictions of Christ."

Is it that He did not know their weakness, their failures, and wanderings, that He was not aware that they would often and sadly fall, grieving themselves and grieving Him? He knew all.

> "My substance was not hid from thee, when I was made in secret, and curiously wrought in the lowest parts of the earth, thine eyes did see my substance, yet being unperfect; and in thy book all my members were written, which in continuance were fashioned, when as yet there were none of them" (Ps. 139:15, 16).
>
> "Like as a father pitieth his children, so the Lord pitieth them that fear him; for he knoweth our frame; he remembereth that we are dust" (Ps. 103:13, 14).

Is it that they were *not* His own children, the purchase of His blood, the gift of His Father? Why, not less than seven times in

this prayer alone, He speaks of them as His own, given to Him
of His Father! Is it that He had not manifested to them His
Father's name, or given to them His Father's Word? Nay, He
had just told the Father in their hearing that He had done *both
the one and the other!* Is it that they had not believed His
Word? He had just declared for them and of them, "they have
received" Thy words, "they have believed that thou didst send
me!" Is it that He had not secured to them the Holy Ghost?

> "I will pray the Father, and he shall give you another Com-
> forter, that he may abide with you for ever" (John 14:16).

Is it that they were not united to Himself, partakers of His grace,
and to be partakers of His glory?

> "The glory which thou gavest me I have given them; that
> they may be one, even as we are one."

And yet hear Him, "I pray not that thou shouldest take them
out of the world." Under all these circumstances, we might have
thought His prayer would have been exactly the opposite; we
might have expected Him to say, "Father, remove My redeemed
ones, translate My treasured portion from the world's corrupted
and corrupting atmosphere, from a scene where tears and conflicts and tribulations and failures and humiliations, and distresses will surround them on every side; Father, I have revealed
Thy love to them; I have fulfilled Thy law; I have magnified
Thy name; I have brought in everlasting righteousness; I have
entitled Thee to send them the Holy Ghost, and to make them
Thy living temples; I have purchased and bequeathed to them
their inheritance; and now, Father, translate them that they
may be with Myself, where no tears can dim their eyes, where no
sorrow can chill their hearts, and where Thou art all and in all!"
We might suppose that *this* would have been the Lord's prayer,
but He does not desire it; on the contrary, He distinctly states,
"I pray not that thou shouldest take them out of the world."

We may learn here at the outset, how very little qualified we are to judge of the ways of God in His dealings with His people; how very little we can understand or fathom the depths of His wisdom, His love, and His goodness; nay, how very much we are in danger, if we keep not closely to His Word, of misunderstanding His dealings with us. Here we are in the world—a world that hated Christ and crucified Him; a world where every sort of evil surrounds us, and where every temptation suited to poor fallen nature besets us on every side; a world which it is utterly impossible to pass through without being sullied on the way, yet we are sent into it by Christ, and being sent into it we hear Him say to His Father and our Father, "I pray not that thou shouldest take them out of the world." It is not a kind world to His people, it is not a holy world, and our passage through it is oftentimes a weary one, weary to ourselves—and may we not add, weary to our God? For we have wearied Him with our iniquities, and make Him to serve with our sins (cf. Isa. 43:23). As easy would it have been for Him to remove us immediately, in the power of that blood which was presented in heaven on our behalf; as easy would it have been for the Lord Jesus, after having perfectly forgiven us, and perfectly justified us, and sanctified us, and adopted us into the family of the great King, and given us to be heirs of God, and joint heirs with Himself; as easy to have brought us away in Himself, with Himself, and for Himself, and to Himself, into the glory which He had with the Father before the world was. Yet He says, "I pray not that thou shouldest take them out of the world."

Truly, there must be many and potent reasons why, under all these circumstances, we should be left here. However, of one thing we may be quite sure, it is for the glory of the Lord we are here, in the world; and if so, depend upon it we are not here at our own charges, depend upon it we are not left to battle in our own strength, nor are we here without the sympathy of Him who is love itself, nor without the saving help of His right hand.

"Whatsoever things were written aforetime were written
for our learning, that we through patience and comfort of the
Scriptures, might have hope" (Rom. 15:4).

Now, we read that when the Lord delivered His people out of
the land of Egypt, He led them by the Red Sea into the wilderness. Refer for a moment to Psalm 107:

"They wandered in the wilderness, in a solitary way; . . .
He led them forth by *the right way*."

It may have been a solitary way, but it was the right way.

"They found *no city* to dwell in; . . .
That they might *go to a city* of habitation; . . .
Hungry and thirsty, their soul fainted in them; . . .
He *satisfieth* the longing soul, and *filleth* the hungry soul
with goodness; . . .
[They sat] in darkness and in the shadow of death, being
bound in affliction and iron; . . .
He *brought them out of darkness* and the shadow of death,
and brake their bands in sunder."

Read Deuteronomy 8:2, 3:

"Thou shalt remember all the way which the Lord thy God
led thee these forty years in the wilderness, to humble thee, and
to prove thee, to know what was in thine heart, whether thou
wouldest keep his commandments, or no. And he humbled
thee, and suffered thee to hunger, and fed thee with manna,
which thou knewest not, neither did thy fathers know; that he
might make thee know that man doth not live by bread only,
but by every word that proceedeth out of the mouth of the Lord
doth man live."

Remember, when our Lord Jesus Christ was upon the earth, in
the days of His flesh, when the heaven was opened unto Him,
and His Father's voice was heard proclaiming, "This is my beloved Son, in whom I am well pleased," when the Holy Ghost
descended like a dove, and abode upon Him, the first thing the
Spirit did was to lead Him into the wilderness to be tempted of
the devil.

> "Though he were a son, yet learned he obedience by the things which he suffered" (Heb. 5:8).

And into the wilderness our Father leads all His children.

> "Behold I will allure her, and bring her into the wilderness, and speak comfortably unto her. And I will give her her vineyards from thence, and the valley of Achor for a door of hope: and she shall sing there, as in the days of her youth, and as in the day when she came up out of the land of Egypt" (Hosea 2:14, 15).

I will mention four reasons, out of many, which we may suppose prompted our Lord to say, "I pray not that thou shouldest take them out of the world."

I. Perhaps this weary wilderness is the only place—certainly it is the *best* place—in which to *teach* us the most important lessons that can be learned outside heaven, and which it is absolutely necessary for every child of God experimentally to learn. And what are they? 1. We are here to learn *our own nothingness,* our weakness, our emptiness, our untold unworthiness; the variety of our corruptions, and the strangeness and greatness of our unbelief. God knows there is no place like the world for teaching lessons like these. 2. We are here to learn the *strength* and *number* of *our enemies.* Verily, they are like giants, and we as grasshoppers, one of them could chase a thousand of us; we are no match for the great trinity of evil—"the world, the flesh, and the devil"; we find ourselves crushed before the moth, bruised reeds are not more weak, and smoking flax not so easily quenched as is the strength of the poor sinner. We wrestle with the strong powers of darkness, and it is well that we should know our own weakness, on the one hand, and the strength and malice of our foes, on the other. 3. We are here to learn—and the world is well suited as the place to teach us—the faithfulness, the love, the care, the longsuffering, and the goodness of our God. Oh! how He holds us, how He keeps us, shelters us, carries us as on eagles' wings, else surely by this time we should have been utterly swallowed up.

II. But there is another reason why the Lord said, "I pray not that thou shouldest take them out of the world." We are *pre-destinated* by our heavenly Father "to be conformed to the image of his Son." In heaven we shall be conformed to His image, as He is, in the glory, but we are left in this world's wilderness to be made conformable to His image in suffering,

> "To know the fellowship of his sufferings, being made conformable to his death" (Phil. 3:10)

—to be like *Him* rejected of the world, to be like *Him* tempted of the evil one, to be like *Him* loving, trustful dependents upon the care and faithfulness of our Father, living a life of faith, drawing upon the Father for hope, for strength, for joy, for peace, for protection; for victory, for everything. Therefore are we in the world.

III. Another reason is, this world belongs to Christ. He has a kingdom *in* the world, though His kingdom is not *of* the world; and He needs servants to serve Him here, He needs ambassadors to go upon His messages, He needs witnesses to testify of the glory of His grace, He needs subjects to do His will, to keep His charge, to be made happy under His rule, and to wait for His coming. Thank God for the privilege of being in the world, to witness for Him where He is rejected, though it be but for a little while! Thank God for the privilege of being allowed to glorify Him in the world (the *only* place in which He asks us to glorify Him), and to go now and then upon His business! Oh! would we had more heart for it, would that we were more true to Him as the subjects of His kingdom.

IV. Another reason is, the world is yours, not only Christ's, but yours: in I Corinthians 3:22, we learn the amazing truth, "the world is yours." God has given it to you as "the *field*" in which you are to sow the seeds of eternal truth and life, and where you are to gather a harvest for the great God. The world is yours—the *battle-plain* where God has placed you to fight the good fight of faith, His own enlisted soldiers, armed with all the armour of God, and where He has promised to make you more than conquerors through Him that loved you (cf. Rom. 8:37). There you are to battle with the prince of darkness, there you are to battle with the flesh and the world. The world is yours,—it is the *great deep* where storms so ofttimes rock us, where billows so ofttimes seem to roll over our souls, where many a sunken rock is hidden, and where many a gallant ship has foundered. We are here to prove the skill of our Pilot. Jesus is at the helm. The world is yours. It is *the school* to which God has sent us to learn most important lessons. We are here to learn *what sin is.* People make a great mistake as to why Christians are in the world; it is not that they may be made angels of, but that they may learn what sin is, and what self is, that they may know experimentally how to wait patiently upon the Lord. Some children of God are sadly tried and exercised in the world. There are some who seem never to be rid of sore temptations, others are afflicted with grievous bodily pain and suffering, others lose all the friends they loved best on earth, others are allowed to outlive the use of their faculties.

"Fear none of those things which ye shall suffer" (Rev. 2:10).

If we had cause to fear them we had never heard Him say, "I pray not that thou shouldest take them out of the world." The answer to all our hearts' disquieting anxieties and disturbing fears is this:

"Be still and know that I am God" (Ps. 46:10).

The world is yours. It is the *hospital* where we can minister to Christ's members, and in ministering to His members we are privileged to minister to Himself.

"I was an hungred, and ye gave me meat: I was thirsty, and
ye gave me drink: I was a stranger, and ye took me in: naked,
and ye clothed me: I was sick, and ye visited me: I was in
prison, and ye came unto me. . . . Inasmuch as ye have done
it unto the least of these my brethren, ye have done it unto
me" (Matt. 25:35, 36, 40).

These are services which can be rendered to God and to His
Christ, only while we are in the world. Who would wish to
forego the privilege, who understands how much he owes? The
world is yours. It is our opportunity for trusting Christ, even
though we walk in darkness and have no light. It is our opportunity for committing to Him our all, for time and for eternity,
and hoping to the end for the grace that is to be brought unto
us at the revelation of Jesus Christ. "The world" is our opportunity for making it manifest that though we have not seen
Him, we love Him better than the things we see. It is greatly
for the Lord's glory that it should be so; therefore, "I pray not
that thou shouldest take them out of the world."

Let us then be content to remain. It costs our loving Christ
far more to have us *here* than it *can* cost us. Remember this!
Our circumstances of trial are His circumstances of trial, and
they call forth all His sympathy; His presence shall surely go
with us. He is never so near His plants as when they are being
pruned by Him; He will never leave us, never forsake us. His
glory is more fully displayed in keeping us from the evil *here,*
than in crowning us with the glory *there.* And if at any time,
under the pressure of great trial, and wearied by reason of the
disappointments and the crushing sorrows of the way, we pray
the Father to take us hence, we are thinking more of our own
ease than of His glory, who said, "I pray not that thou shouldest
take them out of the world."

Now let us enumerate a few of the encouragements our Lord
has left with His people, to support them while they are in the

world. And first (I write as to believing children of God), the question of our salvation is *settled;* we *are* saved!——

> "Saved in the Lord with an everlasting salvation" (Isa. 45:17).

We are not *of* this world, though we are *in* it. We have been translated *out* of the kingdom of darkness, we have been introduced *into* the kingdom of God's dear Son; our title has not to be made out, it has been *already* secured to us. The precious blood is our title, and He who shed it has gone within the veil to present it, as our Representative. Our meetness and qualification for heaven and for glory has not to be bestowed, it has been *already* given. Our meetness is the Holy Ghost who dwelleth in us. The moment the Holy Ghost enters the soul of a believing sinner, that man is as "meet for glory" as if he lived in the school of grace for a thousand years. These considerations are most important.

> "[Let us give] thanks unto the Father, which hath made us meet to be partakers of the inheritance of the saints in light" (Col. 1:12).
> "Things present or things to come cannot separate us from the love of God" (Rom. 8:39);

our inheritance is secure, and,

> "Our fellowship is with the Father, and with his Son Jesus Christ" (I John 1:3).

If we are left here it is because the Lord has need of our emptiness, our weakness, the variety of our temptations and temperaments, the peculiar character of our corruptions, the disappointments, the dangers and difficulties with which His poor people are possessed and surrounded, that it may be made manifest that there never was a case, or a circumstance, or a sorrow, or a sin, or a difficulty, for which there was not a remedy and a supply in His fullness and in His love. Our need suits His fullness, and

His fullness corresponds to our need; there must needs be the infinite variety of cases, and of characters, of temptations, and necessities, which exist among the children of God, in order that there may be full scope, occasion and opportunity for displaying the infinite varieties of the fullness, the love, grace, mercy, and salvation, laid up in the Lord Jesus Christ for His dear people, and that in their relief and deliverance from all their troubles, He might win for Himself an everlasting name.

So long, then, as there remains one lesson to be learned concerning our Saviour's grace, or our own need, so long as the love which passeth knowledge may be more fully known, so long as there is anything to be done for Him, or anything to be suffered in His cause, so long as there is a soul to be comforted, a poor wanderer to be brought home, or a mourner to be cheered, let us be willing to be here, and to tarry our Lord's leisure, even though our lot be cast where Satan dwelleth. His eye is upon us; He will not leave us nor forsake us. He who said "I pray not that Thou shouldest take them out of the world" knows well how to keep us in it.

May our souls drink more into His Spirit and have more dealings with His love, and with His Word, while we remain here, for His name's sake!

26

"I PRAY NOT THAT THOU SHOULDEST TAKE THEM OUT OF
THE WORLD, BUT THAT THOU SHOULDEST KEEP
THEM FROM THE EVIL."—John 17:15

YOU OBSERVE there are two things taken for granted all
through this prayer—first, their conversion to God; and,
secondly, the mutual interest which His people have in Christ,
and which Christ has in them. He does not pray for these things,
He speaks of them as *matters of fact:* "I have given unto them
the words which thou gavest me; and they *have received them,*
and they have known surely that I came out from thee, and *they
have* believed that thou didst send me." Then, with *one* exception, in verse 24, where He prays, "Father, I will that they also,
whom thou hast given me, be with me where I am; that they
may behold my glory, which thou hast given me," all the rest
of the prayer, from beginning to end, is for their protection in
the world, and their sanctification through the truth.

"Keep them from the evil" is the burden of His entire prayer.
"Keep them from the evil" is the boon which He pleads for with
His Father, urging every possible consideration in order that it
may be surely granted. "Glorify thy Son," in keeping them. "I
have given them thy word!" "Keep them." "I pray for them!"
"Keep them." "I am glorified in them!" "Keep them." Holy
Father! "keep them." I plead Thy name. I plead Thy gift of
them to Me. I plead Thy Word. The world hates them. "They
are not of the world, even as I am not of the world." "Keep
them." "I pray not thou shouldest take them out of the world,
but that thou shouldest keep them from the evil." I leave them

here in the world, to learn their own great need, their indescribable weakness and emptiness; I leave them here to learn the strength of the foes with which they have to battle, and from which I have pledged Myself to deliver them; I leave them here, that they may learn their Father's loving, tender, holy keeping. Father! "keep them from the evil."

A most interesting and most important question here suggests itself for our consideration. We may not doubt—indeed, we dare not doubt—that our Lord's prayer for His disciples has been heard and answered; and not for His disciples only. "Neither pray I for these alone, but for them also which shall believe on me through their word." We cannot doubt that the prayer, "keep them," has been registered in the heart of God. Indeed, the relation of Jehovah to His people as their keeper is the burden of many an Old Testament promise. For instance,

> "He will keep the feet of His saints" (I Sam. 2:9);
> "He that keepeth [thee] shall neither slumber nor sleep. The Lord is thy keeper" (Ps. 121:4, 5);
> "He shall preserve thee from all evil: he shall preserve thy soul" (Ps. 121:7).

So, also, the burden of some of the most precious promises of the New Testament has reference to this relationship of the Lord to His people.

> "The Lord is faithful, who shall stablish you, and keep you from evil" (II Thess. 3:3).
> "He is able to keep that which I have committed unto Him against that day" (II Tim. 1:12).

You remember St. Peter's beautiful description,

> "Kept by the power of God through faith unto salvation" (I Peter 1:5).

Such is his inspired account of the security of the Lord's people. Now, as all these promises and engagements had reference to the Lord Jesus Christ in His person and work for sinners, so

His prayer is the seal and the endorsement and confirmation of them. "I pray not that thou shouldest take them out of the world, but that thou shouldest keep them from the evil"; and tenderly they are kept constantly, effectually, triumphantly, they are kept from all evil, all the time they are in the world, else surely the Lord's prayer has not been answered. I do not see how the truth of this can be questioned.

Now if this prayer has been heard, *How is it answered?*

1. The history of the Church of God, and the individual experience of every member of it, sufficiently proves that we are not secured from outward tribulations, distresses, persecutions, obloquy, and even violent assaults from the world, the flesh, and the devil. A glance at the apostle's account in I Corinthians 4: 9–13, will sufficiently evidence this:

> "I think that God hath set forth us the apostles last, as it were appointed to death: for we are made a spectacle unto the world, and to angels, and to men. We are fools . . . we are weak . . . we are despised. Even unto this present hour we both hunger, and thirst, and are naked, and are buffeted, and have no certain dwellingplace . . . being reviled . . . being persecuted . . . being defamed . . . we are made as the filth of the world, and are the offscouring of all things unto this day."

And yet the Lord Jesus prayed, and the Lord Jesus Christ was heard, "Keep them from the evil."

2. The experience of the Church of God, and the individual experience of every member of it, also proves that we are not secured from *spiritual conflicts.* A glance at Ephesians 6 will prove the truth of what I say, even if our own experience did not prove it. In verses 11, 12, we are counseled to

> "Put on the whole armour of God, that [we] may be able to stand against the wiles of the devil. For we wrestle not against flesh and blood, but against principalities, against powers, against the rulers of the darkness of this world, against spiritual wickedness in high places";

and we are not always successful in the struggle. Yet the Lord
Jesus Christ prayed, and the Lord Jesus Christ was heard, "Keep
them from the evil."

3. The experience of the Church of God, and of every individual member of it, also proves that we are not secured from
temptations arising from various sources; they are even called
in Scripture *"fiery trials,"* not only resulting from the malice of
the devil, and the weakness of self, but from contact with the
evil which is in the world, the entanglements of the world, evil
companionships which we cannot get rid of, evil influences, and
evil associations. And yet the Lord prayed, and the Lord has
heard, "Keep them from the evil."

4. Nor are we secured from *humiliating failures* in service.
Witness Peter, how humbling was the failure of that great
apostle. Witness the failure of all the other apostles in the hour
of their Master's need,

> "They all forsook him and fled" (Mark 14:50).

What shameful cowardice; what humiliating ingratitude! Subsequently, in the Acts of the Apostles, we find them disputing
with one another, and the dissension in one instance was so great
between Paul and Barnabas that

> "They departed asunder, one from the other" (Acts 15:39).

And after all his experience of his own weakness, Peter again
failed; he was found dissembling, and was openly rebuked before the whole church. These were truly very sad failures. Yet
the Lord prayed, and the Lord was heard, "Keep them from the
evil."

5. Our experience proves that we are not secured from *grievous bodily suffering,* nor from crushing bereavements, loss of
health, loss of substance, death itself; and *painful* dying. Yet
the Lord Jesus Christ prayed, and was heard, "Keep them from
the evil."

6. We are not secured—surely our own experience endorses what I say—we are not secured from *the burden of self,* we are not secured from the conscious coldness, hardness, and deadness of our own corrupt heart and nature. Is it only the apostle Paul who was compelled to cry,

> "O wretched man that I am! who shall deliver me from the body of this death?" (Rom. 7:24).

Was it only the apostle who had need to confess,

> "We that are in this tabernacle do groan, being burdened" (I Cor. 5:4)?

And yet the Lord Jesus Christ prayed, and was heard, "Keep them from the evil."

7. And, we are not secured from *actual sin!*

> "If we say that we have no sin, we deceive ourselves, and the truth is not in us. . . .
> "If we say that we have not sinned, we make him a liar" (I John 1:8, 10).

Surely it is no empty confession we make day after day in the house of God: "We have erred, and strayed from Thy ways like lost sheep. We have left undone those things which we ought to have done; and we have done those things we ought not to have done; and there is no health in us." And yet the Lord Jesus Christ prayed, and the Lord Jesus Christ was heard, Father, "Keep them from the evil."

Now, if this be so, not one of these, nor all of them together, constitute *evil* to the people of God; or, if evil in themselves, our Lord Jesus Christ's prayer secures that good shall be brought out of the evil, and that all these things

> "Shall work together for good to them that love God" (Rom. 8:28).

Nothing is really evil but that which can separate us from the love of God; I repeat it, nothing on earth or in hell is really evil

to us but that which can separate us from the love of God. And
I pray you

> "Shall tribulations, or distresses, or persecutions, or famine,
> or nakedness, or peril, or sword be able to separate us from the
> love of God which is in Christ Jesus? . . . Nay, in all these
> things we are more than conquerors through him that loved
> us" (see Rom. 8:35, 37, 39).

Shall spiritual conflicts separate us from the love of God?

> "My grace is sufficient for thee; for my strength is made per-
> fect in weakness" (II Cor. 12:9).

Can strong temptations separate us from the love of God? It
is written

> "God is faithful, who will not suffer you to be tempted above
> that ye are able; but will with the temptation also make a way
> to escape that ye may be able to bear it" (I Cor. 10:13).

Can humiliating failures separate us from the love of God?

> "I have prayed for thee, that thy faith fail not" (Luke
> 22:32)

was Peter's security, when Satan desired to have him that he
might sift him as wheat. Nor can grievous diseases separate us
from the love of God which is in Christ Jesus; nor bereavements, nor agonies, for

> "Whom the Lord loveth he chasteneth, and scourgeth every
> son whom he receiveth. If ye endure chastening, God dealeth
> with you as with sons; for what son is he whom the father
> chasteneth not?" (Heb. 12:6, 7).

Not self with all its burdens, nor the flesh with all its corruptions, can separate us from the love of God.

> "I am crucified with Christ" (Gal. 2:20),

and He

"Shall change our vile body, that it may be fashioned like unto his glorious body, according to the working whereby he is able even to subdue all things unto himself" (Phil. 3:21).

Not even our very *sins* can separate us from the love of God, for

"If we confess our sins, he is faithful and just to forgive us our sins, and to cleanse us from all unrighteousness" (I John 1:9).

We may be puzzled and perplexed by God's mysterious dealings with us, we may sometimes misunderstand the dispensations with which He permits us to be exercised, we may sometimes make mistakes as to what has and what had not been promised; but one fact we may rest upon—there is no mistake about this, He has prayed, *"Keep them from the evil."*

What, then, is the blessing for which the Lord Jesus Christ here prayed? and what is the evil from which all His people, all who believe upon Him, are everlastingly secure? From all *spiritual hurt.* You remember, in Psalm 121 which so beautifully sets forth Jehovah as the Keeper of His people, the emphasis is on this (v. 7),

"The Lord shall preserve thee from all evil; *he shall preserve thy soul.*"

That is only evil *to us* which can hurt *the soul;* all the other things which we may think evil, and call evil, shall work together for our good. The evil that can hurt the soul shall never come nigh our dwelling, for the Lord Jesus prayed, "Keep them from the evil." No evil, no hurt, no loss, no spiritual evil, can evermore prevail to injure the soul of any child of God, whether it arise from the evil one, or from the hatred of the world to Christ and to His cause, or from our own poor, wretched, fallen nature, or from the dominion or the consequences of sin. For the first, we have the promise,

"Sin shall not have dominion over you, for ye are not under
the law, but under grace" (Rom. 6:14);

and for the second, there is the fact that sin and the penal consequences of sin are already put away. None of the evils arising
from the snares and blandishments, the attractions, and temptations of the world, can evermore avail to hurt our souls. Not
even the peculiar besetting sins of which each poor child of
God is conscious, and over which he mourns; not even his falls
shall be permitted to hurt his soul.

"Rejoice not against me, O mine enemy: when I fall I shall
arise" (Mic. 7:8).

He that kept the children of Israel in Egypt; He that kept the
Hebrew youths in the fiery furnace; He that kept Daniel in the
den of lions, shall keep His people from the evil that is in
the world, and make them more than conquerors through Him
that loved them.

Temptations can only manifest us to ourselves, failures can
only empty us of self, they cannot deprive us of our Christ;
difficulties can only humble us, and we cannot be humbled too
much; disappointments can only loosen the bonds of the world
around us, and disentangle us from its attractions; bodily pains
and bereavements can only chasten us; dissolution itself can
only deliver us; for

"Where sin abounded grace did much more abound" (Rom.
5:20).

"Father, I pray not that thou shouldest take them out of the
world, but that thou shouldest keep them from the evil."

"Fear not: for they that be with us, are more than they that
be with them" (II Kings 6:16).
"Because thou hast made the Lord, which is my refuge,
Even the Most High, thy habitation;
There shall no evil befall thee,
Neither shall any plague come nigh thy dwelling.

For he shall give his angels charge over thee, to keep thee in all thy ways. . . .

Thou shalt tread upon the lion and adder:

The young lion and the dragon shalt thou trample under feet.

Because he hath set his love upon me,

Therefore I will deliver him:

I will set him on high, because he hath known my name" (Ps. 91:9–14).

"Fear none of those things which thou shalt suffer: behold the devil shall cast some of you into prison, that ye may be tried; and ye shall have tribulation ten days: be thou faithful unto death, and I will give thee a crown of life" (Rev. 2:10).

"Because thou hast kept the word of my patience, I also will keep thee from the hour of temptation, which shall come upon all the world, to try them that dwell upon the earth" (Rev. 3:10).

We may be tempted by unbelief and ignorance, to say, with Jacob of old,

"All these things are against me" (Gen. 42:36);

we may, perhaps, be compelled to feel as he did when he stood before Pharaoh—

"The days of the years of my pilgrimage are an hundred and thirty years: *few and evil* have the days of the years of my life been" (Gen. 47:9).

but, ah! listen to him at the close (48:15, 16): he saith,

"God, before whom my fathers, Abraham and Isaac, did walk, the God which fed me all my life long, unto this day, *the Angel which redeemed me from all evil.*"

That was his testimony to our God, and that shall be the testimony every child of God shall one day render, as we look back upon the way by which the Lord led us, however entangled it may have been, however humbling to ourselves it may have been. Father, Thou didst redeem us from all evil!

Let us, then, come *boldly* with all our personal and peculiar difficulties and sorrows, our temptations and failures, to the throne of grace! He who sits upon that throne knows us fully; He looks within, He sees the evil that we feel, and how it affects us—our wants, our sorrows, our temptations, our fears, our miseries, our distresses. He has left us in the world that we might experience these things, that we might know the evils from which He has pledged Himself to deliver us. We had never known the triumphs of our Deliverer, we had never known the preciousness of His blood, we had never known the saving strength of His right hand, if we had not been made personally and experimentally acquainted with our special and peculiar need. He has left us here that we might have such communion with Himself, as even the glorified in heaven cannot know. Here walking in darkness and having no light, not seeing whither we go, the Holy Ghost enables us to put our hand into His hand, saying, Lord, lead me when Thou wilt, where Thou wilt, and as Thou wilt; in Thy strength, and by Thy grace, I will follow Thee. By-and-by when we come home to heaven He will *glorify us;* but it is only here in the wilderness, in which He has placed us, we can thus *glorify Him. It is not when we are enjoying Christ most that we glorify Him best;* it is when we are in the deepest humiliation by reason of the experience of our failures, when our hearts are consciously cold and dead, when our feelings are all distressing, when our experience is all against us, when we walk in darkness and have no light, when, like Job of old,

> "[We] go forward, but he is not there; and backward, but [we] cannot perceive him: on the left hand, where he doth work, but [we] cannot behold him; and he hideth himself on the right hand, that we cannot see him" (Job 23:8, 9).

Then to take Him upon the mere warrant of His Word and trust Him; *then,* when we have so little reason to be satisfied with ourselves, to take Him for our All in all, our "wisdom, righteousness, sanctification, and redemption," simply resting upon His own greatness, and faithfulness, and mercy, and truth —*truly no angel in heaven can glorify Him, as the poor sinner does who glorifies Him thus.*

Therefore, as He has left us here for this purpose, let us have but one thought, one aim, one object, one prayer, even that He would reveal Himself to us and teach us to live upon Him, and give Him credit for His love, that we might realize more and more the triumphs of His grace, and know assuredly how faithfully He will keep His promise,

> "I will never leave thee, nor forsake thee" (Heb. 13:5).

Often we have been cast down, and yet He has lifted us up; often we have been in circumstances out of which we thought there was no escape, and yet He delivered us; often we have been in dark, dark hours, and yet the light of the glory of God in the face of Jesus Christ *did* shine into us.

He has not changed, and He cannot change—blessed Lord Jesus, glorious Intercessor! He has a large, and helpless, and needy family, He knows it; He would have them know it too. He has fullness of life, and grace, peace, and rest, righteousness, sanctification, and redemption; all this is for them. He has fullness enough to supply all our need, and much more than all our need requires. There is more preciousness in His atoning blood than there is vileness in all our sins, more strength in His saving right hand than could support a thousandfold all our weakness. Oh!

> "[To] be able to comprehend with all saints what is the breadth and length and depth and height; and to know the love of Christ which passeth knowledge, that we might be filled with all the fullness of God" (Eph. 3:18, 19).

He could, if He pleased, immediately remove us, but in that case His glory would not be displayed in saving us from the evil, maintaining His own work in our souls, displaying His power, making His strength perfect in our weakness, and often causing the weakest in His flock to be a terror to Satan and a wonder to the world. Fear not,

"He giveth power to the faint; and to them that have no might he increaseth strength" (Isa. 40:29).

He is all-sufficient; He is "all in all"—our God, Saviour, Friend. He is all eye to watch over us, all ear to hear us, all heart to sympathize with us, and not upbraid us for our failures. Did we live more on the Lord in the exercise of faith, in His holy Word, we would go on our way "rejoicing even in tribulations," and

"Coming up out of the wilderness, leaning on our beloved" (S. of Sol. 8:5).

Let us then come boldly to the throne of grace, and when in the full consciousness of our utter unworthiness, and notwithstanding the difficulties within us and around us, we believe and trust in Him as God's great gift to us, and as our strong salvation, His object in leaving us in this world is well nigh accomplished, and all the evils that befall us in our way shall prove but the breezes and the billows to waft us onward, and bear us to our rest.

27

"THEY ARE NOT OF THE WORLD, EVEN AS I AM NOT OF THE
WORLD."—John 17:16

THIS FACT was evidently one of great importance in our
blessed Lord's mind, for it is the second time we find Him
urging it in behalf of His people. In verse 14, He says, "I have
given them thy word; and the world hath hated them, because
they are not of the world, even as I am not of the world." There
He assigns it as a reason why the world hated His people. And,
here again, He assigns it as a reason why they would be exposed
to much evil from the world, the flesh, and the devil, and He
makes it as an argument with His Father why He should keep
them from the evil.

"They are not of the world"; it is our dear Lord's own account of His people. Do not overlook the stigma which our
Lord's words cast upon the world, or the judgment of it which
they imply. He says in another place,

> "If ye were of the world, the world would love his own; but
> because ye are not of the world, but I have chosen you out of
> the world, therefore the world hateth you" (John 15:19).

Alas, manifestly the great majority of even professing Christians are unmistakably of the world; and yet the Lord says of
His disciples, "They are not of the world." By this He evidently
means not the material world, but the people of the world. The
world follows the things of the world, its principles and its
practices, its pleasures and pursuits; the world has its hopes, its
aims, its ends, and its desires, ay, and its *religion* too, all of them

not of the Father, but of the world; a fearful destiny awaits the world, for we read,

> "The earth also and *the works that are therein* shall be burned up" (II Peter 3:10);

but the Lord says of His people, "They are not of the world."

The Lord's people are taught by the Word of God to regard the principles of this world as not from above, but from beneath. They are taught that its practices, however applauded in the world, are sinful; that its pleasures are mere phantoms, that its pursuits are contrary to the revealed will of God, that its happiness is a mere shadow, that its boasted morality is only a splendid course of sin, that its one aim is self, that its religion is a delusion, and that its end is destruction.

The Holy Ghost enabled the apostles of the Lord (they were simple-minded men) to give utterance to their thoughts, they proclaimed what the Spirit of their Father taught them. They told the world what its true character, weighed in the balances of God's sanctuary, really was: and the world hated them, opposed them, and persecuted them unto death. And depend upon it, if the Lord's people were as faithful and outspoken, as the apostles were, they would find themselves in the same category. We get on with the world, because we are not honest with the world, or faithful to our God and to His truth. If we were to profess in the world what in our conscience we believe, and what we are taught of God concerning it, depend upon it we should find the world would hate us.

But what heavenly consolation, what divine encouragement our Lord's words supply, as we regard them from the *heavenward side*. "They are not of the world"—that implies they *are* of Christ, they *are* of the Father, they *are* of the light, they *are* of the truth, they have received God's Word, they bear Jehovah's name, they are identified with Christ and His cause. It is on this account the world hates them; it is on this account they are exposed to the evil that is in the world. They are left here for the glory of their Father, that they may be monuments to the everlasting grace of His most holy name, of the grace that kept them, of the Spirit that taught them, of the blood that washed them, of the righteousness that covered them, of the gracious faithful God that guided them, and made them more than conquerors over all within them, as well as over all without them, and caused the hatred and opposition of the world only to bring out into divine contrast His tender, constant care, and the all-prevailing intercession of their Christ.

So the Lord pleads. His words are as if He said, My Father, it is solely because Thy people *are Mine,* it is because they have received Thy Word, it is because of their love to Me, because of their identification with My cause, it is solely on this account they are hated by the world, and shall be despised and persecuted in the world; therefore, My Father, keep them, "keep through thine own name those thou hast given me"—"keep them from the evil." Truly it is a most wonderful and precious *secret* which our Lord here reveals, namely, that all the hatred and opposition of the world towards His people, all the plottings and plannings of the evil one against their souls, all the worry, the temptations, the distresses, the tribulations in which they are involved, are simply because "the evil one," "the god of this world," hates Christ, and because he would, if he could, grieve and wound Him through His members. Our Lord lays this fact before His Father in the hearing of His disciples for His people's comfort, and that they might understand the nature and cause of the incessant warfare of which they are conscious, and also to assure them that the enemies of their souls—the world, the flesh, and the devil—would evermore be utterly overthrown, utterly thwarted, utterly confounded in all their confederacies against His people, through His own intercession before the throne.

"They are not of the world." Let us lift up our hearts unto

the Lord. Let us ask Him for the light, and teaching of His
Holy Spirit, while we meditate upon the wondrous words before
us, revealing the true origin, portion, and destiny of God's believing people. And in order that our faith may grow exceedingly, and that we may experience in our own souls the victory
that overcometh the world.

"They are not of the world, even as I am not of the world."
Observe, our glorious Lord here asserts what He has taken for
granted all through His prayer, even the mutual interest and
relationship existing between His people and Himself. He did
not pray for *that;* He takes it for granted all through. What He
prays for is, that His people may enjoy *the fruits and results* of
it, in being kept and sanctified; that we may individually *manifest* it,

> "That the world may believe that thou hast sent me";

that we may anticipate *the fruition* of it. "Father, I will that they
also, whom thou hast given me, be with me where I am; that
they may behold my glory."

The great fact is not to be forgotten, that the Lord Jesus'
interest in us, and our interest in Him, given by our gracious
Jehovah's love before the world was, is the cause and source of
all the manifestations of His grace to us in time, and also of all
the manifestations of His glory to us in eternity. The incarnation of the Son of God was the result of the interest He had in
us;

> "Forasmuch as the children were partakers of flesh and
> blood, he also himself likewise took part of the same" (Heb.
> 2:14).

The gift of the Holy Ghost was also the result of our interest in
Him, for it is written,

> "Because ye are sons, God hath sent forth the Spirit of his
> Son into your hearts, crying, Abba, Father" (Gal. 4:6).

And all He is now doing for us by His intercession in heaven, and all that is to follow in His glorious kingdom hereafter, flows from the first great love that gave us to Christ, and gave Christ to us; and our Lord here pleads His identification of His people with Himself, in order that they may be secured from all evil; "they are not of the world, even as I am not of the world."

I. Let us consider these words, first as referring to *Christ Himself*—"I am not of the world." Our glorious Lord was not of the world as to *His origin*. No! He was "the Lord from heaven," "the King eternal, immortal, invisible, the only wise God," "who only hath immortality, dwelling in the light which no man can approach unto," "who being in the form of God, thought it not robbery to be equal with God." "Of the world?" He *made* the world!

> "In the beginning was the Word, and the Word was with God, and the Word was God . . . All things were made by him . . . And the Word was made flesh, and dwelt among us, (and we beheld his glory, the glory as of the only begotten of the Father) full of grace and truth" (John 1:1, 3, 14).
>
> "I am from above, ye are from beneath" (John 8:23).
>
> "The Lord from heaven . . . I am not of this world" (I Cor. 15:47).

"I am not of the world." His conversation was in heaven: He was in the world, but not of the world; bodily presence was here, but His home was in the heavens, His Father, His throne, His crown, His rest, His portion, were in the heavens; the glorious Lord lived there; no man hath ascended into heaven but "he that came down from heaven, even the Son of man which *is in heaven*." This was not His country; He was not a citizen of earthly cities; He was the King of the "city which hath foundations, whose builder and maker is God," where "they need no candle, neither light of the sun; for the Lord God giveth them light"; "and the Lamb is the light thereof."

He says (v. 11), *"Now I am no more in the world."* He was

just leaving it, and going to another. The glorious home from whence He descended was about to receive Him back again; the harps were waiting, the songs were silent, till He arrived; He was about to go to His Father and our Father, to His God and our God. That "Father's business" had detained Him for a little while, and would for a little longer detain Him here on earth; His people's salvation was not yet fully accomplished, He had yet a great fight to fight, He had yet a great atonement to make, He had yet a great offering to present; but it was as good as done: He was "not of the world," He was on His way home.

II. Now, mark what He also says of *His people,* "they are not of the world." Truly, this is a wonderful statement.

What an high origin our blessed Lord ascribes to His dear people—"They are not of the world, even as I am not of the world." *Their origin* is not of earth.

"Thine they were and thou gavest them me."

They were God's portion, God's inheritance, God's gift, His predestinated companions,

"Predestinated to be conformed to the image of his Son,"

that they might be suited companions for Jehovah; predestinated to share the glory of the Lord Jesus Christ, that they might be the happy children of their Father,

"[They are] born of God" (I John 3:9);
"Partakers of the divine nature" (II Peter 1:4);
"Heirs of God, and joint-heirs with Christ" (Rom. 8:17);

the brothers, sisters, and companions of God's Firstborn; they are the Bride of the Lamb, the members of His Body, the heirs of the promises; all things are theirs, "the world, life, death, things present and things to come, all theirs, because they are Christ's, and Christ is God's." This is their origin; for

"Both he that sanctifieth and they that are sanctified are all *of one:* for which cause he is not ashamed to call them brethren" (Heb. 2:11).

They are "not of the world, even as I am not of the world." No; their Father is *above!* Their home is *above!* Their portion is *above!* Their birth is *from above!*

> "A glorious high throne from the beginning is the place of our sanctuary" (Jer. 17:12),

although born on earth in order to learn many a difficult lesson which could hardly be learned elsewhere—Father, "keep them from the evil," for "thine they were, and thou gavest them me," and they are hated and opposed in the world because "they are not of the world, even as I am not of the world." Wonderful words! full of heavenly comfort. Listen! "Even as I am not of the world." This world *is not our country!* Does not our Great Head seem thus to express Himself associating Himself with His family? "Our conversation is in heaven." We are Thy children, Father! The laws and the liberties of heaven are our privileges, and the glory of heaven our rest! And, because Thou art there, our thoughts are there, our desires are there, our expectations are there, our *hearts* are there, because our *all* is there. What a glorious, loving, condescending, unspeakable gift is Christ! "He is not ashamed to call us brethren." We have all we need in Him. He is everything to the newborn soul, the supreme object of its affections, and the joy and crown of all its hope; on Christ its faith rests, and its portion; its expectation and its fullness is in Him, faith lives where He lives, the eye of faith is watching for Him, the ear of faith is listening for Him, the heart of faith is yearning for Him, and the feet of faith are weary to follow Him, though the poor body may be in the world, tempest-tossed, "fightings without and fears within." "They are not of the world, even as I am not of the world."

"They are not of the world," because *they too are on their way home.* Very soon the journey will be over, and the wilderness be passed, and Jordan shall open its waters for our entrance into the promised land. Here our characteristic is that we

are "strangers and pilgrims," for, saith the Lord, "they are not of the world, even as I am not of the world."

Now, suffer a word of practical application for ourselves. Is this our description? Do we correspond to this sketch? Are we "not of the world?" Oh! this is a very searching question. It is written, "Be not conformed to this world." Are we conformed to it? Do we go its way? Are its tastes, its pleasures, its pursuits, its companions ours? or, have we been transformed by the renewing of our minds? Has light from God fallen down upon us, and in His light do we see light? And having seen light doth the world's light around us seem to be darkness? Are we thanking God "who hath called us out of darkness into His marvelous light"?

"Strangers and pilgrims" are travelers! Are we merely passing through the world, using it, and not abusing it? "Strangers and pilgrims" never think of building, or settling down in the country where they sojourn. Their thoughts are upon the loved ones at home, upon the green fields and sunny smiles at home; home is the thought that fills their eyes, their hopes, their hearts, as they travel through the strangers' far-off land. How is it with ourselves?

"Strangers and pilgrims" are known by their language in the country through which they are passing. It is different from that which is spoken around them—the tone is quite different. Aye, and the dress too, therefore they are oftentimes *a gazing-stock* to those among whom, for a short period, their lot is cast. Their manners too are different, you at once perceive it, it strikes you immediately, you would never take them for inhabitants of the land in which they are strangers and pilgrims—never! They could not be mistaken for a single instant. How is it with ourselves? Are we strangers and pilgrims in this world? Is our language different, our manner different, our attire different? Is it impossible for us to associate with the men of the world without their finding out that while we are in the world we are not of it? This is a very solemn question. If it is otherwise with us, then we are ashamed of the cross, we are ensnared by the world where we ought to be but as passing strangers.

If a stranger and pilgrim in a far-off land meets a fellow citizen by the way, one speaking the same language, wearing the same attire, evidently by his manner belonging to the same country as himself, how delighted he is, what sweet intercourse they enjoy. Imagine yourself in a distant land, far away from all home associations, among utter strangers, whose ways and tastes and manners and language were utterly foreign to you— imagine meeting one of *your own* there, how you would embrace, how you would hold him fast, how soon you would make a companion of him,—you could not do otherwise. How is it with ourselves?· When we meet the children of God here on earth, are they our choice, our delight, our companions?

"Strangers and pilgrims" are not loath to leave the country in which they are sojourning. It would be no unwelcome news to "strangers and pilgrims" to tell them they are called home. It would be no sorrowful tidings to "strangers and pilgrims," that the business for which they were here was done, and that there was no longer any reason why they should not go home at once to where their children are, and their fathers are, and to where the scenes they love best are—they would be *nothing loath*. How is it with us? "Strangers and pilgrims." Are we afraid to die?

> Afraid! to die!—the child of grace,
>   Redeemed by Jesus' dying love,—
> Afraid! to go, behold His face,—
>   Afraid! to tread the courts above!
>
> Afraid! to fling to nature's night,
>   Mortality's cold troubled dress—
> Afraid to take the soaring flight,
>   Robed in a Saviour's righteousness!

> The eagle, bird of strength and light,
> Fears not to lay his plumage by,
> And with new wings attempt his flight—
> And shall a Christian fear to die?

Oh! that the realization of our heavenly destiny may constrain us—and if it doth not, what else can constrain us—to live here below as those who are not their own, but bought with a price, as those of whom the blessed Jesus said on earth, and for whom He is now pleading in heaven, "Father, keep them from the evil," for "they are not of the world, even as I am not of the world."

28

O UR LORD JESUS had just prayed to His Father, His "holy Father," to keep His people from "the evil." He now further pleads that they may be *sanctified* through the truth, on account of the possession of which they were hated. All that remained for prayer was that they might be glorified, and that petition He afterwards presented in verse 24. Thus we have fully expressed our dear Lord's desires for His people; (1) that they might be preserved from all evil while they were in the world; (2) that they might be sanctified through the truth; and (3) that they should be with Him to behold His glory which His Father had given Him,

> "Changed into the same image from glory to glory, even as by the Spirit of the Lord" (II Cor. 3:18).

There is an inseparable connection between these three petitions. All whom He will glorify shall be sanctified through the truth, and kept from the evil that is in the world.

"Sanctify them through thy truth: thy word is truth." Whatever may be the means employed by our heavenly Father for the sanctification of His people, God Himself alone is the agent. We cannot sanctify ourselves any more than we can preserve ourselves, or glorify ourselves. Observe, in verse 19, the exceeding emphasis laid upon the petition He now presents:

> "For their sakes I sanctify myself, that they also might be sanctified through the truth."

This is only one of many passages in which our attention is
called to the paramount importance of the sanctification of God's
people. In Hebrews 10:7,

> "Then, said I, Lo, I come (in the volume of the book it is
> written of me) to do thy will, O God."

What that will is we are told in verse 10:

> "By the which will we are sanctified through the offering of
> the body of Jesus Christ once for all."

And in 13:12,

> "Jesus . . . that he might sanctify the people with his own
> blood, suffered without the gate."

And in I Peter 1:2, we read this account of God's people,

> "Elect according to the foreknowledge of God the Father,
> through sanctification of the Spirit, unto obedience and sprin-
> kling of the blood of Jesus Christ."

Thus we learn that our sanctification by the Holy Ghost is *the
result* of our sanctification in the Lord Jesus Christ.

How strikingly this great truth was pictured in the Old Testament. See Exodus 28:36–38:

> "And thou shalt make a plate of pure gold, and grave upon
> it, like the engravings of a signet, HOLINESS TO THE LORD.
> And thou shalt put it on a blue lace, that it may be upon the
> mitre; upon the forefront of the mitre it shall be. And it shall
> be upon Aaron's forehead, that Aaron may bear the iniquity
> of *the holy things,* which the children of Israel shall hallow
> in all their holy gifts; and it shall be *always* upon his forehead,
> *that* THEY *may be accepted before the Lord."*

Observe the divine reason why holiness to the Lord was always
to be prominent upon the high priest's forehead. It was a
wonderful picture of the complete consecration of the Lord
Jesus Christ as High Priest, who is evermore Holiness unto the

Lord, that His people may be always accepted in Him before the Lord; and, so long as "Holiness to the Lord" is written upon the brow of our ascended Saviour, so long shall we, notwithstanding the iniquity of our holy things (and if the iniquity of our *holy* things, how much more the iniquity of our unholy things), be nevertheless evermore accepted before the Lord.

The sanctification of the Lord's people is a most important matter. In truth, all God's dealings with us in grace seem to have respect unto this.

> If we are *elect,* it is "that we should be holy" (Eph. 1:4);
>
> If *predestinated,* it is that we should "be conformed to the image of his Son" (Rom. 8:29);
>
> If *redeemed* by the Son, it is that we might be "redeemed from all iniquity, and purified unto Himself a peculiar people, zealous of good works" (Titus 2:14);
>
> If *called* by the Holy Ghost, it is with "an holy calling" (II Tim. 1:9);
>
> If the *truth is revealed* unto us, it is that we may be "sanctified through the truth" (John 17:19);
>
> If He *restoreth our souls,* it is that He may "lead us in the paths of righteousness for his name's sake" (Ps. 23:3);
>
> Nay, if even He *chasten* us, it is that "we might be partakers of his holiness" (Heb. 12:10);
>
> "Sanctify them through thy truth."

Now, remember there are two principal uses of the word *sanctification* in Scripture. Primarily, to sanctify is to set apart for God's sole use, and *all* the allusions to sanctification in the Bible have their root in this meaning. Thus God is said to sanctify the seventh day, that is, He set it apart for His own and His people's rest. Thus God is said to sanctify the first-born, that is, He set them apart for Himself and for the peculiar privileges He intended for them. Thus the tabernacle and all its vessels were sanctified; and it is in this sense we understand that remarkable statement made by the Lord Jesus Christ concerning Himself—

"Say ye of him, whom the Father hath sanctified, and sent into the world, Thou blasphemest; because he said, I am the Son of God" (John 10:36).

But there is another meaning of sanctification in Scripture, involving and including the *communication* to the soul of all the blessings for which God has set us apart; and the manifestation of the Holy One Himself, not only *to* us but *in* us. For *these* see Ezekiel 36:23–27.

"I will *sanctify my great name,* which was profaned among the heathen, which ye have profaned in the midst of them; and the heathen shall know that I am the Lord, saith the Lord God, when *I shall be sanctified in you* before their eyes."

And we have the following seven-fold communication of blessings for which they were sanctified, and in the bestowing of which the Lord was to be sanctified in them.

(1) "I will *take you* from among the heathen, and *gather you* out of all countries, and will *bring you into your own land.*

(2) "Then will I sprinkle clean water upon you, and *ye shall be clean:* from all your filthiness, and from all your idols, will I cleanse you.

(3) "A *new heart* also will I give you.

(4) "A *new spirit* will I put within you:

(5) I *will take away the stony heart* out of your flesh, and I will give you an heart of flesh.

(6) "*I will put my spirit within you,*

(7) "And I will *cause you to walk in my statutes,* and ye shall keep my judgments, and do them."

Putting these passages together, we have the full meaning of sanctification; namely, the setting apart of certain persons for blessing, and the manifestation of Jehovah to them *in the communication* of all those blessings for which they were set apart, or sanctified.

In the New Testament also we might refer to many passages, but one will suffice, it contains the whole matter. Here the apostle addresses the people of God as those

"That are *sanctified* by God the Father, and *preserved* in Jesus Christ, and *called*" (Jude 1).

Observe, how the the three Persons of the Trinity are engaged in the sanctification of God's people; the Father sanctifying them, the Son in whom they are preserved, and, the Holy Ghost by whom they are called; in this one passage we have the setting apart, the manifestation of the blessing and the communication; "called," through the Spirit to His eternal glory in the Lord Jesus Christ, in whom they are preserved, and by the Father who hath sanctified them. If this be so, what a divinely perfect work must be the sanctification of God's people, the foundation laid in the incarnation of the Lord Jesus Christ and our union with Him. The manifestation and communication of the blessing is "through the truth," and "the belief of the truth"; and the power by which it is consummated, "the Holy Ghost that dwelleth in us."

As Satan corrupts us through falsehoods, our God sanctifies us through "the truth." Observe, it is not through impressions, or through excitement, or through revelations or visions, or through the sacraments (as, alas! too many teach), or yet through church traditions, we are sanctified. "Sanctify them through *thy truth; thy word is* truth."

Now, *why* is "the truth" the instrument?

It is through the truth the love of God is revealed and shed abroad in our hearts; love is a sanctifying principle, "We love him, because he first loved us"; love is a constraining principle, "the love of Christ constrains us."

The truth is the instrument by which the Holy Ghost is ministered to the soul, therefore, in II Corinthians 3:8, the gospel is called

"The ministration of the Spirit," because it is the means whereby the Spirit is ministered.

In Galatians 3:2, the apostle asks,

> "Received ye the Spirit by the works of the law, or by the hearing of faith?"

implying that they did not receive the Spirit by the works of the law, but that *they did* receive the Spirit by the hearing of faith, that is, the gospel. Again, "the truth" is the means of our sanctification, because faith which purifies the heart is produced by the truth;

> "Faith cometh by hearing, and hearing by the word of God" (Rom. 10:17).

Again, "the truth" supplies hope. In Colossians 1:5, it is thus described,

> "The hope which is laid up for you in heaven, whereof ye heard before in the word of the truth of the gospel."

And you forget not I John 3:3, where we are taught,

> "Every man that hath this hope in him purifieth himself, even as he is pure."

Again, the truth is the means whereby the promises of God are bestowed (see the apostle's argument in II Cor. 7:1):

> "Having *therefore* these promises, dearly beloved, *let us cleanse* ourselves from all filthiness of the flesh and spirit, perfecting holiness in the fear of God."

There is another interesting passage upon this subject in I Peter 1:22, where this principle is also laid down,

> "Seeing ye have purified your souls in *obeying the truth through the Spirit.*"

Thus you perceive we read of sanctification in two senses. In one respect our sanctification is complete, so that nothing can be added to it or taken from it. It is already effected for *all* God's believing people through the one offering of the Lord Jesus Christ, once for all. He is our sanctification as truly as He is our justification, and as completely.

"But of him are ye in Christ Jesus, who of God is made unto us, wisdom and righteousness and sanctification and redemption" (I Cor. 1:30).

Let us keep this fundamental truth always present in our minds; we are complete in Christ as before our God, both as sanctified, and as justified, if we have come to the Lord Jesus Christ by faith. In another respect it is progressive, and is commonly called progressive sanctification. But, in reality, this latter sanctification is the fruit of faith, and its manifestation and development in the heart will evermore be according to our faith, and in the degree in which our minds, and affections, our hopes, and desires are experimentally conversant with the gospel of the grace of God, and as we receive the Lord Jesus Christ into our hearts and live day by day upon His fullness, through the power and indwelling of the Holy Ghost. In Titus 2:11–14 the apostle writes—

"The grace of God that bringeth salvation hath appeared to all men, teaching us that, denying ungodliness and worldly lusts, we should live soberly, righteously, and godly, in this present world; looking for that blessed hope, and the glorious appearing of the great God and our Saviour Jesus Christ; who gave himself for us, that he might redeem us from all iniquity, and purify unto himself a peculiar people, zealous of good works."

Sanctification as it respects our persons, in Christ, is absolutely and everlastingly complete: as the apostle writes in Colossians 2:10,

"Ye are complete in him, which is the head of all principality and power."

The second aspect of sanctification has reference to the *effect* of the truth upon our minds, and hearts, and conduct; and to this the apostle directs our attention in Ephesians 4:23–25 where he fully opens out the subject—

"Be renewed in the spirit of your mind"—

that is, by the entrance and operation of the truth—

"[And] *put on the new man,* which after God is created in righteousness and true holiness. Wherefore putting away lying, speak every man truth with his neighbour: for we are members one of another."

And he then proceeds to enforce practical duties, *which are in fact fruits of faith,* and manifestations of our union with Him who is "Holiness to the Lord."

When He prayed thus, "Sanctify them through thy truth," there can be no doubt our Lord referred specially to the particular truths He had just revealed to them, such as "they are thine . . . Thou gavest them me . . . I am glorified in them . . . They are not of the world even as I am not of the world." Speaking on a former occasion, and in reference to the union between Himself and them, He said,

"*Now are ye clean,* through the word which I have spoken unto you" (John 15:3).

They were already clean in Him; but He earnestly prayed that this great fact of their complete sanctification in Himself might be so fully and constantly realized in their hearts and affections; that it might be a practical power in their lives and conversation, influencing them for happiness, for holiness, and for usefulness. He had spoken of the truth "as his Father's word . . . the words which thou gavest to me . . . the words which I have given them . . . the word which they have received," the word on account of which "the world hath hated them"—and He now asks that it may be the effectual means of their sanctification.

"Thy word is truth." Doth our Lord by this expression mean Himself, or the truth which revealed Him? We have in this Gospel "the Word was God," and "the word of God." Probably in His prayer our Lord refers to His testimony; but He certainly conveys to us by the language He uses, that the Bible of God is as true as the God of the Bible, and that *"the word of God"* is to us in importance only less than *"the Word"* Himself. Would that the Scriptures were more regarded by us in this light. See a remarkable passage in Acts 20:32, bearing on this subject,

"Now, brethren, I commend you to God, and to the word of his grace, which is able to build you up, and to give you an inheritance among all them which are sanctified."

You observe how remarkably the God of the Word, and the Word of God, are identified in that passage. All the ability there attributed to the Word of His grace might be as truly predicated of God Himself as it is of the gospel that reveals Him. Little do we realize how much we owe to the written Word of God.

If we are *begotten* into God's family, it is "by the word of God which liveth and abideth for ever" (I Peter 1:23);

If our souls are *quickened,* "thy word hath quickened me" (Ps. 119:50);

If we are to *grow,* "desire the sincere milk of the word, that ye may grow thereby" (I Peter 2:2);

If we are to be *fed,* "man doth not live by bread only, but by every word that proceedeth out of the mouth of the Lord doth man live" (Deut. 8:3);

If our souls are *enlightened,* "the entrance of thy words giveth light" (Ps. 119:130);

If our hearts are *comforted,* it must be "through patience and comfort of the Scriptures" (Rom. 15:4);

If we are *renewed,* we are "renewed in knowledge" (Col. 3:10);

If we are to be *established,* it must be in the truth;

If we are to be *conquerors,* we overcome by the word of the testimony (Rev. 12:11);

If we are to be *sanctified,* "Sanctify them through thy truth."

The Spirit of God sets before us a very high calling in the matter of sanctification. See Colossians 1:9–12, addressed as you perceive in verse 2, "to the saints"—*sanctified ones*—"for this cause we also, since the day we heard it"—they had received the truth, this it is to which He alludes—"do not cease to pray for you, and to desire that ye might *be filled* with the knowledge of his will, in all wisdom and spiritual understanding." Observe the abundant measure, not only in wisdom, but "in *all* wisdom and spiritual understanding; that ye might walk worthy of the Lord unto all pleasing"—not merely so as to please Him, but unto *all* pleasing "being fruitful in *every good work*"—wonderful language—"and *increasing* in the knowledge of God; strengthened with *all* might, according to his glorious power"— what a measure!—"unto *all* patience and longsuffering with *joyfulness:*

> "Giving thanks unto the Father, which *hath made us meet* to be partakers of the inheritance of the saints in light."

You observe the starting point,—seeing that the Father *"hath made us meet to be partakers of the inheritance of the saints in light,"* then the pathway—"in the knowledge of his will"; "increasing in the knowledge of God." Thus it is we walk with Him thankfully, and rejoicingly, in the holy fruitful path here described for us, which shineth brighter and brighter unto the perfect day (see Prov. 4:18). Always remember it is because of his complete sanctification in Christ, that there is anything like a fruitful walk in the believer on earth, and that just as *his faith apprehends his calling, he will practically walk worthy of it.* See I Thessalonians 5:23, 24:

> "The very God of peace sanctify you wholly; and I pray God your whole spirit and soul and body be preserved, blameless, unto the coming of our Lord Jesus Christ. Faithful is he that calleth you, who also will do it."

It is not a question! *"He will do it."* Observe the new name of God which constitutes the ground of the apostle's petition, and the assurance of his hope—"the God of peace." "Our peace is made," the blood has gone in, we stand "accepted in the be-loved" before the throne, "complete in him." Our God is the God of peace, and just as our faith apprehends this we shall be practical in our walk. "Now the God of peace, that brought again from the dead our Lord Jesus, that great Shepherd of the sheep, through the blood of the everlasting covenant, *make you perfect* in every good work to do his will, *working in you* that which is well-pleasing in his sight, through Jesus Christ" (Heb. 13:20, 21). See the foundation laid, *"the God of peace."* Oh! for faith to apprehend these things, and to know that our peace is made, and that Christ Himself is our peace, and then our walk will be in fellowship and communion with Him who made it.

It is written in Hebrews 12:14, "Follow peace with all men, and holiness, without which no man shall see the Lord." Observe the connection between holiness and peace. We cannot follow either peace or holiness with men if we are not in the enjoyment of peace and holiness with God: one is the fruit of the other;

"Holiness, without which no man *shall see the Lord.*"

There are two most important senses in which this statement is true. If we are not "in Christ," "complete in him," "sanctified through the offering of His body once for all," we shall never "see the Lord." This is positively and absolutely true.

It is also practically true that, as Christians, we shall have no fellowship, no communion, no vision of the Lord, nothing of the light of His countenance falling upon our souls, nothing of the gladness of the joy which many of His children know, if our walk is a loose walk, an unholy walk, a careless walk. The way to enjoy God on earth is to follow holiness. It is not *because* you follow holiness on earth that you are accepted in Christ; do not suppose *that*. You are accepted *in the Beloved!* It is because of the offering of His dear body once for all, we are ever-more sanctified before God, this is a holiness *without* us altogether: existing in Him who is made unto us our sanctification; but if we would be happy, if we would walk in the light and in the enjoyment of fellowship with God, if we wish to see His face, and to have our weary way cheered and gladdened with the light of His countenance, we must follow holiness, for without "holiness no man shall see the Lord."

Holiness is *communion* with God. In II Corinthians 13:14, you have the familiar passage,

> "The grace of the Lord Jesus Christ, and the love of God, and the communion of the Holy Ghost be with you all."

Alas! practically we think far more of our safety than we do of our communion. This is a great mistake.

Again, the Lord is thus earnest concerning the sanctification of His people, because holiness is *communion with God,* and therefore *their holiness is happiness.* "Be ye holy for I am holy." When shall we learn this, and that sin is not more the enemy of God than it is the enemy of the sinner? Holiness is happiness.

Holiness is fruitfulness. In Galatians 5:22, the fruits of the Holy Spirit are summed up:

> "The fruit of the Spirit is love, joy, peace, long-suffering, gentleness, goodness, faith, meekness, temperance."

Holiness is meetness for our inheritance above. In every sense, "without holiness" no man can enter it. What would men say if, while I professed to be about to enter a neighboring kingdom to spend all my life there, they saw me, nevertheless, perfectly careless with regard to learning the laws or customs of that kingdom, ignorant of its language, and unwilling to make myself acquainted with any of the inhabitants of that kingdom who might be sojourning in my neighborhood? What would they think, moreover, if they observed that the more I knew of its language the less I liked it, and the more I knew of its inhabitants the more I avoided them? Would they not say that I was quite beside myself in professing to anticipate any pleasure in spending the rest of my days in that kingdom? Or, suppose they knew me to be a criminal condemned to die, and that all my thoughts and anxieties were engrossed in the effort to obtain a reprieve—at the same time quite overlooking the fact that I had a mortal disease, and never thinking of sending for a physician, so that, in all probability, the very day a reprieve might arrive I would die of my disease; would they not say, What folly, what madness! Yet it is just in this way most professing Christians deal with the things of eternity. They all profess to hope they shall go to heaven at last; all profess to be anxious about the pardon of their sins; but they seem to forget altogether that without holiness they would not be happy in heaven itself.

This subject of personal, practical sanctification is a very important one, although it be humbling; but if we have any real desire to be conformed to the image of God's dear Son, and any real shrinking from the things which are contrary to Him, let us thank God for it.

Earnestly desire the *highest* attainments in the way of personal consecration to God. Remember the high standard set before us, and plead the promise that God "is faithful who also will do it."

Beware of self-exaltation. I believe the Lord does not allow us *to feel* much of the progress of our sanctification, lest we should turn it to self-exaltation. A very material part of our practical holiness consists in humility. It is written (Isa. 57:15),

> "I dwell in the high and holy place, with him also that is of a contrite and humble spirit."

Thus the Lord, the Holy One, acknowledges a close connection between His dwelling place in the atmosphere of holiness, and His dwelling place in the atmosphere of humility. Do not forget *this*.

A main part of our sanctification here on earth, is carried on, and perfected, in learning our sinfulness, experiencing our nothingness, and realizing our corruption, our misery, and our ruin.

We are left here very much in order that we may learn these things.

But, when our Lord Jesus Christ brings us up to God, then we shall learn the fullness of His grace in teaching us; when He shows us the glory to which He has redeemed us, we shall best know, in the dark contrast of what we have been here, how much we owe to grace, and how precious was the blood that saved us. No wonder that it is written,

> "They rest not day or night, saying . . . Thou art worthy . . . for thou wast slain and hast redeemed us to God by thy blood" (Rev. 4:8; 5:9).

And now, if God's Word is truth, and therefore truth because *it is* His Word, let us prize it, read it, love it, hide it in our heart that we may not sin against Him. And may those who know it have grace to proclaim it.

29

"AS THOU HAST SENT ME INTO THE WORLD, EVEN SO HAVE
I ALSO SENT THEM INTO THE WORLD. AND FOR THEIR
SAKES I SANCTIFY MYSELF, THAT THEY ALSO
MIGHT BE SANCTIFIED THROUGH THE
TRUTH."—John 17:18, 19

WITH THESE WORDS our Lord closes the second portion
of His prayer. The first part (vv. 1–6) had reference
exclusively to *Himself*. This second part (vv. 6–20) had reference to His apostles.

First, as men divinely and specially appointed and commissioned for an extraordinary and peculiar office and work,
for which they were also divinely qualified. The Lord conferred
the Holy Ghost upon the apostles in a peculiar manner, and
for a peculiar purpose. They were enabled to work miracles;
they were enabled to discern spirits; they were enabled au-
thoritatively to declare the forgiveness of sins; they were endowed with extraordinary gifts qualifying them for the special
mission upon which the Lord sent them, to be His witnesses to
the ends of the earth. The pretensions of some men to be the
successors of the apostles seems to be a painful and unscriptural
assumption. For the peculiar work to which the Lord appointed
His apostles, He had in a special manner given them His Word,
so they were inspired men. In a special manner He bestowed
upon them His Holy Spirit, so that they had not only extraordinary divine illumination, but they had also extraordinary
divine power.

Now in His prayer for them there were two matters about which the Lord expresses Himself anxious. (1) *Their preservation,* for much depended upon it. He had given them His Word, and they were to be His ambassadors to the sons and daughters of men; they were to bear His testimony to the ends of the earth, and therefore, their preservation in the world was all-important. "Holy Father, keep them." and (2) *their sanctification,* that they might be holy vessels filled with truth. "Sanctify them through thy truth."

But our Lord evidently regards the apostles, in another point of view, even as simple believers, like ourselves. They had the same corrupt nature that we have; they were exposed to the same temptations that we are; they were opposed by the same adversaries—the world, the flesh, and the devil; they had no more righteousness of their own than we have; they had no more power to obtain the pardon of sin by their own merits than we have; they were as weak in themselves, as helpless as we are; they were as dependent upon the mere grace and mercy of their heavenly Father as we are; they were as poor and needy as we are; but they knew it far better than we do, because of the greater amount of grace and spiritual light bestowed upon them.

Thus the Lord's prayer to His Father concerning them enters into their need in *both* characters—as apostles, and as individual believers; and in embracing them, His prayer manifestly includes all the family of God, and all the circumstances of each member in all ages of the world's history; and that this is so may be easily proved. When He said to them

"In the world ye shall have tribulation,"

did He mean His apostles only? Or again,

"These things I have spoken unto you, that in me ye might have peace" (16:33), did He mean His apostles only? Thank God many a soul taught by His Spirit, and comforted in His love can testify to the contrary. So here, when He prays

> "As thou hast sent me into the world, even so have I also sent them into the world; and for their sakes I sanctify myself, that they also might be sanctified through the truth,"

it is evident that while He refers to His apostles specially, yet not exclusively, He also comprehends in His prayer all who in subsequent ages of the Church shall at any time believe upon Him through their word. In this point of view how beautiful the passage is, and how wonderful the truth it contains! Here are two arguments into which all the others from verse 6 seem to flow as streams into an ocean.

> "As thou hast sent me into the world, even so have I also sent them into the world; and for their sakes I sanctify myself, that they also might be sanctified through the truth."

Let us confine our attention at present to the first of these verses only.

Our blessed Lord makes three all-important statements.

I. "Thou hast sent me into the world."

II. "I have sent them into the world."

III. He speaks of a resemblance—a likeness between the Father's sending Him into the world, and His sending His dear people into the world.

> "As thou hast sent me into the world, even so have I also sent them into the world."

I. The first statement is in itself an immense subject—Christ sent into the world. What deep teaching that simple sentence conveys! Let us attend to a few only of the great subjects connected with it.

1. His *pre-existence*, "That thou hast sent me into the world." In Proverb 8, under His name, The Wisdom of God,

we learn that, long before the Lord Jesus Christ was manifested
in human nature, He was the God-man in divine purpose. He
was the Mediator in the covenant of grace long before He was
incarnate, and manifested as Mediator in the fullness of time;
He there speaks of Himself delighting in the sons of men before
the world was. So here His words imply His pre-existence,
"Thou hast *sent me* into the world."

2. He came not of His own accord;

> "Neither came I of myself, but he sent me" (John 8:42).

Our Lord loved to trace His own mission to the Father's love for
His people, and to point out that the fact of His presence here
was but the pledge and seal of that Father's everlasting love,—

> "My meat is to do the will of him that sent me, and to finish
> *his work*" (John 4:34);
> "Wist ye not that I must be about my Father's business?"
> (Luke 2:49);

and when He was about to return,

> "Now I go my way to him that sent me" (John 16:5),
> "God so loved the world that he gave his only begotten Son,"

God sent Him into the world that we might live through Him.

3. Christ was sent and *commissioned.* The apostle (I John
4:14) says,

> "We have seen and do testify that the Father sent the Son
> to be the Saviour of the world."

4. Sent and *qualified.* His qualification was that

> "The fulness of the Godhead dwelt in him bodily" (Col.
> 2:10);

the Holy Ghost without measure was upon Him to anoint
Him;

> "All power in heaven and earth" (Matt. 28:19)

was bestowed upon Him, and

> "Authority to execute judgment also, because he was the *Son of man*" (John 5:27).

5. Christ was sent into the world *officially*. He was sent to be the Prophet, the Priest, and the King.

> "The Lord thy God will raise up unto thee *a Prophet* like unto me, unto him shall ye hearken" (Deut. 18:15).
> "The Lord has sworn and will not repent, thou art *a Priest* for ever after the order of Melchizedek" (Ps. 110:4).
> "Yet have I set my king on my holy hill of Zion" (Ps. 2:6).

6. Christ being sent officially, implies that He was *responsible* for the discharge of the office He had accepted; therefore all that can be done for us by a priest He will do, all that can be done for us by a prophet He will accomplish, all that can be done for us by a king we may depend upon being done. Remember how He loved to use language implying His responsibility for the discharge of His office.

> "I *must* work the works of him that sent me" (John 9:4).

Observe, not I will, but I must.

> "Other sheep I have, which are not of this fold: them also I *must* bring, and they shall hear my voice; and there shall be one fold and one Shepherd" (John 10:16).
> "So *must* the Son of man be lifted up, that whosoever believeth in him should not perish" (John 3:14, 15).
> "All things *must* be fulfilled . . . concerning me" (Luke 24:44).

It is a precious truth, that when the Lord was sent into the world officially to be the Saviour of sinners, He felt His responsibility to discharge the office He had undertaken. If

> "Moses was faithful in all his house as a servant," how much more our glorious "Christ as a Son" (Heb. 3:2, 6).

He is responsible to receive the sinner who comes to him—for this purpose He was sent; He is responsible to wash in His

blood the guilty soul that appeals to Him—for this purpose was
He sent. As well might Aaron discharge his office faithfully
while rejecting an Israelite, as Christ in rejecting a sinner.

7. But from *whence* was He sent? We read He was "in the
bosom of the Father"; He was the brightness of His Father's
glory, and the express image of His person;

> "[He was] in the form of God [and] thought it not robbery
> to be equal with God" (Phil. 2:6).

Such He was, such was the home in which He dwelt, and from
whence He was sent.

8. *Whither* was He sent? Not to the Jewish temple to be
worshiped, but into the world: "Thou hast sent me into the
world"; not into the circle of a family which would recognize
Him and love Him, and sit at His feet, and adore the grace that
brought Him down; but into the world that hated Him; not
into the society of angels and archangels, but into the world; not
even into the solitudes of the wilderness, but into the busy tur-
moil of life: "thou hast sent me into the world," the world
where Satan had triumphed, the world where sin had reigned,
the world where Jehovah's law had been outraged.

9. With what *object* was He sent?

> "[He] was manifested to destroy the works of the devil" (I
> John 3:8);

to

> "Put away sin . . . magnify the law . . . abolish death"
> (see Heb. 9:26; Isa. 42:21; II Tim. 1:10).
> "The spirit of the Lord is upon me, because he hath anointed
> me to preach the gospel to the poor; he hath sent me to heal
> the broken-hearted, to preach deliverance to the captives and
> recovering of sight to the blind, to set at liberty them that are
> bruised, to preach the acceptable year of the Lord" (Luke
> 4:18, 19).

The mission of Christ is the greatest *fact* in our world's
history. The creation was as nothing to this. It was for the great-

est *cause* He was sent—even the glory of God; for the greatest *object*—the salvation of sinners; and for the greatest results— even that He might subdue all things to Himself. *He only* could do it, therefore He was sent; He could do it *only* in our nature, therefore He assumed it; He could do it *in the world* only, therefore He dwelt among us. Here God's law had been trampled upon; here, therefore, He magnified it, both by His life and by His death.

II. The second statement is, "I have sent *them* into the world." The mere mention of this fact in association with the former one is beyond anything I can express in the way of grace. That He should mention them together, "Thou hast sent Me, and I have sent them," is something for faith and hope and love to rest upon. We have seen that Christ was sent into the world. Mark the parallel.

1. We too are sent: and "we are not our own," we are not here upon our own business, or at our own charges. We are sent as Christ's chosen ones, as Christ's redeemed ones, as Christ's adopted ones "into the world."

2. We are not here of our own choice, we did not select our position for ourselves, *He selected it for us.* What comfort to know this. He who sent us into the world could remove us from it in a moment. Having revealed His love to us, having washed us in His blood, and possessed us by His Spirit, He might at once take us where no temptations can assail us, no sin can sully us, and no tear can dim our eye nor sorrow press down our spirit; yet He doth it not, it is not His will. He says (v. 11), "These are in the world, and I come to thee," I leave them behind. He says (v. 15), "I pray not that thou shouldest take them out of the world." Here He goes further, and positively asserts, "I have sent them into the world"; not into the paradise of God, where the tree of life puts forth its leaves for the healing of the nations, but "into the world," where the serpent hides in the foliage of the tree of knowledge: not into the Father's home, where there

is "bread enough and to spare," but "into the world"; not into the society of angels, but into the company of the world: not into the home of purity and love, but into the den of impurity and evil, not even into solitude and retirement, not into peace and into calm, but "into the world." For the world is the school where God's children are taught by the Holy Ghost to know themselves, and learn what sin is.

It is in the world's disappointments, in the world's follies, in the world's temptations, in the world's tribulations, in the world's snares, in the world's sinfulness, and in the world's falsehood, we are taught to learn the corruption of our own hearts, the vanity of the creature, the bankruptcy of self, and the malice of the devil. Here we learn to hate and distrust ourselves, and in the realization of the preciousness of the blood which has washed us, and bought us, to hate ourselves all the more, while we long for the time when, with clear vision, no clouds between, we shall see Him

"Who, though he was rich, yet for our sakes became poor,
that we through his poverty might be rich" (II Cor. 8:9).

Moreover, it is in the world we can best learn to live by faith, to live in hope, and be influenced by the love that comes down to us in our difficulties, pardons our sins, and pledges to us the victory. It is very easy to profess abstract truths; but if ever we are to learn truth profitably, we must learn it experimentally. I might tell you of a beautiful well, I had heard of, sparkling with its living waters, gladdening the region where in God's providence it was placed, but you might tell me, "when I was weary and faint, I *drank of that well"*; how much more then, would you appreciate its value than I could do. I might tell you of a friend, amiable and generous, wealthy and sympathizing, and that he was all or more than I could describe, every one said so who knew him, but you might tell me, "when I was needy and poor and sick, he visited me, and comforted me, and relieved me, and nursed me"; surely, you would know *far more* of him than I did. We are left in the world not only to hear of the Lord Jesus Christ as the Well of life and as the Friend of sinners, but we are here to *drink the waters* and to *prove His love*.

III. The last statement in the text is wonderful—it passeth knowledge. The Lord speaks of the analogy and resemblance between the Father's sending Him into the world, and His sending His people into the world; for He says, "*As* thou hast sent me into the world, even *so* have I sent them into the world." Truly our blessed Lord here opened out His whole heart. He now pleads *for* them what He had already said *to* them in the fifteenth chapter of this Gospel (v. 9):

"As the Father hath loved me, so have I loved you" (John 15:9).

So now He reminds His Father, that even as He had sent His beloved *One*, He was sending His loved *ones;* that as the Father sent Him, His loved One, *into the world*—the weary world, the tempting world, the world of tribulation and of difficulty—so He was sending His loved ones into *the same place*. He reminds the Father with that object He Himself was sent into the world, even for His own glory; and now He tells the Father that it was for the same object He was sending His loved ones into the world, that there they might learn to know His name, to prove His love, and to triumph in His salvation. Moreover, He reminds the Father that as He came down here a dependent upon His Father's bounty, and to live a life of faith on Him; so He was sending His loved ones into the world, and that they were needy, and dependent, and had nothing but what He would give them, O Father, keep them—"Sanctify them through thy truth"; for "As thou hast sent me into the world, even so have I also sent them into the world."

Let us attempt to draw a parallel between these two missions.

The Father sent Christ into the world as His servant; Christ sends His dear people into the world as His servants.

The Father sent Christ into the world to magnify the law, and He did it in the way in which only *He* could do it; Christ sends us into the world to magnify the law.

You may say to me, "How can we magnify the law?" See that poor sinner bowed down to the earth in the very dust under a sense of his own corruption, and wanderings, and inconsistencies. Hear him groan, see him water his couch with tears. Why is it? Because he knows he has grieved God by breaking the law. Oh! how he magnifies that law, he cannot fulfill it as Christ did; he cannot expiate the sin committed against it as Christ did, nor does he need to do so, but God's law is magnified in that heart half-broken under the consciousness of the sad disparity between his own conduct, and God's will and Word.

Christ was sent into the world to *reveal* His Father; and Christ sent His people into the world that they might learn in the face of Jesus Christ to *know* their Father.

Christ was sent into the world to be the way, the truth, and the life, and Christ sends His people into the world that they may walk in that way, enjoy that life, and live upon that truth.

Christ was sent into the world to overcome the world; even so Christ sends His people into the world to overcome the world, and

> "This is the victory that overcometh the world, even our faith" (I John 5:4).

Christ was sent into the world to be the light of the world; and He sent His people to be the light of the world.

> "Let your light so shine before men, that they may see your good works and glorify your Father which is in heaven" (Matt. 5:16).

Christ was sent into the world to be a witness against the world; and so are His people sent by Him into the world to be witnesses against the world. Let us witness against its sins, its follies, its inconsistencies, its God-dishonoring ways, and customs; let us do it with our lips, do and not be ashamed; let us do it in our hearts, and manifest it in our lives. For this cause are we sent.

Christ was sent into the world and *qualified* for His mission. Do you think He will leave His poor people, sent into the same world, *unqualified* for their mission? No, not so long as there is a Holy Ghost, not so long as there is power in the hands of Him unto whom all power in heaven and earth is entrusted; not so long as there is the fullness dwelling in Him, of which His people shall receive "grace for grace."

And lastly, Christ's mission into the world ended in victory —though sin and law, and death, and hell opposed it, it ended in victory; so it shall be with His people; He sent them not into the world to be defeated, not that sin, and the world, and the devil (though they be confederate, and with strong hand) should have the ultimate advantage, but that they might be made more than conquerors through Him that loved them. No angel in heaven was ever sent into the world upon such a mission as that upon which we sinners who believe in Jesus are sent. It is written

"As he is so are we in this world" (I John 4:17).

As He is Conqueror on the throne above, so are we

"More than conquerors through him that loved us" (Rom. 8:37).

And it is our duty, and it is our privilege as believers to know, that He who sent us into the world is able to protect us where we are in the world, able to keep us from falling, and to present us faultless before the presence of His glory with exceeding joy (see Jude 24) and meantime to sanctify us with the truth which tells us of the love that gave Him to us, and will with Him also freely give us all things.

Lord Jesus, give us Thyself in our hearts, Thy faith, Thy love; Thou art the expulsive power which dethrones all other lords; Thy love—the constraining principle which consecrates our lives; Thy faith—the all-conquering principle which overcomes the world into which Thou hast sent us.

30

Our Lord could not love more, say more, do more, plead more.

He had prayed, "Sanctify them through thy truth"; He pleaded (1) the fact of their heavenly origin—"they are not of the world"; (2) their need, "by reason of the dangers to which they would be exposed in the world"; and (3) His object in sending them there. "As thou hast sent me." Now, again, He pleads, "Sanctify them." (4) "For their sakes I sanctify myself, that they also might be sanctified through the truth." There are subjects upon which the Word of God is silent (and even the silence of Scripture is instructive). There are other subjects of which the whole of Scripture, from beginning to end, seems full. If our minds were rightly ordered, we should never desire the knowledge of any matter which our heavenly Father has been pleased to withhold from us; and, on the other hand, we would receive into our inmost hearts, and prize beyond all earthly considerations, every truth He is pleased to reveal for our guidance, warning, comfort, or for His own glory. Now, there are few subjects on which the Spirit of God dwells more frequently, and none seems more important than—*the sanctification of the Lord's people.* It pervades the whole Bible, but so far as I am aware the weightiest passage on the subject is our text. There is a depth and fullness here which can never be fully expressed, even in heaven. Observe, our Lord not only lays the foundation of His people's sanctification in the reality of His own, but He also estimates the fullness and completeness of it by the same standard: "For their sakes I sanctify myself that they also might be sanctified through the truth."

Here are four all-important matters revealed.

I. "I sanctify myself." What does He mean? He was "The Holy One of God . . . Holiness unto the Lord . . . the Most Holy"; it is utterly inconceivable that He could become *more holy* or *more sanctified* than He was, yet He says, "I sanctify myself." His use of the expression throws great light upon what the Spirit of God means by sanctification in Scripture, for certainly this passage is the key to the whole. The meaning here evidently is, I dedicate, I consecrate, I set apart My *whole self,* —My Person, Godhead and Manhood, Soul and Body. I consecrate all Mine offices—if I be a Priest, if I be a Prophet, if I be a King—I set them apart, I wholly dedicate and consecrate all My fullness of grace and glory, all My righteousness, all Mine interest, My very existence, I sanctify for the purpose and object for which I plead, "whatsoever I am; and I am Thy fellow, Lord God of Hosts! whatever My resources; (and 'it pleased the Father that in him should all fullness dwell';) whatever the merit of My blood, and the glory of My name, I absolutely dedicate: I lay down *all* upon the altar of divine and unchangeable love that I may *be* all, *do* all, *suffer* all, *merit* all My people need, and, that I may *pay* all My people owe"; "for their sakes I sanctify myself." Oh! what did He hold back? Nothing! His was a complete surrender; it was an absolute devoting of Himself, all that He was as Son of God, all that He was as Son of Man, all that He was as Mediator, all His fullness, and all His service, His time, His care, His thought, His very life itself He consecrated and set apart, that He might be the sanctification of His people.

You perceive that this is the crowning petition of the many He had presented on behalf of His disciples, and well He knew in what light His Father would regard *the* offering, on the ground of which He prayed. We cannot think too highly of the sacrifice of the Lord Jesus Christ; we cannot rest too fully on the dignity of the Offerer, the worth of the offering, or the benefits that flow from it. We cannot make too much of the blood, or dwell too securely under its protection. The blood of Christ has a *double* efficacy: it is the atonement for sin, and it is the sanctification of the sinner on whose heart it is sprinkled.

"We are justified by his blood" (Rom. 5:9);

and we are sanctified by the blood (see Heb. 13:12). This one offering of Himself includes sin-offering, burnt-offering, meat-offering, peace-offering, *all in one*. His blood cleanseth "from all sin," both from the *guilt* of sin, and from the *filth* of sin, from every kind and degree of sin, and everything contained in sin, its pollution, its demerit, and its consequences; where the blood of the Lamb is applied by faith the Holy Ghost descends and dwells there forever.

Would we did always remember, to the comfort of our souls, that when the Lord Jesus Christ hung upon the cross of Calvary, as an offering for sin, all the iniquities, transgressions, and sins of the Church of God, whether past, present, or future, were laid upon Him. It is written,

"The Lord hath laid on him the iniquity of us all" (Isa. 53:6),

and all were future then! Nay, they were confessed upon His blessed head, even as Aaron confessed all the iniquity, the transgressions, and the sins of Israel, putting them on the head of the scapegoat.

Now, if this was so, and the blood then shed availed to blot out the mighty *whole;*

If our Substitute "rose again from the dead through the blood of the everlasting covenant";

If Christ entered into heaven by His own blood "having obtained eternal redemption for us" (Heb. 9:12);

If He therefore sat down upon the throne of the Majesty in
the heavens, from henceforth expecting till His enemies
be made His footstool;

if, I say, the blood of the everlasting covenant was sufficient to
open a way for the responsible Representative of *all* His people
—how much more is it sufficient for you and me, how much
more is it sufficient to discharge and blot out all the iniquities,
transgressions, and sins of any individual sinner who comes to
the Father by Him, pleading the merit and the acceptance of
His blood! If it was sufficient to free *Him* from all responsibility
concerning it, on whose head the *accumulated whole was laid*
—how much more in the case of the sinner, who, after all, is
but one member in the Body!

Once again observe, it was altogether His *own doing,* "I
sanctify *myself.*" He had the right and the authority, He had the
power; and He had love enough to do it—"I sanctify myself."
No one dictated it to Him, no power moved Him, no prayer invited Him, no welcome awaited Him when He came to put
away our sin by the sacrifice of Himself, no sympathy greeted
Him from those for whom He came to die.

> "Thy time was the time of love" (Ezek. 16:8) when He
> sanctified Himself.

This then seems to be the meaning of "I sanctify myself."
It was His setting Himself apart—all that He was, all that He
had, and all that He could at any time command—devoting
Himself, dedicating Himself, and delighting to do so, for the
persons and for the objects He had in view.

II. "For their sakes!" Every one has an aim, object, and motive for what he does; here we have the Lord distinctly stating in
the hearing of His disciples, what was *His* aim, and what was
His motive for what He did—"For their sakes I sanctify myself." The great truth expressed here is the amazing and transforming fact of the *personal love* of our Lord Jesus Christ for

His people; first for His disciples, and, as in the next verse, for all who shall believe on Him through their word—His infinite delight and complacency in them, and that He had no greater joy than to claim them for His portion, and lay out His fullness for their supply; no deeper wish than to be *for them* to God, all He required of them; and from God *to them,* all that they needed from Him.

"For their sakes," this expression of personal love for His people runs through the whole account of the Lord's work and mission.

> "Ye know the grace of our Lord Jesus Christ, that though he was rich, yet *for our sakes* he became poor, that we through his poverty might be rich" (II Cor. 8:9).

So here our Lord saith, *"for their sakes,"* "to supply all their need out of My own fullness, to make My strength perfect in their weakness, to be the fountain-head of their life, to be their light, and their joy, to be

> " 'Made unto them wisdom, and righteousness and sanctification, and redemption' (I Cor. 1:30),

"To be 'a wall of fire round about them,' so that no evil may befall them,

"To be the glory in the midst of them, so that every blessing may be with them,

"That they may be kept from falling, and presented faultless before the presence of My glory with exceeding joy,

"That they may lack nothing that is good for time or for eternity, in life or in death,

"That they may evermore be filled with all the fullness of God, and kept for Me and the Father forever, 'I sanctify Myself.' "

"For their sakes," and *for their sins*: we read in Galatians 1:4, He "gave himself for our sins," that we might be forgiven; and not only forgiven, but that we might be "justified from all things"; and not only justified, but that we might be adopted, made sons and daughters of the Lord God Almighty; and not only adopted but "sanctified"; not only delivered from destruction, but exalted to holiness; not only saved from hell, but brought to heaven; that His glory might not only be "seen *on us,*" but that it might be "revealed *in us.*" "For their sakes I sanctify myself." Thus our glorious Mediator commits His people into His Father's hands, to be blessed with all blessing according to the Father's own estimate of His dear Son's merit, and the measure of His infinite love for His people, surely, here is rest for the soul, here is life and joy, and peace.

If we are empty, it is not because there is want of fullness in Jesus, or unwillingness to impart it;

If we are poor, it is not because there are not "unsearchable riches" in Christ, or love enough to supply them;

If we are wandering, it is not because there is not grace in Jesus, and infinite readiness to gather and restore us;

If our consciences are accusing us, it is not because there is not the all-atoning blood in Jesus, or the Holy Ghost to apply it.

If we lack *anything,* it is not because He is unable or unwilling to do for us "exceeding abundantly above all we can ask or think," but because we do not "come to him," we do not "ask him," we do not "trust in him"; for He has truly and unchangeably said, "For their sakes I sanctify myself." And His whole object in doing so is, that He may be exclusively *for us,* and that we may come to Him, *as* we will, *when* we will, *where* we will, *for what* we will, and never be refused, and never be upbraided.

31

THAT THEY ALSO might be sanctified." The words evidently imply that His own sanctification was to be the source, ground, reason, and measure of theirs.

Indeed, we find that in all Jehovah's dealings with His people in grace and in glory, the divine rule is to begin with the Lord Jesus Christ; to do unto Him, and with Him, what in His purpose of grace and love He intends to do with us, and thus make Him the fountain-head and source of all our blessings. Thus, God in the first instance unites Christ to Himself, and then in Christ unites Himself to His people, making His own union with Christ the ground, reason, and means of His union with us. Thus again,

Christ is "the first begotten among many brethren," and then we are begotten in Him;

Christ is the "most blessed for evermore," and we "blessed in Him with all spiritual blessings."

First, the Father gave to Christ "to have life in Himself," and then He gave us life in Him:

Christ is first filled with "all the fullness" of God, and then we out "of his fullness have received, and grace for grace";

Christ was first manifested and declared to be the Son of the Father, then we in Him:

Christ crucified for sin, and we "crucified with Him";

Christ risen, we "raised up together with him":

Christ more than conqueror, we "more than conquerors through him":

Christ set down at the right hand of the Majesty in the heavens, we "sitting at God's right hand in the heavenly places in Christ Jesus"; the Holy Spirit descending without measure upon Him, that as "the anointing oil upon the head of Aaron went down upon his beard even to the skirts of his raiment," so we might, through the anointing of our High Priest, enjoy His unction and inherit His blessing; and thus it is also in the matter of our sanctification.

"For their sakes I sanctify myself, that they also might be sanctified."

Now, as there is a close and inseparable *connection* between the Lord Jesus sanctifying Himself, and the sanctification of His people in Him, so there is an *analogy* also—therefore we must carefully remember in what sense Christ sanctified Himself, that we may understand the nature and character of our own sanctification. In a word, then, Christ's sanctification of Himself consists in this—that whereas it

> "Pleased the Father that in him should all fulness dwell"
> (Col. 1:19),

and that whereas as a fact

> "In him dwelleth all the fulness of the Godhead bodily"
> (Col. 2:10),

He did in His love, and in covenant with the Father and the Holy Ghost, absolutely and voluntarily dedicate and set apart His whole person, His inheritance, His offices, His very life itself, to be the everlasting portion and supply for His people's need—their spiritual need, and their temporal need—and to be their divine and inexhaustible dowry for time and for eternity. Therefore, and for this end, the Lord Jesus Christ is to us God's "unspeakable gift," consecrated or sanctified, to be the atonement for our sins, and our everlasting righteousness; sanctified to make our peace with God, to procure our adoption, and bestow on us the Spirit of adoption,—

> "And if children, then heirs, heirs of God, and joint-heirs with Christ" (Rom. 8:17)—

sanctified to be our inheritance of grace on earth, and our inheritance of glory in heaven.

It was on this understanding, and with this object, God the Father sanctified His Son, and sent Him into the world; it was on this understanding, as we gather from the Saviour's words, He "sanctified himself"; and it was on this understanding "the Holy Spirit" was upon Him anointing Him

> "To preach the gospel to the poor; . . . to heal the broken-hearted, to preach deliverance to the captives, and recovering of sight to the blind, to set at liberty them that are bruised, to preach the acceptable year of the Lord" (Luke 4:18);

and therefore it is we find Him pleading as in the text, "For their sakes I sanctify myself, that they also might be sanctified."

The resurrection of the Lord Jesus Christ from the dead, His ascension into heaven, His being there enthroned at the right hand of God, and the subsequent descent of the Holy Ghost upon the day of Pentecost, are just so many pledges and acknowledgments on our heavenly Father's part, that He did not "sanctify himself" in vain, but that His offering was accepted, His prayer heard, and His desire fulfilled. A few testimonies of the Spirit of God on this point will be sufficient, and we select them out of many. See Hebrews 10:10,

> "By the which will we are sanctified, through the offering of the body of Jesus Christ once for all."

See also I Corinthians 6:11 where, having given a list of some of the vilest crimes of which humanity is capable, He says,

> "Such were some of you: but ye are washed, but ye are sanctified, but ye are justified *in the name* of our Lord Jesus, and by the Spirit of our God."

Keeping these texts in view, we learn in the first place, that the sanctification of the people of God is *"complete* in Christ" without any reference to their own attainments, or even the degree of their faith. The apostles speak of all believers at Corinth, and there were many degrees of faith and of spiritual attainments among them. Our sanctification in Christ is therefore complete without any reference to the *degree* of faith (supposing us to be really believers in the Lord Jesus Christ), and it is everlastingly complete. Moreover, it is also evident from these texts, that it is through the offering and sacrifice of our blessed Lord Jesus Christ that we are thus sanctified; our sanctification consists in fellowship with Him, and in the participation and enjoyment of all that He is. In I Corinthians 1:30, this truth is stated in so many words, "Of him"—that is of God the Father—"are ye *in* Christ Jesus" (the foundation of all our blessing consists in being in Christ Jesus. The moment we receive God's testimony concerning Christ Jesus this union is consummated, our standing henceforth is in Christ Jesus, and "neither death nor life . . . nor things present, nor things to come, can separate us . . .) who of God is made unto us wisdom, and righteousness, and sanctification, and redemption: that, according as it is written, He that glorieth, let him glory in the Lord"; again, John 1:12, compared with verse 16, tells us the same truth—"as many as *received him,* to them gave he power to become *the sons of God,* even to them that believe on his name"; thus believing on His name, receiving Him, and being the child of God, are synonymous terms. When a man believes on Jesus he receives Jesus, and receiving the Lord Jesus Christ he is a child of God. Then verse 16:

> "Of his fulness have all we received, and grace for grace"
> (John 1:16),

first *Himself* and then His *fullness!* This is the true ground of the believer's sanctification. Hebrews 2:11 is also a very remarkable scripture:

> "Both he that sanctifieth and they who are sanctified are all of one"—

they have one Father—God; they have one life—the divine life; they have one strength—Jehovah's strength—made perfect in their weakness; they have one grace, that is *all* grace; and they have one glory—"the glory which thou gavest me I have given them, that they may be one, even as we are one . . . for which cause he is not ashamed to call them brethren." The life of sanctification is, therefore, plainly *a life of faith,* a faith that lays hold upon the fact that the Lord Jesus Christ sanctified Himself, in order that those who believed on Him might in Him be sanctified also; and thus the faith that lays hold upon Him for sanctification before God, lives upon Him for practical sanctification day by day, "Lord, increase our faith!"

It follows therefore that, according to the purpose and will of Him with whom we have to do, the "Holy, Holy, Holy, Lord God Almighty," we, as believers in the Lord Jesus Christ, cannot be more sanctified than we are.

Oh! that we might drink into this great fact. The reason is a very simple one, it is because the ground of our sanctification is not anything that *we* are, anything *we* have attained unto, or can possibly attain unto even by faith; the entire ground of our sanctification in the sight of God consists in what the Lord Jesus Christ *is,* and what the Lord Jesus Christ *has done* for us; thus He expresses Himself upon this subject,

> "For their sakes I sanctify myself, that they also might be sanctified."

Neither can we be more dearly loved; not even in glory shall we be more dear to our heavenly Father than we are now here below, tempest-tossed as we are, and tried and troubled with "fightings without, and fears within."

Neither can we be more "perfect" or "accepted" even in glory; for it is written, "Ye are complete in him which is the head of all principality and power."

Neither can we be made more *meet* for glory than His grace has already made us: the moment we came as poor sinners to the

Lord Jesus Christ and received Him, He "was made unto us wisdom, and righteousness, and sanctification, and redemption," in the fullest and in the divinest sense thereof, and in the fullest and divinest measure thereof. Yea,

> "He *hath made* us meet to be partakers of the inheritance of the saints in light" (Col. 1:12).

It is just as we receive these things simply, intelligently, and obediently into our minds, our hearts become affected, and *"the fruits of faith which are by Jesus Christ" abound in our lives and conversation "to the praise and glory of God."*

Now, as our Lord Jesus Christ's motive in the sanctification of Himself was in order that believers might be sanctified, His object *must* be accomplished and attained; and therefore, as believers in Him, our sin is entirely put away as if it had never existed—

> Removed "as far as the east is from the west," from us (Ps. 103:12)—

in every sense of the word *from us:* for either our sin was laid upon the Lord Jesus Christ, or it was not. Which is true?

Either the Lord Jesus Christ made His soul an offering for our sin, that He might make an end of sin, or He did not. Which is true?

Either the Lord Jesus Christ was raised from the dead—God, in this way, publicly acknowledging that His offering was accepted, that justice was satisfied, the sin atoned for, and blotted out in the precious blood of Christ—or it was not so. Which is true? And if the sin was laid on Jesus, it cannot be laid on the believer, who is identified with Him in God's sight; if justice was satisfied by the sacrifice of Christ, justice will never demand the sacrifice of the sinner; if Jesus was raised from the dead because of our justification, who is to condemn us?—"Who shall lay anything to the charge of God's elect? . . . For Christ has died, yea rather is risen again, who is even at the right hand of God, who also maketh intercession for us" (Rom. 8:33, 34). Most blessed is the argument of the apostle upon this subject, in Romans 6:4, "We are buried with him by baptism into death." The baptism he speaks of is the baptism in the Holy Ghost, whereby we are united to Jesus in His death and resurrection. The baptism that we perform with water is *the symbol,* the memorial, the illustration of it, God's own blessed ordinance appointed to assure us of the great reality it represents;

"We are buried with him by baptism into death: that like as Christ was raised up from the dead by the glory of the Father, even so we also should walk in newness of life."

A few precious texts upon this subject must now claim our attention, see Hebrews 13:12,

"Jesus . . . that he might sanctify the people with his own blood, suffered without the gate."

How wonderfully this harmonizes with what He says here, "For their sakes I sanctify myself, that they also might be sanctified." He went forth without the gate, He gave His whole person an atonement upon the cross. Is it any wonder the Holy Ghost should testify for Him to the praise of the glory of His grace, that His believing people *"are sanctified* by his blood?" Romans 3:24, 25,

"Being justified freely by his grace, through the redemption that is in Christ Jesus: whom God hath set forth to be a propitiation through faith in his blood, to declare his righteousness for *the remission* of sins that are past, through the forbearance of God."

The blood not only sanctified us, but *justified* us. This is the keynote of the song in heaven (Rev. 1:5, 6):

"Unto him that loved us, and washed us from our sins in his own blood, and hath made us kings and priests."

Why, the blood does everything for us, consecrates us kings and priests, justifies us, sanctifies us, and gives us the victory! (Rev. 12:11).

You may remember how even "the shadow of good things to come," in the Old Testament times, taught the complete sanctification of the people of God, through the blood of Jesus. In Leviticus 16:30 we read,

> "On that day shall the priest make an atonement for you, to cleanse you, that ye may be *clean from all your sins before the Lord.*"

It was on the great day of atonement, when the sins of all Israel were confessed upon the scape-goat, the blood of his fellow having been presented within the veil as an atonement for them; and if the shadow of the atonement of the Lord Jesus Christ effected so much, well argues the apostle in Hebrews 9:14,

> "How much more shall the blood of Christ, who through the eternal Spirit offered himself without spot to God, *purge your conscience* from dead works to serve the living God?"

Again, see II Corinthians 5:21,

> "[God] hath made him to be sin for us, who knew no sin; that we might be made the righteousness of God in him."

You observe the *double* transfer, our sin transferred to Him, His cross being the consequence; His righteousness transferred to us, and the highest summits of eternal glory shall be the consequence, for we read in Hebrews 1:3,

> "When he had by himself purged our sins; [He] sat down on the right hand of the Majesty on high."

And it is written,

> "To him that overcometh"—we overcome by the blood— "will I grant to sit with me in my throne, even as I also overcame, and am set down with my Father in his throne" (Rev. 3:21).

From all these Scriptures it is divinely evident that our sanctification is the fruit and result of *the sacrifice of the Lord Jesus Christ*. And that in Christ Jesus the believer in Him is as pure as the blood of Christ can cleanse him, as righteous as the righteousness of Christ can make him, and as complete as the mediatorial fullness of the Lord Jesus Christ can render him. Truly this is a most important matter, and prayerfully to be learned. Moreover the work of the Holy Ghost *in us*, which is consequent upon the work of the Lord Jesus Christ for us, is not intended to be an opposition ground of confidence, a rival standard of peace within the soul, but to enlighten our minds, to remove the veil from our hearts, and to discover to us what God *hath given* to us in Jesus, that we may

> "With open face beholding as in a glass the glory of the Lord, be changed into the same image, even as by the Spirit of the Lord" (II Cor. 3:18),

that He may feed us and comfort us with Christ, forming Christ in us, ministering to us His fullness according to our daily need, and teaching us how to draw out of Christ's strength for our weakness, and find mercy in Him to help in time of need. The Holy Ghost has nothing—I speak with humility, but this is true —the Holy Ghost has *nothing to draw upon* for sinners redeemed by the blood of Christ but the fullness of that same Lord Jesus Christ, of whose fullness He is sent here to communicate to His people "grace for grace," testifying of the Lord Jesus, and thus begetting and drawing forth our faith, and hope, and love, having first created them within us in order to fix them on Christ, crown them with Christ, satisfy them with Christ, and thus form Christ in our hearts, "the hope of glory."

Our Father's purpose concerning the Lord Jesus Christ is that in Him all our fullness should dwell; and, therefore, our life, righteousness, sanctification, and peace, are in the heavens;

Our Father's purpose concerning us is that we should see and know that this is so, and that we should act accordingly; drawing by faith upon the fullness of Christ, till we are

"Filled with all the fulness of God" (Eph. 3:19);

Our Father's purpose concerning the Holy Ghost, when He sent Him to be our Comforter, was that He might make these things so plain, clear, and precious to us, that the life we now live in the flesh, we might live henceforth by the faith of the Son of God, who loved us and gave Himself for us. The Holy Ghost supplies us with *no ground of confidence apart from Christ,* sets up no standard for the soul to rest in, or find comfort from, as a rival to Him. The mission of the Comforter is not to supply an independent, additional, or even a concurrent ground of peace and confidence, but simply to discover to us and give us grace to avail ourselves of the discovery, of the boundless salvation laid up for us in Christ. How many dear children of God are troubled because they look for the graces of the Holy Ghost within them as a ground for comfort, rather than to Him who is their High Priest before the throne in heaven, and whose fullness is indeed their portion, and their peace.

In Leviticus 8:22–24, we have the consecration of Aaron, the Old Testament picture of Christ's sanctifying Himself:

"He brought the other ram, the ram of consecration: and Aaron and his sons laid their hands upon the head of the ram, and slew it"—

(No sanctification, but through the blood; moreover you will observe it takes "Moses and Aaron," "the ram," "the altar," and all the other appliances here enumerated to make up the type of Christ sanctifying Himself that His people might be sanctified)—

"And Moses took of the blood of it, and put it upon the tip of Aaron's right ear, and upon the thumb of his right hand, and upon the great toe of his right foot. And he brought Aaron's sons, and Moses put of the blood upon the tip of their right

> ear, and upon the thumbs of their right hands, and upon the great toes of their right feet: and Moses sprinkled the blood upon the altar round about."

And verse 30,

> "And Moses took of the anointing oil, and of the blood which was upon the altar, and sprinkled it upon Aaron, and upon his garments, and upon his sons, and upon his sons' garments with him; and sanctified Aaron, and his garments, and his sons, and his sons' garments with him."

The ear consecrated by that blood to listen to what poor sinners had to say for evermore; the hand consecrated to minister to their wants, and the feet touched with the same consecrating blood, thus devoted to go up and down on their business, and to transact their affairs with God for evermore; then the oil was put upon the blood signifying that the Holy Ghost was bestowed, in consequence of that blood being shed and sprinkled.

Now compare chapter 14 (v. 2),

> "The law of the leper in the day of his cleansing."

The leper was a picture of the sinner. There was no healing for a leper but by God Himself, no earthly physician could meet his case. If a leper is to be cleansed, *the lamb must be slain.* Now observe verses 13–18,

> "And he shall slay the lamb in the place where he shall kill the sin offering, and the burnt offering, in the holy place":

(the identification of the lamb with the sin offering and the burnt offering is to be noted, and in the holy place) :

> "For as the sin offering is the priest's, so is the trespass offering: it is most holy. And the priest shall take some of the blood of the trespass offering, and the priest shall put it upon the tip of the right ear of him that is to be cleansed [the leper] and upon the thumb of the right hand, and upon the great toe of his right foot: and the priest shall take some of the log of oil, and pour it into the palm of his own left hand: and the priest

shall dip his right finger in the oil that is in his left hand, and shall sprinkle of the oil with his finger seven times before the Lord: and of the rest of *the oil* that is in his hand shall the priest put upon the tip of the right ear of him that is to be cleansed, and upon the thumb of his right hand, and upon the great toe of his right foot, and *upon the blood* of the trespass offering":

(observe that connection) :

"And the remnant of the oil that is in the priest's hand he shall pour upon the head of him that is to be cleansed; and the priest shall make an atonement for him before the Lord."

It is impossible that the truth in our text could have been more distinctly or more beautifully shadowed forth than it is in this Old Testament law for "the cleansing of the leper"—the identification of the priest and the leper, and the connection between the sanctification of the one and of the other, is most striking. Here then we learn that the true secret of Christian life is identification with Christ, and the practical and consecrated walk of the Christian is as he lives on Christ, as he abides in Christ, and as he lives for Christ. It is only as Christ abides in us we are enabled to do this. You remember His own word in John 15:4, "Abide in me, *and* I in you." His abiding in us is the secret power by which we abide in Him, and this mutual abiding is carried on by the Holy Ghost the Comforter, who dwelleth in us; whereby Christ abides in us and enables us, attracts us, and seals us into union with and abiding in Himself.

"The anointing which ye have received of him abideth in you, and ye need not that any man teach you: but as the same anointing teacheth you of all things, and is truth, and is no lie, and even as it hath taught you, *ye shall abide in him*" (I John 2:27).

32

"Sanctified through the truth."—John 17:19

THE APPOINTED MEANS through which His people are
sanctified—"through the truth."
In Ephesians 5:25–27, the apostle writes,

> "Christ . . . loved the church, and gave himself for it; that
> he might sanctify and cleanse it with the washing of water *by
> the word,* that he might present it to himself a glorious church,
> not having spot or wrinkle, or any such thing; but that it should
> be holy and without blemish." Observe the means—"With the
> washing of water by the word."

"Through the truth." The Word of God is the appointed
means for cleansing and purifying the heart; the washing of
water or ordinance of baptism only represents as in a figure the
action of the Word (the truth as it is in Jesus) in cleansing the
soul. Remember this. Indeed the passage before us is a key to
the true meaning of the ordinance.

The text may be interpreted in three ways—

I. "that they . . . might be sanctified through the truth,"
that is, through the truth just stated, even the great fact—"For
their sakes I sanctify myself." It was no mere profession of an
interest in His people, it was no mere boast, but a divine fact,
He *did* sanctify Himself for their sakes. And this great fact, and
"truth," was to be the means and source of their sanctification.

II. "Through the truth" may refer to the whole gospel as
revealing what the Lord Jesus Christ had done, was doing, and
would do for sinners. This was to be the means for engaging

His people's affections, quickening their souls, and purifying their hearts to the end of time.

III. Or "through the truth" may be understood as rendered in the margin, that they might be "truly sanctified."

Consider the subject in reference to this threefold interpretation.

I. "That they might be sanctified through the truth"—that is, through the great fact that the Lord has just stated—"For their sakes I sanctify myself." His was a complete, an unreserved, a voluntary consecration, and setting apart of His whole person, human and divine, on the stipulation and understanding that His people might have the full enjoyment of all He was, and of all the fullness He contained. Our glorious Lord utters these words in prayer; He stands, as it were, beside His burnt offering, He lays His hand upon the head of the victim and He claims for His people a full equivalent for the travail of His soul,— namely, the putting away of their sins, the bestowing upon them His own divine righteousness, the inhabitation of the Holy Ghost, and the supply of every grace which could be necessary for their complete, absolute, and everlasting sanctification in the sight of God. In I Thessalonians 5:23, we have the apostle's prayer for the complete sanctification of the Lord's people.

> "The very God of peace sanctify you *wholly;* and I pray God your whole spirit and soul and body be preserved blameless unto the coming of our Lord Jesus Christ";

and he adds,

> "Faithful is he that calleth you, who also *will do it."*

This prayer of the apostle seems to be merely the response of the Holy Ghost to our Lord's own pleading, when He said, "For their sakes I sanctify myself that they also may be sanctified through the truth." And truly,

> "Faithful is he who hath promised, who also will do it" (I Thess. 5:24).

Again, we read in I Corinthians 1:30,—

> "Of him are ye in Christ Jesus, who of God is made unto us wisdom, and righteousness, and sanctification, and redemption."

So true it is that the great and wondrous fact our Lord had just stated in prayer is evermore the ground and source of the complete sanctification of His people.

II. "Through the truth," as the appointed means for effecting this object so dear to our Saviour's heart,—the sanctification of His people. By "the truth" is meant the facts and doctrines of the everlasting gospel. Many things are true; these are emphatically *"the truth,"* as there are many books; but this is emphatically *the Book,* the Bible. No doubt "the truth," of which the Lord Jesus Christ is specially the substance, is what is here alluded to—"the truth," revealing to us His everlasting, condescending, unchanging love, and what that love led Him to do for us, even to lay down His life that we might live through Him; "the truth," revealing to us that He is now at the right hand of God, and His object in being there is that He might ever live to make intercession for us; "the truth," revealing to us the grandeur and majesty of the salvation He has accomplished, and the union which He has effected between Himself and His people, that they might evermore dwell in Him, and He in them, as members of His Body, of His flesh, and of His bones, and that they might inherit all things who live by virtue of that union.

It is evermore the truth of Christ and His salvation, received into our minds by the operation of the Holy Ghost, by which we are practically separated from all evil, and consecrated unto God. All the fruits of gospel sanctification are *"fruits of faith."* Observe how strikingly this connection is brought out in Colossians 1:4–6; the apostle says,

> "Since we heard of your *faith* in Christ Jesus, and of the *love* which ye have to all the saints, for the *hope* which is laid up

> for you in heaven, whereof ye heard before in *the word of the
> truth* of the gospel; which is come unto you, as it is in all the
> world; and bringeth forth *fruit,* as it doth also in you, *since the
> day ye heard of it,* and knew the grace of God in truth."

Since they knew the word of the truth of the gospel, since they
knew the grace of God in truth, faith was the result—faith in
Jesus; and love was the result of faith—love to all the saints;
and hope was a result—hope laid up for them in heaven; and
fruitfulness was a result; and, finally, another result is added in
verse 10, a

> "Walk worthy of the Lord unto all pleasing."

So that it is evident the word of the truth of the gospel is the
means by which the believer is practically consecrated to God.

It is only so far as we have real scriptural knowledge of the
Lord Jesus Christ, through the Truth, that we believe on Him;
and in our real believing on the Lord Jesus Christ, it is that we
have fellowship with Him; and in real fellowship and communion with the Lord Jesus Christ, consists *the very life and
essence* of gospel sanctification. As we live in Jesus we live on
Jesus, and we enjoy communion with Him in living on Him; in
proportion as we do so we cannot sin; for we live to God. The
mind fully occupied with the love of God in Christ cannot be
occupied with sin; the eye filled with the beauty of Jesus, while
fixed upon that beauty, cannot be attracted by earthy and sinful
things; the heart engaged in contemplating Jesus, while so employed, is above the earth: that soul dwells consciously in God,
and stands upon its high places; and, therefore, it is that the
Lord Jesus Christ prays, "sanctify them through thy truth."

Every development and department of this gospel-sanctifica-
tion is brought about through the operation of the Truth. In
II Peter 1:4, we learn that it is through the knowledge of the
Truth we are made

> "Partakers of the divine nature."

Again (I Peter 1:23), we read,

> "Being born again, not of corruptible seed, but of incorruptible, by the word of God, which liveth and abideth for ever"—

in other words, by "the truth." In verse 22 we read,

> "Seeing ye have purified your souls in obeying the truth."

Observe the connection; obedience to the truth—faith in the truth—is the means of purifying the soul. See also Acts 15:9,—

> "Purifying their hearts by faith."

In I John 3:3, you have the same thing said of hope. What is hope but that principle of the divine life which lays hold upon the promises, and expects them, and specially the promise of our own blessed Master's coming again in glory?—

> "Every man that hath this hope in him, purifieth himself, even as he is pure."

And if we speak of love, what is that which produces love in the soul, or love to God? "We love him because" we *believe* that "he first loved us." In II Corinthians 5:14 we read of this love of Christ, that it is a constraining principle, leading us to live for Him who died for us.

"The truth" is the element in which the Christian lives and walks. The beloved disciple expresses it in one word;

> "I have no greater joy than to hear that my children walk in truth" (III John 4).

The belief of the Truth is, moreover, the seal of the believer's adoption and the earnest of his inheritance. See Ephesians 1: 13, 14:

> "In whom ye . . . trusted, after that ye heard the word of truth, the gospel of your salvation: in whom also after that ye believed, ye were sealed with the Holy Spirit of promise, which is the earnest of our inheritance."

"The entrance of thy word giveth light" and when we dwell in light and walk in light, we dwell in the element in which God Himself dwells, "who dwelleth in the light." It is into God's own marvelous light He leads the soul when the truth enters into any mind.

Light! discovering to us what we are, that we may fly from self.

Light! discovering to us what sin is, that we may loathe it.

Light! discovering to us what Satan is, that we may not be ensnared by his devices.

Light! discovering to us what the world is, that we may not be entrapped by its delusions.

Light! unveiling hell, that we may fly from it to our refuge.

Light! discovering an opened heaven, and Him who beckons us in;

> "If we walk in the light, as he is in the light, we have fellowship one with another, and the blood of Jesus Christ his Son cleanseth us from all sin" (I John 1:7).

The Truth into which the Lord introduces us tells us that "God is love," "and that he commended his love to us in that while we were yet sinners Christ died for us"; it tells us of a Saviour who saves to the uttermost all that come unto God by Him (see Heb. 7:25); it tells us of blood that meets our need, and has made our peace with God; it tells us of home and rest where He who loved us is all in all; and that even the way by which we are journeying thither, is surrounded with "angels and archangels and the company of heaven." With open face we behold as in a glass the glory of the Lord; and as we drink into the spirit and rejoice in the truth, "we are being changed into the same image, from glory to glory, as by the Spirit of the Lord." Therefore He prays, "Sanctify them through thy truth."

How can the eyes that are fixed upon God in Christ engage in sin? How can the ears that are listening to His voice be attentive to iniquity? How can the hands that clasp His feet "pull at sin as with a cartrope"? How can the feet anointed to follow Him, and whose bonds He has unloosened, wander willfully into the byways of sin and error? When we are led astray, it is because the eye is not on Christ, the ear is not listening to Christ, and the heart is not filled with Christ, and then, alas! alas! other things come in; but when we are engaged with the Truth as it is in Jesus, in the light and teaching of the Holy Ghost, sin and self lose their attractiveness; and when the world, the flesh, and the devil present to us their temptations, we shall feel as David did when the three worthies broke through the Philistines' hosts and brought him the water for which he had thirsted from the well of Bethlehem;

> "[He] poured it out to the Lord, and said, My God forbid it me, that I should do this thing: shall I drink the blood of these men that have put their lives in jeopardy?" (I Chron. 11:18, 19).

This will be the answer of conscience and of the heart to every lust. Is not this the blood of my Lord Jesus Christ, "who gave himself for my sins, that he might deliver" me "from this present evil world"?

III. "Sanctified through the truth," that is, *truly sanctified,* so it is rendered in the margin. The sanctification which our Lord Jesus Christ pleaded for on His people's behalf, and with which alone He can be satisfied, is sanctification in the *true sense,* that which will meet all their need from regeneration unto glory. He will have no substitution of forms or ceremonies, or washings, or cleansings. He will be content with nothing less than that they shall be "truly sanctified." Whatever deficiency there may be in them, whatever corruptions, whatever infirmities, whatever failures they may suffer from, He here tells His Father, and tells us, there is enough in Him to counterbalance them, "For their sakes I sanctify myself, that they also might be *truly* sanctified." Nothing less than our being truly sanctified will compensate Him for the travail of His soul, and nothing in His view is to be truly sanctified but what involves identification with Himself. For "their sakes I sanctify myself, that they also might be truly sanctified." His people's sanctification must be according to the measure of the fullness of the supply laid up in Himself for their benefit.

Union with our Lord Jesus is the root and source of His people's sanctification. "From me is thy fruit found." Jesus living in us, who once died for us; Jesus Christ "revealed in us," "formed in us," operating in us, speaking with our words, looking out with our eyes, loving with our hearts, ministering with our hands, and walking with our feet, is our complete and practical sanctification. Oh! to be able to say, "It is no more I that live but Christ that liveth in me."

We have the believer's sanctification clearly traced from the beginning, so far as it applies to our earthly history, in Galatians 1:15, 16,

> "It pleased God, *who separated me from my mother's womb*" —the moment he had existence, separated by God, set apart then and there—*"and called me by his grace"*—the result and fruit of His setting Him apart in love—*"to reveal his Son in me."*

This is true practical sanctification, and this is evermore its order. The God of all grace, because of His great love, sets apart His child the moment he has existence, and then in time calls him by His grace through the Truth, tells him *he is a child,* and then, in the knowledge of his adoption, reveals the Son of God not only *to him* but *in him.* This is the being *"truly sanctified,"* of which the Lord speaks, and here He concludes His prayer, so far as it has special reference to His disciples.

It will help us to have clear ideas on this subject to remember that when He prays for their sanctification, (1) He does not pray that their *persons* might be sanctified, for this simple reason, their persons had been sanctified. "Sanctified by God the Father" (Jude 1). "Separated, sanctified from their mother's womb." This sanctification of the persons of His people was not a matter for prayer, it had been already effected by God's own sovereign gracious act (see Eph. 1:3, 4). *No mediator was necessary in order to this!* We need to learn these things, for we live at a lower rate than our God has provided for us. If we are to be sanctified through the truth *we must know the truth.* The Lord did not pray that the persons of His people might be sanctified through the truth, for this simple reason, *they had been "sanctified* by God the Father," and "chosen in Christ Jesus before the world was."

(2) He does not pray for an increased degree of their sanctification in Himself. That was impossible! They could not be more sanctified in the sight of God than they were. The apostle, addressing believers at Corinth, speaks of them all as "sanctified in Christ Jesus," one as much as another; no possible ground exists for degrees in reference to the sanctification of believers in Christ Jesus—

> "He is made unto them sanctification . . . ye are complete in him" (see I Cor. 1:30; Col. 2:9).

(3) Neither does He pray for the sanctification of *the natural man.* The natural man never can be sanctified.

> "That which is born of the flesh is flesh" (John 8:6).

Make what you will of it, it cannot rise higher than the nature and principle from which it has its beginning;

> "Flesh and blood cannot enter into the kingdom of God" (I Cor. 15:50).

If the Lord does not refer to the natural man, much less does He mean the natural body when He says, "Sanctify them." We await the morning of the resurrection for the sanctification of the body, then

> "This corruptible must put on incorruption, and this mortal
> must put on immortality" (I Cor. 15:53).

Not for sanctification of their persons; not for increase of their
sanctification; not for the sanctification of the natural man; not
for the sanctification of their poor flesh doth He pray, but for
the illumination and consequent sanctification of their minds
and hearts "through the truth." Thus also the apostle prays for
believers at Ephesus,

> "That the God of our Lord Jesus Christ, the Father of glory,
> may give unto you the spirit of wisdom and revelation in the
> knowledge of him: the eyes of your understanding being en-
> lightened; that ye may know what is the hope of his calling"
> (Eph. 1:17, 18).

Oh! it is the knowledge of our standing in Christ, the realization
of our completeness in Him, and the conscious possession of
promises, all yea and amen to us in Him, which are the operating
principles upon the practical walk of the believer:

> "Having therefore these promises, dearly beloved, let us
> cleanse ourselves from all filthiness of the flesh and spirit, per-
> fecting holiness in the fear of God" (II Cor. 7:1).

The practical walk and life of the Christian is the result and development of the complete sanctification the believer possesses,
in the Lord Jesus Christ. The more we apprehend this, the more
we walk in the light, and in the conscious possession of this, according to the truth, the more will our walk be worthy of our
high and holy calling.

Let us endeavor to keep in mind the following all-important
matters:

1. Evidently, all those for whose sins Christ has satisfied,
shall be "sanctified through the truth." Those for whom He has
made satisfaction He will undoubtedly sanctify.

2. What it cost Him so much to procure, He will hardly fail
to *effect;* what it required such labor and pains, and suffering,

and humiliation to accomplish, He will not be likely to neglect. If a man lays out millions of money in purchasing a property, he is not likely easily to let it go. Depend upon it the Lord Jesus Christ spent too much pains, laid out too much precious blood for the purchase of His people, and for the sanctification of His people, to be easily deprived of them. Who is to deprive Him of them? In virtue of His mediatorial office, He is over all principalities and powers, and every name that is named, not only in this world, but also in that which is to come.

3. Again, what a motive *this* fact ought to be to stimulate us to use the means God has provided, in order that we might walk with God closely and in fellowship. If it be a matter so near the Saviour's heart, can we be careless on a matter that doth so deeply interest Him, and in which not only His honor but our own happiness is involved? No child of God can be happy while he is walking carelessly; his own peace is not less at stake than his Father's honor.

4. Again, the truth which reveals Jesus to us as our sanctification, is God's own appointed means for accomplishing Christ's prayer, for our practical sanctification; for He says, "Sanctify them through thy truth," and

> "For their sakes I sanctify myself, that they also might be sanctified through the truth."

Oh! let us value "the truth"—God's own truth written for us as in letters of blood, witnessed by the Holy Ghost sent down from heaven, which the wisdom of God hath devised, and the love of God, the grace of God, and the power of God hath bestowed. Let us value the truth. If we let it go, we let go the means of our own sanctification. "Buy the truth and sell it not"; if we let it go, we let go the means of our comfort. Oh! contend for the truth, the simple "truth as it is in Jesus." Men and devils devise other ways and means for sanctifying the soul; God's means is obedience to "the truth."

But, it may be asked, is this sanctification through the truth always discernible? To the well-instructed mind it may be so, but truly one of the last lessons we learn in the school of Christ is to recognize in our humiliations, our failures, our emptyings, and in the producing causes of our sighs and tears, some of God's own appointed or permitted means for our true sanctification.

Again, it may be asked, Is this sanctification through the truth always progressing? Undoubtedly! The Lord never allows any work to which He has put His hand to stand still; but we are very apt to make many great mistakes as to this progressing sanctification. Depend upon it we are never more practically or truly sanctified, than when we are most disgusted with ourselves, and when in conscious need and bankruptcy we are leaning most confidingly, and unreservedly, on the Lord Jesus Christ, and with no other warrant for doing so than is to be found in God's testimony concerning Him as given to us by the Spirit of God in *the truth.* This sanctification of the believer consists as much in the daily discovery of himself, and that he is nothing but sinful need, as in teaching him that "Christ is all and in all." Perhaps when we are near the end of our earthly education in the school of Christ we are beginning to know this, but young believers are apt to look rather at what they suppose to be the testimony of the Spirit of God *within them concerning themselves,* than at the testimony of the Spirit of God *without them concerning Christ;* and thus in ignorance and unbelief they draw disparaging, disheartening conclusions concerning themselves because of "the truth" which the Spirit of God discovers to them of themselves.

If we are walking in the light, the light will discover the truth, and make "all things manifest." The Spirit of God cannot show us a more abominable picture than we are in ourselves,

"The heart is deceitful above all things, and desperately wicked: who can know it? I the Lord search the heart" (Jer. 17:9, 10), and even He cannot afford to show us self but by degrees, and in the measure in which He reveals Jesus to us, because self is so abominable, it would crush us to realize it, scarcely could faith outlive the discovery; but as He reveals us to ourselves, He doth also discover to us God's salvation, supplying promises of grace to meet the infirmity and the ruin of our nature; and as we rise to fuller and worthier views of sinful self, apprehending at the same time more fully "the things for which we are apprehended in Christ Jesus," *our practical sanctification goes on;* and I know of no practical sanctification on earth beyond that, at which that believer has arrived, who in the fullest realization of his own unworthiness can nevertheless say with the apostle,

> "I know whom I have believed and am persuaded that he is able to keep that which I have committed unto him against that day" (II Tim. 1:12).

God's order is "Sanctified by God the Father, preserved in Christ Jesus and called" (Jude 1).

> "Called . . . by our gospel to the obtaining of the glory of our Lord Jesus Christ" (II Thess. 2:14).

33

"NEITHER PRAY I FOR THESE ALONE, BUT FOR THEM ALSO
WHICH SHALL BELIEVE ON ME THROUGH THEIR
WORD."—John 17:20

W E HAVE NOW arrived at a third part of our Lord's prayer. From verse 1 to 6, His petitions had peculiar reference to Himself; from verse 6 to 20, to His disciples; and from this verse to the end they embrace His whole Church.

We have great depths to explore through the remainder of this chapter. Our Lord reserved His highest petitions to the close of His prayer, and until His great heart had taken in and embraced all the company of His redeemed. We may gather from the fact of the Lord's petitions rising higher and higher in the scale of glory as He approaches the close of His prayer, that the more He thinks of His people, and the more He exercises Himself, as Mediator, in their behalf, the more is His heart drawn out to their need and to themselves.

A cursory view of the whole prayer will help our minds to an intelligent understanding of the great theme before us. He who is addressing the Father had lain in His bosom from all eternity, and now, in the hearing of His disciples, He is pleased to utter transactions which had taken place between the Father and Himself before the world was:

"O Father, glorify thou me, with thine own self, with *the glory which I had with thee before the world was*" (v. 24);

"Father, I will that they also, whom thou *hast* given me, be with me where I am; that they may behold my glory, which thou hast given me; *for thou lovedst me before the foundation of the world"* (v. 24). Again, He speaks of the highest act of God's love and grace towards His people as consisting in the fact of His having given them to Him: "I have manifested thy name unto the men which thou gavest me out of the world; thine they were, and thou gavest them me" (v. 6).

And this is repeated again and again—see verse 9, "I pray . . . for them which thou *hast given me;* for they are thine": and in verse 11, "Holy Father, keep through Thine own name those whom *thou hast given me"*: and in verse 12, "Those that *thou gavest me* I have kept": and in verse 24, "I will that they also, whom thou hast *given me,* be with me where I am." Moreover, He speaks of His having manifested to them His Father's name, and of having given to them His Father's Word, as the immediate consequence of His having received them as His Father's gift, "I have manifested thy name unto *the men which thou gavest me* out of the world" (v. 6); and, "I have given unto them the words which thou gavest me" (v. 8). Then He prays for their safety, "Holy Father, keep them"; He prays for their sanctification, "Sanctify them through thy truth"; for their union, "That they all may be one"; and He demands their glory, for He says, "Father, I will that they also, whom thou hast given me, be with me where I am."

Our dear Lord might have asked anything for His people that either the power or love of God could supply; He was willing to ask the best things for them, and He merited that they should obtain any blessing He might be pleased to demand for them of His Father. Yet He doth not ask for worldly riches, nor long life, nor great influence; He doth not ask for them the possession and enjoyment of the things which this poor, mistaken world runs riot in order to obtain; He doth not ask that they should be exempt from trial, and difficulties, and temptations, and disappointments. On the contrary, He says, "I pray not that thou shouldest take them out of the world"; but He does pray that they may be *kept* in the Father's name, and that they may be *sanctified* through the Father's truth, that they might be *united* in the Father's love, and that ultimately they might *behold the Father's glory.*

In this beautiful and comprehensive petition, we may each read our own names, if indeed we are believers in the Lord Jesus Christ. The weakest believer and the feeblest, may hear his own name presented before the Lord, and his own case considered and provided for, as truly, and as fully, as was the name and the case of the disciple whom Jesus loved. "Neither pray I for these alone, but for them also which *shall believe* on me through their word."

Consider again:—

I. The Person praying, and the character in which He prays.

II. The persons for whom He pleads, as He describes them— "those who shall believe on him."

III. The means and instrumentality by which they shall believe—"through their word."

I. *The Person.* He who here presents Himself, and opens out His whole heart before His heavenly Father, was personally and essentially the only begotten Son of God; but He does not pray in this character. Deity could not pray; Deity could not receive from any one; but He who was Deity had become man; and here He who was God-man prays to His Father and our Father, to His God and our God, as Mediator; in accordance with the offices He had undertaken and assumed in the covenant between Father, Son, and Holy Ghost, and in reference to the relationships in which He stood then and there towards those for whom He prayed.

Christ now prayed as "the head of his body the church." In the natural body it is the head which thinks for all the other members: the head provides for them, feels for them, sees for them, receives nourishment for them; and here, as Head of the Church, Christ pleads for all the members of His mystical Body, for as the natural body is not one member but many, so also the mystical Body of Christ is not one member but many; and the Head is Christ.

All the concerns of all His members were before Him when He uttered this prayer; and all His fullness was for their benefit, He knew it and would have them know it also; He was now, as Head of His Church, about to lay down His life the substitute for His people. Not one name of all the many names of all the members of that mystical Body, not one case of all their many cases was overlooked or forgotten in His great heart.

He prays as their Representative. He does represent His people; He merits all things for them, and He here claims for them all that He merits. Surely if we did but meditate more on the Lord Jesus Christ as He is here set before us, we could not but have confidence in Him; we could not distrust or fear Him; we could not entertain a hard thought of Him.

II. Consider *the persons* for whom He prays. "Those who shall believe on me." They are here described in a three-fold point of view, namely, in reference—

1. To the time when they believed.
2. The Object on whom they believed.
3. The instrumentality by which they believed.

Remember we have here the Lord Jesus' *own* description of the persons for whom He prays. "Those who shall believe on me."

(1) Mark the time, "who *shall* believe." They had not yet believed. They did not yet know Him, and had not come to Him —not one of them. As God loves His people in His own election view of them, so Christ prays for them. What encouragement is here for those who pray for unconverted relatives! Some of us have children who as yet know not the Lord, parents who have not yet believed, friends very dear to us who have never come to Him: He prayed for those who knew Him not, and believed not on Him. His prayer for them brought the Holy Ghost to them that they might believe; and He who had promised Jesus,

> "Ask of me, and I shall give thee the heathen for thine inheritance, and the uttermost parts of the earth for thy possession" (Ps. 2:8),

saith also to us in His Word, "Whatsoever ye shall ask in My Son's name I will do it." First He prays for His people in their unbelief, that they *may* believe; and then He prays for them when they *do* believe

> "That the eyes of [their] understanding being enlightened; that [they] may know what is the hope of his calling, and what the riches of the glory of his inheritance in the saints" (Eph. 1:18).

(2) The Object on whom they were to believe. "I pray for them . . . which shall believe *on me*";

He does not say, which shall believe in God, but *"on me"*;

He does not say, which believe the Word of God, but *"on me"*;

He does not say, who believe in their salvation, but *"on me."* Here we learn the faith that justifies is faith in *the Person* of the Lord Jesus Christ. Who is there, except a few professed infidels, who do not tell you they believe in God?—who, in this country, but a few professed infidels, do not say they believe in the Word of God? We may quite satisfy ourselves that we believe in God, and in the Word of God; and in our own ultimate salvation; and yet we may not be included in our Lord's prayer, because He does not say, "I pray for them which shall believe" —in God, or in the Word of God, or in their own salvation, but—*"on me."*

Not that to believe in God, or in the Word of God, and in the fact of our own salvation, is not our privilege and duty. Oh, no! But when we believe in Him, we believe in God in a different sense; we believe in the Word of God as a different thing, and for a different object. We believe in God as loving us when we were sinners, and giving His Son to die; we believe in the

Word of God as the truth revealing this fact; we believe in our salvation as the end of our faith; but we believe on the Lord Jesus Christ as the Saviour who took our place, died in our stead, was wounded for our transgressions, whose blood cleanseth from all sin, and who, in resurrection glory, now stands before the throne as our Representative, Himself the object of all-justifying faith. Alas! how many talk of believing in God, and in His Word, who have never believed on the Lord Jesus Christ, and have never taken refuge in Him for their salvation.

There are several passages of Scripture which bear upon this truth. Let us quote a few:

> "Be it known unto you therefore, men and brethren, that through this man is preached unto you the forgiveness of sins: and *by Him,* all that believe are justified from all things" (Acts 13:38, 39).

In Romans 3:24, 25, we read,

> "Being justified freely by his grace, through the redemption that is in Christ Jesus: whom God hath set forth to be a propitiation through *faith in his* blood."

Observe how justifying faith is limited to the Lord Jesus Christ as its object, and to faith in His blood. John 3:16 is a passage familiar to us all:

> "God so loved the world, that he gave his only begotten Son, that whosoever believeth *in him* should not perish, but have everlasting life";

and verses 35, 36,

> "The Father loveth the Son, and hath given all things into *his* hand."

That is what we are to believe—it is God's testimony concerning Christ. Next follows what we are to believe concerning Him,

"He that believeth on the Son *hath* everlasting life: and he
that believeth not the Son shall *not* see life; *but the wrath of
God abideth on him,*"

even though he profess to believe in God, and his Bible, and
though he profess to be sure of his own salvation! "Neither pray
I for these alone, but for them also which shall believe *on me.*"

There are four acts of the mind in reference to the Lord Jesus
Christ, wherein consists the essence of justifying faith. First,
there is knowledge—see Isaiah 53:11:

"By his knowledge [or by the knowledge of Himself] shall
my righteous servant justify many; for he shall bear their iniquities."

See also John 17:3:

"This is life eternal, that they might know thee the only true
God, and Jesus Christ whom thou hast sent."

This knowledge is conveyed to us in the gospel. Angels came
down at the nativity of the Lord Jesus Christ, and sang,

"[We] bring you good tidings of great joy, which shall be to
all people, for unto you is born this day, in the city of David, a
Saviour, which is Christ the Lord" (Luke 2:11).

This knowledge we must possess before we can have any justifying faith in Him: all faith in Christ is grounded upon the
knowledge of Christ. "I know," says the apostle, "whom I have
believed." If he did not know Him, he could not believe upon
Him. We must know Jesus Christ as set forth in God's Word
ere we can possibly believe upon Him. This, then, is the first
act of the soul, in reference to justifying faith,—acquaintance
with Christ, in the *knowledge of Him,* as gathered from the
Word of God, knowledge as to who He is, what He has done,
and what He has promised.

Next follows *the assent of the heart* to what we know of Him,
and this is called *"believing* on him" as contrasted with mere

knowledge. When we know what is declared concerning the Lord Jesus Christ—His love, His life, and His work—then follows *the assent of the heart* to what we know. Thus the apostle states it in I John 5:10, 11:

> "He that believeth not God hath made him a liar; because he believeth not the record that God gave of his Son. And this is the record, that God hath given to us eternal life, and this life is in his Son."

We must first know the facts recorded, and the assent of the heart to those recorded facts is called "believing on him."

The third act of the soul follows—namely, *accepting Him on whom we believe*—in other words, receiving the Lord Jesus Christ:

> "As many as received him, to them gave he power to become the sons of God, even to them that believe on his name" (John 1:12).
>
> "I know whom I have believed, and am persuaded that he is able to keep that which I have committed unto him" (II Tim. 1:12).

In the beautiful description of the faith of the early patriarchs (Heb. 11:13) we have all three acts of the kind enumerated:

> "These all died in faith, not having received the promises, but having *seen them afar off*"—

there is the eye of the understanding, the intelligent acquaintance with truth, the knowledge of the fact that God had promised; "and *were persuaded of them*"—there is the believing of them; and thirdly, they *"embraced them"*—took them in, accepted them.

The fourth act of the soul in reference to the Lord Jesus Christ is to trust in Him—resting on Him, reposing, relying on Him, as being what the promises declare Him to be. Thus it is written (Eph. 1:13, 14),

"In whom ye also trusted, *after* that ye heard the word of truth, the gospel of your salvation."

This then is what true faith is: *knowing* what God has said, *believing* what we know, *accepting* what we believe, and then rolling ourselves, and our burdens, our poor weary heart and soul *upon Him on whom we believe.* For all who do so the Lord Jesus prayed, not for His disciples alone, but "for all them also which shall believe on me through their word."

But here an objection meets us. Someone will say, we cannot believe of ourselves, we cannot know, we cannot receive, we cannot repose upon the Lord Jesus Christ, or rest in Him of our own selves. True! you *"will not,"* and therefore cannot, but the gospel itself is the very means and instrument by which God *produces* this knowledge and this believing, and bestows the ability to receive and repose our souls on the Lord Jesus Christ. "Faith comes by *hearing,"* knowledge comes by *hearing,* receiving the Lord Jesus Christ comes by *hearing* of Him; and the repose of the soul upon Him for salvation is the simple result of hearing and believing that He is the Saviour,

"Able to save to the uttermost all that come unto God by him" (Heb. 7:25).

The entreaties of the gospel, the warnings of the gospel, the commands of the gospel are God's means for quickening sinners' souls, begetting divine faith in their hearts, and ministering to them the Holy Ghost; and all the fruits of a righteous walk, and the hopes of a happy eternity flow from believing in the Lord Jesus Christ.

Do we speak of comfort? "Let not your heart be troubled; ye believe in God believe also in me." See God's appointed channel for the supply of all His comforts to your soul!

Do we desire to be holy and pure?—

"Every man that hath this hope in him [Jesus] purifieth himself, even as he is pure" (I John 3:3);

faith in Him is the fountain-head of all purity. Do we desire to be filled with the Holy Ghost?

> "In the last day, that great day of the feast, Jesus stood and cried, saying, If any man thirst, let him come unto me, and drink. He that *believeth on me,* as the scripture hath said, out of his belly shall flow rivers of living water. But this spake he of the Spirit, which they that *believe on him* should receive" (John 7:37–39).

Do not rest satisfied with general notions of truth, or with vague ideas of believing in God. The justifying object of faith is the Lord Jesus Christ. And our believing on the Lord Jesus Christ demonstrates our interest in all His salvation work, for He says, "Neither pray I for these alone, but for them also which shall believe on me through their word." If you want to know whether or not you are a child of God, ask yourself another question. "Do I believe on the Lord Jesus Christ?" The weakest believer is interested in Christ as truly and as much as the strongest believer, for He prays for those who believe on Him without any reference to the degree of their faith: He says nothing about it.

Again, when Jesus becomes the entire object of our faith, it implies two things: (1) The conscious deficiency of our own merit (if we had merit of our own we need not lean upon Him). (2) The all-sufficiency of His merit on whom we believe. Oh! let us fetch in Christ to our hearts by faith, lay hold on Christ, receive Christ, live on Christ, that "out of his fulness we may all receive, and grace for grace."

(3) We have also the description of those for whom the Lord Jesus Christ prayed, in connection with *the instrumentality* by which they believed. It is not every faith that is divine faith; it is not every believer that is included in the Lord's prayer; it is not every one who calls himself a believer that is alluded to; when He says "those who believe," He means those only who

believe on Him *"through their word."* I know no more important truth for the days in which we are living than this, and I
dwell upon it because it is most precious and essential. Now observe the faith, *the only faith* our Lord Jesus Christ acknowledges, is faith begotten by *the teaching of the Word which He
had given to His disciples;* "for I have given unto them the
words which thou gavest me"; "and I pray for them which shall
believe on me *through their word";* not through traditions; not
through human systems; not through improvements; not
through churches, and ministers, but "through their word";
not, of course, the word of which they were the *authors,* but the
Word of which they were the *preachers,* and of which they were
the *penmen.*

Remember,

(1) It is the gospel of the grace of God, "the record," God's
testimony concerning the Lord Jesus and His love and that "he
died for our sins and rose again for our justification," *which
makes believers.* This gospel is the instrument in the hands of
God for producing faith and

> "Is the power of God unto salvation to every one that be-
> lieveth" (Rom. 1:16).

(2) No other faith whatever, however much religiousness
there may be about it, no faith grounded on any other communication is accounted by the Lord Jesus Christ to be the faith
of His people. It is faith exclusively through *"their word"* of
which He speaks, and therefore *no other believers, whatever
they may believe, but only those who believe through the Word
of God, were prayed for by the Lord Jesus on this occasion:*
"Neither pray I for these alone, but for them also which shall
believe on me through their word."

Oh! I feel the power and importance of this statement, and
the necessity that exists for insisting on it in this our day, when
such strange and confusing doctrines are preached, founded

upon I know not what—revelations, theories, new discoveries dogmas, councils, or decretals having no agreement with the Word which our Lord Jesus Christ gave to His apostles. Such faith is not founded on revelation, but delusion; it is not faith, it is unbelief; it is not wisdom, it is folly; it is not salvation, it is ruin. *Believers in other words or in other teaching than what the apostles taught, are none of Christ's believers; and they are none of those for whom Christ prayed;* "Neither pray I for these alone, but for them also which shall believe on me through their word." Oh, how this statement of our blessed Lord magnifies the value of the Scriptures!

34

"THAT THEY ALL MAY BE ONE; AS THOU, FATHER, ART IN
ME, AND I IN THEE, THAT THEY ALSO MAY BE
ONE IN US."—John 17:21

WE READ in Exodus 28:29, that the high priest was bound
by the law of his office whenever he approached God in
worship to bear about him

> "The names of the children of Israel in the breastplate of
> judgment upon his heart . . . for a memorial before the Lord
> continually."

And here we have his great Antitype, the Lord Jesus, presenting
Himself before His Father; and having gathered into His heart
every name and case of all His believing ones to the end of time,
He now expresses His whole heart's desire for them before God:
"That they all may be one; as thou, Father, art in me, and I in
thee, that they also may be one in us."

It is a vast effort for human thought to conceive or for human
language to utter, even in a remote degree, the immensity of
the grace here expressed by the Lord Jesus Christ in reference
to His blood-bought ones, and the unspeakable glory here
claimed by Him for the weakest and the feeblest true believer in
His Word. Let us endeavor, the Lord helping us, to approach
the subject by degrees, and as best we can.

Our Lord's prayer must have been answered. He could not
pray in vain. And if this be so, then it is a divine fact, a most
blessed reality, that all His believing people *are one,* according
to His own words, "even as thou, Father, art in me, and I in

thee." But what does He mean by these words? What is the force of them?

(1) The Lord does not here speak of an absolute, complete, and perfect *uniformity* between believers in His name. If He did, His prayer had not been answered, for no such uniformity exists. (2) He does not speak of a union between the different *sects* and denominations of the professing Christian church—if He did, His prayer has not been answered, for alas! no such union exists. For my own part, I believe sects and denominations to be the result of the devil's attempt to mar and hinder as far as possible the visible union of the Church of God: and that they all have their root in our spiritual pride and selfishness, our self-sufficiency and our sin. (3) The Lord does not pray that His people should be more united in His Father's purpose, because this would be *impossible*. It is a most precious truth, and one which the Scriptures treat of most fully, that the Father always saw His people as united to Himself in the Lord Jesus Christ. In this view of them He elected them, and in this view of them He

> "Blessed [them] with all spiritual blessing in heavenly places
> in Christ" (Eph. 1:3).

He has never regarded Jesus apart from His Church, nor His Church apart from Jesus; and He never will and never can do so. (4) The Lord doth not pray that His people may be more united one to another and to Himself *in fact,* no need for this, because they are in fact united. Why then, you ask, does He use such language—"that they all may be one"? The answer is this: in our heavenly Father's dealings with His people in grace, He always hath regard to the righteousness, the fullness, and mediation of the Lord Jesus Christ our Saviour. In all His outgoings to us, both in His purposes and in His performances, He hath evermore had respect unto the Lord Jesus Christ as being in Himself alone the *meritorious cause* of all our blessings, and His priestly intercession on our behalf as the divinely arranged *channel* by which they are to flow in upon our souls. You remember after the Lord had spoken wondrous things by the prophet in the way of promise and grace concerning the people of Israel, revealing what He would do for them, and in them, He says,

> "Thus saith the Lord God; I will yet for this be enquired of by the house of Israel to do it for them" (Ezek. 36:37).

Thus, in like manner, whatsoever blessings have been secured to us in Christ, all are to be enjoyed by us *as received at His hands, and obtained for us through His intercession.* Thus we are told of our Great High Priest that,

> "He is able to save to the uttermost all that come unto God by him, seeing he ever liveth to make intercession for them" (Heb. 7:25),

and therefore our Lord here prays, "that they all may be one"; first, because He was Himself the ground of this union; secondly, because His prayer was the appointed and suitable channel through which the benefits of it were to be enjoyed; thirdly, that we might understand what a costly and divine blessing this union is; and lastly, that our hearts might be assured as to the certainty and abiding character of this union, seeing Christ desired and prayed for it. Oh! for faith while we listen that we may henceforth rejoice in the privileges and blessings which our union with Christ and with each other involves. His prayer did not make this union a fact, but it was the divinely appointed means of communicating the enjoyment of the fact to His believing people, that in apprehending their union, they might *manifest it.*

First, there is that union which all the Lord's believing people have one with another as members of the same body, as children in the same family, as living stones in the same spiritual temple, the foundation stone of which is the Lord Jesus Christ. In

Ephesians 3:15, we have this thought of the family brought out,

> "Of whom the whole family in heaven and earth is named";

a family composed not only of living believers, but including those who shall believe for ages to come: "Neither pray I for these alone, but for them also which shall believe on me through their word"; and not only of present and future believers in the Lord Jesus Christ, but the family includes all who have died in the faith, and are gone before—the family in heaven as well. In Colossians 1:20, we read:

> "Having made peace through the blood of his cross, by him to reconcile all things unto himself; by him, I say, whether they be things in earth, or things in heaven."

The whole subject is beautifully sketched in Ephesians 2: 14, 15:

> "He is our peace, who hath made both one, and hath broken down the middle wall of partition between us; having abolished in his flesh the enmity, even the law of commandments contained in ordinances; for to make in himself of twain one new man, so making peace."

Here is first, union between Jew and Gentile, and then between both with God: for He adds,

> "And that he might reconcile both unto God in one body by the cross, having slain the enmity thereby."

But it may be asked, How can such union as this really exist, seeing it is made up of persons of divers nations, of divers ages, and of divers circumstances? The bond of union between the people of the Lord Jesus Christ is not a visible or corporeal one, but it is not the less close and real on that account. There are seven grounds of union binding the children of God to each other.

1. In Ephesians 4:3, *"the unity of the Spirit."* The same Holy

Ghost dwells in all—*"in* one Spirit we are all baptized into one body" (I Cor. 12:13).

2. In Ephesians 4:13, *"the unity of the faith."* All the children of God have their trust, hope, and confidence fixed on the same Father; all speak of the same righteousness, all plead the same blood; they are all born of promise, and are "children by faith." Oh! how much more there is to unite the children of God than there is to separate them, if they could only believe it.

3. In Acts 4:32, we read of the early believers (a picture of the case as it ought to be), *"they were of one heart."*

4. In Colossians 2:2, *"knit together in love."* Love unites the children of God, wherever they meet; whenever they recognize each other they cannot help loving one another, notwithstanding all their peculiarities, and all their differences. When hearts and hearts are drawn together, and they speak one to the other of the one hope, the one glorious home, oh! how they cleave to one another, and the unity of love is manifest and felt.

5. In Ephesians 4:3, *"The bond of peace";* sweet peace, of which our Lord said, "Peace I leave with you, my peace I give unto you." Oh! it is a heavenly bond; strangers cannot intermeddle with it.

6. In I Corinthians 1:10, "perfectly joined together in the *same mind."*

7. And in the *same judgment.*

These things lay deeply in our Lord's heart when He prayed "that they all might be one"; and the Holy Ghost has recorded it in His Word, that we may have them evermore in our hearts also. Shame upon us that our union is not more manifested, seeing there are so many heavenly bonds cementing us together, and from which we are absolutely unable to disengage ourselves!

Second, there is union between the body, made up as it is of many members, and the glorious Head Himself. In Colossians 1:18 we read,

"He is the head of the body, the church: who is the beginning, the firstborn from the dead; that in all things he might have the pre-eminence."

Again, in 2:19, the apostle finds fault with certain persons at Colosse, for

"Not holding the Head, from which all the body by joints and bands having nourishment ministered, and knit together, increaseth with the increase of God."

In Ephesians 4:13, we have this union described in its consummation:

"Till we all come in the unity of the faith, and of the knowledge of the Son of God, unto a perfect man, unto the measure of the stature of the fulness of Christ,"

and verse 15:

"Speaking the truth in love, may grow up into him in all things, which is the head, even Christ."

Oh, what union is here! We know something of it as it exists in the natural body; where the head sees for the whole body, thinks for the body, provides for the body, receives nourishment for the body, and where if the head be honored the whole body is honored, for "if one member be honoured all the members rejoice with it," See I Corinthians 12:12–14, 21:

"As the body is one, and hath many members, and all the members of that one body, being many, are one body: so also is Christ. For by one Spirit are we all baptized into one body, whether we be Jews or Gentiles, whether we be bond or free; and have been all made to drink into one Spirit. For the body is not one member, but many . . . the head cannot say to the feet, I have no need of you."

The Head of the spiritual mystical Body being united to it, thinks for it, provides for it, sees for it, rules it, receives the nourishment for it, and from the Head, by joints and bands, the whole Body and its members receive the nourishment ministered; the anointing upon the Head comes down upon the members, and the glory upon the Head shall yet be the glory of the members. Beautiful union; the Lord prays that it may be enjoyed by His people!

Third. "As thou, Father, art in me, and I in thee." Here are divine words, very difficult to open out. The Lord Jesus Christ speaks as Mediator, as the Days-man between God and us, for He speaks in prayer. In another place (14:11) He uses similar language,

> "Believe me that I am in the Father, and the Father in me."

And here He prays that as the Father is in Him, and He is in the Father, so His people may be one with Him, and with the Father. He could not ask more: I believe there is nothing beyond this possible; and I suppose if more were possible, and if there were anything beyond, that His blood could merit for us, or His love secure, we should have it.

If we refer to the I and II Epistles to the Thessalonians we read,

> "The church of the Thessalonians which is in God the Father, and in the Lord Jesus Christ" (I Thess. 1:1),

and, in II Thessalonians 1:1, the same language occurs:

> "The church of the Thessalonians in God our Father, and the Lord Jesus Christ."

The amazing truth here expressed is, that there is a union between Christ and His people, which can be compared only to the union between the Father and the Son. "As thou, Father, art in me, and I in thee." Now there is an *as* of similitude and likeness, and there is also an *as* of equality. The *as* here is not the *as* of equality—only the Father, the Son, and the Holy Ghost can be united in equality; but it is the *as* of similitude and likeness. The expression is used in the same way in Matthew

5:48: "Be ye . . . perfect, even as your Father which is in heaven is perfect." It does not mean, Be as perfect as God, but a perfection of likeness and similitude; as also, in the prayer commonly called the Lord's prayer, "Forgive us our trespasses, as we forgive them that trespass against us."

There is a threefold union between the Lord Jesus Christ and His Father, and He will have a counterpart to each of them in the union between His people and Himself. This subject is very deep. If the Spirit of God would only shine upon our minds, what a feast for our souls we should gather from it!

1. The highest union in existence, and the closest possible, is the union between the Man Christ Jesus, and the Second Person in the Trinity, the Son of God. This is what is termed the hypostatic union. The human nature complete in all its fullness, and the divine nature complete in all its attributes, are united in one glorious Person; the Godhead not interfering with the essentials of the manhood, and the manhood not interfering with the essentials of the Godhead; but both natures remaining complete in their perfection of one Person—the Lord Jesus Christ—who is in all points like unto His brethren because He is man, and also in all points one with and equal to the Father because He is God: and this union doth not destroy or hinder the human feelings of the man, nor doth the manhood dim the luster and the glory of God. This union is altogether ineffable and inconceivable, but it is clearly revealed for the obedience and joy of faith.

Now the Lord will have the union between Himself and His people to correspond in all respects with this; and even as His human nature is united to the Godhead in His own person, so are all His believing people united to Him, as "members of His body, of His flesh, and of His bones"—that even as the manhood and the Godhead are united in one person—JESUS—which is the highest conceivable union, so is there like union between all believers in Jesus, and the human nature, which is united to the Godhead in His person. And this seems to be the full meaning of His words, "that they all may be one; as thou, Father, art in me, and I in thee." Oh! what blessings must outflow from such a fountain! What crowns, what glories, what enjoyments must result from such a union!

"For ye are Christ's, and Christ is God's" (I Cor. 3:23).

2. There is a love union between the Father and the Son,—the union of dear affection and of mutual delight. Oh! how the Father and the Son delight in each other! The Scripture is full of this (John 3:35):

"The Father loveth the Son, and hath given all things into his hand."

And in Isaiah 42:1:

"Behold my servant, whom I uphold; mine elect, in whom my soul delighteth."

Hear the announcement of it from heaven at the Jordan:

"This is my beloved Son, in whom I am well pleased" (Matt. 3:17).

And in John 1:18,

He is spoken of as being "in the bosom of the Father."

Moreover, the love is mutual; for in John 14:31, it is written,

"That the world may know that I love the Father."

Now the Lord Jesus will have such union of love between His people, Himself, and His Father that, even as the love of the Father flows down upon us in and through Christ, so our love shall go back to Him, to crown Him, and bless Him; that thus we may dwell in God, and find no rest, no portion, no enjoyment but in His love,—there to live, and rest, and nestle evermore, finding our all in Him.

"God is love, and he that dwelleth in love dwelleth in God, and God in him" (I John 4:16).

Oh! nothing less than this will satisfy His love whose name is love; and nothing less than this can ever satisfy redeemed souls —the objects of that love.

3. There is a union of will between the Father and the Son. It consists in the inexpressible agreement and consent of Their wills. They are diverse in person, but they never differ in thought, or aim, or end, or object, or motive. This is our Lord's meaning in John 5:19, a passage so much perverted by Socinians:

"The Son can do nothing of himself, but what he seeth the Father do."

And (v. 30),

"I can of mine own self do nothing."

He would not, He could not act apart, or think apart, or wish apart from His Father; there is perfect unity of will, perfect unity of heart, perfect unity of purpose.

Now, Christ will have the counterpart in His people. Even as He could say, Not as I will, but as Thou wilt, so He will have us say (not in word only but in truth also), "Father . . . not our will, but thine be done." Oh, it would be heaven on earth if we had more of this entire submission to the Father's will! If we would only see with our Father's eyes, and hear with our Father's ears, and move as it were by the direction of our Father's mind, what a heaven our earth would be! Thus it was with Jesus. It was His "meat and drink" to do His Father's will, and He will have it the meat and drink of His people also. Happy people that are in such a case! That was a blessed privilege which we read of as enjoyed by Israel in Old Testament times—"a people near" unto God; here is a far higher privilege, even a people dwelling in God, and God in them, "Even as thou, Father, art in me, and I in thee." This is more than fellowship, this is more than communion, *it is union*—union with God in Christ; the manhood being the link between Jehovah on the throne, and the members of Christ; while from our living and anointed Head of His Church, all blessings shall and must flow down throughout eternity on us, and unending praises and adoration shall ascend through Him from us to God by the Holy Ghost, who dwelleth in us.

Truly unspeakable are the consequences flowing from this union.

(1) *The relationship* into which it introduces us. In reference to it our Lord said,

> "I ascend unto my Father, and your Father; and to my God, and your God" (John 20:17).

(2) *The portion* to which this relationship entitles us,

> "Heirs of God, and joint-heirs with Christ" (Rom. 8:17).

And this not an inheritance apart from Christ, but possessed in Christ, and with Christ. It is written, "The Father loveth the Son, and hath given *all things* into his hand." And we are in Him, "heirs of God, and joint-heirs with Christ." Again, it is written—

> "Let no man glory in men. For all things are yours; . . . the world, or life, or death, or things present, or things to come; all are yours; and ye are Christ's; and Christ is God's" (I Cor. 3:21–23).

(3) *The privileges* we have through this union. "Through him we both"—Jew and Gentile, one Body,—"have access"—the word means we are taken by the hand by One who hath a right to introduce us, and presented before the throne—

> "Have access by one Spirit unto the Father" (Eph. 2:18).

(4) *The interest* in God which this union confers upon us, we dwell in God, and God in us, and in dwelling in God and

God in us, we dwell in love, and love in us, "for *God is love*" (cf. I John 4:12, 13, 16).

(5) Perfect *knowledge* of God is thus secured to us; we shall know God immediately and intimately.

> "Then shall I know, even as also I am known" (I Cor. 13:12).

(6) *The sources of enjoyment* into which this union introduces us, even into "all the fulness of God," because "it pleased the Father that in him"—the Mediator between us and the Deity—"should all fulness dwell," and

> "Of his fulness have all we received, and grace for grace" (John 1:16).

We occupy a position only one degree further from God than Jesus Himself: nay, we can hardly be said to be one degree further, for, *in Jesus,* God dwells in us and we dwell in God.

(7) *The security.* Professors talk about believers being lost. Is it not monstrous to suppose that He will lose one of His members?

> "No man ever yet hated his own flesh; but nourisheth it and cherisheth it, even as the Lord the church" (Eph. 5:29).

What shall separate us? Will Christ separate Himself from God? When Christ separates Himself from God, then His people may be separated from Christ, not till then, for His prayer is "that they all may be one: *as thou, Father, art in me, and I in thee.*"

(8) What a glory life is—*our life!* eternal life! "the divine nature!"

> "Your life is hid with Christ in God" (Col. 3:3),

and "when Christ who is our life shall appear, then shall we also appear with him in glory."

> "What manner of persons ought we to be in all holy conversation and godliness?" (II Peter 3:11).

How ought we who have received the Lord Jesus Christ, and God's fullness in Him, to walk? "As ye have received Christ Jesus the Lord, so walk ye in Him."

What a new and even awful character sin assumes, when committed by a child of God! It is not like ordinary sin, it is so inexpressibly abominable, aggravated as it is by the peculiar position toward God which that sinner occupies. Alas for sin against such love, and against such union! Remember, that this union involves and secures a Father's chastening rod for erring children. Will our Father treat us "as bastards, and not sons" when we sin thus against Him?

May our faith be greatly increased by these weighty truths, and as we believe may we "make God, even the Most High, our habitation," and be assured that no evil shall happen unto us, for He that hath made us one with His dear Son, will never leave us or forsake us. Be careful for nothing, *for two worlds* wait upon us.

35

"THAT THEY ALL MAY BE ONE; AS THOU, FATHER, ART IN
ME, AND I IN THEE, THAT THEY ALSO MAY BE ONE
IN US; THAT THE WORLD MAY BELIEVE
THAT THOU HAST SENT ME."
—John 17:21

OUR BLESSED LORD'S prayer, here, is concerning those who
had believed on Him, and all who shall to the end of time
believe on Him through the words which He had given to His
apostles, even the Word of God, "that all may be one," by
which He evidently means, as indeed He most fully expresses,
not only that all His believing people shall be united *one to
another,* whether believers in Old Testament time or in New
Testament days; whether Jew or Gentile; whether believers in
the past, the present, or the future; whether they had their
home in heaven now, or were still wandering upon the earth,
that all should be united as children of the same heavenly
family, of which He Himself is the Firstborn; all having the
same Father, all to enjoy the same portion, all to be gathered
into the same home, all to partake of the same joys, and having
kindred sympathies, that all should be one—united together as
members of the same mystical Body, of which He Himself was
the Head. Members various, it may be, in their degrees of
strength, and knowledge, and beauty, and usefulness, but each
member in its place, each member having the proper proportion
and growth, so as to carry out the symmetry of the whole Body;
each member ministering to the other, caring for the other,
necessary to the other; each member interested in the prosperity

of the other,—making one beauteous whole, of which the Lord Himself was to be the risen Head and crown.

He would have all united together as living stones in the same spiritual temple, of which He Himself is the foundation and the top-stone; stones gathered from different quarries, not uniform in size, or shape, or even in material, but gathered together and cemented in love; the Builder of the temple, and the Maker of it, God; the Light of it, Himself; and the anthems, the praises of a redeemed people.

He would have all one, as branches of the same living vine, of which He Himself is the Root, evermore and through all eternity putting forth, through them, and by them, His beauty, His fragrance, and His fruitfulness. He would have all united together; the smallest spray in all that living tree is necessary to its beauty and symmetry, and united to the root as truly and as closely as any of the main branches; and there God Himself will rest in His love, and sit down under its shadow with great delight.

But our Lord evidently means *more* than this, because He says, "that they all may be one," and not only so, but one "as thou, Father, art in me, and I in thee, that they also may be one *in us*," possessing the same nature, the same affections, the same will, the same character, and enjoying the same fullness. These are wonderful words, they are

> "As high as heaven; what canst thou do? deeper than hell;
> what canst thou know?" (Job 11:8).

Nothing remained, after this request, but that He should say, as He does in verse 24,

> "Father, I will that they also, whom thou hast given me, be
> with me where I am."

We need to be reminded that our Lord's prayer is not the origin of the union of which He speaks, or the cause of it; but the fruit and result of it. He is not praying that a union might be established between Himself and His people which hitherto had not existed, but that the union which was always in the mind and purpose and heart of God, and on the ground of which Christ came down to be the Saviour, and the Holy Ghost to be the Comforter, *should be enjoyed* and manifested by His believing people. He would by His words scatter heavenly light round about them, and within them, that they might walk in the light as He Himself was in the light, and as the beloved apostle teaches us in his First Epistle that thus we might have

"Fellowship . . . with the Father, and with his Son Jesus Christ" (I John 1:3).

Our Lord leads us in prayer to the fountain-head and source of fellowship with God in those mysterious words, "that they also may be one *in us.*" I need not tell those who are acquainted with their Bibles that the Lord is using scriptural language, and that He is referring directly to the familiar mode of expression by which the Persons in the Godhead are frequently described. You have it first in Genesis 1:26,

"And God said, Let *us* make man in our image, after our likeness";

in 3:22,

"The Lord God said, Behold, the man is become as one of *us*";

in 11:7,

"Let *us* go down, and there confound their language."

See also in Isaiah 6:8–10, in the record of the vision which the prophet had of the manifestation of the glory of the Lord:

"Also I heard the voice of the Lord, saying, Whom shall I send, and who will go for *us?* Then said I, Here am I; send me. And he said, Go, and tell this people, Hear ye indeed, but understand not; and see ye indeed, but perceive not. Make the heart of this people fat . . ."

It is very interesting to trace the quotations of this passage from
the Old Testament, in the New, and thus learn who are meant
by *"us."* The prophet Isaiah tells us (6:1), "Jehovah sitting
upon a throne" and (v. 8), *"I heard the voice of Jehovah* saying, Whom shall I send, and who will go for *us?"* In John
12:39–41, the passage is quoted as referring to Christ:

> "Therefore they could not believe [on Christ], because that
> Esaias said again, He hath blinded their eyes, and hardened
> their heart; that they should not see with their eyes, nor under-
> stand with their heart, and be converted, and I should heal
> them. *These things said Esaias when he saw his glory, and
> spake of him,"*

evidently the Lord Jesus Christ. And again, in Acts 28:25, 26,
the apostle Paul quotes the same in reference to the Holy
Ghost:

> *"Well spake the Holy Ghost* by Esaias the prophet unto our
> fathers, saying, Go unto this people, and say, Hearing ye shall
> hear, and shall not understand; and seeing, ye shall see, and
> not perceive."

Observe the beautiful proof here of the existence and union
of *three Persons* in the Godhead, the "us" of our Lord's Prayer,
—Jehovah the Father, Jehovah the Son, and Jehovah the Holy
Ghost.

Now here our Lord prays that His people may also be one,
using the same language, you perceive, *"one in us!"* The union
of the mystical Body of believers to their Head is personal
union, their souls and bodies are united to the soul and the
body of the Lord Jesus Christ—our souls to His soul, our bodies
to His body, our spirits to His Spirit; thus our whole persons
are united to His whole person, even as His whole person God-
man is united to the Godhead, His manhood united to the Son,
who is one in the Father, and His Spirit united to and dwelling
in His people—that thus we might be truly one, and, not only

one with each other, but also *"one in us"*—as truly, as effectually, as eternally, as beneficially, as mutually, "one, as we are" —*"one in us."*

These words express and imply consequences and communion with God throughout eternity, in the contemplation of which one can scarcely breathe. Deity itself—the fountainhead from whence the Spirit-soul and the body of the believer are to draw; Christ in our nature, the Days-man between the Godhead and the sinner, laying His hand upon both—and Himself the channel through which all unctions and blessings are to flow; the fullness of the Godhead dwelling in Him bodily, our supply; the indwelling power of the Holy Ghost the Comforter, in the believer, our power; that fullness flowing in, until in the unspeakable language of the apostle, we are "filled with all the fulness of God."

Let us, for our own souls' profit, consider some few of the practical conclusions to which truth like this naturally leads us. First, we have revealed to our faith and hope here the highest blessing and source of blessing that even God Himself can bestow upon us. It is union with Himself; and this is more than all things else. Union with God in Christ is more than *all grace* and more than *all glory,* because all grace in time and all glory in eternity shall flow from this. We read in verse 22 a passage which, I conceive, contains one of the deepest of the many deep sayings of Christ: "And the glory which thou gavest me I have given them; *that they may be one, even as we are one."* Evidently, this union is more than the glory given, which is but a means to it. It is a divine reality; and by-and-by, when it shall be fully manifested, Jesus shall "see of the travail of his soul, and shall be satisfied." Meantime, faith may take its highest range, hope may soar to its loftiest flight, and love embrace its fullest portion; yet nothing that faith can reach, or hope aspire to, nothing that love itself is able to comprehend, can possibly exceed what this union with God secures—"That they also may be one *in us"* forevermore. Wonderful! wonderful! the believer's union with God in Christ! It is the foundation gospel truth of revelation; and it is well adapted to fill our thoughts, hearts, hopes, and affections with Christ, by whom "God dwelleth in us and we in God," and who thus introduces it in His prayer that we, listening to Him by faith, may be lifted out of the things of time, and that our desires may soar away unto the things of eternity. Oh, how humbly ought we to walk with our God—how loosely to the things of earth! What manner of persons ought we to be, in all holy conversation and godliness! And if the apostle could say, "Pass the time of your sojourning here in fear; forasmuch as ye know that ye were not *redeemed* with corruptible things, as silver and gold, from your vain conversation received by tradition from your fathers; but with the precious blood of Christ, as of a lamb without blemish, and without spot"; and if the Holy Ghost could say that "God will be sanctified in those who draw *near* to him," how much more in those who are not only "redeemed by the blood" of Jesus, not only made near to God, but are one with Him in God.

> "As thou, Father, art in me, and I in thee, that they also may be one in us."

It is in the reception into our hearts by faith of truths like these the power of practical consecration consists, and we are sanctified as we apprehend, through the teaching of the Holy Ghost, the high position into which the love of God has called us.

Now if, as believers, we are

> "In God the Father and in our Lord Jesus Christ" (I Thess. 1:1),

and if our Lord prayed that *all* who believe on Him should be so, truly the blessing is secure, and the answer certain;—let us then avail ourselves of our position. Our welfare here is not more our own concern, than it is His. Hath He not said,

> "He that toucheth you toucheth the apple of mine eye"?
> (Zech. 2:8).

Have we cares?

> "Cast all your care upon him; for he careth for you" (I Peter
> 5:7).

Have we need? Bring all your need to Him. Are we weak?
Help has been laid on One that is mighty.

We may go to God at all times, and under all circumstances;
for if He has united us with Himself, He has opened a way of
access to Himself *for His own sake*. Even for His own sake He
will not neglect us or refuse us.

If all believers are in God, then are we related one to the
other in Christ, by a far closer and more lasting tie than any
earthly relationship. Mere earthly relationships shall be severed
by-and-by; death will do it for time, and the day of judgment
will do it for eternity; but those who are related in God can
never part, can never meet for the last time, can never say
farewell forever.

If indeed we are in God, we are brothers and sisters in Christ
Jesus; "let us love one another"; let us "bear . . . one another's burdens, and so fulfil the law of Christ"; let us sympathize with one another; let us remember He has promised to
acknowledge from His throne,

> "Inasmuch as ye have done it unto one of the least of these
> my brethren, ye have done it unto me" (Matt. 25:40).

Let us not wrong or misjudge our brethren; and, above all, let
us take heed that we offend not one of the little ones who believe in Jesus;

> "[For] in heaven their angels do always behold the face of
> my Father which is in heaven."

If we be in God, let us live on God; let us not live on a
miserable daily pittance when we have the fullness of God for

our portion. Let us live on God, that we may live for God; and forsaking all other lords, all other loves, all other portions, let us "walk worthy of our calling," as those who are "not their own, but are bought with a price." And let us evermore pray "that God may be glorified in us, and we in Him"; that He may shed abroad His love more and more in our hearts; that He may communicate to us His joy and peace; that He may manifest Himself in us more and more by the Holy Ghost; that He may increase our knowledge of Himself; that we may be "renewed in knowledge day by day," and be established in the communion of the Holy Spirit, till we are

> "Able to comprehend with all saints, what is the breadth, and length, and depth, and height; and to know the love of Christ which passeth knowledge" (Eph. 3:18, 19).

And let us return love to Him for love. The only thing we can give to God is our love. Everything else we have belongs to Him, but our hearts are our own, and He delights in our love. "We love him because he first loved us."

And let us love one another more, and not be disheartened when we see apparent divisions between the people of God; there is a much closer union between them, than any of us suspect, or than the world has the least idea of. It is true, misconceptions, misconstructions, and prejudices tend to divide the children of God one from another, pity that it is so. Yet they are truly united.

Ask them what about sin! They will *all* tell you, with one voice, "It is the abominable thing we hate."

Ask them of Jesus! They will *all* tell you His "name is as ointment poured forth."

Ask them of His blood! They *all* agree about it! that it is *"the precious blood,"* and that it has spoken peace to their consciences; to that blood they all fly in every time of difficulty, and sorrow, and danger, and fear.

Ask them of righteousness! They know no righteousness but "his righteousness only."

Ask them of love! They tell you of the "love that passeth knowledge"—*His love.*

Ask them of rest! They all tell you they expect no rest till they rest in Him. Surely this is *true* union. Wherever you find a child of God over the whole earth, "Jew or Gentile, barbarian, Scythian, bondman or freeman, male or female," you will find they are all at one in these, the only and all-essential principles of gospel light and truth. Pity it is that with so much to unite them, very trifles are so often allowed to separate them. *"An enemy hath done this."*

The Lord's prayer shall be fully answered by-and-by, and there shall be the fullest manifestation of this union. "I in them, and thou in me, that they also may be one in us."

36

I T WAS TO BE EXPECTED that a prayer in which our Lord evidently opens out all His heart, and pleads all His Father's covenant engagements with Him, should contain more or less reference to every matter which the purposes and promises of Jehovah had pledged Him to; and that all the dispensations of divine grace would be embraced, and comprehended in His petitions. Our Lord was now pleading, with His hands as it were upon the sacrifice on the altar, and claiming upon the ground of His own infinite merit, all that the love of God in Christ had intended and prepared for His creatures.

There are unspeakable promises and dignities of grace and glory attaching to the Lord Jesus Christ in connection with His titles and royalties. I may remind you of *four* principal ones, into which all the others merge.

Jesus Christ is *"the Son of God,"* and as the Son of God He is the Firstborn, the "King of Saints," and the Head and the Husband of His Body the Church. This is His highest title, and prerogative.

But He is also *"the Son of Abraham,"* and as the Son of Abraham He is by birthright "the King of the Jews," and shall be "the glory of his people Israel."

But He is also *"the Son of David,"* and as the Son of David He is "King of kings and Lord of lords," "the desire of all nations," and the "light to lighten the Gentiles."

But He is also *"the Son of man,"* and as Son of Man He shall yet be "the King of all the earth," and the Creator and Head of "a new heaven and a new earth, in which dwelleth righteousness."

Our Lord had prayed for His believing people of all times and ages, all those who should believe on Him through the gospel—confining His prayer to believers in the gospel; He prayed for them that they might be united to one another, and to Himself, according to the divine pattern, "As thou, Father, art in me, and I in thee, that they also may be one in us." Now He further contemplates *a result to the universe* from their union one with another, and with Himself, "that the world may believe that thou hast sent me."

The promise made by God to Christ as Son of God contained a great deal more than that He should be the Head of His Church, and Head over all things to His Church, though that was the chief promise, the fruition of which was His chief object in coming down from heaven to die. But we find, in Psalm 2:7–9, Jehovah thus addressing His Son,—

> "I will declare the decree . . . Thou art my Son; this day have I begotten thee. Ask of me, and I shall give thee the heathen for thine inheritance, and the uttermost parts of the earth for thy possession."

Again, promise was made to Christ as the Seed of Abraham; the apostle, in Galatians 3:16 teaches that when the promise was made to Abraham, and to his seed,

> "He saith not, And to seeds, as of many; but as of one. And to thy seed, *which is Christ*":

therefore the promise to the seed of Abraham was in reality a promise to Christ; and it was on this wise,

> "In thy seed shall all the families of the earth be blessed" (Gen. 12:3).

Accordingly, in Romans 4:13, this promise is interpreted by the Holy Ghost,

"That he [Abraham] should be the heir of the world."

This was secured to him in his seed, Christ: therefore Christ is the heir of the world.

Again, as Son of David, there is a promise of a somewhat similar character made to Christ, to which the psalmist alludes very distinctly in Psalm 72: "Give the King thy judgments, O God, and thy righteousness unto the king's Son" (v. 1). Verses 8, 9—

> "He shall have dominion also from sea to sea, and from the river unto the ends of the earth. They that dwell in the wilderness shall bow before him; and his enemies shall lick the dust."

Verses 11, 17–20—

> "Yea, all kings shall fall down before him; all nations shall serve him . . . His name shall endure for ever: his name shall be continued as long as the sun; and men shall be blessed in him: all nations shall call him blessed. Blessed be the Lord God, the God of Israel, who only doeth wondrous things. And blessed be his glorious name for ever: and let the whole earth be filled with his glory."

And so it shall be,

> "Amen, and Amen. The prayers of David the son of Jesse are ended" (Ps. 72:19, 20).

Again, promise is made to the Lord Jesus, as the Son of Man (see Dan. 7:13, 14):

> "I saw in the night visions, and, behold, one like the Son of man came with the clouds of heaven, and came to the Ancient of days, and they brought him near before him. And there was given him dominion, and glory, and a kingdom, that all people, nations, and languages should serve him: his dominion is an everlasting dominion, which shall not pass away, and his kingdom that which shall not be destroyed."

This kingdom in which Christ's people are to reign as kings and priests with Him, is associated with, and results from, the sacrifice of Himself! In Psalm 22 this is very clearly brought out. The well-known quotation of this Psalm by our blessed Lord upon the cross, "My God, my God, why hast thou forsaken me," proves Him to be the person speaking, or spoken to throughout it. In verses 27, 28, we read,

> "All the ends of the world shall remember and turn unto the Lord: all the kindreds of the nations shall worship before thee. For the kingdom is the Lord's: and he is the governor among the nations."

Evidently this was part of the covenant arrangement, on the understanding of which the Lord Jesus Christ came down from heaven to be the Mediator between God and man, and the Saviour of sinners. Nor is this teaching peculiar to the Old Testament. In Philippians 2, we have the exaltation of our Lord Jesus Christ to universal dominion associated with, and resulting from, His great sacrifice.

> "Wherefore God also hath highly exalted him, and given him a name which is above every name: that at the name of Jesus every knee should bow, of things in heaven, and things in earth, and things under the earth; and that every tongue should confess that Jesus Christ is Lord, to the glory of God the Father."

Again, see Revelation 5:13, where we have a chorus of the whole creation when Jesus takes the throne,

> "And every creature which is in heaven, and on the earth, and under the earth, and such as are in the sea, and all that are in them, heard I saying, Blessing, and honour, and glory, and power, be with him that sitteth upon the throne, and unto the Lamb for ever and ever."

And in Revelation 11:15, we have the accomplishment of the mystery of God.

> "The seventh angel sounded; and there were great voices in heaven saying, The kingdoms of this world are become the

kingdoms of our Lord, and of his Christ; and he shall reign for ever and ever."

It is hardly necessary to seek further evidence that the Lord must have had these promises and performances in His mind, and in His heart also, when He prayed "that the world may believe that thou hast sent me."

Sometimes the world is put for all those who are saved out of mankind, by union with the Lord Jesus Christ,—His elect people; as, for instance, in II Corinthians 5:19: "God was in Christ, reconciling the world unto himself, not imputing their trespasses unto them." There *the world* means the family of the blessed in Christ,—of whom the psalmist says,

> "Blessed is he whose transgressions are forgiven; whose sin is covered. Blessed is the man unto whom the Lord imputeth not iniquity" (Ps. 32:1, 2).

The blessed ones of God are there called *the world.* Sometimes *the world* is used to define and describe willful unbelievers, rejecters, and neglecters of the Lord Jesus Christ:

> "The whole world lieth in wickedness [*i.e.,* in the wicked one]" (I John 5:19).
> "If any man will be a friend of the world, he is the enemy of God" (James 4:4).

Sometimes by *the world* the Spirit of God means the *Gentiles,* as contrasted with the *Jews* (Rom. 11:12); sometimes the heathen who have not heard of His fame or seen His glory (Isa. 66:19).

What, then, does our Lord mean when He prays "that *the world* may believe that thou hast sent me"? He evidently does *not* mean His disciples; He had already prayed for them. He does *not* mean those who shall believe on Him through their word; He had prayed for them:

> "Neither pray I for these alone; but for them also which shall believe on me through their word; that they all may be one;

as thou, Father, art in me, and I in thee, that they also may be one in us."

Evidently, believers are a peculiar people, and a high calling and a peculiar privilege is theirs! Union in one Body of which He Himself is the Head, even as He and His Father are united, *"that they also may be one in us."*

Again, He does *not* mean the willfully unbelieving world, rejecting Christ:

> "He that believeth not is condemned already . . . he that believeth not . . . the wrath of God abideth on him,"

is the testimony in John 3:18 and 36. Well, then, to whom does He allude as the world? As I understand Scripture, I conceive He alludes to both Jews and Gentiles in general, and in their national character; first to "Israel, to whom blindness in part has happened till the fulness of the Gentiles be come in"; and then to the Gentiles, who, through the Jews, being brought to the knowledge of the Lord, are also to be gathered in, "as doves to their windows": for

> "If the fall of them be the riches of the world, and the diminishing of them the riches of the Gentiles; how much more their fulness?" (Rom. 11:12).

You remember a beautiful promise to this effect in Isaiah 49:6, 7:

> "It is a light thing that thou shouldest be my servant to raise up the tribes of Jacob, and to restore the preserved of Israel: I will also give thee for a light to the Gentiles, that thou mayest be my salvation unto the end of the earth. Thus saith the Lord, the Redeemer of Israel, and his Holy One, to him whom man despiseth, to him whom the nation abhorreth, to a servant of rulers, Kings shall see and arise, princes also shall worship, because of the Lord that is faithful, and the Holy One of Israel, and he shall choose thee."

Observe, He does not ask that the world may be one with Himself; that prayer is limited and confined to those who did believe, and who shall believe on Him through the Word. But He now prays in reference to the result and influence which the manifested glory of His people shall yet have upon the world, "that the world may believe that thou hast sent me."

Again observe, and this is also very important, the means by which the world is to be brought to this true sense and conviction of Jehovah having sent His Son to be the Saviour of the world, is not the preaching of the gospel, but the manifested union of the Church of God with one another, and with Christ in the Father. Not faith, but vision; not the preached Word, but the effects of the preached Word in the children of the Lord God Almighty, united in one. Even "as thou, Father, art in me, and I in thee, and they also one in us." In the vision of the union of the Church of God with its Head, in the apprehension of our happiness, and in the light of our glory, the world shall be convicted or convinced. And this is but half the truth; for see Ephesians 3:8–11,

> "Unto me . . . is this grace given, that I should preach among the Gentiles the unsearchable riches of Christ; and to make all men see what is the fellowship of the mystery, which from the beginning of the world hath been hid in God, who created all things by Jesus Christ: to the intent that [not only the world may believe, but that] now unto *the principalities and powers in heavenly places* might be known by the church the manifold wisdom of God, according to the eternal purpose which he purposed in Christ Jesus our Lord."

The Church of Jesus Christ, washed in His blood, clothed in His beauty and in His glory, united to Himself as Head, and in Him as Head to the Father, and manifested to the universe, is to be the everlasting monument of the love of God, upon which not only the world shall read that God sent His Christ, but on which the angels and principalities and powers in heavenly places shall contemplate and be made acquainted with the manifold wisdom of God. Christ is to be glorified in His saints and admired in all those that believe, and Jehovah will summon all the universe to behold His redeemed in Jesus and to admire and worship Him for what His love could do, what His grace could do, what His blood could do.

Thus it is written, Revelation 3:12,

> "Him that overcometh will I make a pillar in the temple of my God, and he shall go no more out: and I will write upon him the name of my God, and the name of the city of my God, which is new Jerusalem, which cometh down out of heaven from my God: and I will write upon him my new name."

The world shall see and admire and believe the love which passeth knowledge; and angels, and principalities, and powers in heavenly places shall behold and admire also. In Revelation 21:23, 24, we have the same truth in figure; it is written of that city of which we have been speaking:

> "The glory of God did lighten it, and the Lamb is the light thereof. And the nations of them which are saved shall walk in the light of it: and the kings of the earth do bring their glory and honor into it"—

"That the world may believe that thou hast sent me." And in verse 23, "That the world may *know* that thou hast sent me, and hast loved them, as thou hast loved me." Observe the distinction still maintained between His own,—the members of His Body, and the world, which beholds their beauty and happiness, their unity and their glory.

The prophetic order in which all this is to take place seems to be: First, the fulfillment of the immediate hope of the Church, the return of our Lord, as we read in I Thessalonians 4:15–17; then afterwards His returning with them, II Thessalonians 1:7–10,

> "To be glorified in his saints, and to be admired in all them that believe."

Thus the saints of God will be the medium in, and through whom the Lord Jesus' beauty and glory shall so shine forth as to be admired, "admired in all them that believe." Then the glory and restoration of Israel. See Isaiah 60, "Arise, shine; for thy light is come, and the glory of the Lord is risen upon thee"; "and the Gentiles shall come to thy light, and kings to the brightness of thy rising." See also Isaiah 19:22–25:

> "The Lord shall smite Egypt; he shall smite and heal it: and they shall return even to the Lord, and he shall be entreated of them, and shall heal them. In that day there shall be a highway out of Egypt to Assyria, and the Assyrian shall come into Egypt, and the Egyptian into Assyria; and the Egyptians shall serve with the Assyrians. In that day shall Israel be the third with Egypt and with Assyria,"

the two great enemies of Israel, all through her history, were Egypt and Assyria; she was in bondage in Egypt, and led captive into Assyria,—

> "In that day shall Israel be the third with Egypt and with Assyria, even a blessing in the midst of the land; whom the Lord of hosts shall bless, saying, Blessed be Egypt my people, and Assyria the work of my hands, and Israel mine inheritance."
>
> "That the world may believe that thou hast sent me."

"He must reign, till he hath put all enemies under his feet" (I Cor. 15:25). And all who do not bow to the scepter of His grace shall be trodden down under the rod of His power.

> "As I live, saith the Lord, every knee shall bow to me, and every tongue shall confess to God" (Rom. 14:11).

Very interesting it is to observe the two agencies mentioned in this Gospel; whose testimony and witness in the earth are to result in the conversion, or the conviction of all mankind. One is the Holy Ghost. In John 16:8–11, we read,

> "When he is come, he will convict [such is the original] the world of sin, and of righteousness, and of judgment: of sin, because they believe not on me; of righteousness, because I go to my Father, and ye see me no more; of judgment, because the prince of this world is judged."

And the other shall be the glorified people of Christ as in our text: "they also may be one in us: that the world may believe that thou hast sent me." Yes, every tongue shall confess it, either to their everlasting confusion, "Behold, ye despisers, and wonder, and perish," or to the everlasting happiness of those

> "Who have fled for refuge to lay hold upon the hope set before them" (Heb. 6:18),

even to Him who

> "Shall have put down all rule and all authority and power . . . till he hath put all enemies under his feet" (I Cor. 15: 24, 25);

when, having abolished death and banished sin, and having destroyed the works of the devil, He shall deliver up the kingdom (for the conquest and redemption of which He left His throne and became man) to God, even the Father:

> "Then shall *the Son* also himself become subject unto him that put all things under him, that God may be all in all" (I Cor. 15:28).

"I in them, and thou in me," and they in us; "that the world may believe that thou hast sent me."

This subject seems to suggest three practical lessons for ourselves.

1. Evidently, the Lord here implies that the only Bible the world reads is the character of Christians,—their likeness to Himself. Are we doing the world justice? The world will not be brought to a sense of its ruin, nor to any practical sense of the goodness of God in sending Christ, but by the manifestation of His grace in His people. Are we manifesting Christ? Are

we living epistles, known and read of all men? You perceive it lay much upon the heart of Jesus that His people should be so manifestly one with one another, and one with Himself, that the world might take knowledge of them—"that the world may believe that thou hast sent me."

2. Another is in reference to our divisions. May God forgive us for and correct our divisions! Nothing gives greater occasion to the outside world, than the differences between professing Christians. The bickerings and contentions between men and women of different sects and denominations of the visible church of God, has always been one of the world's greatest hindrances. Instead of looking on, and being constrained to confess, "See how these Christians love one another," the world has too much reason to say, "See how they carp at one another, see how they judge one another, see how they malign one another."

3. The honor of Christ, and the happiness of the world, as well as the dignity of the Church of Christ, demand that we should lay aside our wrangling, and gather round our Head. Oh! let our lives and conversation be more Christlike, and our hearts more knit together in

"The unity of the Spirit in the bond of peace" (Eph. 4:3).

It is written,

"By this shall all men know that ye are my disciples, if ye have love one to another" (John 13:35).

37

"AND THE GLORY WHICH THOU GAVEST ME I HAVE GIVEN
THEM; THAT THEY MAY BE ONE, EVEN AS WE ARE
ONE."—John 17:22

O UR LORD here expresses all His heart. Union is still His
theme—union with God and with Himself and in Himself—this alone can satisfy His great love and travail for us.
"That they all may be one" (v. 21); "that they . . . may be
one in us" (v. 21); "that they may be one, even as we are
one" (v. 22); "that they may be made *perfect in one*" (v. 23).

Union with God Almighty is the greatest and fullest of all
conceivable blessings, and the source and spring from whence
all other blessings must flow.

Union with God was the highest grace vouchsafed to the
Lord Jesus Christ Himself; and all His personal and mediatorial dignities, and fullness, are results flowing from *that* union;

And our union with Christ in God's everlasting purpose
(and all believers have union with Him) is the source of all
blessing which has been, or is, or shall ever be bestowed upon
us, and of all the glory to be revealed to us or in us, whatever
that glory may be. *"And the glory which thou gavest me I
have given them, that they may be one,* EVEN AS WE ARE
ONE."

Here Christ tells His Father, in our hearing, the amazing
fact, that He has bestowed on us the glory given by the Father
to Him, that it may be the element in which we are to be
qualified for union and communion with the Father Himself.
Thus every believer in Jesus Christ shall be united to God as

closely and as blessedly as it is possible for the creature to enjoy.

There are four unions revealed to us in the Word of God, and here we read how divine grace and love have connected them most marvelously and most closely with one another.

First, the incomprehensible union, nowhere described or defined, but simply stated for the obedience of our faith, namely, the mutual union and indwelling of the three Persons in the Godhead; Father, Son, and Holy Ghost; the triune Jehovah, immortal, invisible, possessing all divine attributes—eternity, omniscience, omnipotency. The *second,* the mutual union and indwelling of the Man Christ Jesus with the second Person of the blessed Trinity, the Son of God, making one glorious *Person,* God-man, the Lord Jesus Christ, our Saviour, the Captain of our salvation, the Author and Finisher of our faith. The *third* is the mutual union and indwelling between Himself and His believing people; as the members of His mystical Body, He having taken our nature into heaven, we are one with Him *there,* and He with His Holy Spirit dwelleth within us evermore, He is one with us *here.* The *fourth* is the union and mutual membership and intercommunion of all of the believing people of God one with another; and this union obtains, whether we speak of those who have gone before, Abraham, Isaac, and Jacob, etc., or those who are at present upon the earth, believing, or of the future ingathering of all who shall at any time believe on the Lord Jesus Christ; for He says, "Neither pray I for these alone, but for them also which shall believe on me through their word; *that they all may be one.*"

When we trace back this union to its divine source, and mark the connection from beginning to end, it is impossible to conceive, much less to express, the breadth, and length, and depth, and height of the love of God contained, and revealed and bestowed therein. Here are believers of every age, united together in one Body, under one headship, the Lord Jesus Christ;

and He who is our Head, united to the second Person of the blessed Trinity, and in Himself God-man personally; united in His manhood, to all His believing people, and united in His Godhead, evermore with the Father, the Source from whence our life descends, and the fullness from whence all our blessings flow. The fact is unspeakable, and the glory that *must* follow from it inconceivable! This the love of God hath accomplished, and this the love of God hath revealed.

Perhaps there is no passage in the Word of God which affords a higher view of this subject than the passage we are considering. We have been in the habit of regarding glory as the end and ultimate climax of all that the grace and love of God can do for us, or cause us to attain unto. If such has been our idea, we are altogether wrong; here we are taught that there is something *beyond glory,* even UNION WITH THE GOD OF GLORY; and that the glory given to Christ has been given by Christ to His people as a means and qualification for the realization, the enjoyment, and the manifestation of *union with the Father.* "The glory which thou gavest me I have given them; that they may be one, even as we are one." Everything here is grace, but oh, what grace! We read of the "riches of grace," and we read of "the riches of the glory of grace," and truly it is here expressed.

Our Lord had already pleaded the fact of a people being given to Him, and of power over all flesh being vested in Him for their benefit. In verse 4, He spake of a work being given Him to do on their behalf; we know what that work was, even

> "To finish the transgression, and to make an end of sins, and to make reconciliation for iniquity, and to bring in everlasting righteousness, and to seal up the vision and prophecy, and to anoint the most Holy" (Dan. 9:24).

In verse 8: of *words* given to Him and taught to them,—even the glorious gospel, the testimony of the love of God in Christ to sinners, given to Christ to be confirmed and fulfilled, and given by Christ to His people as finished and fulfilled, to be believed and enjoyed. He had spoken (14:16) of another gift to them, the gift of the Holy Ghost, *"another Comforter"* to dwell with them and be in them forever. And finally, in our text, of *glory,* "the glory which thou gavest me I have given them; that they may be one, even as we are one . . . that the world may know that thou hast sent me, and hast loved them, as thou hast loved me." What a climax of bliss and fullness of uncreated glory passing all knowledge and all description is now set before us as the everlasting rest which the love of God has prepared for those who wait for Him!

We may infallibly gather the amazing fact, that the glory He has given us, and which had been given to Him by the Father, is to be the element, in which we shall reach unto the attainment, and enjoyment of union and communion with the Father in Him. Just as the union of Christ with God is the foundation of all the grace and glory given to Him as man, so our union to Christ is to be the foundation and source of all the grace and glory to be yet bestowed on us, His members, through all eternity. Our union with Christ is more than *all grace* and *glory;* for all communicable grace, and all conceivable glory, are to flow from it.

Salvation is a great and unspeakable grace and blessing, but it is only one result of our union with Christ. Justification from all sin is a great and unspeakable blessing, but it is only another result of our union with Christ.

Sanctification is a great and unspeakable grace and blessing, but it is only a preliminary qualification and fitness for union and communion with God.

> "As many as received him, to them gave he power [the right, the privilege, the authority] to become the sons of God, even to them that believe on his name" (John 1:12);

and

> "If children, then heirs; heirs of God, and joint-heirs with Christ" (Rom. 8:17);

Christ's fullness flowing to Him from union with His Father, and our fullness flowing to us from union with Christ in whom all fullness dwells.

Let us endeavor to approach this mysterious subject by degrees. "The glory which thou *gavest* me, I have given them." Observe the glory He speaks of, is such as He could *receive;* and such as He could and did, and will *bestow.* Now Christ hath a glory which is incommunicable. As the second Person of the blessed Trinity our Lord possesses the essential glory of the Godhead. This is glory He could not receive because it was, from all eternity, essentially His own. It cannot, therefore, be the glory to which He here alludes; for He speaks of it as *received.*

Again, as God-man Mediator, the Son of God incarnate in the Man Christ Jesus, our Lord hath a personal glory which, although received, is and ever must be peculiar to Himself and incommunicable—

> "The glory as of the only begotten Son of God . . . The firstborn from the dead; that in all things he might have the pre-eminence" (John 1:14; Col. 1:18).

Moreover, the glory of our Christ as *the Head of the Church* is also peculiar to Himself; and the glory of our Lord Jesus Christ as *Mediator,* whereby He became the treasury and receptacle of all the fullness of the Godhead bodily, for His people, is peculiar to Himself. But there is also glory given to Him relatively,—glory given to Him who is the Son of God, and who is our Lord Jesus Christ, and given to Him for the special object and purpose that He should dispense it to His believing people, till out of His fullness they receive, and grace for grace.

Now, if we except the glory which is incommunicable, which He hath as the second Person of the Trinity, and the glory also incommunicable which He possesses as God-man in His own glorious person, we know of no limit we can assign to His words, "The glory which thou gavest me I have given them; that they may be one, even as we are one."

Now what is this glory? Read it in the glorious titles which our heavenly Father has given to Him,

"The Prince of Life,"
"The Prince of Peace,"
"The King of Glory,"
"The Everlasting Father,"
"The Bridegroom,"
"The Saviour" of the world,
"Our Redeemer" and our sanctification,
"The Resurrection and the Life,"

> "The brightness of his [the Father's] glory, and the express image of his person" (Heb. 1:3).

Read it in the *names* by which His Father calls Him:

> "Mine elect, in whom my soul delighteth" (Isa. 42:1).
> "My beloved Son, in whom I am well pleased" (Matt. 3:17).
> "My servant, whom I uphold" (Isa. 42:1).
> "My salvation unto the end of the earth" (Isa. 49:6).

Read it, as implied in *the position* to which Jehovah has exalted Him,

> "[God has] given him a name which is above every name: that at the name of Jesus every knee should bow" (Phil. 2:9, 10).
> "[God exalted him to his own right hand in the majesty of the heavens] far above all principality, and power, and might, and dominion, and every name that is named, not only in this world, but also in that which is to come; and hath put all things under his feet" (Eph. 1:20–22).

Read the glory given to Him in *the prerogatives* with which His Father has endowed Him:

"All power is given unto me in heaven and in earth" (Matt. 28:19);

"The Father judgeth no man, but hath committed all judgment unto the Son" (John 5:22);

"I have laid help upon one that is mighty" (Ps. 89:19);

"As the Father hath life in himself; so hath he given to the Son to have life in himself" (John 5:26);

"It pleased the Father that in him should all fulness dwell" (Col. 1:19);

"God giveth not the Spirit by measure unto him" (John 3:34).

Read the glory given to Him in *the offices* to which He hath been consecrated.

"PROPHET"—to teach us all our Father's mind, and to reveal to us all our Father's grace.

"This is my beloved Son: hear him" (Mark 9:7).

"Priest [Jesus] glorified not himself to be made an High Priest; but he that said unto him, Thou art my Son; today have I begotten thee" (Heb. 5:5).

"PRIEST"—to transact God's affairs with man, and man's affair with God; to make atonement for sin; to present His own merits in our behalf as a sweet savour, in the fullness of which He intercedes before the throne, and by-and-by, to come back and bless us; to put the Father's name upon us forevermore.

"KING"—to put down our foes; King—to reign in our hearts; King—to reign over the universe, and to ride "upon the heaven" for our help. Oh, think of the glory!

And why was this glory given to Him? It was not for Himself. He is none the richer for all this; it was a *stoop* for the Son of God *to accept such offices,* or to be the recipient of such glory. He made Himself less than the Father, by taking a nature which could receive anything from the Father. Why, then, did He receive all these things? Not to enrich Himself; but that His people might be enriched, and yet not as apart from Him, but as united to Him; therefore, it was as our treasury and as our trustee!—for He says,

"The glory which thou gavest me I have given them";

He accepted the glory given to Him only because He was their Head: and He holds it for them, that they may enjoy it, and be blessed in His fullness.

What, then, is the glory He has given to His people?

All the glory arising from the fact that

"[He who was] in the form of God, [and] thought it not robbery to be equal with God: but made himself of no reputation, and took upon him the form of a servant, and was made in the likeness of men: and being found in fashion as a man, humbled himself [literally, emptied himself] and became obedient unto death, even the death of the cross" (Phil. 2: 6–8);

All the fruits of that infinite sacrifice which hath satisfied justice, glorified the law, and commended the love of God,

"In that while we were yet sinners Christ died for us" (Rom. 5:8);

All the fruits of His conquest of death and hell, and the world and the flesh;

All the fruits of His glorious resurrection and ascension, and constant intercession;

All the fruits of His exaltation to the right hand of the majesty in the heavens,—

All the glory redounding from this He has given to us.

He, who is the image of the invisible God, will yet stamp upon His people the image of the invisible God, for to this are they

"[Predestinated even] to be conformed to the image of his Son" (Rom. 8:29).

All His resurrection offices in heaven are exercised with a view to His people, and they shall have the benefits;

All the fullness of His grace has been received in order to be communicated to them, and so it shall be, for "the glory which thou gavest me I have given them." He speaks of it as *done* because it is sure.

All the glory given by Jehovah to Christ and laid up in Christ is intended for His people, settled upon His people, secured to His people, and either has been dispensed, is being dispensed, or shall be dispensed, till they *are perfected in one*.

"The glory which thou gavest me I have given them, . . . that they may be one, even as we are one." It means union with Christ's person, participation in Christ's fullness, the communication of Christ's glory given to His people—"that they may be one"—(1) one with each other. He has slain the "enmity, even the law of commandments contained in ordinances," which separated believing Gentiles from believing Jews, that He might

> "Make in himself of twain one new man, so making peace"
> (Eph. 2:15).

(2) As being one with each other in *Him;* who is one with the Father, "one in us."

> "Made nigh by the blood of Christ . . . having forgiven [us] all trespasses; blotting out the handwriting of ordinances that was against us, which was contrary to us, and took it out of the way, nailing it to his cross" (Eph. 2:13; Col. 2:13, 14);

and having bestowed divine power on His people by His gift of the Holy Ghost, He opened

> "A new and living way, which he had consecrated for us, through the veil" (Heb. 10:20);

and thus with every incapacity overcome, the divine nature bestowed, every barrier removed, and His redeemed made gloriously nigh, He prays, "that they also may be one even as we are one." Only think of it! It must mean that they may evermore be found partaking of the same holiness, enjoying the same happiness, interested in the same honors, blessed in the same vision, dwelling in the same place, enjoying the same fullness. And this is the end of all His travail, the answer to all His prayer, and the result of all His imparted glory—"that they may be one, even as we are one." How do our divisions shame us, how does the want of union amongst the people of God mar their glory! Did Christ thus long for manifested union, and shall true believers in the Lord Jesus Christ sever the one from the other, about every petty difference and dispute, which narrow-mindedness, bigotry, selfishness, or the malice of the world and the devil have invented and magnified?

Finally. Let us suggest some inferences arising from what is here said, "that they all may be one." The Lord's prayer is not for strong believers, or for deeply taught Christians only; but for the weakest, and the feeblest, and the most unlearned of all the redeemed family. "Neither pray I for these alone, but for them also which shall believe on me through their word; that they *all* may be one," the weak and the strong in one glorious bond of union by the Spirit, through the Saviour, to the Father.

Oh! think of the blessed prospect here opened out to *all* believers.

All believers in Jesus Christ are equally redeemed, one as much so as another;

Equally justified, one as much so as another;

Equally sanctified in the sight of God, one as much so as another;

And they shall be equally glorified, one as much so as another;

"For whom he justified, them he also glorified";

Equally happy, for God shall be their inheritance, and His fullness shall be their portion;

Equally filled; equally folded;

"For the glory which thou gavest me I have given them; that they may be one . . . I in them, and thou in me, that they may be made perfect in one."

O God the Holy Ghost, deal with our souls; teach us to believe these things; teach us to claim them; teach us to receive them; teach us to *reflect* them. And, O God, teach us what confidence we may repose in Thee; Thou didst all these things for us when we were Thine enemies; and if Thou didst give to us Thy Son, that He might give to us the glory that Thou gavest Him, that we might be one with Thee, wilt Thou "not with him also freely give us all things"? (Rom. 8:32). O Lord, bless us, and feed our souls for the Lord Jesus Christ's sake, that He "may be glorified in us, and we in him, according to the grace of our God, and the Lord Jesus Christ."

38

"I IN THEM, AND THOU IN ME, THAT THEY MAY BE MADE
PERFECT IN ONE; AND THAT THE WORLD MAY KNOW
THAT THOU HAST SENT ME, AND HAST LOVED
THEM, AS THOU HAST LOVED ME."—John 17:23

THUS DOTH our blessed Lord conclude the supplicatory part
of His prayer. Here, in the presence of His disciples, He enters into the details of covenant settlements arranged with His
Father before the world was, and to fulfill the conditions of
which He came down from heaven to take our nature and die
in our place, establishing a divine, personal, and everlasting
union with His people thus united *in Himself* to each other,
and to His heavenly Father also.

This consummation was the joy set before Him, for which
He "endured the cross, despising the shame."

For this He had given them the glory which His Father had
given Him, "that they may be one, even as we are one" (v. 22).
And now, on the eve of His sacrifice, and on His way to the
altar, He thus emphatically expresses His whole heart concerning them. "I in them, and thou in me, that they may be made
perfect in one; and that the world may know that thou hast
sent me, and hast loved them, as thou hast loved me."

Even Christ Himself could ask no more,

God Himself can give no more.

The indwelling power of the Holy Ghost can enable the
believer to enjoy no more than Christ here asks for His people. Having uttered the prayer, He ceases to supplicate, and

might well say, as His great forerunner did, "the prayers of David, the son of Jesse, are ended."

"I in them." Amazing indwelling!—not only My love in them, Mine interests with them, My fullness, My Spirit, their portion,—but I Myself in them, the inexhaustible Fountain of their holiness, and happiness, the fullness of their glory, their inheritance, and their crown! "I in them"—not only *with* them forever, not only *for* them, and against all those that are opposed to them, not only *near* them, but "in them," as their very life and glory,

In them as the head doth live in the members of the body,

In them as the glory fills the temple of the Lord,

In them evermore, the incarnate fullness of God in their souls.

"I in them"—*in all of them,* the least of them as well as the greatest, the most ignorant of them as well as the most instructed. "I in them"—in them as their portion forever.

Oh! it is very, very blessed to dwell upon these sayings of our divine Lord, "I in them, and thou," My life, My felicity, My perfection, and My glory, "in me." Christ in our nature is the bond uniting His people to the fountain of Deity: just as the Lord Jesus Christ as man receives His fullness by immediate union and communion with the fountain of Deity, so His people shall evermore receive their fullness from immediate union and communion with the incarnate Son of God.

Just consider! Christ *in* His believing people as the Father is *in* Him. The Father was the life of Christ.

> "As the living Father hath sent me, and I live by the Father: so he that eateth me [note the figure illustrating union] even he shall live by me" (John 6:57).

Moreover, the Lord Jesus Christ speaks of His Father as His strength and power. How often we find Him in the Psalms addressing Him and saying,

"Jehovah, my strength . . . My stronghold . . . My rock."

Now, as the Father was the strength of Christ, so is Christ the strength of the soul that trusts in Him, and He promises to make His strength perfect in weakness. Jehovah was the Sustainer and Preserver of Christ:

> "Behold my servant, whom I uphold; mine elect, in whom my soul delighteth; I have put my spirit upon him . . . I will hold thine hand, and will keep thee" (Isa. 42:1, 6).

So is the Lord Jesus Christ the Upholder of His people. We read they are "preserved in Jesus Christ" (Jude 1). Just as Noah was preserved in the ark, as Lot was preserved in Zoar, and as the manslayer was safe in the city of refuge, so the soul that trusts in Jesus is safe—safe forever; for Jesus is his Stronghold and his Rest, as the Father is the Stronghold and the Rest of Jesus. The Father was in Christ, speaking and working.

> "Believest thou not that I am in the Father, and the Father in me? the words that I speak unto you I speak not of myself: but the Father that dwelleth in me, he doeth the works. Believe me that I am in the Father, and the Father in me: or else believe me for the very works' sake" (John 14:10, 11).

So is it with the soul that trusts in the Lord Jesus; Christ lives and works in that man, as the apostle says, "It is no more I that live, but Christ liveth in me" (see Gal. 2:20). Moreover, the Father was in Christ reconciling the world unto Himself. The Father was in Christ in His incarnation; in the wilderness, and on the cross, in His triumph over death and hell, and so is Christ in His people; He is identified with them and they also with Him in all He did, and suffered and achieved, so that when He died upon the cross they were *"crucified with Christ";* when He rose from the dead they *"were raised up together with Him";* when He sat down at God's right hand, they also were made to sit together with Him in heavenly places (see Eph. 2:6), identified with Him for grace here, and for glory there. "I in them, and thou in me, that they may be made perfect in one."

Our Lord mentions two objects He had in view in praying for this manifested union of His people with each other in Him, and with the Father. The first as regards *them,* for their complete happiness and everlasting security, "that they may be made perfect in one." The second as regards the world, that the manifest union between the Father and His people in Christ, might convince the world "that the world may know that thou hast sent me, and hast loved them, as thou hast loved me." Let us examine these things.

First, as regards His people, *"that they may be made perfect in one."* All God's creatures were created perfect—when He created the angels they were perfect, but they were only creatures, therefore not immutable and they fell. When God created man He created him perfect, but he was only a creature; he was not immutable, therefore when temptation assailed him he also fell. Why did angels fall? They were not made perfect *in one.* Why did man fall? He was not made perfect *in one.* Behold the salvation of God! and how divine grace has provided that there shall be no future fall, no more tears in that new world He is about to introduce, no more suffering, no more sin in that new heaven and new earth—"That they may be made perfect in one"; God Himself, the center of their existence, and the circumference of their fullness;

God Himself, as a wall of fire round about them, their security forevermore;

The incarnate Son, the divine channel by which God's fullness shall flow into them;

The Holy Ghost, the Comforter, the divine agent by which that fullness shall be communicated. Thus made perfect in one, God Himself must fail before His children can fall, Christ's fullness must be exhausted before His members can fail. The Holy Spirit must be overcome before our happiness in God can be hindered, or the heart that trusts Him be disappointed, for we are made "perfect in one."

Our Lord's words evidently refer not to mere creature blessings, but to supercreation grace—not to created fullness, but to union and communion with Himself in God. God dwelling in us and we in God, is henceforth to be the source and supply of the perfection of Christ's redeemed. (See I Thess. 1:1.) This is our glorious position, and promised portion,

> "To be filled with all the fulness of God" (Eph. 3:19).

But not only is union with God in Christ intended, union with each other also must exist, "that we might be made perfect in one." No individual believer, however great his need or his capacity for grace, could receive or contain all the fullness of God. The whole Body in all its members must be united to the Head, that

> "*All* . . . having nourishment ministered, and knit together, [may increase] with the increase of God" (see Col. 2:19).
>
> "In the unity of the faith, and of the knowledge of the Son of God, we *all* come unto a *perfect man,* unto the measure of the stature of the fulness of Christ, and grow up into him in *all* things" (see Eph. 4:13–15).

It is

> "With *all saints* we must comprehend the love of Christ that passeth knowledge, that we may be filled with all the fulness of God" (see Eph. 3:18, 19).

"Made perfect in one."

Men have formed professing Christian bodies and formularies and creeds, we have our tests of fellowship, our uniformity of ritual, and our conformity to selected standards of faith and practice; but the union of which our Lord Jesus Christ speaks has God for its center, Christ and His fullness for its supply, and the Holy Ghost indwelling for its power. Thus only can we be made "perfect in one," and filled with all the fullness of

God. Himself, our life and light, and portion; His heaven of heavens our home, and His attributes our defense through Christ by His Spirit, "made perfect in one," and never more to be assailed by Satan, sin, or sorrow, in the rest that remaineth for the people of God (see Heb. 4:9): and the countless ages of eternity as they roll over shall witness us enjoying more and more that fullness into which the love of God in Christ shall have introduced us forevermore.

The second object our Lord had in view in the manifested union of His people with Himself was "that the world may know that thou hast sent me, and hast loved them, as thou hast loved me." Our blessed Lord here embraces in His prayer vast generations yet to come. Evidently His words have reference to future dispensations of grace, and to men and women yet unborn on our earth, for it is written that

> "In the dispensation of the fulness of times he [God] will gather together in one all things in Christ, both which are in heaven, and which are on earth; even in him" (Eph. 1:10).

He had spoken in verse 8 of His own disciples thus, "they have known surely that I came out from thee, and they have believed that thou didst send me." And now He declares His purpose "that *the world* also may know that thou hast sent me." There is, however, a difference in the dispensations of grace, to which our Lord refers. The disciples believed "because of his word," and we, like the disciples, are born in a day when it is our privilege to take the Word of God as the ground of our hope and confidence. Those who now believe on our Lord Jesus Christ the absent One! the rejected One! are all

> "Baptized by one Spirit into one body" (see I Cor. 12:13).

"They are made perfect in one";

> "We are all the children of God by faith in Christ Jesus" (Gal. 3:26).

But when the day shall come when all the promises to the people of God shall be fulfilled, and we shall be manifested, in union with Him and be like Him; our voices, features, affections, and our very bodies like unto His own glorious body, changed

> "According to the working whereby he is able even to subdue
> all things unto himself" (Phil. 3:21),

then the world shall know; but this knowledge will not be the result of faith, but of vision. No suffering for Christ then— no casting in their lot with a rejected Saviour then—the King shall have returned, and His people's union with Him shall be manifested, and the world shall see what it never saw before, and learn what it never knew before, that God sent His Son for a new creation great and worthy of Him, whose name is Love, and that He who came to fulfill it loved the lost sinners for whom He died with a love that passeth knowledge, and that the Father also loved them even as He loved the Son!

We may enumerate several hindrances to the world's reception of the revealed facts that God "sent his Son into the world to save sinners"; and that He loves His redeemed people even as He loves Christ. First, the permitted power of Satan over the minds, bodies, and characters of men and even over the Lord's people: it puzzles the world, and, no wonder, to see evil so rampant. Another hindrance arises from the fact that in the long-suffering of God execution is not speedily visited where sin is committed.

> "Because sentence against an evil work is not executed
> speedily, therefore the heart of the sons of men is fully set in
> them to do evil" (Eccles. 8:11).

Another difficulty presenting itself is the absence of the King. The world knows that the people of God confess their love to Christ, and believe in Christ's love to them, and yet their King remains away in a far-off country; He seems to the eye of sense to have forgotten all about them, leaving them to toil in the wilderness, and to struggle with the world, the flesh, and the devil.

Another great hindrance arises from the want of conformity in God's children to the image of their Father. Alas! that the world should see so little in us to recommend to them our Father's character, and our Saviour's name. Again, the circumstances of the Lord's people are a great difficulty: some of those who love God best, and who serve Him most, seem to have nothing but trouble all their days; their way on earth is a weary one, and their path a dark path, so far as the world's observation goes; while perhaps those who have no care, and indeed little thought for God, seem to have all prosperity,

> "Their eyes stand out with fatness: they have more than heart could wish" (Ps. 73:7).

The great love of God to His people is not displayed; and the world mocks at the notion that such love exists, when it sees nothing but conflict, tears, and failure, and hears nothing but the sighing of the prisoners, or perhaps the murmurings of the discontented and unbelieving. The manifestation of the sons of God is not yet!

But the day is coming when all this shall be set right, when the Lamb of God shall put Satan down manifestly and forever, when execution shall be visited immediately upon all rejecters of the grace of God,

> "Gather . . . first the tares, and bind them in bundles to burn them: but gather the wheat into my barn" (Matt. 13:30);

when it will be no longer said the King is absent,—the King shall be here! As the lightning shineth from the one end of the heavens to the other, so shall the coming of the Son of Man be (see Luke 17:24). The day is coming when His own hand

> "Shall wipe away [all] tears . . . and the rebuke of his
> people shall he take away from off all the earth" (Isa. 25:8),

and when it shall be manifest even to the eye of sense how great
a purpose was in the mind of the Father when He sent Christ,
and how great a work was accomplished by the Son of God
when He bowed His head upon the cross and gave up the ghost,
and that it was for a great object the Holy Spirit descended to
seal sinners to the day of redemption.

It is written,

> "The earnest expectation of the creature waiteth for the
> manifestation of the sons of God" (Rom. 8:19);

And again,

> "Of his own will begat he us with the word of truth, that *we*
> should be a kind of *firstfruits* of his creatures" (James 1:18).

It is written of Israel as a nation,

> "If the casting away of them be the reconciling of the world,
> what shall the receiving of them be, but life from the dead?"
> (Rom. 11:15).

How much more, when the Church is manifested and "made
perfect in one." The day is coming when it shall be so:

> "All flesh shall see the salvation of God" (Luke 3:6);

our Lord is anticipating it in His prayer—"I in them, and thou
in me, that they may be made perfect in one, and that the world
may know that thou hast sent me, and hast loved them, as thou
hast loved me." O world! because thou hast seen, thou hast
believed; "but thrice blessed are they that have not seen and yet
have believed."

And this leads us to consider the second thing that the Lord
desires the world should learn from the manifested union of His
people, namely, "that thou . . . hast loved them, as thou hast
loved me." Wonderful words of unspeakable import! It is a fact

yet to be revealed to and known by the world that Jehovah, the Father, loves the believer in the Lord Jesus Christ, even as He loves the Lord Jesus Christ HIMSELF! Do we professing Christians *now believe* this gospel of our glory, even that our Father in heaven never loved and never will love His own Christ, apart from us? And that He never regarded us and never will regard us apart from Christ? That we are beloved of the Father as being *one* with His Christ,

> "As he hath chosen us in him before the foundation of the world, that we should be holy and without blame before him in love: having predestinated us unto the adoption of children by Jesus Christ to himself, according to the good pleasure of his will, to the praise of the glory of his grace, wherein he hath made us accepted in the beloved" (Eph. 1:4–6),

and that He will continue to love us so through a coming eternity, even as He loves the Lord Jesus Christ. And that He will never change in His love meantime, notwithstanding all the infirmities of which we complain; notwithstanding all the shortcomings we confess; notwithstanding all the inconsistencies which weary us, and notwithstanding all the chastening hidings of His face. For He loves us as He loves Christ, notwithstanding the peculiarities in our circumstances, many of which puzzle us, and puzzle others. He will never cease to love us, because He will never cease to love Christ. His love for us is infinite, and there are no degrees in infinity!

Now, since this is truly so, let us learn to depend upon our Father's love at all times, and under all circumstances. Let us confide to our Father our cares, our distresses, our anxieties. Let us be in love with our Father, who has been so much in love with us, and let us expect great things from the love that loves, even as Christ is loved, and love and wait upon our Father.

> "Eye hath not seen, nor ear heard, neither have entered into the heart of man the things which God hath prepared for them that love him" (I Cor. 2:9).

He has already given us three pledges of His love in the gift of His Son, in the gift of His Spirit, and in the gift of His Word. Oh, what must remain to us of blessing, where we have already such pledges of His love!

One word more. It is to those who do not yet believe on the Lord Jesus Christ, who have never come to Him, who do not trust Him—"why will ye die?" Love opens its arms to welcome you, why will you go away? Everlasting grace supplicates you to come and find rest for your souls, why turn a deaf ear? Jesus' prayer has gone up,—it is registered in heaven, not only for His disciples but "for them also who shall believe on me through their word, that they all may be one." Why will you continue to reject the testimony which the Holy Ghost came down to bear witness to? "The testimony of Jesus is the spirit of prophecy."

Oh, that in study of His Word, every unbeliever may be persuaded to believe in Christ, to receive Christ, to trust in Christ, to be one with God in Christ, and happy with Him forever!

39

"FATHER, I WILL THAT THEY ALSO, WHOM THOU HAST GIVEN
ME, BE WITH ME WHERE I AM; THAT THEY MAY BEHOLD
MY GLORY, WHICH THOU HAST GIVEN ME: FOR
THOU LOVEDST ME BEFORE THE FOUNDA-
TION OF THE WORLD."—John 17:24

OUR DIVINE LORD having pleaded "the glory which thou gavest me I have given them; that they may be one, even as we are one: I in them and thou in me, that they may be made perfect in one"—and having declared that their manifested union, and their consummated bliss, would be the means whereby the world should know how great was the work which God sent His Son to accomplish, and how inconceivable the love was wherewith they were loved, thus enfolding and enshrining them in the very love wherewith He had Himself been loved: He now whispers to His Father's heart the ultimate object for which He was here on earth in our nature, and for the attainment of which He was about to lay down His life, "Father, I will that they also, whom thou hast given me, be with me where I am; that they may behold my glory, which thou hast given me: for thou lovedst me before the foundation of the world."

He had prayed for the realization and manifestation of their union with each other, in Him and with God in heaven; He does not pray for the *fact,* He had no need to pray for that; He Himself was the pledge on earth of the indissoluble union of His people with their heavenly Father. And, oh, what a proof He was just then giving of how close that union was! Our Lord was in the immediate anticipation of Gethsemane: the dark shades of Calvary were gathering round His blessed soul, yet nothing could disengage His thoughts from His beloved people; He was thinking not of Himself but of them, not even the prospect of the glory into which He was about to return could make Him forget them; He had said in the early part of His prayer, "Glorify thou me with thine own self, with the glory which I had with thee before the world was." The time was come, soon, very soon, the everlasting gates shall be opened to the King of glory, and He shall take His place at the right hand of God, amidst the hallelujahs of angels, and archangels, and the company of heaven, yet is He thinking of His dear people, and pleading for them; His language clearly conveys that He would not be satisfied with the glory itself unless they are with Him, participating in His felicity, and beholding His glory. He had said as much to them before,

> "I go to prepare a place for you. And if I go and prepare a place for you, I will come again, and receive you unto myself; that where I am, there ye may be also" (John 14:2, 3).

The Head and the members must be together, "Father, I will that they also, whom thou hast given me, be with me where I am" (in My divine nature, and where I shall soon be in My human nature); "that they may behold my glory, which thou hast given me."

"Father, I will"; this manner of addressing God is peculiar to Christ. We find no parallel to it in any of the recorded prayers of Old or New Testament saints. Indeed we must feel conscious that such language uttered by a mere creature would be entirely unbecoming, if not absolutely irreverent and profane, but as used by our Lord on this occasion they express the last will and testament of God's beloved Son, whispered into His Father's heart, concerning His redeemed. A short time previously He told His disciples of His will in reference to them and during the term of their separation.

> "Peace I leave with you, my peace I give unto you: not as the world giveth, give I unto you. Let not your heart be troubled, neither let it be afraid" (John 14:27).

Now He tells His heavenly Father what His will was with regard to their future, "Father, I will that they also, whom thou hast given me, be with me where I am; that they may behold my glory, which thou hast given me."

We all hope to be one day in heaven. What is the character of that heaven for which *we* hope? On this depends the true character of our religion. Is our heaven the heaven of the Mohammedan, where we expect *carnal* ease and pleasures, and all things that minister to the natural taste and appetite, where we shall have music and dancing, and the excess of such pleasures as men follow after here,—if this be the heaven we anticipate, then, a life of carnal indulgence is about the fittest preparation for it. Or is the heaven we anticipate the undefined and indescribable *apprehension* the world imagines—a negative felicity, not so much an existence of positive enjoyment with God as an escape from damnation—a sort of heaven we would fain postpone as long as possible, seeing we much prefer the things we have, and enjoy, to the things we have not seen, and do not realize or desire? If this is the heaven we anticipate, then the undefined religion of the world is about the natural preparation for it. But the heaven of the child of God, the man whose soul is born from above, the man whose eyes are enlightened with divine light, and whose heart is instructed with divine truth, is here described in one sentence, "To be with Christ, and to behold his glory."

The great Apostle of the Gentiles was caught up to the third heaven, and saw what he could not describe; but you will observe that ever after his thought of heaven was this—*to be with Christ:*

> "I have a desire to depart, and to be with Christ, which is far better" (see Phil. 1:23).

"With Christ." Our blessed Lord Jesus Himself seems to have had no more perfect way of expressing what heaven was than, *"where I am."* When He would cheer the forgiven and dying thief, and awaken the note of triumph in his heart, the promise was,

> "Today shalt thou be *with me* in paradise" (Luke 23:43).

And now when He would tell all His loving heart's desire, all His last will, to His heavenly Father, He thus expresses Himself, "Father, I will that they also, whom thou hast given me, be *with me* where I am; that they may behold my glory."

> "And reflecting as a mirror the glory of the Lord, we shall be changed into the same image from glory to glory" (see II Cor. 3:18).

If this be indeed the heaven we are anticipating, let us ask ourselves what is our title to it? There must be a title corresponding to the dignity of the position into which we are about to enter. Away with all merit of our own!—human merit could give no title to be with Christ, and to behold His glory. All our charities, observances of ordinances, prayers, and services, even were they perfect and spotless, which they are not, could give us *no* title to such a position. There is but one title to heaven, the blood and righteousness of the Lamb,—have we received Him? are we united to Him? Only one name is recognized there! the name which is above every name, have we learned it? do we plead it?

Again. If this is the heaven we anticipate, what is our meetness for it? Would we be happy there? It is a very solemn question, and one we ought in all sincerity to ask ourselves. Suppose the God of all grace were this moment to introduce us to where Christ is, that we might be with Christ, beholding His glory, would serving Him be our happiness? Would the employments of heaven suit our taste? Alas, the employments which most suit the tastes of many have no place there; where Jesus is all in all. Do we care for His society here? The long days of eternity in heaven are spent in praise, ascribing

> "Blessing and honour, . . . and power . . . to him that sitteth upon the throne" (Rev. 5:13),

magnifying His holy name, and with unspeakable adoration worshiping Him that

> "Made us kings and priests to God and to his Father" (Rev. 1:5).

Do we enjoy this sort of thing now? If not, what reason have we for supposing we would enjoy it there?

> "Ye must be born again" (John 3:3)

if the heaven Jesus speaks of—as being with Him, and beholding His glory—is to be our consummated happiness. Even here on earth the true believer's heaven consists in being with Jesus, beholding Him by faith. That beautiful passage, in II Corinthians 3:18, thus describes the Christians' heaven here—

> "We all, with open face beholding as in a glass the glory of the Lord, are changed into the same image from glory to glory, even as by the Spirit of the Lord." *

The Word of God, the gospel of His grace, displays Jesus, there the eye of faith sees Him, and there the heart of faith learns to enjoy Him. At the best we see but through a glass darkly, at the best our spiritual vision is very dim, and our glimpses of Him but fitful, passing things. Yet, after all, it is our heaven on earth to see and enjoy even a little of Jesus, and have Him with us in spirit, even "though now we see him not."

* Rather, "reflecting as a mirror."—R. V.

In the times of sorrow, when no earthly comforter is near;
in hours of temptation, when the world, the flesh, and the devil
are too strong for us; in seasons of conflict, when we realize that

> "We wrestle not against flesh and blood, but against princi-
> palities, against powers, against the rulers of the darkness of this
> world, against spiritual wickedness in high places" (Eph.
> 6:12);

in times of conscious weakness and failure; in hours of sickness,
when

> "Weary days and weary nights are appointed to us,"

and we seem to draw nigh to the valley of the shadow of death,
—how sweet it is to behold Jesus, to see the glory of His grace
and love as He is revealed in His Word: and find Him "all in
all," all we want, *as* we want Him, *where* we want Him, *when*
we want Him, and *forevermore.*

But if such beholding of Him, and such communion with
Him is our privilege here in the wilderness, what will it be by-
and-by to behold His unveiled face in the glory, to be revealed
no longer as in a glass darkly, no longer as afar off, but with
Him, beholding His glory—the summit of felicity, the enjoyment of eternity.

This beholding does not merely mean that we shall be spec-
tators. In Isaiah 65:1, the word implies participation in that
which we behold,

> "I said, Behold me, behold me, unto a nation that was not
> called by my name."

And not only is participation implied, but assimilation. The
apostle John tells us,

> "When he shall appear we shall be like him; for we shall see
> him as he is" (I John 3:2);

this is the believer's heaven. "Father, I will that they also, whom
thou hast given me, be with me where I am; that they may
behold my glory."

"Thine eyes shall see the King in his beauty: they shalt behold the land that is very far off" (Isa. 33:17);

"We shall be able to comprehend with all saints what is the breadth, and length, and depth, and height; and to know the love of Christ, which passeth knowledge, that we may be filled with all the fulness of God" (Eph. 3:18, 19).

We shall see the salvation of God; we shall know the depths from which it has plucked us; we shall realize the heights to which it has exalted us; we shall

"Apprehend that for which [we are] apprehended of Christ Jesus" (Phil. 3:12);

we "Shall sit down [with Abraham and Isaac and Jacob] in the kingdom of God" (Luke 13:29); shall enter through the gates into the city; and never feel ashamed in their company, evermore complete in Jesus we shall have our portion where He is all in all. Oh, what glory! We shall wear the white robe—"the best robe"; and receive "the crown which the Lord, the righteous Judge, shall give to us in that day, and not to us only, but to all those who love His appearing"; we shall even ascend the throne on which He sits! for

"Unto him that overcometh will I grant to sit with me in my throne, even as I also overcame, and am set down with my Father in his throne" (Rev. 3:21).

Oh, what glory! We shall drink from

The river of the water of life that floweth "clear as crystal, proceeding out of the throne of God, and of the Lamb" (Rev. 22:1);

we shall sit down under the shadow of the tree of life, and banquet upon its fruits and be filled with God. Oh, that glory! which "eye hath not seen, nor ear heard, neither hath entered into the heart of man to conceive!" We shall "stand together on the sea of glass, having the harps of God," and singing our new song, the song that "no man can learn but those who are redeemed from among men."

A most important and precious part of this subject remains, namely, the ground upon which our blessed Master thus claims us for the glory. He pleads *atonement* and *substitution.* He who knew no sin was about to be made sin for us that we might be made the righteousness of God in Him (see II Cor. 5:21) and have all the benefits thereof. He pleads the fulfillment of covenant arrangements, and everlasting settlements between Himself and the Father. We are too apt practically to overlook or ignore these great facts—indeed, the majority of professing Christians seldom get beyond the notion of a merciful God and Saviour. The Lord Jesus Christ here introduces us to a just God and yet a Saviour (see Isa. 45:21). Observe once more His arguments; He pleads His relationship—"Father." Remember it was because of His Sonship He was ordained to be our teacher,

> "This is my beloved Son, hear him" (Mark 9:7).

It was because of His Sonship He was anointed to be King.

> "I have set my King upon my holy hill of Zion. . . . Kiss the Son lest He be angry" (Ps. 2:6, 12).

It was as the Son of the Father He was consecrated High Priest,

> "The word of the oath . . . maketh the Son, who is consecrated for evermore" (Heb. 7:28).

Again He pleads His Father's everlasting love,

> "Thou lovedst me before the foundation of the world."

Already He had pleaded His finished work,

> "I have finished the work which thou gavest me to do" (v. 4),

He pleads, "thine they were and thou gavest them me." *Seven* times He alludes to this truth in His prayer. Then He pleads, "I have given unto them the words which thou gavest me." Finally, He pleads, "The glory which thou gavest me I have given them." And then He declares to His Father the object He has had in view, and for the attainment of which He was about to die, and

> "The joy . . . set before him [for which He] endured the cross, despising the shame" (Heb. 12:2);

"that they may be one, even as we are one," and "that they may be with me where I am, and that they may behold my glory." "Father, I will." That will is registered in the heart of God! That "I will" has been endorsed in the resurrection of Christ! That "I will" has been attested and sealed by the Holy Ghost sent down from heaven, and it is recorded for the encouragement of our faith in God's most true and faithful Word. Now let us strengthen our *faith* by dwelling on His words, "Father, I will that they also, whom thou hast given me, be with me where I am; that they may behold my glory." Many there be that seem to say unto our souls, We will they shall *not* be with Jesus where He is, to behold His glory. Memory! Conscience! The broken law! Opportunities neglected! Mercies abused! God forgotten! Each in turn seems to say, I will you shall *not* be with Jesus. Failure upon failure! Sin upon sin! Inconsistency upon inconsistency! All seem to challenge us, You shall never be with Jesus! But our God and Father puts the will of His dear Son against all the opposers of our souls and tells us that neither death nor life, nor things present or to come, shall separate us from His love (see Rom. 8:39). Encourage *your joy.*

> "Being justified by faith, we have peace with God, through our Lord Jesus Christ" (Rom. 5:1).

Encourage *your hope.*

> "We rejoice in hope of the glory of God!" (Rom. 5:2).

Anchor your tempest-tossed soul here where hope maketh not ashamed. A few more rising and setting suns and we shall be with Christ. "The Lord himself shall be thine everlasting light and the days of thy mourning shall be ended"; those weary hands shall take the crown, those feeble knees shall bear thee through the golden streets, and those lips shall praise Him. "I will," blessed "I will!" The world, the flesh, and the devil may say I will not, while Jesus says, "I will."

What a practical subject this is! Shall we spend our eternity with Him, beholding His glory?

> "What manner of persons ought we to be in all holy conversation and godliness?" (II Peter 3:11).

Shall the eyes that are to look on Jesus be busy with objects that displease Him? Shall the ears that are to listen to His welcome be busy with sounds that dishonor Him? Shall the members that are to minister to Him in the glory, work at sin here as it were with a cart rope? O God forbid!

Lastly, one word to those who have not believed in Jesus. You have not come to Him, and you cannot anticipate with us the joy of being with Him, beholding Him, and participating in His glory. Yet the Son of God came down to *where you are;* He left the heavens and came into the world, and those to whom He came gave Him no welcome,

> "The Son of man had not where to lay his head" (see Matt. 8:20).

Unasked He came, and "his own received him not"; now He has gone up where He was before, having

> "Led captivity captive . . . received gifts for men; . . . even for the rebellious also, that the Lord God might dwell among them" (Ps. 68:18).

He has by His offering of Himself, made it a just thing with God to forgive and receive you; He invites you to come to be with Him *where He is,* to claim His precious blood as the ground of your acceptance, His blessed name as your introduc-

tion to God, and His faithfulness and truth as your argument.
Now "why will you die," why continue to reject Him? why per-
sist in saying,

> "Go thy way for this time; when I have a convenient season,
> I will call for thee" (Acts 24:25)?

Oh, think of this! It is His registered will in heaven that every
poor sinner who believes upon Him, who takes Him as God's
gift of salvation (which He is) shall be with Him *where He is,*
beholding that glory which the Father gave Him, who loved
Him before the foundation of the world, and who loves all poor
sinners who love Jesus.

40

"O RIGHTEOUS FATHER, THE WORLD HATH NOT KNOWN
THEE: BUT I HAVE KNOWN THEE, AND THESE HAVE
KNOWN THAT THOU HAST SENT ME."—John 17:25

THE SUBJECTS suggested here are very many, and precious
beyond all description to the "believer." As our blessed
Lord began His prayer, so He ends it, calling on His "Father."
It was an endearing relationship, it is a tender tie, but in His
case most of all. Never before from the days of eternity did such
a Son, and under such circumstances, address such a Father. You
remember how beautifully a Father is portrayed in the parable
of the Prodigal Son. He saw His wandering child afar off, when
no other eye could recognize him; He ran to meet him, and put
His arms around his neck, and kissed him, when no other arms
would receive him. *God was that Father!*

"I have surely heard Ephraim bemoaning himself" (Jer.
31:18).

No other ear in heaven or earth could hear him! Now these
were *sinful* children. With what listening ears, with what love,
with what sympathy, think you, did the Father in heaven regard
the supplication of His only begotten Son, His holy One, His
spotless One.

It is the God-man that prays, He who had taken our own
nature, and humbled Himself to be made in the likeness of men
—and it is as Mediator He prays. As the divine Son, the second
Person of the blessed Trinity, "equal to the Father as touching
His Godhead," *He could not pray:* it would be incongruous His

doing so; He could ask for nothing He had not; He could receive nothing that did not essentially belong to Him. It is true that as the second Person of the blessed Trinity, the eternal Son might address the first Person as His eternal Father, being begotten before all worlds; but not so the God-man Mediator Christ Jesus, whose incarnation is not attributed in Scripture to the first Person, but to the Holy Ghost, also to His own act; as it is written—

> "The Holy Ghost shall come upon thee, and the power of the Highest shall overshadow thee: therefore also that holy thing which shall be born of thee shall be called the Son of God" (Luke 1:35).

And again, Hebrews 2:14,

> "Forasmuch then as the children are partakers of flesh and blood, he also himself likewise *took part* of the same."

When, therefore, our blessed Lord here supplicates His Father, He prays as Head of His Church, and in the same sense in which He teaches us to address Him in what is commonly called the Lord's Prayer:

> "My Father, and your Father; . . . my God, and your God" (John 20:17).

We cannot be too clear upon this most important subject. The prayer before us is, therefore, a prayer of faith; He who uttered it lived by faith.

> "He was the author and finisher of faith" (Heb. 12:2).

One of the objects He had in coming down from heaven into our nature was to teach us how that Father might be known and trusted.

"O righteous Father." In thus addressing God, our Lord pleads the promises made to Him by His Father according to covenant, everlasting settlements, entered into before the world was. He had finished the work His Father had given Him to do, and He now claims from a righteous God the equivalent of blessing for those for whom He labored. It is like His language in Psalm 17:1:

> "Hear the right, O Lord, attend unto my cry, give ear unto my prayer, that goeth not out of feigned lips."

When He prayed, Father, keep them and sanctify them, His plea was, "Holy Father, keep . . . those whom thou hast given me." And why? Because Jehovah had pledged Himself to Christ by His *holiness* (see Ps. 89:35), and He claims the pledge. But here, when He expresses the desire that His people may have the full reward of His own travail, and that they may be with Him where He is, He appeals to the righteousness of God —"O righteous Father." His appeal is founded on HIS *own merit.* He was about to be made an offering for sin, and to bear in His own body upon the tree the tremendous penalty due to all "the iniquities, the transgressions and sins," of those He represented, and for whom He pleads. "My Father, My righteous Father, the hour has come; I am on My way to Calvary; I am about to pour out My soul unto death. I am about to drink to the last dregs the cup of Thine indignation against the sins of My people; I am about to suffer, the just for the unjust, that I may bring sinners unto God: Father, I am about to blot out in My own blood, the handwriting of ordinances which is against My people, and which is contrary to them, taking it out of the way, and nailing it to My cross. I am about to spoil principalities and powers, and make a show of them openly, triumphing over them on the cross. I am about to magnify Thy holy law, which they have broken, and all this in accordance with our everlasting covenant. 'O righteous Father,' I appeal to Thee that as Thou dost accept Mine offering, they may be with Me where I am, to behold My glory!"

Consider how complete must be His atonement, and how perfect His satisfaction for sin, when He can thus claim from the righteousness of God such an equivalent for His people! Oh! remember, and forget not, that God's righteousness is now pledged to bestow upon every believer in the Lord Jesus Christ all that He has merited in His life, and in His death, for sinners who believe on Him. In this blessed fact Christ rested, and here He pleads it with His righteous Father, that His people's faith may rest there also, and that we may realize that when we pray, we are not merely dealing with a God who is gracious and merciful, but with a righteous Father, who is

> "Faithful and just to forgive us our sins, and to cleanse us from all unrighteousness" (I John 1:9).

It was pure mercy in God to provide a Saviour when man had sinned; it was pure mercy in God to promise that Saviour; it was pure mercy in God to send Him; but, having provided, having promised, having sent Him to be a propitiation through faith in His blood, and *having accepted* His offering and raised Him from the dead, it is no mere mercy in God to give the benefit to those sinners who believe on Him,—it is *justice* to Christ, though it is mercy to them. Now, the Lord here rests our salvation upon the faithful promise of the faithful Promiser.

> "In hope of eternal life, which God, that cannot lie, promised before the world began" (Titus 1:2).

A promise which must have been made to Christ Himself, for there was no one else to promise to. See also Isaiah 42 where the Lord, speaking to Christ, pledges Himself that He will hold His hand, call Him in righteousness, keep Him, and give Him a covenant to the people, for a light of the Gentiles,

> "To open the blind eyes, to bring out the prisoners from the prison, and them that sit in darkness out of the prison house" (Isa. 42:7).

The Lord promised Christ that He would do this. It was pure grace in the Lord to make that promise; but now Christ was come to fulfill the conditions of the covenant, and make an end of sin, and He appeals to His righteous Father to secure to Him and to His believing people all the benefits of His passion.

Take a few passages of Scripture to illustrate how this truth is pressed upon our attention by the Holy Spirit, in the New Testament first, as to the forgiveness of our sins. It is written,

> "If we confess our sins, he is faithful and *just* to forgive us our sins" (I John 1:9).

Why? Because Christ has suffered in our place, it would be injustice to Christ if He did not. Second, as to our justification from all things, it is written, that through the propitiation of Christ, God is

> "*Just,* and the justifier of him which believeth in Jesus" (Rom. 3:25, 26).

Third, as to the vengeance of God upon those who oppose our souls, and the rest to be enjoyed by us when our warfare is over, and our fight is done, it is written,

> "It is a *righteous* thing with God to recompense tribulation to them that trouble you; and to you who are troubled rest with us, when the Lord Jesus shall be revealed from heaven with his mighty angels, in flaming fire taking vengeance on them that know not God, and that obey not the gospel of our Lord Jesus Christ" (II Thess. 1:6–8).

Fourth, as to the acceptance of our poor services rendered in Christ's name, it is written,

> "God is not *unrighteous* to forget your work and labour of love" (Heb. 6:10).

Fifth, as to the promised crown for which we hope, it is written,

> "Henceforth there is laid up for me a crown of righteousness, which the Lord, the *righteous* Judge, shall give me at that day: and not to me only, but unto all them also that love his appearing" (II Tim. 4:8).

Our Lord's words in the passage before us are in complete harmony with these passages of Scripture, for having declared His will that His people might be with Him where He was, to behold His glory; He now seals and crowns His claim by an appeal to His *"righteous* Father!" A righteousness so perfect that when man sinned and the Lord Jesus Christ presented Himself as a Substitute to atone for the sinner and for the sin, God would not abate one jot of the penalty due; judgment was brought to the line and righteousness to the plummet (see Isa. 28:17), and, He who was in the form of God was wounded for our transgressions; He was bruised for our iniquities, the chastisement of our peace was upon Him (see Isa. 53:5). And He now appeals to that same righteousness, that seeing justice has been satisfied, and the broken law vindicated, His people for whom He died may not have one title less than God the righteous Father knew His own righteous Son deserved. So great is the salvation of God! Here let us rest our hearts, our hopes, and our confidence, for here Christ Himself rested.

But the words of our blessed Master refer to what follows as well as to what precedes them. "O righteous Father, *the world hath not known thee."* What a mysterious fact this is! The Creator of the world unknown by the world, the Benefactor of the world a stranger in our midst, and not from want of evidence,

> "The heavens declare the glory of God; and the firmament showeth his handiwork" (Ps. 19:1).

His messengers proclaimed Him, and

> "God, who at sundry times and in divers manners, spake in times past unto the fathers by the prophets, hath in these last days spoken unto us by his Son" (Heb. 1:1).
> "He that hath seen me hath seen the Father" (John 14:9).

And yet, "O righteous Father, the world hath not known thee."

"He was in the world, and the world was made by him, and
the world knew him not. He came unto his own, and his own
received him not" (John 1:10, 11).

Not of the Gentiles only is it written that they knew not God,
but of Israel!

"The ox knoweth his owner, and the ass his master's crib;
but Israel doth not know, my people doth not consider" (Isa.
1:3).

For thirty-three years God in our own nature lived in our
world, and taught, and worked, and yet after all how comparatively small was the success of His ministry! How few there
were in the hour of trial even among His own chosen disciples
to watch with Him even for one hour!

We might easily ask curious and unprofitable questions very
difficult to answer as to why it was, and how it was, that God
could permit this; how in the midst of light men are so often
found walking in darkness: how is it possible for such a God,
so full of love, and grace, and power, to permit such a state of
things to exist: how He could suffer His position here to be
usurped so long by

"The god of this world . . . the spirit that now worketh in
the children of disobedience" (II Cor. 4:4; Eph. 2:2).

Just see how Christ treats this question. He doth not attempt to
fathom it. As on another occasion He said,

"I thank thee, O Father, Lord of heaven and earth, because
thou hast hid these things from the wise and prudent, and hast
revealed them unto babes. Even so, Father: for so it seemed
good in thy sight" (Matt. 11:25, 26).

So here He answers all with one word, *"Righteous* Father."
Infinite wisdom, power, love, and rectitude has guided all that
Father has done, and all He was doing or would do. There is a
parallel passage in the Old Testament which throws a consider-

able light upon our Lord's words here, where, after promises made to Him—very wonderful—including

"Thou art my servant, O Israel, in whom I will be glorified";

our Lord is represented as answering,

"Then I said, I have labored in vain, I have spent my strength for nought, and in vain: yet surely my judgment is with the Lord, and my work with my God" (Isa. 49:3, 4).

Thus in the prayer before us our Lord commits Himself and His work *"to him that judgeth righteously,"* and would have us silence all our misgivings, and unravel all our difficulties, thus

"Shall not the judge of all the earth do right?" (Gen. 18:25).

Clouds and darkness may be round about God, but

"Righteousness and judgment are the habitation of his throne" (see Ps. 89:14).

"O righteous Father, the world hath not known thee." How sad a state of things is here described. Perhaps we say this refers to the world of heathendom, the world of past ages of darkness. Well! and how is it with *ourselves?* We grant that there is a vast difference between the days of darkness and ignorance which "God overlooked," and the times in which our lot is cast; we are surrounded with light, and compassed with privileges, but how is it with ourselves? What do we know about God? I do not ask what do we know about a God;

"There be gods many, and lords many" (I Cor. 8:5),

but I ask, and I ask myself, what do we know of *the God of the Bible?* What do we know experimentally of Him? What do we know of God as our "righteous Father"? Do we know Him as our Father? We can have no experimental knowledge of God, but as we have soul-communion with Him as "our Father." What degree of communion have we with God? Alas, the thoughts, the words, the works, the tastes, the likings, and the dislikings of too many evidence that they know little practically of God, and have very little practically of communion with "the Father."

Ignorance of God is the root and source of all the evil existing in the world. And in this one sentence our Lord expresses that solemn fact, "O righteous Father, the world hath not known thee." What is profligacy, but a filthy stream flowing from ignorance of God? What is the love of the world, and of the things of the world? What is infidelity? What is sensuous religion—a religion of forms and ceremonies, and bowings and turnings, but fruits growing out of ignorance of God? Continued ignorance of God must finally exclude us from heaven, for it is written, and it is a solemn statement,

"The kingdom of God is *within you*" (Luke 17:21).

Now, if the kingdom of God doth not take possession of us *here*, we can never enter into it *there*. "O righteous Father, the world hath not known thee."

On the other hand the *knowledge* of God is the root and source of all bliss, the means of justification (Isa. 53:11), the earnest of glory, and the meetness for glory, the characteristics of "the children" and "the fathers" in God (I John 2:10). "This is life eternal, to know thee, the only true God, and Jesus Christ, whom thou hast sent."

"Acquaint now thyself with him, and be at peace" (Job 22:21).

Yea, through the knowledge of God peace and mercy are multiplied, and in the knowledge of God we are made partakers of the divine nature (see II Peter 1:2–4).

The world hath not known thee; "*But I have known* thee, and these have known that thou hast sent me." On this wide earth there was not one solitary being but Himself who knew that Father. When God looked down upon the world He had made, there was not one heart beating in sympathy with His own, but the heart of that beloved Son who was addressing Him.

"No man knoweth the Son, but the Father; neither knoweth any man the Father, save the Son, and to whomsoever the Son will reveal him" (Matt. 11:27).

"O righteous Father, I have known thee." Yes, He came from His bosom; He knew Him well. Who can describe that perfect, boundless, inconceivable knowledge? "I know Thee, and I delight in Thee—I can trust Thee—I can commit all to Thee. 'I have known thee,' I know all Thy perfections, I know all Thy degrees, Thy counsels, Thy purposes, Thy gentleness, Thy long-suffering, Thy grace, Thy love, Thy kindness, 'Thy thoughts that are to usward'; I know them, and I want My people to know them, and because I know Thee, I appeal to Thee as My 'righteous Father,' that Thou wilt, for My own sake, and for the sake of the great atonement made to Thy justice, gather all my believing people to be with Me where I am, that they may behold My glory; for I have known Thee, and these have known that Thou hast sent Me." This was the Saviour's prayer. "These have known that thou hast sent me." Very limited was their knowledge, yet He will give the best account of them. Our dear Lord takes credit not only for what He had done for them, but for what He was yet about to do for them through His Holy Spirit, unto the fullness of the purpose of His boundless love.

41

"And I have declared unto them thy name, and will declare it: that the love wherewith thou hast loved me may be in them, and I in them."
—John 17:26

Yes, He had told them, and He tells us what it is, "Father!" God desires to be thought of by us as a Father, spoken to as a Father, trusted in as a Father, loved as a Father, and obeyed as a Father, and our Father's name is "Love." Our Lord has told us

> "God so loved the world that he gave his only begotten Son, that whosoever believeth in him should not perish, but have everlasting life."

"I have declared unto them thy name, and *will declare it,*" referring, no doubt, to the further manifestations of His Father's grace in His own death upon the cross for sinners, His resurrection from the dead as the Lord of life and glory, and the consequent gift of the Holy Ghost who was to lead them into all truth, "to dwell" with them, and to "be in them . . . a well of living water springing up into everlasting life," and forevermore. Whatever we shall know of God, in time or in eternity, Jesus will be the Teacher; whatever we shall see of God, Jesus will be the Manifestor, whatever we shall enjoy of God, Jesus will be the Medium; "I have declared unto them thy name, and *will* declare it."

Observe how the results of His doing so are grouped about this statement and promise! First, "These have known that thou hast sent me." It is characteristic of the "little children" that "they have known the Father"; and the highest characteristic of the "fathers" in God is the same. They have known the Father, only they have known Him longer and better (I John 2:13, 14). How is this? "I have declared unto them thy name." Second, they shall be "with me." None who are ignorant of God can ever be with Jesus. Third, they shall "behold my glory"; none shall behold the glory of Jesus who are not acquainted with God. Fourth, "That the love wherewith thou hast loved me may be in them." What is to produce that love but the knowledge of it? And fifth, "'I in them,' the seal of all their blessedness, the fullness of all their joy, the crown and consummation of all Thy purposes towards them, the fruition of all that great salvation Thou hast provided for them."

The dispensation of shadows is past and gone, and we have been listening to the words of "God manifest in the flesh,"

> "God hath spoken unto us by his Son" (Heb. 1:2).
> "God, who commanded the light to shine out of darkness, hath shined in our hearts, to give the light of the knowledge of the glory of God in the face of Jesus Christ" (II Cor. 4:6).

It is written in the latter part of Exodus 34 that when Moses came down from his interview with God his face shone so that the children of Israel could not look at him, although he wist not that his face shone. Here (*in the Bible*) we have God's own portrait, for He upon whose face we gaze by faith is the image of the invisible God, the brightness of the Father's glory, the express image of His Person, and the Manifestor of His Father's name. This Word is God's mirror, where the Spirit reveals Him, that we may see the glory, even the goodness of the Lord. It is the written record of what Jesus hath declared concerning the Father's name and the Father's love. And the light by which we behold the vision is the Holy Ghost.

Even here on earth as we contemplate Christ in His Word, we are changed into the image of His glory. How much more when no longer as through a glass darkly, no longer as at a distance, but with Him where He is, beholding His glory, shall we be *altogether* like Him,

> "Changed from glory to glory, even as by the Spirit of the Lord."

Yes, by-and-by, when this poor veil of flesh shall be removed, when we know as we are known, and love as we are loved, we shall have the full fruition of that which our God, in Christ, purposed for our happiness.

Let us learn to prize more and more the glorious gospel of the blessed God. It is the means whereby God doth impart to us the knowledge of Himself; whereby He doth establish fellowship with us in Christ, revealing Himself to us as in a mirror, and stamping His image upon our souls;

It is the means whereby He doth impart to us the Holy Ghost, and shed abroad in our hearts His love;

It is the means whereby Christ Himself is formed in our souls, the hope of glory. There is nothing beyond it, as a possessed blessing and privilege, but the fruition of the glory it proclaims to us.

To that fruition He evidently alludes here. "I have declared unto them thy name, and will declare it: that the love wherewith thou hast loved me may be in them, and I in them." Our Lord's final purpose concerning His people, as here expressed, reaches far beyond the circumstances of time, and far above the region of thought; it can only be fulfilled in the fruition of the beatific vision; "The love wherewith thou hast loved me . . . in them, and I in them." Observe! *not* the love wherewith Thou hast loved *them* . . . vast! indescribable! unspeakable as that love had been; *not* the full realization of its length and breadth and depth and height, although this shall surely be enjoyed; *not* that Thou shouldst love them as Thou hast loved Me,—no need to ask for that—*this love was theirs.* Our Lord had told His

Father (see v. 23) that He would have even the world know "that thou hast loved them, as thou hast loved me." He was, Himself, the seal and pledge of the love wherewith the Father had loved them, and it was no part of His work or mission to procure it. No, it is "that the love wherewith thou hast loved me *may be in them";* meaning not only the love of God to Christ should be bestowed upon them, and the full participation and realization of that love enjoyed by them, but more, *much more,* even that God's love for Christ "may be in them." Known by them? Yes. Realized by them? Yes; but more—possessed by them, as bestowed *on Him. The very love wherewith God Himself loved Christ given down into the hearts of Christ's people!* and with Himself "that the love wherewith thou hast loved me may be in them, and I in them"; He himself evermore dwelling in them, the chosen shrine of His Father's love.

This shall be the crowning fruit of that union for which our Lord had been praying. (1) "I in them, and thou in me, *that they may be made perfect in one."* (2) *"That the world may believe that thou hast sent me,"* (3) *"and that thou hast loved me."* (4) *"That the love wherewith thou hast loved me may be in them,"* (5) *"and I in them,"* as its resting place forever.

See in how many ways, and by how many means He has provided and secured that His people shall be one with Him. By *incarnation:*

> "Forasmuch . . . as the children are partakers of flesh and blood, he also himself likewise took part of the same" (Heb. 2:14).

By *the Holy Ghost,* the Comforter whom I will send unto you from the Father, He dwelleth with you, and shall be in you (see John 14:16, 17). By *His Word:* you remember His answer to Judas' question,

> "Lord, how is it that thou wilt manifest thyself unto us, and not unto the world? Jesus answered and said unto him, If a

man love me, he will keep my words: and my Father will love him, and we will come unto him, and make our abode with him" (John 14:22–24).

And finally, in *His Father's love!* "The love wherewith thou hast loved me . . . in them, and I in them." Our Lord Jesus Christ could ask no more, and the fullness of the communicable blessing of Deity can impart no more than He here prays for. The beloved disciple seems to express the same truth when he wrote

> "Whosoever shall confess that Jesus is the Son of God, God dwelleth in him, and he in God . . . God is love; and he that dwelleth in love dwelleth in God, and God in him" (I John 4:15, 16).

May God evermore keep us in memory of these things, till we enjoy the fruition of them with Himself. We here learn that *union* with the Lord Jesus Christ is salvation, and that there is no salvation where this union does not exist. We learn, moreover, that the union between Christ and His people has its foundation in the ineffable union between Father, Son, and Holy Ghost, in the blessed Trinity. This union of the Three in One is first let down to the Lord Jesus Christ, the Mediator between God and man, who is *both* God and man in *one Person,* and then this union descends from the Lord Jesus Christ to the members of His mystical Body, that is, to sinners of every age and of every clime, who hear His Word and believe on Him. (See v. 20.) He is their Saviour; He is their Husband; He is their Head, and they are "the members of His body, and of His flesh, and of His bones . . . I in them, and thou in me."

Moreover, we learn here that the primal reason and ground of our redemption by Christ is God's own immutable interest in and love for us. This fact was pleaded, verse 6, "Thine they were, and thou gavest them to me."

Again, we learn here that the Father's gift of His people to Christ in order to be redeemed by His blood and evermore united to Himself and in Himself to God was regarded by Christ as the special pledge of His Father's love to Him. This He also pleads when claiming that we may be with Him where He is, and that we may behold His glory: "For thou *lovedst me* before the foundation of the world" (v. 24). Now, since God's love to Christ is the foundation of our salvation, let us not be cast down when we find difficulties within, and trial without, for God's love to us

> Is the love of God "which is in Christ Jesus our Lord." And therefore, "neither death, nor life, nor angels, nor principalities, nor powers, nor things present, nor things to come, nor height, nor depth, nor any other creature shall be able to separate us from" His love (Rom. 8:39).

And finally, remember that it is Christ's interest in us even more than our interest in Christ, which is the source and security of our union and blessedness in Him, and the hope and the earnest of our inheritance. Accordingly He prays, "That the love wherewith thou hast loved *me* may be in them, and I in them" (v. 26).

> "Therefore let no man glory in men. For all things are yours; whether Paul, or Apollos, or Cephas, or the world, or life, or death, or things present, or things to come; all are yours" (I Cor. 3:21–23).

Why? because Christ is yours? No, but because

> *"Ye are Christ's; and Christ is God's"*

Christ's interest in us is therefore the foundation of our interest in Christ. Always begin at the beginning, go to the Fountainhead if you want to be happy. Our God is love, and God's love to Christ, and Christ's interest in us, are the everlasting pillars of our salvation and security.

When we are painfully conscious of the hardness of our hearts, and the coldness of our love to Him who first loved us, let us remember and not forget what is here taught us and promised to us. A day is coming when *God's own love to Christ* shall be in us, and we, too, shall love Christ with the love wherewith His Father loves Him: this shall be the reward of His travail, and there He will rest forever, inhabiting the praises of His people, and enshrined in their hearts, dwelling in the very love wherewith His Father loved Him.

Christ and perfect love must be evermore together; where He dwells, love dwells, the Father dwells; the Holy Ghost dwells, God dwells, and we shall dwell! "The love wherewith thou hast loved me . . . in them." "And I in them!" Their everlasting perfection with God!

Thus He would express His ultimate purpose and the consummation of all His desires for His people, "I in them," evermore "in them"; their Light in the wilderness, their strength in the conflict, their hope, their joy, their portion in time; but also in them when I and they are with Thee in "the glory which I had with thee before the world was; Thou in me, and I in them [*dwelling in*] *the love wherewith thou hast loved me.*"

Oh, it dazzles the understanding to think what the love of God in Christ has provided for us sinners! Will you, reader, neglect and reject Him? Many, many to this very hour do practically reject Him, yet He opens His arms and His heart to them still, and says,

> "Come unto me, all ye that labor and are heavy laden, and I will give you rest" (Matt. 11:28).

Poor weary ones, come and find in the Father's name, which Christ doth declare unto you, all the grace your souls need for time; and when time shall be no more, all the glory which He has promised to those that love Him.

> "At that day ye shall know that I am in my Father, and ye in me, and I in you" (John 14:20).

Amen.

GOSPEL DIALOGUE BETWEEN MR. D. L. MOODY AND REV. MARCUS RAINSFORD

I

Mr. M.—What is it to be a child of God? What is the first step?

Mr. R.—Well, sir, I am a child of God when I become united to the Son of God. The Son of God prayed (John 17:20, 21) that all who believed upon Him should be one with Him, as He was one with the Father. Believing on Jesus, I receive Him, and become united to Him (John 1:12, 13); I become, as it were, a member of His Body. I am an heir of God, a joint-heir with Christ (Eph. 5:30; I John 5:1; Gal. 3:26).

Mr. M.—What is the best definition of faith?

Mr. R.—Trust in the Son of God, as the Saviour He has given to us. Simple trust, not only in a creed, but in a Person. I trust my soul to Him. I trust the keeping of my soul to Him. God has promised that whosoever trusts Him, mercy shall compass him on every side (Ps. 32:10).

Mr. M.—Does not the Scripture say that the devils believe? (James 2:19).

Mr. R.—They believe the truth, do they not? They believe that Jesus was manifested to destroy them; and they "tremble." I wish we believed as truly and as fully that God sent His Son into the world to save us.

Mr. M.—What is it to "trust"?

Mr. R.—I take it to mean four things:

(1) Believing on Christ: that is, taking Him at His Word.

(2) Hoping in Christ: that is, expecting help from Him, according to His Word.

(3) Relying on Christ: that is, resting on Him for the times

455

and ways, and circumstances in which He may be pleased to fulfill His promises according to His Word.

(4) Waiting on Christ: that is, *continuing* to do so, notwithstanding delay, darkness, barrenness, perplexing experiences, and the sentence of death in myself (II Cor. 1:9). He may keep me waiting a while (I have kept Him a long time waiting); but He will not keep me waiting always. Believing in Him; hoping in Him; relying upon Him; and waiting for Him—I understand to be trusting in Him.

Mr. M.—Can all these friends here believe the promises?

Mr. R.—The promises are true, whether we believe them or not. We do not make them true by believing them. God could not charge me with being an unbeliever, or condemn me for unbelief, if the promises were not true for me. I could in that case turn round and say: "Great God, why did You expect me to believe a promise that was not true for me?" And yet the Scriptures set forth unbelief as the greatest sin I can continue to commit.

Mr. M.—How are we "cleansed by the blood"?

Mr. R.—"The blood is the life." The sentence upon sinners for their sin was, "The soul that sinneth it shall die." That we might not die, the Son of God died. The blood is *the poured-out life of the Son of God,* given as the price, the atonement, the substitute, for the forfeited life of the believer in Jesus Christ. Any poor sinner who receives Christ as God's gift is cleansed from all sin by His blood.

Mr. M.—Was the blood shed for us all?

Mr. R.—"There is a fountain filled with blood,
        Drawn from Immanuel's veins;
    And sinners plunged beneath the flood,
        Lose all their guilty stains.

    "The dying thief rejoiced to see
        That fountain in his day;

> And there may we, though vile as he,
> Wash all our sins away."

Mr. M.—Some may think that this is only a hymn, and that it is not Scripture. Did the Lord ever say anything similar to what the hymn says?

Mr. R.—He said, "I have given you the blood upon the altar to make an atonement for your souls" (Lev. 17:11). That was said of the picture of the blood of Christ. And at the Last Supper our Lord said His blood was "the blood of the new testament which is shed for you and for many, for the remission of sins." (Matt. 26:28; Luke 22:20; and John 6:37. See also Rom. 3:25, and 5:9; Heb. 9:12; Rev. 1:5.)

Mr. M.—What is "the gift of God"?

Mr. R.—There are three great gifts that God has given to us—
(1) His blessed Son (John 3:16).
(2) The Holy Ghost, "the promise of the Father," that we might understand the unspeakable gift bestowed on us when He gave His Son.
(3) He has given us His holy Word.
The Holy Ghost has inspired the writers of it that we may read and hear and know the love that God has to us, "in that while we were yet sinners Christ died for us." We could not have the Son for our Saviour unless God gave Him. We could not understand the gift of God unless the Holy Ghost had come to quicken us and teach us; and this He does through the Word.

Mr. M.—How much is there in Christ for us who believe?

Mr. R.—In Him dwelt "all the fullness of the Godhead bodily" —fullness of life, of righteousness, of sanctification, of redemption, title to heaven, and meetness for it; all that God wants from us, and all that we want from God, He gave in the person of Christ.

Mr. M.—How long does it take God to justify a sinner?

Mr. R.—How long? The moment we receive Him we receive authority to enroll ourselves among the children of God (John 1:12); and are then and there justified from all things (Acts 13:39). The sentence of complete justification does not take long to pronounce. Some persons profess to see a difficulty in the variety of ways in which a sinner is said to be justified before God: (1) Justified by God; (2) Justified by Christ; (3) Justified by His blood; (4) Justified by grace; (5) Justified by faith; (6) Justified by works.

Justification has reference to a court of justice. Suppose a sinner standing at the bar of God, the bar of conscience, and the bar of his fellow-men, charged with a thousand crimes.

(1) There is the Judge: that is God, who alone can condemn or justify: "It is God that justifieth" (Rom. 8:33). That is justification by God.

(2) There is the Advocate, who appears at court for the sinner; the Counselor, the Intercessor: that is Christ. "Justified by Christ" (Gal. 2:17 and I John 2:1).

(3) There is next to be considered the ground and reason on account of which the Advocate pleads before the Judge. That is the merit of His own precious blood. That is justification by His blood (Rom. 5:9).

(4) Next we must remember the law, which the Judge is dispensing. The law of works? Nay, but the law of grace and faith. That is justification by His grace (Rom. 3:24).

(5) And now the Judge Himself pronounces the result. "Be it known unto you that through this man is preached unto you the forgiveness of sins; and by him all that believe are justified from all things" (Acts 13:38, 39). Now for the first time the sinner at the bar knows the fact. This is justification by faith (Rom. 5:1).

(6) But now the justified man leaves the criminal's dock. He does not return to his prison or to his chains. He walks forth from the courthouse a justified man; and all men,

friends or foes, are made aware that he is free. That is "justification by works" (James 2:24).

Mr. M.—A man says: "I have not found peace." How would you deal with him?

Mr. R.—He is really looking for the wrong thing. I do not look for peace. I look for *Christ;* and I get peace with Him. Some people put peace in the place of Christ. Others put their repentance or prayers in the place of Christ. *Anything* put in the place of Christ, or between the sinner and Christ, is in the *wrong place.* When I get Christ, I possess in Him everything that belongs to Him, as my Saviour.

Mr. M.—Some think they cannot be Christians until they are sanctified.

Mr. R.—Christ is my sanctification, as much as my justification. I cannot be sanctified but by His blood (Heb. 13:12; see also 9:13). There is a wonderful passage in Exodus 28:36-38. The high priest there represented in picture the Lord Jesus Christ. There was to be placed on the forefront of the mitre of the high priest, when he stood before God, a plate of pure gold, and graven upon it, as with a signet, the words: "Holiness to the Lord." My faith sees it on the forefront of the mitre on the brow of my High Priest in heaven. "And it shall be upon Aaron's forehead, that Aaron may bear the iniquity of the holy things, which the children of Israel shall hallow in all their holy gifts; and it shall be always upon his forehead, that *they* may be accepted before the Lord." That was for Israel of old! *That* on the brow of Jesus Christ is for me. Yes, for me, "That I may be accepted before the Lord." As I believe this truth it purifies my heart, it operates on my affections and my desires; and I seek to walk with Him because He is my sanctification before God, just as I trust in Him as my justification, because He shed His blood for me.

Mr. M.—What is it to believe on His name?

Mr. R.—His name is His revealed self. We are informed what

it is in Exodus 34:5, 6. Moses was in the mount with God; and He had shown him wonderful things of kindness and of love. And Moses said, "O God, show me thy *glory.*" And He said, "I will make all my *goodness* pass before thee." So He put Moses in the cleft of the rock, and proclaimed the name of the Lord: "The Lord, the Lord God, merciful and gracious, longsuffering, and abundant in goodness and truth, keeping mercy for thousands, forgiving iniquity and transgression and sin"—there it is, root and branch—"and that will by no means clear the guilty." That is His name; His glory He will not give unto another; to believe in the name of the Lord is just to shelter under His promises.

Mr. M.—What is it to "receive the kingdom of God as a little child"?

Mr. R.—Well, I do not believe in a little child being an innocent thing. I think it means that we are to receive it in all our need and helplessness. A little child is the most dependent thing on earth. All its resources are in its parents' love: all it can do is to cry; and its necessities explain the meaning to the mother's heart. If we interpret its language it means: "Mother, wash me; I cannot wash myself. Mother, clothe me; I am naked and cannot clothe myself. Mother, feed me; I cannot feed myself. Mother, carry me; I cannot walk." A mother may forget her sucking child, "yet will I not forget thee" (Isa. 49:15). This it is to receive the Kingdom of God as a little child—to come to Jesus in our helplessness and say: "Lord Jesus, wash me!" "Clothe me!" "Feed me!" "Carry me!" "Save me, Lord, or I perish."

Mr. M.—A good many say they are going to try. What would you say to such?

Mr. R.—God wants no man to "try." Jesus has already tried. *He* has not only tried, but He has succeeded. "It is finished." Believe in Him who has made an end of sins, making reconciliation for iniquity, finishing transgression, and bringing in everlasting righteousness (cf. Dan. 9:24).

Mr. M.—If people say they are "going to try," what would you say to them?

Mr. R.—I should say, Put trusting in the place of trying, believing in the place of doubting; and I should urge them to come to Christ as they are, instead of waiting to be better. There is nothing now between God the Father and the poor sinner but the Lord Jesus Christ; and Christ has put away sin that I may be joined to the Lord. "And he that is joined unto the Lord is one spirit" (I Cor. 6:17). "And where the Spirit of the Lord is, there is liberty" (II Cor. 3:17).

II

At the last after-meeting in Down Lodge Hall, Mr. Moody resumed his questioning of Mr. Rainsford. "I have tried," he said to the people, "to put the truth before you in every way I could think of. Now I want to put a few questions to Mr. Rainsford that relate to the difficulties that some of you have."

Mr. Rainsford, on taking his stand beside the evangelist, said he prayed to God to give him grace to answer aright.

Mr. M.—About the last thing an anxious inquirer has to contend with is his feelings. There are hundreds here very anxious that this Mission should not close until they are safe in the Kingdom; but they think they have not the right kind of feeling. What kind of feeling should they have?

Mr. R.—I think there are several of those present who can say that they found a blessing in the after-meetings through one verse of Scripture. I will quote it as an answer to Mr. Moody's question. "Who is among you that feareth the Lord, that obeyeth the voice of his servant, that walketh in darkness, and hath no light? let him trust in the name of the Lord, and stay upon his God" (Isa. 50:10). Some of you may be walking in darkness; that is how you feel. What is God's command? "Let him trust in the name of the Lord, and stay upon his God." If I am to trust God in the darkness, I am to trust Him anywhere.

Mr. M.—You would advise them, then, to trust in the Lord—whether they have the right kind of feeling or not?

Mr. R.—If I were to think of my feelings for a moment, I should be one of the most miserable men in this hall to-night. My feelings are those of a sinful, corrupt nature. I am just to believe what God tells me, in spite of my feelings. Faith is "the evidence of things not seen"; I might add, "the evidence of things not felt."

Mr. M.—Some may say that faith is the gift of God, and that they must wait till God imparts it to them.

Mr. R.—"Faith cometh by hearing" (Rom. 10:17). The Word of God is the medium through which faith comes to us. God has given us Christ; and He has given us His Spirit and His Word: what need is there to wait? God will give faith to the man who reads His Word and seeks for His Spirit.

Mr. M.—What then should they wait for?

Mr. R.—I do not know of anything that they have to wait for. God says: Come now; believe now. No, no; there is nothing to wait for. He has given us all He has to give; and the sooner we take it the better.

Mr. M.—Perhaps some of them think they have too many sins to allow of their coming.

Mr. R.—The Lord Jesus has put away sin by the sacrifice of Himself. "As far as the east is from the west, so far hath he removed our transgressions from us" (Ps. 103:12). Why do we not believe Him? He says He has "made an end of sins." Why do we not believe Him? Is He a liar?

Mr. M.—Is unbelief a sin?

Mr. R.—It is the root of all sin.

Mr. M.—Has a man the power to believe these things if he will?

Mr. R.—When God gives a command, it means that we are able by His grace to do it.

Mr. M.—What do you mean by "coming" to Christ?

Mr. R.—Believing in Him. If I were to prepare a great feast in this hall to-morrow night, and say that any man that comes to it would have a grand feast and a five-pound note besides, there would not be any question as to what "coming" meant. God has prepared a great feast. He has sent His messengers to invite all to come; and there is nothing to pay.

Mr. M.—What is the first step?

Mr. R.—To believe.

Mr. M.—Believe what?

Mr. R.—God's invitation; God's promise; God's provision. Let us believe the faithfulness of Him who calls us. Does God intend to mock us, and make game of us? If He did so to one man it would hush all the harps in heaven.

Mr. M.—Suppose the people do "come," and that they fall into sin to-morrow?

Mr. R.—Let them come back again. God says we are to forgive till seventy times seven. Do you think the great God will do less than He commands us to do?

Mr. M.—If they truly come, will they have the desire to do the things they used to do before?

Mr. R.—When a man really receives Christ into his heart, he experiences "the expulsive power of a new affection." The devil may tempt him to sin; but sin has lost its attraction. A man finds out that it does not pay to grieve God's Holy Spirit.

At this stage of the conversation Mr. Moody called on all who were willing to come to Christ for salvation to manifest their desire by rising. "It seems to me," he said, "that every one of you must either accept or reject the Saviour." Quite a number responded to the call. When Mr. Moody asked all who had received definite blessing during the fortnight's Mission to stand, almost the entire body of those occupying the large central reserved section rose *en masse.* It was a very stirring sight, and must have greatly rejoiced the hearts of Mr. Moody and his co-workers. Pointing to the great company of young disciples before him, Mr. Moody said to Mr. Rainsford, "What would you advise them to do?"

Addressing himself to the audience, Mr. Rainsford said: "When you were little babes, if you had had no milk, no clothing, and no rest, you would not have lived very long. You are now the result of your fathers' and mothers' care. When a man is born in the family of God, he has life; but he needs food. 'Man doth not live by bread alone.' If you do not feed upon God's promises you will be of no use in God's service: it will be well for you if your life does not die out altogether before long. Then you need exercise. If you only take food, and do no work, you will soon suffer from what I may call spiritual apoplexy. When you get hold of a promise, go and tell it to others. The best way for me to get help for myself is by trying to help others. There is one great promise that young disciples should never forget: 'He that watereth shall be watered also himself' (Prov. 11:25)."

Mr. M.—How are they to begin?

Mr. R.—I believe there are some rich ladies and rich gentlemen on the platform. When such persons are brought to the Lord they are apt to be ashamed to speak about salvation to their old companions. If our Christian ladies would go among other ladies; Christian gentlemen among gentlemen of their own class; noblemen among noblemen; and so on—we should see a grand work for Christ. Each of you has some friends or relations whom he can influence better than anybody else can. Begin with them; and God will give you such a taste for work that you will not be content to stay at home: you will go and work outside as well.

Mr. M.—A good place to start in would be the kitchen, would it not? Begin with some little kitchen meetings. Let some of you get fifteen or twenty mothers together, and ask them to bring their young children with them. Sing some of these sweet hymns; read a few verses of Scripture; get your lips opened; and you will find that streams of salvation will be breaking out all around. I always think that every convert ought to be good for a dozen others right away.

Mr. R.—Let me tell a little incident in my own experience. I was once asked to go and see a great man and tell him about Christ. He did not expect me, and if I had known that, perhaps I should not have had the faith to go at all. When I went he was very angry, and very nearly turned me out of the house. He was an old man, and had one little daughter. A few weeks afterwards he went to the Continent, and his daughter went with him. One day when he was very ill he saw his daughter looking at him, while the tears rolled down her cheeks. "My child," he said, "what are you crying about?" "Oh, Papa, you do not love the Lord Jesus Christ! I am afraid you are going to hell." "Why do you say that?" "Do you not remember when Mr. Rainsford called to see you, and you were very rude to him? I never saw you so angry. And he only wished to speak to you about Jesus." "Well, my child, you shall read to me about Jesus." If that man has gone to heaven—I do not say whether he has or not—the only light he had he got from his little daughter. You set to work, and you cannot tell what may be the result, by the blessing of God.

III

Mr. M.—As a good many people were helped when I asked some questions of Mr. Rainsford at Wandsworth as to what

it is to be a Christian, I am going to ask him a few more
to-night. Mr. Rainsford, how can anyone make room in his
heart for Christ?

Mr. R.—First, do we really want Christ to be in our hearts? If
we do, the best thing will be to ask Him to come and make
room for Himself. He will surely come and do so. "I can do
all things through Christ which strengtheneth me." "Without me ye can do nothing" (Phil. 4:13; John 15:5).

Mr. M.—Will Christ crowd out the world if He comes in?

Mr. R.—He spake a parable to that effect. "When a strong man
armed keepeth his palace (the poor sinner's heart) his goods
are in peace: but when a stronger than he shall come upon
him, and overcome him, he taketh from him all his armor
wherein he trusted [unbelief, false views of God, worldliness, and love of sin], and divideth his spoils" (Luke 11:21,
22). The devil keeps the heart because Christ desires it for
His throne—until Christ drives him out.

Mr. M.—What is the meaning of the promise—"Him that cometh unto me I will in no wise cast out"? (John 6:37).

Mr. R.—I think we often put the emphasis upon the wrong
word. People are troubled about how they are going to
COME, when they should put the emphasis on HIM to whom
they are coming. "Him that cometh unto *me* I will in no wise
cast out": no matter how he may come. I remember hearing
this incident at an after-meeting. A gentleman was speaking
to an anxious inquirer, telling him to come to Christ, to *trust*
in Christ; but the man seemed to get no comfort. He said that
was just where he found his difficulty. By and by, another
friend came and spoke to the anxious one. All he said was:
"Come to *Christ;* trust in *Christ.*" The man saw it in a min-
ute. He went and told the other gentleman, "I see the way
of salvation now." "Tell me," said he, "what did that man say
to you?" "Well, he told me to trust in Christ." "That is what
I told you." "Nay, you bade me *trust* in Christ and *come* to

Christ; he bade me trust in *Christ* and come to *Christ*." That made all the difference.

Mr. M.—What does Christ mean by the words *"in no wise"*?

Mr. R.—It means that if the sins of all sinners on earth and all the devils in hell were upon your soul, He will not refuse you. Not even in the range of God's omniscience is there a reason why Christ will refuse any poor sinner who comes to Him for pardon.

Mr. M.—What is the salvation He comes to proclaim and to bestow?

Mr. R.—To deliver us from the power of darkness and the bottomless pit, and set us upon the throne of glory. It is salvation from death and hell, and curse and ruin; but that is only the half of it. It is salvation to God, and light, and glory, and honor, and immortality, and from earth to heaven.

Mr. M.—If the friends here do not come and get this salvation, what will be the true reason?

Mr. R.—Either they are fond of some sin which they do not intend to give up, or they do *not* believe they are in a lost condition and under the curse of God, and therefore do not feel their need of Him who "came to seek and to save that which was lost." Or they do not believe God's promises. I have sometimes asked a man, "Good friend, are you saved?" "Well, no, I am not saved." "Are you lost?" "Oh, God forbid! I am not lost." "Where are you, then, if you are neither saved nor lost?" May God wake us up to the fact that we are all in one state or the other!

Mr. M.—What if any of them should fall into sin after they have come to Christ?

Mr. R.—God has provided for the sins of His people committed after they come to Christ as surely as for their sins committed before they came to Him. Christ "ever liveth to make intercession for all that come unto God by him." "If we say that we have no sin, we deceive ourselves, and the truth is not in us. If we confess our sins, he is faithful and just to forgive us our sins, and to cleanse us from all unrighteousness." For, "if any man sin, we have an *ADVOCATE* with the Father— Jesus Christ, the righteous: and he is the propitiation for our sins" (Heb. 7:25; I John 1:8, 9; 2:1, 2). He will take care of our sinful, tried, and tempted selves if we trust ourselves to Him.

Mr. M.—Is it not said that if we sin willfully after we have received the knowledge of the truth, "there remaineth *no more* sacrifice for sins?"

Mr. R.—Yes. Paul wrote it in the Epistle to the Hebrews (10: 26). Some of them were trifling with the blood of Christ, reverting to the types and shadows of the Levitical law, and trusting to a fulfilled ritual for salvation. He is not referring to *ordinary acts of sin.* By sinning willfully he means, as he explains it, a *"treading under foot the Son of God,"* and a total and final apostatising from Christ. Those who reject or neglect Him will find no other sacrifice for sin remaining. Before Christ came the Jewish ceremonies were shadows of the good things to come; but Christ was the substance of them. But now that He has come to put away sin by the sacrifice of Himself, there is no other sacrifice for sin remaining for those who reject Him. God will send no other Saviour and no further atonement; no second "fountain shall be opened for sin and uncleanness." There remains, therefore, nothing for the rejecter of salvation by Christ, but a "fearful looking-for of judgment."

Mr. M.—There are some who say they do not know that they have the right kind of faith.

Mr. R.—God does not ask us if we have the right kind of faith. He tells us the right thing to believe, and the right faith is to believe the *right thing,* even what God has told us and promised us. If I told you, Mr. Moody, that I had found a hymn-book last night, you would believe me, would you not? (Mr.

Moody: Yes.) Suppose I said it was the valuable one *you* lost the other night, you would believe me also just the same. There is no difference in the kind of faith; the difference is in the *thing believed.* When the Son of God tells me that He died for sinners, that is a fact for my faith to lay hold of: the faith itself is not the thing to be considered. I do not look at my hand when I take a gift and wonder what sort of a hand it is. I look at the gift.

Mr. M.—What about those people who say their hearts are so hard, and they have no love for Christ?

Mr. R.—Of course they are hard and cold. No man loves Christ till he believes that Christ loves him. "We love him, because he first loved us" (I John 4:19). It is the love of God shed abroad in our hearts by the Holy Ghost that makes the change.

Mr. M.—Paul said he was "crucified with Christ." What did he mean?

Mr. R.—Oh, that is a grand text! Thank God, I have been "crucified with Christ." The cross of Christ represents the death due to the sinner who had broken God's laws. When Christ was crucified, every member of His Body was crucified; but every believer that was, or is, or shall be, is a member of Christ's Body, of His flesh, and of His bones (Eph. 5:30). Again, we read (I Cor. 12:26, 27): "Whether one member suffer, all the members suffer with it; or one member be honored, all the members rejoice with it. Now ye are the body of Christ, and members in particular." So, when Christ was crucified for sin, I was also crucified in Him; and now I am dead and gone as far as my old self is concerned. I have already suffered for sin in Him. Yes, I am dead and buried with Christ. That is the grand truth that Paul laid hold upon. I am stone dead as a sinner in the sight of God. As it is written (Rom. 7:4): I am "become dead to the law by the body of Christ, that I might be married to another, even to him who is raised from the dead, that I should bring forth fruit unto God." "I am crucified with Christ; nevertheless I live; yet not I, but Christ liveth in me" (Gal. 2:20); and God Himself commands me so to regard my standing before Him as His believing child. In Romans 6:10, 11: "In that he [Christ] died, he died unto sin once: but in that he liveth, he liveth unto God. *Likewise reckon ye also yourselves to be dead indeed unto sin, but alive unto God* through Jesus Christ our Lord."

Mr. M.—Should not a man repent a good deal before he comes to Christ?

Mr. R.—"Repent a good deal!" I do not think any man repents in the true sense of the word till he loves Christ and hates sin. There are many false repentances in the Bible. We are told that Pharaoh repented when the judgment of God came upon him, and he said, "I have sinned"; but as soon as the judgment passed away he went back to his sin. We read that Balaam said, "I have sinned." Yet "he loved the wages of unrighteousness." When Saul lost his kingdom he repented: "I have sinned," he said. When Judas Iscariot found that he had made a great mistake, he said, "I have sinned, in that I have betrayed innocent blood," yet he went "to his own place." I would not give much for these repentances; I would rather have Peter's repentance. When Christ looked upon His fallen saint it broke his heart, and he went out and wept bitterly. Or the repentance of the prodigal when his father's arms were around his neck, and his kisses on his cheek, and he said, "Father, I have sinned against heaven and before thee, and am no more worthy to be called thy son."

Mr. M.—What is your title to heaven?

Mr. R.—The person, the life, death, and righteousness of the God-Man, the Son of God, my Substitute, and my Saviour.

Mr. M.—How do you obtain that?

Mr. R.—By receiving Him. "As many as received him, to them

gave he authority to become the sons of God, even to them that believe on his name" (John 1:12).

Mr. M.—What is your meetness for heaven?

Mr. R.—The Holy Ghost dwelling in my heart is my fitness for heaven. I have only to get there; and I have, by this great gift, all tastes, desires, and faculties for it. I have the eyes to contemplate it; I have the ears for heaven's music; and I can speak the language of the country. The Holy Ghost in me is my fitness and qualification for the splendid inheritance for which the Son of God has redeemed me.

Mr. M.—Would you make a distinction between Christ's work for us and the Spirit's work in us?

Mr. R.—Christ's work for me is the payment of my debt; the giving me a place in my Father's home, the place of sonship in my Father's family. The Holy Spirit's work in me is to make me fit for His company.

Mr. M.—You distinguish, then, between the work of the Father, the work of the Son, and the work of the Holy Ghost?

Mr. R.—Thanks be to God, I have them all, and I want them all—Father, Son, and Holy Ghost. I read that my heavenly Father took my sins and laid them on Christ; "The Lord hath laid on him the iniquity of us all." No one else had a right to touch them. Then I want the Son, who "his own self bare my sins in his own body on the tree." And I want the Holy Ghost: I should know nothing about this great salvation, and care nothing for it, if the Holy Ghost had not come and told me the story, and given me grace to believe it.

Mr. M.—What is meant when it says that Christ saves "to the uttermost"?

Mr. R.—That is another grand truth. Some people are troubled by the thought that they will not be able to hold out if they come to Christ. There are so many crooked ways, and pitfalls, and snares in the world; there is the power of the flesh and the snare of the devil. So they fear they will never get home.

The idea of the passage is this. Suppose you are on the top of some splendid mountain, very high up. You look away to where the sun sets, and you see many a river, and many a country, and many a barren waste between. Christ is able to save you through and over them all, out and out, and beyond —to the uttermost.

Mr. M.—Suppose a man came in here just out of prison: all his life he has been falling, falling, till he has become discouraged. Can Christ save him all at once?

Mr. R.—It is just as easy for Christ to save a man with the weight of ten thousand sins upon him and all his chains around him, as to save a man with one sin. If a man has offended in one point, the Scripture says he is guilty of all (James 2:10).

Mr. M.—If a man is forgiven, will he go out and do the same thing tomorrow?

Mr. R.—Well, I hope not. All I can say is that if we do, we shall smart for it. I have done many a thing since the Lord revealed Himself to my soul that I should not have done—I have gone backward and downward; but I have always found that it does not pay when I do anything that grieves my heavenly Father. I think He sometimes allows us to taste the bitterness of what it is to depart from Him. And this is one of the many ways by which He keeps us from falling.

Mr. M.—What do you consider to be the great sin of sins?

Mr. R.—The Word of God tells us that there is only one sin of which God alone can convince us. If I cut a man's throat, or if I steal, it does not need God to convince me that that is a sin. But it takes the power of the Holy Ghost to convince me that not to receive Christ, not to love Christ, not to believe in Christ, is the sin of sins, the root of sins. Christ said, "When the Spirit is come, He will convince the world of sin, *because they believe not on Me*" (cf. John 16:8, 9).

Mr. M.—What do you mean by the Word of God?

Mr. R.—The Son of God is the Word of God incarnate: the Bible is the Word of God written. The one is the Word of God in my nature; the other is the Word of God in my language.

Mr. M.—If a man receives the Word of God into his heart, what benefit is it to him, right here tonight?

Mr. R.—The Father and the Son will make their abode with him; and he will be the temple of the Holy Ghost. Where he goes the whole Trinity goes; and all the promises are his. "Man doth not live by bread alone; but by every word that proceedeth out of the mouth of God" (Matt. 4:4; Luke 4:4).

Mr. M.—Who is it that judges a man to be unworthy of eternal life?

Mr. R.—*Himself!!* There is a verse in Acts 13 that is worth remembering: "Seeing ye put it [the Word of God] from you, and judge *yourselves* unworthy of everlasting life, lo, we turn to the Gentiles" (v. 46). God does not judge us unworthy. He has given His Son for our salvation. When a man puts away the Word of God from him and refuses to receive Christ into his heart, he judges *himself* unworthy of salvation.

Mr. M.—I understand, then, that if a man rejects Christ tonight, he passes judgment on himself as unworthy of eternal life?

Mr. R.—He is judging himself unworthy while God does not so consider him. God says you are welcome to eternal life.

Mr. M.—If anyone here wants to please God tonight how can he do it?

Mr. R.—God delights in mercy. Come to God and claim His mercy in Christ; and you will delight His heart.

Mr. M.—Suppose a man says he is not elected?

Mr. R.—Do you remember the story of the woman of Canaan? Poor soul, she had come a long journey. She asked the Lord to have mercy on her afflicted child. He wanted to try her faith, and He said: "I am not sent but to the lost sheep of the

house of Israel." That looked as if He Himself told her that
she was not one of the elect. But she came and worshiped
Him, saying, "Lord, help me!" and He helped her there and
then (Matt. 15:22–28). No; there is no election separating
between the sinner and Christ.

Mr. M.—Say that again.

Mr. R.—*THERE IS NO ELECTION SEPARATING BE-
TWEEN THE SINNER AND CHRIST.*

Mr. M.—What is there between the sinner and Christ?

Mr. R.—Mercy! Mercy!

Mr. M.—That brings me near to Christ.

Mr. R.—So near that we cannot be nearer. But we must claim
it. In John 6:39, 40, we get God's teaching about election.
"This is the Father's will which hath sent me, that of all
which he hath given me I should lose *nothing,* but should
raise it up again at the last day." He will do His work, you
may depend upon it. Then in the next verse we read: "And
this is the will of him that sent me, that *every one* which
seeth the Son, and *believeth* on him, may have everlasting
life: and I will raise him up at the last day." That is the part
I am to take; and when I have done so, I shall know the
Father's will concerning me.

Mr. M.—What do you mean by the *new birth?*

Mr. R.—I judge it by what I know of the *old birth.* I was born
of human parents into the human family; so I belong to
Adam's race by nature and by generation, and I inherit
Adam's sin and curse accordingly. The *new birth* is from my
union by faith with the second Adam; but this is by *grace,*
not nature: and when I receive the Lord Jesus Christ I am
born of God, not by generation but by regeneration. As I
am united to the first Adam by nature and generation; so I am
united by faith through grace and regeneration to the Second
Adam, and inherit all His fullness accordingly.

Mr. M.—What is the meaning of being "saved by the blood"?

Mr. R.—A gentleman asked me that in the inquiry room: "What do you mean by 'the blood'?" It is the poured-out life of the Son of God—forfeited as the atonement for sinners' sins.

Mr. M.—Is it available now?

Mr. R.—Yes, as much as ever it was.

Mr. M.—You mean it is just as powerful today as it was eighteen hundred years ago when He shed it?

Mr. R.—If the blood of Abel cried out for vengeance against his slayer, how much more does the blood of Christ cry out for pardon for all who plead it? "It cleanseth [present tense] from all sin."

Mr. M.—How do you get faith?

Mr. R.—By hearing God's Word. "Faith cometh by hearing; and hearing by the word of God" (Rom. 10:17).

Mr. M.—How do you get the Holy Ghost?

Mr. R.—In the same way as you get faith. The Holy Ghost uses the Word as the chariot by which He enters the believer's soul. The gospel is called "the ministration of the Spirit" (II Cor. 3:8).

Mr. M.—Is the Word of God addressed to all here?

Mr. R.—"He that hath an ear, let him hear what the Spirit saith to the Churches" (Rev. 3:22).

Mr. M.—What is the gospel?

Mr. R.—"Good tidings of great joy, which shall be to all people." If our gospel, proclaiming life, pardon, and peace, is not as applicable for salvation to the vilest person here as to the greatest saint in London, it is not Christ's gospel we preach.

Mr. M.—What reason does the Scripture give for the gospel being hid to some?

Mr. R.—It is "hid to them that are lost: in whom the god of this world hath blinded the minds of them which believe not, lest the light of the glorious gospel of Christ, who is the image of God, should shine unto them" (II Cor. 4:3, 4). May God open all our eyes, and take away the veil of unbelief with which the devil may be blinding any of us!

Mr. M.—Are there not many who give an intellectual assent to all these things, and who yet have no power and no divine life?

Mr. R.—An intellectual assent is not faith. I have never found anyone who really believed God's Word who did not get power in believing it. People may *assent* to it; but I do not admit that that is believing it. I do not think there is any man or woman here who really believes the gospel of the grace of God, who has not been taught it by the Holy Ghost. I could easily cross-examine any one of those "intellectual believers" who imagines he believes God, but really does not; and he would break down in a few minutes.

Mr. M.—For whom, then, did Christ die?

Mr. R.—For *"the ungodly"* (Rom. 5:6).

Mr. M.—Why is salvation obtained by faith?

Mr. R.—That it might be by grace. "For this cause it is of faith, that it may be according to grace" (Rom. 4:16, R.V.).

Mr. M.—What is the meaning of Christ dying for us?

Mr. R.—As our Substitute; in our place; *in our stead.*

Mr. M.—How may a man know if he has eternal life?

Mr. R.—By not treating God as if He were a liar when He tells us He has given us eternal life in His Son (I John 5:10–12).

Mr. M.—What is the means by which the new birth we were speaking of is effected?

Mr. R.—"Of his own will begat he us with the *word of truth"* (James 1:18). "Being *born again,* not of corruptible seed, but of incorruptible, by the *word of God* . . . and this is the word, which by the gospel is preached unto you" (I Peter 1:23, 25).